Cosmopolitan Place Making in Australia

Jock Collins · Branka Krivokapic-Skoko ·
Kirrily Jordan · Hurriyet Babacan ·
Narayan Gopalkrishnan

Cosmopolitan Place Making in Australia

Immigrant Minorities and the Built Environment in Cities, Regional and Rural Areas

palgrave
macmillan

Jock Collins
University of Technology Sydney
Broadway, NSW, Australia

Branka Krivokapic-Skoko
Charles Sturt University
Bathurst, NSW, Australia

Kirrily Jordan
Australian National University
Galston, NSW, Australia

Hurriyet Babacan
James Cook University
Townsville, QLD, Australia

Narayan Gopalkrishnan
Social Work and Human Services
James Cook University
Cairns, QLD, Australia

ISBN 978-981-15-8040-6 ISBN 978-981-15-8041-3 (eBook)
https://doi.org/10.1007/978-981-15-8041-3

This Palgrave Macmillan imprint is published by the registered company Springer Nature Singapore Pte Ltd.
The registered company address is: 152 Beach Road, #21-01/04 Gateway East, Singapore 189721, Singapore

Preface

This book investigates cosmopolitan place making, the historical and contemporary impact of minority ethnic communities on the built and social environment in Australian cities, rural and regional areas. Australia is one of the great countries of settler immigration, with more immigrants than most other nations: indeed, only Switzerland and Luxembourg have a higher immigrant share of the population among Western nations. Most research about immigration looks at the impact of immigrants on the economy (jobs, growth, productivity) and society (crime, conflict, social cohesion). This book presents another take on immigration by looking at how immigrants from minority backgrounds have transformed the built environment of the suburbs, towns and neighbourhoods where they settle, changing the way that Australian cities, suburbs and towns look and feel while at the same time changing the social landscape of Australian society. Immigrants are transformed by the experience of settling in a new society and, in turn, transform the places that become their new homes, particularly evident in the places and spaces created by immigrant communities for private or community use. The overall objective of this book is to record the impact of ethnic minorities on the built environment in Australian cities and rural and regional areas, and to investigate the (changing) social uses of this ethnic heritage. Here, the focus is on minority immigrant communities. By this, we mean those immigrants who do not come from English-speaking Western societies, particularly the British and Irish colonial immigrants—Anglo-Celtic immigrants—who have dominated Australian immigration intakes, until recent decades, for over two centuries, and still arrive in Australia in large numbers. While the concept of minority immigrant communities is not without problems—many immigrants born in the United Kingdom, for example, may have Asian or West Indian or other ethnic and cultural heritage, and be Muslim, Hindu or from other non-Christian religious backgrounds—this approach permits the gaze of our study to focus on a relatively overlooked and increasingly important domain of immigrant place making. But at the same time the society into which new immigrants settle is a post-colonial society, with a long history of Indigenous settlement prior to subsequent waves of immigration. The cosmopolitan perspective adopted for this book means that we situate the minority migrant presence within the Indigenous and Anglo-Celtic immigrant communities of all Australian places and spaces.

In the cities, we investigate what we call ethnic precincts such as Chinatown as a clustered suburban form of Australia's minority immigrant community heritage. While most immigrants settle in Australia's large cities, we also wanted to look at the places and spaces they create in Australia's rural and regional areas. However, place making is more than constructing or converting buildings for private or community use by new immigrant communities. It is much more than architecture or heritage. It is also about the social interactions that occur within these places. In both the Australian cities and the 'bush' (an Australian colloquial term for non-metropolitan dwellers), we wanted to investigate how the places built or developed by minority ethnic communities become an integral part of the lives of peoples of diverse Indigenous and ethnic backgrounds of Australian cities, and rural and regional areas.

Because Australian immigration is perhaps Australia's most contentious area of public policy, the immigrant presence in Australian metropolitan and regional cities and rural towns is also often contentious. This is probably most evident in the protests to proposals by Australia's Islamic communities—many of them new immigrants from a minority background—to build new Mosques in suburbs and regional towns. Indeed, most opposition to the place making of immigrant minorities relates to buildings used for religious purposes. The focus on the impact of minority ethnic communities on the built environment is partly because it is contested but also because non-Anglo-Celtic immigration is more visibly different to that of British and Irish immigration. Australia has a long history of formal and informal racism that shapes both immigration policy and the reception of immigrant minority communities. This racism is similar but different to ways that the initial waves of British and Irish immigrants reacted to the Indigenous communities who were living here. Often the community and private buildings constructed by new immigrants provide a safe place where immigrant communities can live and socialise, but over time often become places and spaces for social interaction of people in the neighbourhood from very diverse cultural backgrounds.

In order to study the impact of minority ethnic communities on the built environment, we focus our attention on three Australia states—New South Wales, Western Australia and Queensland—and take as case studies suburban, regional and rural sites in each state. We then investigate how the (changing) immigrant presence led to changes in the built environment in the form of new buildings or the repurposing of existing buildings. There are a number of questions to investigate here: How and why were each of the sites developed? What changes have there been in the social uses of these buildings, spaces and places over time? What was the resulting interaction with local and national regulatory regimes and the responses by other communities in the neighbourhood? The case studies offer numerous examples in which places built and used by non-Anglo-Celtic immigrants and their descendants have become sites of informalised inter-ethnic exchange and interaction. In reflecting on each site's history, social use and role in intercultural exchange, we show the extent to which non-Anglo-Celtic immigrant minorities have literally changed the face of Australian neighbourhoods—both physically and socially. As such, the places and spaces built by or transformed by these immigrants challenge narratives of 'Australianness' that represent multicultural place making as a foreign incursion into an otherwise Anglo-Celtic landscape. They are physical embodiments of the complex, embedded and sometimes long-standing and contradictory relationships of immigrant minorities within their local communities, in neighbourhoods that were also transformed by the immigrant arrivals that displaced Indigenous peoples living there centuries earlier. We hope to better understand the historical and contemporary aspects of cosmopolitan place making in Australia's rural and urban social landscape.

Broadway, Australia — Jock Collins
Bathurst, Australia — Branka Krivokapic-Skoko
Galston, Australia — Kirrily Jordan
Townsville, Australia — Hurriyet Babacan
Smithfield, Australia — Narayan Gopalkrishnan

Acknowledgements

The research for this book was financed by a four-year Australian Research Council Linkage Grant. We also had funding and support from the National Trust of Australia (WA), the Community Relations Commission for Multicultural Australia, the National Trust of Australia (NSW) and the Department of the Premier and Cabinet, Qld. There are numerous individuals who gave their time, energy and knowledge to assist with the research over the years; we are very grateful for their support. In particular, we would like to acknowledge the support of: Mr. Enzo Sirna, of the National Trust of Australia (WA), whose enthusiasm and tireless support for the project were critical to its successful completion; Mr. Tom Perrigo, also of the National Trust of Australia (WA), who was the first person to recognise the importance of this research and to pledge funding and support for it; and Mr. Warren MacMillan—formerly of the Department of the Premier and Cabinet, Queensland, for invaluable support with the Queensland fieldwork. Katherine Watson provided her excellent editing skills to this manuscript, though we take responsibility for whatever faults and errors remain. Jan Rath provided invaluable networking opportunities for discussion of theoretical and policy insights into the relationships between immigrant communities and public and private space in the metropolises of the world.

Contents

Abbreviations

ABS	Australian Bureau of Statistics
ANM	Australian National Movement
ASIO	Australian Security Intelligence Organisation
BCC	Brisbane City Council
BHP	Hill Propriety Company Ltd
BigN	Business Improvement Group of Northbridge
BME	Bacchus Marsh Express
CALD	Culturally and Linguistically Diverse
CARM	Caboolture and Redcliffe Multicultural
CBD	Central Business District
CCA	Cathay Community Association
CCTV	Closed-Circuit Television
CCQ	Chinese Club of Queensland
CNN	Cable News Network
CSC	Caboolture Shire Council
CWA	Chung Wah Association
CYL	Chinese Youth League
DIA	Department of Indigenous Affairs
DIEA	Department of Immigration and Ethnic Affairs
DPC	Department of Premier and Cabinet
EPRA	East Perth Redevelopment Authority
FECCA	Federation of Ethnic Community Councils of Australia
FFMT	Fremantle Fishermen's Memorial Trust
FYROM	Former Yugoslav Republic of Macedonia
HCWA	Heritage Council of Western Australia
ICOMOS	International Council on Monuments and Sites

IMRO	Internal Macedonian Revolutionary Organization
KMT	Kuomintang
LAP	Local Action Plan
MAQ	Multicultural Affairs Queensland
MWA of NSW	Macedonian Welfare Association of New South Wales
NBHP	Northbridge History Project
NSW	New South Wales
NSW DECC	New South Wales Department of Environment and Climate Change
NZ	New Zealand
OECD	Organisation for Economic Co-operation and Development
Qld	Queensland
RSL	Returned and Services League
SHFA	Sydney Harbour Foreshore Authority
TAB	Totalisator Agency Board
TAFE	Technical and Further Education
TNSW	Tourism New South Wales
UK	United Kingdom
WA	Western Australia
WAMMCO	WA Meat Marketing Co-operative Limited
WAPC	Western Australian Planning Commission
WUFC	Wollongong United Football Club

List of Figures

List of Tables

CHAPTER 1

Place Making, Migration and the Built Environment: An Introduction

Places reflect the people who live there, their history and their experiences. The built environment of the neighbourhood in the city, suburb or town provides the physical setting by which and in which we live our lives. There are emotional, physical and community interactions in this space which determine our well-being, our identity and civic participation. The built environment is strongly influenced by the social, political and economic influences of the time and often reflects issues of power, resources, ideas and values.

Immigration and immigrant experiences constitute an important element of the way places and spaces are conceived, imagined, constructed and transformed. Memory, nostalgia, estrangement, isolation, participation, dislocation and hope are elements that influence place making. Therefore, in the post-migration period, places are constructed from the contradictory forces of the familiar and unfamiliar, resulting in culturally hybrid places where individuals, community, state and national identities are negotiated and change. The place making of immigrant minorities is even more contradictory and challenging than when immigrants come from the dominant cultural backgrounds, such as British immigrants in Australia. In one sense, the contribution of immigrant minorities to the built environment can be viewed as an attempt at social participation and inclusion through control of, access to and use of public spaces (Babacan 2006).

J. Collins et al., *Cosmopolitan Place Making in Australia*,
https://doi.org/10.1007/978-981-15-8041-3_1

The expression of ethnic and cultural difference in the landscape—what Dunn (1999, p. 15) called the 'spatialisation' of multiculturalism—is evident in Australia in many ways. Although it is rarely recognised in research on Australia's built heritage, prior to European arrival Indigenous Australians developed the built environment over millennia—some 60,000 years—constructing shelters out of natural materials and building elaborate stone fish traps and ceremonial sites. The British colonial myth of terra nullius—empty land—denied the many thousands of years of Indigenous place making across the continent and their care and management of the Australian landscape (Babacan and Gopalkrishnan 2017; Gammage 2012; Pascoe 2018). While industrial development, urbanisation and natural weathering have seen the disappearance of much of this heritage, many of the stone structures remain intact today. Nonetheless, colonisation has meant that the most dominant influence on the Australian built environment has undoubtedly been the architectural styles and forms originating from the United Kingdom and Western Europe. Perhaps unsurprisingly, it is the styles of British colonial architecture, in particular, that are most commonly recognised as Australia's built heritage.

However, since the earliest decades of colonisation, non-Anglo-Celtic immigrants and their descendants have also left their mark on Australia's built environment. We refer to these non-Anglo-Celtic immigrants as immigrant minorities. Their impact in transforming Australia's built environment is the central focus of this book. For example, despite recent protests against the development of mosques and Islamic schools in Australia, they are hardly a new feature. Temporary mosques were built across the Australian outback soon after the arrival of 'Afghan' cameleers in the mid- to late-nineteenth century, and the first permanent mosque was opened as early as 1899 (Dunn 1999, p. 233). Today, arguably the most obvious of the places built by ethnic and religious minorities are the grand places of worship, such as the Auburn Gallipoli Mosque in Sydney's West, or the Guru Nanak Gurdwara in Woolgoolga on the north coast of New South Wales. But immigrant minorities have also built less immediately striking facilities including cultural centres, social clubs, schools and aged care facilities, restaurants and shops. Together, these sites can be understood as 'multicultural monuments' (Dunn 1999, p. 2)—records of Australia's cultural diversity in its built environment. Non-Anglo-Celtic immigrants have also brought unique architectural and landscaping styles to Australia's residential centres (see Armstrong 1998;

Pascoe 1987, pp. 178–181; Sandercock and Kliger 1998) and even to suburban backyards (Graham and Connell 2006; see also Morgan et al. 2005; Pascoe 1987, pp. 180–181).

Australian architect and academic Susan Stewart and colleagues have also noted the 'invisible' impacts of non-Anglo-Celtic immigrants on the built environment. For example, while some sites may be 'visually unremarkable' and show no obvious signs of Australia's cultural diversity, they are 'culturally heterogenous in their production and habitation', having been designed through a process of cross-cultural negotiation (Stewart et al. 2003, p. 240). For planning researcher Leonie Sandercock, all of these patterns of spatial diversity are signs of a 'mongrelization', a new condition of cities 'in which difference, otherness, fragmentation, splintering, multiplicity, heterogeneity, diversity, plurality prevail' (Sandercock 2003, p. 1). They are also a reflection of the super-diversity of contemporary Australian life and of Australian society (Vertovec 2007).

While this book focuses on sites built by non-Anglo-Celtic ethnic groups, there is a complex overlap between ethnic and religious diversity. Hence, many of the sites examined are places of worship built and used by non-hegemonic ethnic groups who also have non-hegemonic religious affiliations. In this sense, multicultural monuments may also be monuments to religious diversity, with expressions of both ethnic and religious difference in the built environment being a testament to Australia's immigration history.

The spatial impacts of Australian multiculturalism had received little public or academic attention. Tamara Winikoff (1992, p. 140) has suggested that in research on the Australian built environment there has been 'an obvious bias in favour of British influence', with the 'material evidence of ethnic minority settlement... rarely celebrated'. Walter Lalich (2003), too, has argued that while inadequate academic attention has been paid to ethnic community organisations in Australia, even less attention has been given to the buildings and physical infrastructure they have created. Lalich argues that this reflects the cultural hegemony of Anglo-Celtic Australians and an Anglo-centric approach to research.

Similar critiques exist in the heritage realm. Renowned geographer David Lowenthal dubbed it a 'heritage crusade' (1998, p. ix). Interest groups have regularly lobbied to have buildings, towns or natural spaces listed on the numerous 'heritage' registers that now exist at local, national and even international levels. According to Lowenthal, such listings may recognise and validate peoples' attachments to place, enshrining symbols of shared identity and allowing the consolation of tradition in difficult times (Lowenthal 1998, p. 1).

Heritage listings may also have significant practical implications. They may confer status on heritage sites—particularly important in the context of heritage tourism—as well as attracting privilege in resource allocation and political influence in development decisions. However, just as the spatial aspects of multiculturalism have been under-researched in the social sciences, the places built by non-Anglo-Celtic Australians have been largely ignored by heritage professionals. As the Australian Heritage Commission found in 1994: 'the history of many minority groups is relatively invisible in registers of significant places as though the history of such groups is not seen as being of broad public interest and importance' (Johnston in Lalich 2003, p. 9).

Part of the explanation for this lack of attention lies in definitions of heritage that have privileged the age of structures over their significance to local communities. For example, Helen Armstrong argued that the dominant understanding of heritage in Australia in the mid-1990s 'derived from the ICOMOS (International Council on Monuments and Sites) model where antiquity, excellence and rigorous evaluation criteria' prevailed (Armstrong 1994a, p. 480). Heritage assessments based on this model emphasised 'historic, scientific and archaeological value… rather than social value' while the 'concept of social heritage significance [or] what is valued by the community' was inadequately understood (Armstrong 1994a, p. 480; see also Sandercock and Kliger 1998). Researchers in other Western nations have reached similar conclusions. In the United States and New Zealand (NZ), Dolores Hayden (1995) and Michael Hartfield (2001), respectively, have argued that official definitions of heritage have prioritised 'elite' or 'western' heritage at the expense of the heritage places of socially marginalised groups. Babacan and Gopalkrishnan (2017) point out that political struggles over heritage and space play out through structures of difference, discrimination, power and inequality.

Since the 1990s there have been increasing calls among both social scientists and heritage professionals to recognise and examine the social, cultural and political significance of places built by ethnic minorities. In the heritage realm, Hartfield (2001) has argued strongly for the expansion of definitions of heritage away from the age of structures to include places that are identified as significant by local communities, particularly focusing on the inclusion of non-hegemonic ethnic groups (see also Hartfield and Kindon 2003). This approach recognises that what constitutes 'heritage' is socially constructed and gives equal value to both places deemed significant by heritage 'experts' and those felt to be heritage by local communities.

Official definitions of heritage in Australia have begun to recognise these concerns. For example, in 1999 the Burra Charter, the document developed by Australia ICOMOS—the peak body for heritage professionals in Australia—to guide in the management of places of cultural significance, was updated to recognise the cultural significance not only 'embodied in the place itself' but also in its 'fabric, setting, use, associations, meanings, records, related places and related objects' (Australia ICOMOS 1999). The Burra Charter recognised that cultural heritage is living and always changing (Australia ICOMOS 1999).

In practice, the operationalisation of notions of heritage by heritage agencies and professionals increasingly recognises the cultural context of built sites, incorporating the social use of sites and even the prevailing legislative climate as aspects of a place's heritage (see, for example, National Trust of Australia [NSW] 2007). Some local governments and state heritage agencies began to commission studies of multicultural sites. For example, the Heritage Branch of the New South Wales Department of Planning commissioned studies into the thematic histories of Greek, Italian and Chinese immigrants in New South Wales (NSW), with the studies including research on significant buildings (see Pesman and Kevin 1998; Turnbull and Valiotis 2001; Williams 1999).

In the social sciences, several geographers and urban researchers both in Australia and overseas focused their attention on places built and used by ethnic and religious minorities. For example, Kevin Dunn (1999) examined the politics of mosque development in several Sydney suburbs (see also Dunn 2001a, b, 2003, 2004). Helen Armstrong has explored questions of immigrants' sense of place (1994b, c, 1997, 2002), while other researchers examined the history and politics of buildings such as Muslim schools (Rath et al. 2001), Hindu mandirs (Naylor and Ryan 2003) and Buddhist temples (Beynon 2007) in predominantly Christian countries. Lalich (2003) researched the emergence of community facilities as a result of the collective action of non-Anglo-Celtic ethnic groups in Sydney. He referred to the clubs, schools, places of worship and childcare that immigrant minorities funded and built as ethnic community capital, a subset of ethnic social capital. Lalich documented the financing, management and the social usage of these places and spaces, including the extent to which bridging and bonding social capital occurred in them. Babacan and Gopalkrishnan (2011, 2017) have explored the spatial elements of a sense of belonging, identity and fear. Babacan and Babacan (2012) focused attention on the link between citizenship, equal valued status and place for ethnic minorities in Australia. Law et al. (2011) examined culturally diverse groups' impact on natural environments, agricultural land use, natural resource management and rural landscapes in Far North Queensland ethnic communities. Gopalkrishnan and Babacan point to the complexity of place and space nationally and internationally and the impact it has on relationships. The authors explore the impacts of place on marriage arrangements in the Indian community in Australia (Babacan and Gopalkrishnan 2012; Gopalkrishnan and Babacan 2007).

Following the pioneering work of Kay Anderson (1990, 1991), several researchers have studied the representation of ethnicity in ethnic precincts (Dunn 1998; Ip 2005; Mak 2003), while ethnic precincts' complex economic, social and political environments have become a growing area of research (Chang 2000; Conforti 1996; Fitzgerald 1997; Fong 1994; Frenkel and Walton 2000; Kinkead 1993; Lin 1998; McEvoy 2003; Zhou 1992). Several studies have also explored the potential of Chinatowns and other ethnic precincts to attract both tourist dollars and investment capital (Collins and Kunz 2005, 2006; Kunz 2005; Rath 2007; Rath et al. 2018). Korean immigrant entrepreneurs in the restaurant industry in Sydney cluster around Eastwood, Strathfield and Campsie—the suburbs with the highest concentration of Korean immigrants—and a block of a few streets in the Sydney Central Business District which has Korean language street names but little by way of other Korean iconography (Collins and Shin 2014). Much of the recent research has been influenced by the 'mixed embeddedness' approach which emphasises how different regimes of regulation in different cities and countries shape the contours of immigrant entrepreneurship (Kloosterman and Rath 2001). A recent study of the role of Chinese and Asian ethnic entrepreneurs in suburban place making in Toronto, Canada (Zhuang 2019) demonstrated how the institutional framework plays a role in shaping ethnic retail places and the spatial and physical outcomes of ethnic entrepreneurship. Other studies have investigated how neighbourhoods have been gentrified (Hackworth and Rekers 2005; Zukin et al. 2009; Bridge et al. 2011; Sakizlioglu and Uitermark 2014; Hochstenbach 2015; De Oliver

2016) and streetscapes transformed (Hagemans et al. 2015; De Koning 2015; van Eck et al. 2020) by newly arrived immigrant minorities and immigrant entrepreneurs.

These studies provide enormously useful insights into contests over space and the role of place in both economic competition and the social construction of identity and belonging. However, many focus their research on the specificities of one place or immigrant group. While this allows detailed and focused analysis, it loses the valuable insights that can be gained through comparative research. Moreover, almost all studies of multicultural place making have focused on sites in large cities, with less focus on regional cities and rural towns. This is not surprising given the urban settlement of most immigrants in most countries, leading to the inadequate attention to regional and rural immigration research (see, for example, Black et al. 2000). However, this book consciously attempts to rectify this urban bias in research on minority immigrant place making by also putting the spotlight on immigrant minorities in regional cities and rural towns. Despite the smaller numbers of regional and rural immigrants, immigration has had a significant impact on regional and rural Australia for a long period. For example, Italian (Kelley 2001) and German (Borrie 1954), Indian (de Lapervanche 1984) and Chinese immigrants (Lancashire 2000; Frost 2000) have played a significant role in the historical development of the Australian agricultural sector.

As Dunn (1999, p. 17) has previously noted, while 'the spatial dimension of Australia's ethnic diversity' has been neglected in academic research, 'a documentation of all spatial reflections would be a mammoth task'. While this book seeks to move beyond existing studies that focus on a particular site or ethnic group, it attempts to strike a balance between depth and breadth. Focusing on several sites in three Australian states, it demonstrates that places built and used by non-Anglo-Celtic immigrants and their descendants are crucial aspects of Australia's built and social landscape, with each of the sites in this study contributing to their local communities in complex and diverse ways.

The analysis of case studies in this book supports Anderson's (1990) concerns that the representation of ethnicity in public space may be racialised and shaped by a (changing) political climate of planners, regulators and politicians with their own agendas. But the key point of departure here is that immigrants are not passive victims: they transform their new neighbourhoods while they themselves are changed by them. The book highlights the agency that immigrants have in shaping their own destiny in the literal form of the buildings that they erect or renovate in the neighbourhoods where they live, work, eat, pray and socialise. We look at the places of worship they build, at the restaurants and shops they develop and decorate with signage and iconography, the social and sporting clubs they build for recreation purposes and the ethnic neighbourhoods that develop and emerge with their dragons, lanterns and foreign language signposts. Our analysis shows that while the emergence and development of ethnic places and spaces may entrench negative ethnic stereotypes or reinforce ideas of cultural difference for some visitors, the same sites may be interpreted by others as an opportunity to challenge Anglo-Celtic cultural exclusivity and narrow definitions of Australianness and belonging. Importantly, they may also be seen by members of the associated co-ethnic population as claiming space and asserting community pride. The findings of our book support Meethan's (2001, p. 27) analysis that symbols of ethnicity are 'multivocal, that is, they have the capacity to carry a range of different, if not ambiguous and contradictory meanings'. With the possibility for such multiple interpretations, the focus shifts to the merits of the design process itself and to the importance of a role for the state. At the same time, the authenticity of ethnic places and spaces is viewed as multivocal, as ethnic authenticity is also subject to multiple interpretations (Wang 1999; Boyle 2003; Zukin 2010). Jan Rath and his colleagues identify 'a certain "therapeutic", aestheticised notion of diversity' in recent transformation of Amsterdam's commercial streetscape (van Eck et al. 2020).

1.1 Australia's Changing Patterns of Immigrant Settlement

With the United States, Canada and New Zealand, Australia has maintained a strong settler immigration policy since the end of World War II though temporary immigrants have increased dramatically in the last decade. In 2018, there were 7.3 million migrants—29% of the Australian population—that were born overseas and are first generation immigrants (Australian Bureau of Statistics [ABS] 2019). Only Luxembourg and Switzerland exceed this migrant presence among OECD countries (OECD 2019). Moreover, more than 60% of the population of Australia's largest cities—Sydney, Melbourne, Perth, Adelaide and Brisbane—are either first generation immigrants or their Australian-born children.

One of the most urbanised nations in the world, 67% of Australians live in capital cities (ABS 2020)—with immigrants more likely to live in urban areas than non-immigrants. Of the 1,379,055 international migrants Australia received between 2011 and 2016, 85.52% settled in the greater capital cities, which also attracted many internal migrants from elsewhere in Australia. Greater Sydney and Greater Melbourne, the nation's top two global cities, received more than 50% of Australia's migrants. Only 14.5% of international migrants settled outside the capital cities (Tuli 2019).

It is not only the relatively large size of the Australian immigration intake that is important in understanding the impact of immigrants on the built environment, it is also the diversity of the immigration intake. Australia has one of the most diverse and changing immigrant populations, with the Australian immigration net catching people from all corners of the globe. As a British colony, the largest source countries for Australian post-war immigrants have been the United Kingdom and Ireland which have dominated annual immigration intakes in the last seven decades. Government assistance meant that many British immigrant families could travel to Australia by ship for ten pounds: the so-called 'ten-pound Poms' (Appleyard 1988; Hammerton and Thomson 2005; Jupp 2004). New Zealand is also a key source country, a consequence of the close geography and the shared history as British colonies. The Trans-Tasman Economic relationship also means that unlike immigrants from all other countries, any New Zealanders who want to come to Australia can do so. The annual target for permanent immigrants does not include the NZ intake. In the 1950s and 1960s, immigrants from countries in Southern and Western Europe—particularly Greece, Italy and the former Yugoslavia—came in large numbers. In the 1970s and 1980s, immigrants from Asian countries—particularly Vietnam—began to feature prominently as Australia rescinded the White Australia policy. Today India and China feature at the top of the 'top ten' countries of immigrant arrival (Doherty and Evershed 2018) with the largest Australian immigrant populations born in England, China, India, New Zealand, Philippines, Vietnam, South Africa, Italy, Malaysia and Scotland (ABS 2019). However, the immigration net is cast to more than 100 countries each year.

With this national diversity of the immigration intake comes linguistic, cultural, religious and ethnic diversity of newly arrived immigrant generations. There is also class diversity among Australia's immigrant arrivals. Millionaires go to the top of the queue through the visa pathway of the

Business Migration Program, generally under-subscribed. In the first post-war decades, a *chain migration* process (Price 1963) meant that young, lowly-educated male unskilled or agricultural workers from Greece, Italy and Yugoslavia would arrive in Australia as immigration pioneers. They would easily find unskilled factory jobs in Australian cities—many would hold more than one job—and save up to bring their brothers, then their cousins and parents. Over decades, whole families would move from the Greek islands, from the south of Italy or from Serbia or Croatia to settle in Australian suburbs where the next generations would be born. The Vietnamese boat people—refugees—in the 1970s and early 1980s also found factory work fairly easily, particularly in the cities of Melbourne and Sydney. As Australia entered the globalisation agenda under the guidance of the Hawke and Keating Labor Governments (1983–1996), manufacturing jobs declined, and the services sector expanded. Australian immigration policy shifted from a focus on family reunion to that of skilled migration. Increasingly the skilled migrants needed a university degree to be accepted as a permanent Australian resident. The numbers of skilled migrants from China and India increased significantly. Many of these had previously been in Australia on temporary visas—often student or working holiday maker visas—and made the eventual transition to a permanent visa. Indeed, the other key change in Australian immigration policy in the past two decades is the growth of immigrants arriving on temporary visas. In the last decade the annual number of migrants on temporary visas exceeded those on permanent visas by a factor of three to one (Collins 2014). At the same time, Australia has permitted a small number of refugees to arrive on a humanitarian visa. Today Australia accepts over 18,000 refugees each year. These refugees often arrive from the Middle East, Africa, Asia and Central America with an experience of displacement and trauma, their family networks fractured and dispersed across the globe. Refugees experience the highest rates of unemployment of any immigrant arrivals after settlement.

1.2 Racialisation of Australian Immigration Policy and Australian Immigrants

The history of Australian immigration is the history of formal and informal, individual and institutional racism. At the birth of the Australian nation at Federation in 1901, the common denominator of united disparate factions was the White Australia policy: the promise that

Australia would only take in white immigrants. This legislation was developed in response to the Chinese immigrant settlement related to the gold boom of the 1880s, when one in four adults in Victoria was Chinese (Choi 1975; Collins 2002). The number of Chinese in Australia dropped dramatically in coming decades when most of the non-Indigenous population and the majority of new immigrants were British and Irish in origin. At the beginning of the post-war immigration programme—designed to add 1% to the Australian population per year—the White Australia policy was still in operation. The first minister for Immigration—Arthur Calwell—promised that nine out of ten post-war immigrants would come from Britain. While the White Australia policy began to erode during the 1960s, it was not until the election of the Whitlam Labor Government (1972–1975) that the White Australia policy was formally and finally abandoned. However, it was not until the arrival of Vietnamese 'boat people'—refugees from the Vietnam War who were mostly ethnic Chinese and/or supporters of the South Vietnam regime—that large numbers of 'Asian' immigrants began to arrive in Australia for the first time since 1901.

Since that time the number of 'non-white' immigrants from all corners of the globe has increased. The 2016–2017 immigrant intake shows that the 'top ten' countries of new immigrant arrivals are led by India and China and include the Philippines, Iraq, Syria, New Zealand, Pakistan and Vietnam. Many immigrants from New Zealand are Maori. Regional data demonstrates clearly the global spread of the Australian immigration net. 58,232 permanent immigrants arriving in 2016–2017 came from countries in Southern and Central Asia, 37,235 came from countries in North-East Asia and 31,488 came from countries in South-East Asia. In addition, 28,525 came from North Africa and the Middle East, 25,174 from North-West Europe, 16,445 from Oceania and Antarctica, 11,369 from sub-Saharan Africa, 9687 from the Americas and 7306 from Southern and Eastern Europe (Liddy 2018).

The character of Australia's immigrant arrivals is shaped in a large part by the visa pathways that they take to get the rights to live in Australia temporarily or permanently. In turn, these pathways are largely influenced by the financial, human, social and linguistic capital these immigrants possess. The government annually sets the number of permanent immigrants it will accept—currently around 160,000 per annum—and divides this number between four streams: the skilled stream, the business stream, the family stream and the humanitarian (refugee) stream. The big change in the past two decades is the decline in share of the family stream (family reunion) in annual immigration intakes and the increase in the skilled stream, as Australian governments attempt to more closely align immigration policy with its globalisation agenda (Collins 2013). The business stream ensures that millionaires can always go to the top of the immigration queue, though the intake is relatively small (a few thousand per year) and the target quota always under-subscribed. The humanitarian or refugee stream has increased from 13,700 for over a decade to 18,750 in 2018–2019 despite the politically contested debate over refugees that has dominated Australian federal politics since the turn of the century (Babacan et al. 2009; Marr and Wilkinson 2003; Marr 2011). Refugees experience greater settlement difficulties than other immigrants, partly due to their (relative) lack of financial, social, linguistic and human capital and partly due to the racialisation of the refugee programme and in turn the racialisation of refugees, particularly those asylum seekers who arrive by boat (boat people) (Hartley and Pedersen 2015; Gopalkrishnan and Babacan 2015).

The Australian temporary migrant intake has increased so dramatically in the past two decades that temporary migrants outnumber those arriving under the permanent programme by three to one or more (Collins 2014, 2019; Mares 2016). This is a very big change for a country whose immigration model was based on immigrant settlement for nation building, with a strong focus on the chain migration of family reunion.

This book explores how the increasing and changing cultural diversity of Australian society—mostly a product of Australia's immigration intakes—impacts on the built environment of Australian cities, suburbs and towns and how this in turn impacts on the social environment of Australian society. The key point of departure here is the dynamic complexity of new immigrant intakes. Vertovec (2007, p. 1024) introduced the concept of 'super-diversity' to underline the level and kind of complexity of the contemporary British immigration experience which poses significant challenges for both policy and research: '[s]uch a condition is distinguished by a dynamic interplay of variables among an increased number of new, small and scattered, multiple-origin, transnationally connected, socio-economically differentiated and legally stratified immigrants who have arrived over the last decade'. Accordingly, we need to unpack Australia's immigration experience in the nuanced way described above, in order to identify and analyse the super-diversity of the immigrants themselves and their uneven and often contradictory relationship with Australian society, in order to understand the (super-diverse) way that they transform Australian society and themselves simultaneously. This in turn impacts on and is reflected in changing immigrant settlement patterns, and changes in the variety of ethnic, class, religious and social resources that they possess, which in turn affects where they live—the neighbourhoods into which they settle—and, subsequently, changes the way that the built environment of the neighbourhood is transformed and the social environment is transformed in part because of the social relations that occur in the buildings, places and spaces that immigrants own and control.

Immigration adds to the cultural, ethnic, religious and linguistic diversity of Australian society. The implication of this finding for this book is that the places and spaces that immigrants build or occupy will reflect this diversity. This is particularly true of places built by immigrants for worship: churches, mosques, temples, synagogues, gurdwaras and so on. The 2016 national census found that three-fifths of the Australian population (61%, or 14 million people) self-identify as having a religion or spiritual belief. Christianity is the dominant religion in Australia: 86% of religious Australians—12 million people—identifying as Christians. Of these more than two in five (43%) are Catholic and one quarter Anglican (25%). Just over two million Australians indicated a religion other than Christianity, with Islam (600,000 people), Buddhism (560,000), Hinduism (440,000), Sikhism (130,000) and Judaism (90,000) the largest non-Christian religions. Sikhism is in fact the fastest-growing religion in Australia since 2011 (74% increase) ahead of Hinduism (60% increase). But the religious diversity does not stop there with other Australians identifying as Baha'i, Mandaean, Druse, Zoroastrianism and Yezidi or with Paganism, Wiccan, Animism and Druidism, Taoism, Confucianism, Ancestor Veneration and Shinto and Australian Aboriginal traditional beliefs (ABS 2018).

Linguistic diversity also accompanies immigration. While English is the dominant language in Australia, many people speak a language other than English within their families and communities. 2016 Census data shows that Australians speak over 300 languages and about 21% of Australians speak a language other than English at home, with Mandarin, Arabic, Cantonese, Vietnamese, Italian and Greek the most common (ABS 2017). One manifestation of this linguistic diversity on the built environment of Australian society is the non-English script and iconography on many shop fronts or other buildings in the suburban and town streets in metropolitan, regional and rural areas. This is particularly the case for immigrant-owned restaurants and retail outlets found across Australia. It is most evident in the ethnic precincts of Australia's major cities. All of these cities have a Chinatown and most have a little Italy (Collins 1992) or Little Greece (Collins and Castillo 1998; Collins et al. 2001).

Despite the end of an explicitly racialised immigration policy, attitudes of racism and prejudice and discriminatory practices towards immigrant minorities continue. For example, one recent survey of 1000 Australians found that one in 10 are 'highly Islamophobic' and have a fear or dread of Muslims, although the great majority of Australians feel comfortable having a Muslim as a family member or close friend (Hassan and Martin 2015).

1.3 Immigrant Entrepreneurship in Australia

One of the major and most visible ways that immigrants transform the built environment of Australian neighbourhoods is via immigrants who start up their own business, particularly those who own or rent shops and business premises in the main streets of Australian suburbs, cities and towns. Australia's history of immigrant entrepreneurship is as old as immigration itself. From the outset immigrants set up restaurants, retail outlets and factories, initially serving their co-ethnic community with goods and services that were not locally available—the so-called *ethnic niche* market—before breaking out of this market niche to serve customers in the broader society into which they settled. In the nineteenth century, many of these immigrant businesses arose in the ethnic neighbourhoods of the city such as the Chinatowns that emerged in Sydney and Melbourne (Choi 1975; Fitzgerald 1997).

As well as transforming public space and residential areas, non-Anglo-Celtic immigrants and their descendants have also had a dramatic influence on Australia's commercial spaces, with the businesses they have established along suburban shopping strips or high streets a key feature of many neighbourhoods. In some instances, these businesses have become iconic places in the local landscape. As Collins (2003) has described, in the mid-twentieth century the Greek milk bar and Chinese restaurant became key symbols of increasing immigrant diversity in almost every Australian suburb and country town. In this way, Chinese and Greek entrepreneurs have been the 'vanguard of cultural diversity' in this country, pushing forward into largely Anglo-Celtic Australian suburbs, cities and towns as the front lines of the wave of increasing cultural diversity that was a product of sustained, large-scale Australian immigration.

Blocked from access to the labour market because of formal or informal racial discrimination, many immigrants from minority backgrounds started up their own business in Australia and other western countries. They opened restaurants and retail outlets, built factories and bought land for farms and vineyards (Gopalkrishnan and Khakbaz 2007). In this sense, the impact of immigrant minorities on the built environment of Australian cities, suburbs and towns is in large part a product of the history of immigrant entrepreneurship in Australia. Where ethnic minority enterprises have been clustered together in particular geographic areas, they have often formed what can be referred to as 'ethnic precincts' such as Sydney's Chinatown or Little Italy (Collins and Castillo 1998; Collins 2005; Collins and Kunz 2005, 2006; Kunz 2005). The built form of ethnic precincts is often quite different from the ethnic diversity of the surrounding neighbourhood, being characterised by clusters of small businesses associated with an ethnic group. In many cases, ethnic precincts are also host to ethnic clubs and associations (Lalich 2003) or places of worship identified strongly with the area's ethnic identity. In this way, the impact of immigrant minorities on the built environment in Australian cities, suburbs and towns is in large part a product of the history of immigrant settlement in Australia and the complex religious, cultural, ethnic and linguistic diversity—the increasing super-diversity—that accompanied that settlement. The streetscape may also be increasingly associated with visual signs and symbols of the area's ethnic character, including foreign language signs (see, for example, Lou 2007; Wise and Velayutham 2009; Wise 2010, 2011) and ethnically themed public art, shopfronts and street furniture (Kunz 2005). As Dunn (1999, p. 16) describes, these areas 'may develop a feel, a reputation or an identity linked to a non-hegemonic culture'.

While most immigrant entrepreneurs, like most immigrants, establish their businesses in Australia's largest cities, immigrant entrepreneurs also have a strong history in regional and rural Australia. A century ago Lebanese hawkers (Batrouney 1987) and Afghan traders took their wares in their horse-drawn wagon or on camel-back to homesteads across regional and rural Australia. Germans (Borrie 1954) started the wine industry in South Australia and Italians began growing wine in the Griffith region in South West NSW (Kelley 2001), wine regions that thrive today. Italians had a strong presence in sugar cane growing in Queensland (Vasta et al. 1992) while Sikhs pioneered banana growing in Coffs Harbour region of northern NSW (de Lapervanche 1984) before transforming their farms into growing blueberries as the market for bananas declined.

The immigrant entrepreneurship experience in Australia—and many other countries—is shaped in part by the racialisation of immigrant minorities. This is particularly evident in the case of Chinese immigrant entrepreneurs after the adoption of the White Australia policy at Federation in 1901 (Collins 2002). Explicitly discriminatory factory laws pushed Chinese immigrants into furniture factory businesses and restaurants by excluding them from owning businesses in other sectors of the economy. But the racialisation of immigrant minorities in Australia has been uneven and has changed over time (Gopalkrishnan 2019; Babacan and Herrmann 2013). It is mediated by class, religious, linguistic, cultural, generational and other differences—including visa pathways—within and between minority immigrant groups. Today immigrants from China and India outnumber other immigrant arrivals, including immigrants from Britain and New Zealand. The class character of Chinese and Indian immigrants is very different today than previous decades or centuries. Most have university degrees and arrive under the skilled component of the permanent immigration intake or as students or temporary skilled immigrants. Their rates of entrepreneurship are like or lower than the Australian average, largely because their human capital opens good jobs in the primary Australian labour market. For many immigrant entrepreneurs, the move to set up a business is driven more by the fact that their access to the labour market is blocked by formal or informal racial discrimination (Booth et al. 2012) than by a passion for entrepreneurship or a family history of entrepreneurship. This blocked mobility thesis is most evident in the case of refugee entrepreneurs, who arrive in Australia with relatively lower levels of financial, human, social and linguistic capital and face considerable formal and informal racial discrimination which leads them to have the highest unemployment rates of non-Indigenous Australians. Despite these barriers, refugees have the highest rate of entrepreneurship of any visa category of immigrant arrivals (Collins 2017; Collins et al. 2017).

But racialisation and blocked mobility is only part of the explanation for rates of immigrant entrepreneurship. A recent survey of over 300 Muslim immigrant entrepreneurs in Sydney found that 56% of informants had experienced unemployment prior to setting up a business and 45% of Muslim entrepreneurs reported experiences of discrimination in their place of work on the basis of their religion, with two-thirds of these informants leaving their jobs due to experiences of discrimination. Additionally, half of the Muslim entrepreneur informants agreed with the statement that 'Islamic culture is a barrier to employment' (Alaslani and Collins 2017). Nevertheless, the other half of informants did not reference experiences of racial discrimination in employment or society as a major factor in their trajectory to entrepreneurship. This and other Australian research suggests that the uneven rates of immigrant entrepreneurship in Australia are shaped by differences in the group characteristics of immigrants and the employment opportunities that they face when they arrive in Australia (Waldinger et al. 1990) as well as by the ethnic and class resources (Light and Gold 2000; Light and Rosenstein 1995) that immigrants can accumulate and mobilise once settled in Australia, as well as by their individual and family experiences of entrepreneurship prior to emigration to Australia. In addition, different immigrant groups at different times in different countries face different regimes of regulation and different experiences of immigrant settlement—what Kloosterman and Rath (2001) refer to as mixed embeddedness—that impact on their immigrant entrepreneurial experiences.

1.4 Multiculturalism vs Cosmopolitanism

Australia adopted a policy of multiculturalism in the 1970s. This policy replaced the policy of assimilation that the architects of the post-war Australian immigration programme introduced in 1947 to sell large-scale immigration to the Australian people, promising that immigrants would receive no special treatment and that they were expected to live and act like other (white, British) Australians. However, the serious disadvantage of immigrant minorities faced in health, education, employment, the law, religion and other aspects of Australian life under assimilation policy—not to mention the fact that immigrant minorities were dissuaded from publicly expressing their ethnic and cultural heritage in the areas of dress, diet, dance and dialect—meant that the contradictions of assimilation policy became strongly evident (Martin 1978). Immigrant groups—supported by progressive Australian organisations including the trade union movement—pushed for change. A short interregnum of integration policy replaced assimilation before the Whitlam Labor Government (1972–1975) not only formally ended the white Australia immigration policy but also introduced the foundations of Australian multiculturalism, led by Immigration Minister Al Grassby. The philosophy of multiculturalism was that migrant difference was to be acknowledged and celebrated and that a raft of policies and programmes were required to support the settlement of immigrant minorities and their families. It was not until the election of the Conservative Fraser Government (1975–1983) that the programmatic and policy bones of Australian multiculturalism was built on the philosophical skeleton introduced by Grassby. Education programmes, translation services, media and broadcasting services, the funding of ethnic community organisations and the increasing organisational power of ethnic politics via the Federation of Ethnic Community Councils of Australia (FECCA) were established by the Fraser Government and enthusiastically embraced by the Hawke (1983–1991) and Keating (1991–1996) Labor Governments.

Ethnic communities had made their mark on the built environment through building or transforming buildings as places of worship, ethnic community, social, sporting or recreational clubs, museums or meeting places in Australia since the middle of the nineteenth century. The period of multiculturalism encouraged minority immigrant communities in this regard. At the same time, minority immigrant entrepreneurs were transforming the main streets of suburbs, cities and towns.

But there was also a contradiction at the heart of Australian multiculturalism. The clear advantage of multiculturalism over assimilation was its recognition of the cultural, linguistic, religious and ethnic difference of the immigrant minorities, its promotion of the need to respect that difference and its policy dimension in the form of migrant-specific programmes and services designed to reduce inequality of outcomes of immigrant minorities. Ethnic community organisations and their leaders played a leading role in this regard, though organisations were often run by older generation patriarchs who did not include women and younger generations easily. This was unarguably an improvement on the assimilation days but reified the notion of ethnicity to an essentialist, stereotypical and often static notion that did not permit a sufficiently nuanced, complex assessment of the ways that minority immigrant communities added to the super-diversity of Australian society and Australian neighbourhoods.

The concept of cosmopolitanism permits a more nuanced approach to contemporary immigrant diversity in Australia. Whereas cosmopolitans were once thought of as mobile and upper-class elites—business class cosmopolitans—the term can also apply to the multiple practices of all kinds of people in local environments, not just elites. Delanty (2009) argues that a cosmopolitanism perspective puts an emphasis on the expectation of mutual transformation of people and place by all cultures and peoples without neglecting the inequities that emerge because of globalisation. It is this sense of cosmopolitanism that we apply in this book. The idea of 'vernacular cosmopolitans' was put forward by Werbner (2006), who recognised the open approach to diversity taken by people living cosmopolitan lives, going back through history. This concept has been buttressed with the idea of 'actually existing cosmopolitans' who share common human culture (Sobe 2009, pp. 6–7; see also Werbner 2008). This form of vernacular cosmopolitanism (Reid 2015, p. 724; Reid 2016, p. 196; Reid and Sriprakash 2012, p. 2) is based on Appadurai's (1996) notion of ethnoscapes (shaped by tourists, immigrants and refugees). While most often used in the urban context, cosmopolitanism resonates with historical and contemporary regional and rural society (Krivokapic-Skoko et al. 2018).

1.5 Methodology

The research conducted for this book draws on both primary and secondary sources including key informant interviews, visitor surveys, observation and analysis of existing materials (census data, newspaper articles, existing research and other records). Fieldwork was conducted in three Australian states: Western Australia (WA), New South Wales (NSW) and Queensland (Qld). In each state, an urban, regional and rural site was chosen within which to investigate the impact of immigrant minorities on the built environment. Given the long history of—and current importance of—Chinese immigration to Australia, Chinatowns were the key urban focus in Sydney's Haymarket (NSW), Northbridge in Perth (WA) and Fortitude Valley in Brisbane (Qld). Freemantle was also chosen as an urban site in Perth, given the interests of our WA Industry Partner, the National Trust of Australia (WA). The regional sites chosen were Port Kembla in NSW, which is in Wollongong, the major city 90 km south of

Sydney, Cairns in Qld and Kalgoorlie in WA. The rural sites were Griffith in NSW, Caboolture in Qld and Katanning in WA.

In preparing this book, 60 semi-structured in-depth interviews have been conducted with relevant stakeholders. Interview questions were tailored to each respondent. Interviews were recorded on a voice recorder and later professionally transcribed. Transcriptions were then analysed manually and thematically. The sampling of interview participants was purposive, with participants chosen based on their relevance to the research questions and aims. Respondents were selected using a networking methodology to gain access to several informants in government agencies and community organisations. They include relevant state and local government officials (cultural planners, heritage officers, and place marketers) as well as representatives from ethno-specific organisations or management committees associated with each site and/or individual users of the sites.

The research for this book has also involved carrying out 100 surveys of visitors to two urban sites. While the original research design included 100 surveys in each of the rural and regional sites in Western Australia and New South Wales as well, initial visits to the sites (particularly the Griffith Italian Museum and Cultural Centre) demonstrated that this would be impractical due to lower visitor numbers. Ten surveys were carried out at the Griffith Italian Museum and Cultural Centre during the Festa Delle Salsicce when visitor numbers were unusually high. While the results are useful, the significant amount of time invested for the small number of surveys completed led to the decision to limit the surveys to two urban sites (Chinatown and Northbridge) where visitors are virtually constant rather than episodic.

Two alternative approaches to survey sampling include 'to deliberately construct a sample which is representative of its population' by using existing data such as census figures, or to sample randomly 'so that pure chance determines who is approached and every case has an equal chance of being selected' (Sapsford 2007, pp. 9–10). In carrying out research for this report, the best approximation of random sampling has been achieved by conducting face-to-face surveys with visitors walking down the main streets of Chinatown and Northbridge (Dixon Street and James Street, respectively) at different times of the day (from 8.00 a.m. to 9.00 p.m.) and week (including both weekdays and weekends). Participants were stopped randomly as they passed the researcher, with the next passer-by stopped as soon as the researcher had finished each interview. While this technique eliminated any potential researcher bias in the choice of people approached, it should be noted that the 'randomness' of this method is compromised to the extent that passers-by choose whether or not to stop (with their decisions possibly influenced by the gender, ethnicity or appearance of the researcher) or are unable to be interviewed because of language differences. In the ten surveys carried out at Griffith's Festa Delle Salsicce, participants self-selected to respond to the face-to-face survey.

The sample size of 100 visitors to each urban site was chosen to adequately record a range of views and experiences but is not large enough to be assumed representative. In particular, the condition that survey participants had at least conversational English meant that the Chinatown surveys were not at all representative of non-English-speakers' views. The use of the survey to record a range of perspectives rather than produce a representational sample is reflected in the use of survey data to highlight several different views rather than measure the percentage of instances in which a certain view was expressed. The exception to this rule is where responses to pre-coded demographic questions in the survey have been analysed with the software package SPSS in order to determine frequencies for each response. Responses to open-ended questions have been analysed manually and thematically, as per the analysis of interview responses and observations described above. Responses to open-ended questions were recorded in full or paraphrased using keywords.

Primary research for this book has also involved periods of observation in each site in Western Australia and Queensland, with researchers recording their own detailed impressions of the sites, who they are used by (at different times of the day or week or during special events) and for what purposes (social, economic, religious, cultural). Observation as a research method may be 'non-participant'—in which data are collected by the researcher without engaging with other people—or 'participant'—in which the researcher interacts with others in the setting (Carson et al. 2001, p. 132; see also Marshall and Rossman 2006). In this research, observations were sometimes participatory (being drawn from researcher participation in management committee meetings for particular sites, or researcher participation in special dinners or dances held at the sites) and sometimes passive (such as observation of the use of public spaces in Northbridge and Chinatown by visitors at different times of the day or week). Observations were recorded either in written notes or on a voice recorder and were made at the event where appropriate or otherwise as soon after the event as possible (always before the next day).

The qualitative research undertaken for this book has included three types of sampling; the sampling of case studies; the sampling of interview participants; and the sampling of survey respondents. The latter two have been described above. In Western Australia and New South Wales, the case studies chosen for empirical research have been selected in consultation with industry partners: the National Trust of Australia (WA) and the National Trust of Australia (NSW). Locations (suburbs or towns) were chosen across urban, regional and rural New South Wales and Western Australia, with the inclusion of regional and rural cases designed to redress the urban bias in much immigration research. Informal meetings were then held in each location with representatives from local ethnic and multicultural associations, local councils and local branches of state government community service providers to identify specific sites that were deemed significant to non-Anglo-Celtic residents.

In Queensland, the major fieldwork was conducted around the key areas: Cairns and hinterland, the Sunshine Coast, Caboolture, Brisbane and the Gold Coast. A detailed search was undertaken to excavate the history of immigrant settlement in Fortitude Valley (urban site), Cairns and Cairns Hinterland (regional site) and Caboolture (rural site). This was followed up with collection of information on the impact of the immigrant communities on the built environment, using local archival work with newspapers and libraries, calls for information via ethnic community organisations, and local media. Key informant interviews were conducted at the three sites including government officials, community organisations, community leaders as well as ethnic entrepreneurs. Two case studies were identified in each location and detailed data on each site was generated through key informant interviews, focus group discussions and visitor surveys.

The cosmopolitan approach also means that we focus on Indigenous, Anglo-Celtic immigrant and minority immigrant interaction and history in these urban, regional and rural sites. The focus is not on heritage sites of great architectural importance—though we do look at multicultural monuments, museums and other places and spaces—but rather on the everyday transformation of neighbourhoods, the way a simple house will be transformed into a mosque, a building repurposed as a social and recreational club by the minority immigrant community.

The structure of the book is as follows: Chapter 2 presents the NSW case studies, Chapter 3 the Queensland case studies and Chapter 4 the Western Australian Case studies. In Chapter 5, we conclude our study be reflecting on what our research has told us about cosmopolitan place-making in Australia. In each site, we look first at the Indigenous history and then the immigrant history before outlining the way that these immigrant minorities have transformed the built environment and constructed monuments to their presence along the way. But we are also interested in exploring the dynamics of multicultural social interaction that occurs in these places built by or transformed by minority immigrants. Because these places and spaces are open to the public, we include their take on the ethnic authenticity of their experience in these cosmopolitan places and spaces.

References

Alaslani, M. A., & Collins, J. (2017). The Blocked Mobility Hypothesis and Muslim Immigrant Entrepreneurship in Sydney, Australia. *Review of Integrative Business and Economics Research, 6*(3), 333–357.

Anderson, K. (1990, October). 'Chinatown Re-oriented': A Critical Analysis of Recent Redevelopment Schemes in a Melbourne and Sydney Enclave. *Australian Geographical Studies, 28*(2), 137–154.

Anderson, K. (1991). *Vancouver's Chinatown: Racial Discourse in Canada, 1875–1980*. Montreal: McGill–Queens University Press.

Appadurai, A. (1996). *Modernity at Large: Cultural Dimensions of Globalization*. Minneapolis: University of Minnesota Press.

Appleyard, R. (1988). *The Ten Pound Immigrants*. London: Boxtree.

Armstrong, H. B. (1994a, July 13–15). Sustaining Urban Heritage in Multicultural Cities. In S. Neary, M. Symes, & F. Brown (Eds.), *The Urban Experience: A People-Environment Perspective* (pp. 479–485). Proceedings of the 13th Conference of the International Association for People-Environment Studies, University of Manchester. London: E & FN Spon.

Armstrong, H. B. (1994b). Cultural Continuity in Multicultural Suburban Places. In K. Gibson & S. Watson (Eds.), *Metropolis Now*. Sydney: Pluto Press.

Armstrong, H. B. (1994c). The Myths of Heritage: Inconsistencies in a Multicultural New World. *Polemic, 5*(2), 83–101.

Armstrong, H. B. (1997). Migrant Heritage Places in Australia. *Historic Environment, 13*(2), 12–24.

Armstrong, H. B. (1998). Migrant Placemaking: A Mode of Communication. In G. Gumpert & S. J. Drucker (Eds.), *The Huddled Masses: Communication and Immigration*. Cresskill, NJ: Hampton Press.

Armstrong, H. B. (2002). Landscapes of Hope: Migrant Spaces on the Margins. In S. Akkach (Ed.), *De-Placing Difference: Architecture, Culture and Imaginative Geography*. Proceedings of the Third International Symposium of The Centre for Asian and Middle Eastern Architecture, Faculty of the Professions, The University of Adelaide, South Australia. Adelaide, SA: University of Adelaide.

Australia ICOMOS. (1999). *The Burra Charter: The Australia ICOMOS Charter for the Conservation of Places of Cultural Significance*. http://www.icomos.org/australia/burra.html. Accessed 21 May 2008.

Australian Bureau of Statistics (ABS). (2017). *Census Reveals a Fast Changing, Culturally Diverse Nation*. https://www.abs.gov.au/ausstats/abs@.nsf/lookup/media%20release3. Accessed 20 March 2020.

Australian Bureau of Statistics (ABS). (2018). *Census Reveals Australia's Religious Diversity on World Religion Day*. https://www.abs.gov.au/AUSSTATS/abs@.nsf/mediareleasesbyReleaseDate/8497F7A8E7DB5BEFCA25821800203DA4?OpenDocument. Accessed 19 March 2020.

Australian Bureau of Statistics (ABS). (2019). *Australia's Population by Country of Birth: Key Statistics*. https://www.abs.gov.au/ausstats/abs@.nsf/Latestproducts/3412.0Main%20Features22017-18?opendocument&tabname=Summary&prodno=3412.0&issue=2017-18&num=&view=. Accessed 10 March 2020.

Australian Bureau of Statistics (ABS). (2020). *Interesting Facts about Australia's 25,000,000 population*. https://www.abs.gov.au/websitedbs/D3310114.nsf/home/Interesting+Facts+about+Australia%E2%80%99s+population. Accessed 18 March 2020.

Babacan, H. (2006). Locating Identity: Sense of Space, Place and Belonging. *International Journal of Diversity in Organisations, Communities and Nations, 5*(5), 113–124.

Babacan, H., & Babacan, A. (2012). Equal Valued Status: Belonging, Identity and Place. In N. Steiner, R. Mason, & A. Hayes (Eds.), *Migration and Insecurity: Citizenship and Social Inclusion in a Transnational Era* (pp. 149–168). London: Routledge.

Babacan, H., & Gopalkrishnan, N. (2011). Creating belonging: Safety, Racism and Social Cohesion. In A. Babacan & H. Tahiri (Eds.), *Community Safety in Multicultural Australia: Counter Terrorism, Social Cohesion and Belonging* (pp. 99–116). Newcastle upon Tyne, UK: Cambridge Scholars Press.

Babacan, H., & Gopalkrishnan, N. (2012). Transnational Love and Marriage in the Australian-Indian Diaspora. In A. K. Sahoo, M. Baas, & T. Faist (Eds.),

Indian Diaspora and Transnationalism (pp. 183–209). Jaipur, India: Rawat Publications.

Babacan, H., & Gopalkrishnan, N. (2017). Prevailing Paradigms: Enforced Settlement, Control and Fear in Australian National Discourse. In A. Fischer-Tahir & S. Wagenhofer (Eds.), *Disciplinary Spaces Spatial Control, Forced Assimilation and Narratives of Progress Since the 19th Century* (pp. 189–220). New York: Columbia University Press.

Babacan, H., Gopalkrishnan, N., & Babacan, A. (2009). *Situating Racism: The Local, National, and the Global*. Cambridge: Cambridge Scholar's Press.

Babacan, H., & Herrmann, P. (2013). Nation State, Social Cohesion and Cultural Diversity. In H. Babacan & P. Hermann (Eds.), *Diversity and the State* (pp. 19–37). New York: Nova Science Publishers.

Batrouney, E. (1987, February–March). Lebanese in Australia—Particularly at Albury. *Albury and District Historical Society Bulletin* (Nos. 247 & 248).

Beynon, D. (2007). Centres on the Edge: Multicultural Built Environments in Melbourne. In S. Velayutham & A. Wise (Eds.), *Everyday Multiculturalism Conference Proceedings, Macquarie University 28–29 September 2006*. Centre for Research on Social Inclusion. Sydney: Macquarie University.

Black, A., Duff, J., Saggers, S., & Baines, P. (2000). *Rural Communities and Rural Social Issues: Priorities for Research*. Canberra: Rural Industries Research and Development Corporation.

Booth, A., Leigh, A., & Varganova, E. (2012). Does Ethnic Discrimination Vary Across Minority Groups? Evidence from a Field Experiment. *Oxford Bulletin of Economics and Statistics, 74*(4), 547–573.

Borrie, W. D. (1954). *Italian and Germans in Australia*. Sydney: Angus & Robertson.

Boyle, D. (2003). *Authenticity: Brands, Fakes, Spin and Lust for Real Life*. London, UK: Flamingo.

Bridge, G., Butler, T., & Lees, L. (Eds.). (2011). *Mixed Communities: Gentrification by Stealth?* Bristol: Policy Press.

Carson, D., Gilmore, A., Perry, C., & Gronhaug, K. (2001). *Qualitative Marketing Research*. London, CA and New Delhi: Sage.

Chang, T. C. (2000). Singapore's Little India: A Tourist Attraction as a Contested Landscape. *Urban Studies, 37*(2), 343–368.

Choi, C. Y. (1975). *Chinese Migration and Settlement in Australia*. Sydney: University of Sydney Press.

Collins, J. (1992). Cappuccino Capitalism: Italian immigrants and Australian Business. In S. Castles, C. Alcorso, G. Rando, & E. Vasta (Eds.), *Australia's Italians: Culture and Community in a Changing Society* (pp. 73–84). Sydney: Allen and Unwin.

Collins, J. (2002, February). Chinese Entrepreneurs.: The Chinese Diaspora in Australia. *International Journal of Entrepreneurial Behaviour & Research, 8*(1/2), 113–133.

Collins, J. (2003). Australia: Cosmopolitan Capitalists Down Under. In R. Kloosterman & J. Rath (Eds.), *Immigrant Entrepreneurs: Venturing Abroad in the Age of Globalization*. Oxford and New York: Berg/University of New York Press.

Collins, J. (2005, June 10). *Ethnic Precincts as Contradictory Tourist Spaces: The Case of Sydney Australia*. Paper to the COMPAS/ISCA Seminar Series, Oxford University.

Collins, J. (2013). Rethinking Australian Immigration and Immigrant Settlement Policy. *Journal of Intercultural Studies, 34*(2), 160–177.

Collins, J. (2014, December 2). Report Marks Australia's Shift from Settler to Temporary Migrant Nation. *The Conversation*. https://theconversation.com/report-marks-australias-shift-from-settler-to-temporary-migrant-nation-34794. Accessed 18 March 2020.

Collins, J. (2017, December 20). *Private and Community Sector Initiatives in Refugee Employment and Entrepreneurship*. Lowy Institute Report. https://www.lowyinstitute.org/publications/private-and-community-sector-initiatives-refugee-employment-and-entrepreneurship. Accessed 20 March 2020.

Collins, J. (2019). *Six Facts That Tell a Different Immigration Story Than We Hear from Politicians*. https://www.abc.net.au/news/2019-03-21/australian-immigration-what-do-the-numbers-tell-us/10919970. Accessed 20 March 2020.

Collins, J., & Castillo, A. (1998). *Cosmopolitan Sydney: Explore the World in One City*. Sydney: Pluto Press.

Collins, J., & Kunz, P. (2005, May 26–28). *Spatial Dimensions of the Commodification of Ethnicity in the City: Producers, Consumers and the Critical Infrastructure in Four Sydney Ethnic Precincts*. Paper to IMISCOE Cluster B6 Workshop on Ethnic, Cultural, and Religious Diversity, Amsterdam.

Collins, J., & Kunz, P. (2006). *Ethnic Entrepreneurs, Ethnic Precincts and Tourism: The Case of Sydney, Australia* (Unpublished).

Collins, J., Mondello, L., Breheney, J., & Childs, T. (2001). *Cosmopolitan Melbourne: Explore the World in One City*. Sydney: Big Box Publishing.

Collins, J., & Shin, J. (2014). *Korean Immigrant Entrepreneurs in the Sydney Restaurant Industry*. A Final Report to Sushi Bay Pty Ltd. Sydney: UTS Business School.

Collins, J., Watson, K., & KrivokapicSkoko, B. (2017). *From Boats to Businesses: the Remarkable Journey of Hazara Refugee Entrepreneurs in Adelaide: Full Report*. Sydney: Centre for Business and Social Innovation, UTS Business School.

Conforti, J. M. (1996). Ghettos as Tourism Attractions. *Annals of Tourism Research, 3*(4), 830–842.

De Koning, A. (2015). 'This Neighbourhood Deserves an Espresso Bar Too': Neoliberalism, Racialization, and Urban Policy. *Antipode, 47*(5), 1203–1223.

Delanty, G. (2009). *The Cosmopolitan Imagination: The Renewal of Critical Social Theory*. Cambridge: Cambridge University Press.

De Lapervanche, M. (1984). *Indians in a White Australia*. Sydney: George Allen & Unwin.

De Lepervanche, M. (1975). Australian immigrants 1788 to 1940: Desired and Unwanted. In E. L. Wheelwright & K. Buckley (Eds.), *Essays in the Political Economy of Australian Capitalism* (Vol. 1). Sydney: Australia and New Zealand Book Company.

De Oliver, M. (2016, May). Gentrification as the Appropriation of Therapeutic 'Diversity': A Model and Case Study of the Multicultural Amenity of Contemporary Urban Renewal. *Urban Studies, 53*(6), 1299–1316.

Doherty, B., & Evershed, N. (2018, March 24). The Changing Shape of Australia's Immigration Policy. *The Guardian*. https://www.theguardian.com/australia-news/2018/mar/24/australias-fierce-immigration-debate-is-about-to-get-louder. Accessed 10 March 2020.

Dunn, K. M. (1998). Rethinking Ethnic Concentration: The Case of Cabramatta, Sydney. *Urban Studies, 35*(3), 503–527.

Dunn, K. M. (1999). *Mosques and Islamic Centres in Sydney, Representations of Islam and Multiculturalism* (Unpublished PhD thesis). The University of Newcastle.

Dunn, K. M. (2001a). Examining Local Inter-Communal Relations, Place Making and Citizenship. In K. M. Dunn (Ed.), *Proceedings of the Civics and Citizenship in Geography Conference* (pp. 35–38). Conference Papers No. 16. Sydney: The Geographical Society of NSW.

Dunn, K. M. (2001b). Representations of Islam in the Politics of Mosque Development in Sydney. *Tijdschrift voor Economische en Sociale Geografie, 92*(3), 291–308.

Dunn, K. M. (2003). Using Cultural Geography to Engage Contested Constructions of Ethnicity and Citizenship in Sydney. *Social and Cultural Geography, 4*(2), 153–165.

Dunn, K. M. (2004). Islam in Sydney: Contesting the Discourse of Absence. *Australian Geographer, 35*(3), 333–353.

Fitzgerald, S. (1997). *Red Tape, Gold Scissors: The Story of Sydney's Chinese*. Sydney: State Library of New South Wales Press.

Fong, T. P. (1994). *The First Suburban Chinatown: The Remaking of Monterey Park, California*. Philadelphia: Temple University Press.

Frenkel, S., & Walton, J. (2000). Bavarian Leavenworth and the Symbolic Economy of a Theme Town. *The Geographical Review, 90*(4), 559–581.

Frost, W. (2000). *Migrants and Technological Transfer: Chinese Farming in Australia, 1850–1920* (Working Paper 100/00, Faculty of Business and Economics). Melbourne: Monash University.

Gammage, B. (2012). *The Biggest Estate on Earth: How Aborigines Made Australia*. Sydney: Allen & Unwin.

Gopalkrishnan, N. (2019). Cultural Competence and Beyond: Working Across Cultures in Culturally Dynamic Partnerships. *International Journal of Community and Social Development, 1*(1), 28–41.

Gopalkrishnan, N., & Babacan, H. (2007). Ties That Bind: Globalisation, Love and Transnationalism. *Identities: Global Studies in Culture and Power, 14*(4), 505–526.

Gopalkrishnan, N., & Babacan, H. (2015). Cultural Diversity and Mental Health. *Australasian Psychiatry, 23*(Suppl. 6), 6–8.

Gopalkrishnan, N., & Khakbaz, K. (2007). Migrant Women and Small Business: Way of Life or a Choice? *International Journal of Diversity in Organisations, Communities and Nations, 7*(5), 1–6.

Graham, S., & Connell, J. (2006). Nurturing Relationships: The Gardens of Greek and Vietnamese Migrants in Marrickville, Sydney. *Australian Geographer, 37*(3), 375–393.

Hackworth, J., & Rekers, J. (2005). Ethnic Packaging and Gentrification: The Case of Four Neighborhoods in Toronto. *Urban Affairs Review, 41*(2), 211–236.

Hagemans, I., Hendriks, A., Rath, J., & Zukin, S. (2015). From Greengrocers to Cafés: Producing Social Diversity in Amsterdam. In S. Zukin, P. H. Kasinitz, & X. Chen (Eds.), *Global Cities, Local Streets: Everyday Diversity from New York to Shanghai* (pp. 90–119). New York: Routledge Research Partners.

Hammerton, J., & Thomson, A. (2005). *Ten Pound Poms: Australia's Invisible Migrants*. Manchester: Manchester University Press.

Hartfield, M. (2001, April). *But Whose Heritage Is It Anyway?* Paper presented at the International Community Development Conference, Rotorua, New Zealand.

Hartfield, M., & Kindon, S. (2003). A Participatory Approach to the Assessment of Built Heritage: An Example from Wellington, Aotearoa/New Zealand. *PLA Notes, 46*, 67–72.

Hartley, L., & Pedersen, A. (2015, July). Asylum Seekers and Resettled Refugees in Australia: Predicting Social Policy Attitude from Prejudice Versus Emotion. *Journal of Social and Political Psychology, North America, 3*. https://jspp.psychopen.eu/article/view/476. Accessed 19 March 2020.

Hassan, R., & Martin, B. (2015). *Islamophobia, Social Distance and Fear of Terrorism in Australia: A Preliminary Report*. Adelaide: University of South Australia.

Hayden, D. (1995). *The Power of Place: Urban Landscapes as Public History*. Cambridge, MA and London: The MIT Press.

Hochstenbach, C. (2015). An Anatomy of Gentrification Processes: Variegating Causes of Neighbourhood Change. *Environment and Planning A, 47*(7), 1480–1501.

Ip, D. (2005). Contesting Chinatown: Place-Making and the Emergence of 'Ethnoburbia' in Brisbane, Australia. *GeoJournal, 64*, 63–74.

Jupp, J. (2004). *The English in Australia*. Cambridge: Cambridge University Press.

Kelly, B. (2001). Italians in the Riverina. In J. Jupp (Ed.), *The Australian People: Encyclopedia of the Nation, Its People and Their Origins* (pp. 497–499). Cambridge: Cambridge University Press.

Kinkead, G. (1993). *Chinatown: A Portrait of a Closed Society*. New York: Harper Perennial.

Kloosterman, R., & Rath, J. (2001). Immigrant Entrepreneurs in Advanced Economies: Mixed Embededdness Further Explored. *Journal of Ethnic and Migration Studies, 27*(2), 189–201.

Krivokapic-Skoko, B., Reid, C., & Collins, J. (2018). Rural Cosmopolitism in Australia. *Journal of Rural Studies, 64*, 153–163.

Kunz, P. (2005). *Ethnic Entrepreneurs, Ethnic Precincts and Tourism: Missed Opportunities from Sydney* (Unpublished PhD thesis). Sydney: University of Technology.

Lalich, W. F. (2003). *Ethnic Community Capital* (Unpublished thesis). Sydney: The University of Technology.

Lancashire, R. (2000). European-Chinese Economic Interaction in a Pre-Federation Rural Agricultural Setting. *Rural Society, 10*(2), 229–243.

Law, L., Babacan, H., & McIntyre-Tamwoy, S. (2011). *Culturally Diverse Communities and Sustainable Natural Resource Use*. Report, Reef and Rainforest Research Centre and James Cook University. Cairns, Qld: James Cook University.

Liddy, M. (2018). *Chart of the Day: Where Do Migrants to Australia Come from?* https://www.abc.net.au/news/2018-08-20/where-do-migrants-to-australia-come-from-chart/10133560. Accessed 19 March 2020.

Light, I. H., & Gold, S. J. (2000). *Ethnic Economies*. San Diego: Academic Press.

Light, I. H., & Rosenstein, C. (1995). *Race, Ethnicity, and Entrepreneurship in Urban America*. New York: Aldine de Gruyter.

Lin, J. (1998). *Reconstructing Chinatown: Ethnic Enclave, Global Change*. Minneapolis: University of Minnesota Press.

Lou, J. (2007). Revitalizing Chinatown into a Heterotopia: A Geosemiotic Analysis of Shop Signs in Washington, D.C.'s Chinatown. *Space and Culture, 10*(2), 170–194.

Lowenthal, D. (1998). *The Heritage Crusade and the Spoils of History* (2nd ed.). Cambridge: Cambridge University Press.

Mak, A. (2003). Negotiating Identity: Ethnicity, Tourism and Chinatown. *Journal of Australian Studies, 77*, 93–100.

Mares, P. (2016). *Not Quite Australian: How Temporary Migration is Changing the Nation*. Melbourne: Text Publishing.

Marr, D. (2011). *Panic*. Melbourne: Black Books.

Marr, D., & Wilkinson, M. (2003). *Dark Victory*. Sydney: Allen & Unwin.

Marshall, C., & Rossman, G. B. (2006). *Designing Qualitative Research*. London: Sage.

Martin, J. (1978). *The Migrant Presence*. Sydney: George Allen and Unwin.

McEvoy, D. (2003, September 15–19). *The Evolution of Manchester's 'Curry Mile': From Suburban Shopping Street to Ethnic Destination*. Paper presented to Eighth International Metropolis Conference, Vienna.

Meethan, K. (2001). *Tourism in Global Society: Place, Culture, Consumption*. New York: Palgrave.

Morgan, G., Rocha, C., & Poynting, S. (2005). Grafting Cultures: Longing and Belonging in Immigrants' Gardens and Backyards in Fairfield. *Journal of Intercultural Studies, 26*(1–2), 93–105.

National Trust of Australia (NSW). (2007). *Cultural Context Conference*. http://www.nsw.nationaltrust.org.au/events/cultural-conference/. Accessed 24 June 2008.

Naylor, S., & Ryan, J. R. (2003). Mosques, Temples and Gurdwaras: New Sites of Religion in Twentieth-Century Britain. In D. Gilbert, D. Matless, & B. Short (Eds.), *Geographies of British Modernity: Space and Society in the Twentieth Century* (pp. 168–184). Malden, MA and Oxford: Blackwell.

Organisation for Economic Co-operation and Development (OECD). (2019). *Compare Your Country: International Migration*. https://www1.compareyourcountry.org/migration/en/1/all/default. Accessed 18 March 2020.

Pascoe, B. (2018). *Dark Emu: Aboriginal Australia and the Birth of Agriculture*. Broome, WA: Magabala Books.

Pascoe, R. (1987). *Buongiorno Australia: Our Italian Heritage*. Richmond, Vic: Greenhouse Publications.

Pesman, R., & Kevin, C. (1998). *A History of Italian Settlement in NSW*. Report for the Heritage Office of NSW. http://www.heritage.nsw.gov.au/06_subnav_05.htm. Accessed 21 May 2008.

Price, C. (1963). *Southern Europeans in Australia*. Canberra: Australian National University Press.

Rath, J. (Ed.). (2007). *Tourism, Ethnic Diversity and the City*. New York: Routledge.

Rath, J., Bodaar, A., Waagemakers, T., & Yan Wu, P. (2018). Chinatown 2.0: The Difficult Flowering of an Ethnically Themed Shopping Area. *Journal of Ethnic and Migration Studies, 44*(1), 81–98.

Rath, J., Penninx, R., Groenendijk, K., & Meyer, A. (2001). *Western Europe and Its Islam*. Leiden and Boston: Brill.

Reid, C. (2015). Cosmopolitanism and Rural Education: A Conversation. *International Journal of Inclusive Education, 19*(7), 721–732.

Reid, C. (2016). Teachers' Work in the Age of Migration: A Cosmopolitan Analysis. In D. R. Cole & C. Woodrow (Eds.), *Super Dimensions in Globalisation and Education* (pp. 191–206). Springer 9789811003103.

Reid, C., & Sriprakash, A. (2012). The Possibility of Cosmopolitan Learning: Reflecting on Future Directions for Diversity Teacher Education in Australia. *Asia-Pacific Journal of Teacher Education, 40*(1), 15–29.

Sakizlioglu, N. B., & Uitermark, J. (2014). The Symbolic Politics of Gentrification: The Restructuring of Stigmatized Neighborhoods in Amsterdam and Istanbul. *Environment and Planning A: Economy and Space, 46*(6), 1369–1385.

Sandercock, L. (2003). *Cosmopolis II: Mongrel Cities of the 21st Century*. London: Continuum.

Sandercock, L., & Kliger, B. (1998). Multiculturalism and the Planning System, Part 2. *Australian Planner, 35*(4), 223–227.

Sapsford, R. (2007). *Survey Research* (2nd ed.). London: Sage.

Sobe, N. W. (2009). Rethinking 'Cosmopolitanism' as an Analytic for the Comparative Study of Globalization and Education. *Current Issues in Comparative Education, 12*, 6–13.

Stewart, S., Hanna, B., Thompson, S., Gusheh, M., Armstrong, H., & van der Plaat, D. (2003). Navigating the Sea of Diversity: Multicultural Place-making in Sydney. *International Journal of Diversity in Organisations, Communities and Nations, 3*, 239–252.

Tuli, S. (2019, April 1). Migrants Want to Live in the Big Cities, Just Like the Rest of Us. *The Conversation*. http://theconversation.com/migrants-want-to-live-in-the-big-cities-just-like-the-rest-of-us-113911. Accessed 18 March 2020.

Turnbull, C., & Valiotis, C. (2001). *Beyond the Rolling Wave: A Thematic History of Greek Settlement in NSW*. Report for the Heritage Office of NSW. http://www.heritage.nsw.gov.au/06_subnav_05.htm. Accessed 21 May 2008.

van Eck, E., Hagemans, I., & Rath, J. (2020). The Ambiguity of Diversity: Management of Ethnic and Class Transitions in a Gentrifying Local Shopping Street. *Urban Studies*.

Vasta, E., Rando, G., Castles, S., & Alcorso, C. (1992). The Italo-Australian Community on the Pacific Rim. In S. Castles, C. Alcorso, G. Rando, & E.

Vasta (Eds.), *Australia's Italians: Culture and Community in a Changing Society* (pp. 215–231). North Sydney: Allen & Unwin.
Vertovec, S. (2007). Super-Diversity and Its Implications. *Ethnic and Racial Studies, 30*(6), 1024–1054.
Waldinger, R., Aldrich, H., Ward, R., et al. (Eds.). (1990). *Ethnic Entrepreneurs: Immigrant Business in Industrial Societies*. Newbury Park, CA: Sage.
Wang, N. (1999). Rethinking Authenticity in Tourism Experience. *Annals of Tourism Research, 26*(2), 349–370.
Werbner, P. (2006). Vernacular Cosmopolitanism. *Theory, Culture & Society, 23*(2–3), 496–498.
Werbner, P. (2008). *Anthropology and the New Cosmopolitanism*. Oxford and New York: Berg.
Williams, M. (1999). *Chinese Settlement in NSW*. Report for the Heritage Office of NSW. http://www.heritage.nsw.gov.au/06_subnav_05.htm. Accessed 21 May 2008.
Winikoff, T. (1992). Big Banana and Little Italy: Multicultural Planning and Urban Design in Australia. In S. Gunew & R. Fazal (Eds.), *Culture, Difference and the Arts* (pp. 130–146). Sydney: Allen & Unwin.
Wise, A. (2010). Sensuous Multiculturalism: Emotional Landscapes of Inter-Ethnic Living in Australian Suburbia. *Journal of Ethnic and Migration Studies, 36*(6), 917–937.
Wise, A. (2011). 'You Wouldn't Know What's in There Would You?' Homeliness and 'Foreign' Signs in Ashfield, Sydney. In K. Brickell & A. Datta (Eds.), *Translocal Geographies: Spaces, Places, Connections*. Farnham: Ashgate.
Wise, A., & Velayutham, S. (Eds.). (2009). *Everyday Multiculturalism*. Houndmills, Basingstoke, Hampshire, and New York, NY: Palgrave Macmillan.
Zhou, M. (1992). *Chinatown: The Socioeconomic Potential of an Urban Enclave*. Philadelphia: Temple University Press.
Zhuang, Z. C. (2019). Ethnic Entrepreneurship and Placemaking in Toronto's Ethnic Retail Neighbourhoods. *Tijdschrift voor Economische en Sociale Geografie, 110*, 520–537.
Zukin, S. (2010). *Naked City: The Death and Life of Authentic Urban Places*. New York: Oxford University Press.
Zukin, S., Trujillo, V., Frase, P., Jackson, D., Recuber, T., & Walker, A. (2009). New Retail Capital and Neighborhood Change: Boutiques and Gentrification in New York City. *City & Community, 8*(1), 47–64.

CHAPTER 2

Immigrant Minorities and the Built Environment in New South Wales

As Australia's most populous state and the place where most immigrants to Australia settle, New South Wales is the obvious starting point for an investigation of the impact of minority immigrant communities on the built environment of urban, regional and rural places and spaces. While multicultural place making may be expressed through building clubs, museums and places of worship—all aspects that will be explored in this chapter on New South Wales—perhaps the most visible (and certainly the most well researched) manifestations of spatial diversity are the ethnic precincts and ethnic neighbourhoods of major urban centres. Most immigrant settlement in most countries has been urban, and many countries of immigrant settlement have a long history of Chinese presence. Many cities around the world have a Chinatown (Anderson 1990, 1991; Fong 1994; Lin 1998; Zhou 1992; Collins and Kunz 2005, 2006; Kunz 2005; Rath 2007; Rath et al. 2018). Sydney's Chinatown is thus the point of departure for this chapter and this book. Chinatown is an ethnic precinct that has evolved, developed and been transformed for over one hundred and fifty years. An ethnic precinct is characterised by a clustering of immigrant business enterprises and immigrant community activities related to immigrant community settlement patterns. In this section, we explore in depth the precinct's history, social use and regulatory environment as backdrops to its changing built environment. In this way, we follow a well-worn path of analysis.

J. Collins et al., *Cosmopolitan Place Making in Australia*,
https://doi.org/10.1007/978-981-15-8041-3_2

Ethnic precincts like Chinatown are thus a key site of the commodification and marketing of ethnic diversity in cities of significant immigration. They are a prime focus for the production and consumption of the ethnic economy, a commodification of place and space where the symbolic economy of space (Zukin 1995) is constructed in representations of ethnicity and 'immigrantness'. Ethnic precincts are fundamentally contradictory places and spaces, reflecting the contradictions around the concept of ethnicity itself. So-called ethnic groups are in fact very diverse and not homogenous, or, as Fainstein et al. (2003, p. 246) put it, represent 'the tension between differentiation and homogeneity'. One contradiction relates to the competing conceptions of ***authenticity***: Does the built environment of Sydney's Chinatown represent an authentic representation of Chinese culture? The raison d'être of developing an ethnic precinct is to create a place and a space with an appealing ethnic smell, sound and sensibility, such that visiting this place in the city means experiencing the culture of one of Sydney's Chinese immigrant communities. As Boyle (2003, p. 3) argues, '[t]he point is that many of us—and an increasing proportion of the Western world—want to experience it ourselves. We want it real'. The challenge of the ethnic precinct is to recreate/represent an authentic ethnic experience of place by developing a symbolism, an ambiance and an experience that credibly coincides with wider expectations about or images of that ethnic group. For an ethnic precinct to be a vital part of urban tourism, it must have credibility in the eyes of those locals and tourists who use the space. That credibility—which could be measured quantitatively by return visitation, by the economic success of the ethnic enterprises or by attendances at precinct ethnic festivals—is in turn linked to the extent to which the ethnic precinct is seen as authentic by locals and tourists. This then leads to the question: 'authentic to whom?'

Second, there is the problem or contradiction of legitimation. Who speaks for a particular ethnic authenticity? How is that ethnicity to be symbolically represented? Who decides, and who controls the 'ethnic voice' in the city within resident ethnic groups of complex diversity? This problem is underscored by the fact that there are over 100 different Chinese ethnic community groups and associations in Sydney (Collins 2007, p. 78).

In order to address these multivocal viewpoints related to Chinese ethnicity we draw on in-depth interviews with Chinese Australians and local council staff (see Appendices 1 and 2), and a survey of 100 visitors to the area. Unlike most earlier research on ethnic precincts, we ask 'how do visitors experience the built environment and atmosphere of the precinct?' and 'is social value undermined by commercialisation, ethnic theming and the commodification of ethnicity?'

The next two Sects. (2.2 and 2.3) deal with two very different cases. We first look at Port Kembla as the NSW regional site and then at Griffith as the NSW rural site to see how changing patterns of minority immigrant settlement have impacted on the built environment in both places.

Prior to immigration, Indigenous peoples lived in what we now call Australia for some 60,000 years. As the previous chapter indicated, there was great diversity within the people of the First Nations. The original inhabitants of the City of Sydney and the Haymarket area where Chinatown is located were the Gadigal people while there were about 29 clan groups, collectively referred to as the Eora Nation, living in what today is Greater Sydney. There are 2412 Indigenous people living in the City of Sydney or 1.1 per cent of the population today. Port Kembla is located in land of the Dharawal Nation. Today the Indigenous population of Wollongong is 5348 or 2.5 per cent of the population. Griffith is located within the lands of the Wiradjuri Nation. Today the 1228 Indigenous people living in Griffity City comprise about 0.6 per cent of the population and are descended from the Wiradjuri Nation and also from other language groups such as the Yota, Ngyiampaa and Paakantji. Like the following sections, this one begins with a brief introduction to immigration and cultural diversity in Chinatown before turning to a consideration of the built environment. Interview and survey data give new insights into the way place is interpreted by both those involved in the social production of space and those passing through as consumers. Sydney's Chinatown and its use of 'mono-ethnic' theming can be compared to Perth's Northbridge, an ethnic precinct where processes of ethnic representation in public space have attempted to embrace multi-ethnicity.

2.1 Minority Immigrants and the Built Environment in Sydney's Chinatown

2.1.1 Immigration and Sydney's Chinatown

The history of Sydney's Chinatown is the history of both Chinese immigrant settlement and Chinese immigrant entrepreneurship. Sydney's Chinatown has a long history dating back to the first major wave of Chinese immigration to Australia, with the first concentration of Chinese businesses developing around The Rocks near the ports in Sydney Harbour in the 1860s[1] (Collins 2002; Collins et al. 1995, pp. 41–43; Collins and Castillo 1998; Fitzgerald 1997). Of the Chinese who settled in Sydney, those who set up shop in The Rocks were a minority. In 1878, one report indicated that there were 86 Chinese working in boarding houses and shops catering to people moving through the ports. But there were an additional 874 Chinese living in Sydney at the time (Fitzgerald 1997, p. 23). Nonetheless, in the 1880s, the concentration of Chinese shops and residences in The Rocks 'was beginning to make of George Street North a tentative Chinatown'[2] (Fitzgerald 1997, p. 24).

The concentration of Chinese shops and homes in Sydney was, in large part, an organic response to the patterns of trade and commercial opportunity. Accordingly, it continued to change and adapt as new commercial opportunities sprung up elsewhere in the city. While Chinese businesses had been developing in The Rocks, some Chinese had also settled in the Haymarket area at the southern end of the city and in adjacent Surry Hills. When the city's fruit and vegetable markets moved to the area in 1869, Chinese entrepreneurs established cookshops and lodging houses in the surrounding area to cater for the suburban market gardeners who visited the city to sell their produce. Meanwhile, the number of Chinese passing through the ports was declining, so, as City of Sydney historian Shirley Fitzgerald notes, 'the decline of The Rocks and the emergence of the Haymarket area as Sydney's second Chinatown reflected the changing balance between sojourning and staying' (Fitzgerald 1997, p. 88). Over time, the area around Goulburn, Campbell and Wexford Streets became a major Chinese centre, with Chinese businesses coming to include not only lodging houses and cookshops but also Chinese herbalists, furniture workshops, grocery stores, butchers and gambling and opium 'dens'[3] (Fitzgerald 1997, p. 89).

Sydney's Chinese settlements became a place for Chinese residents and families, too. Some long-standing and reputable Chinese businesses kept branches in both The Rocks and Surry Hills, and in some cases the proprietors chose to live in The Rocks (Fitzgerald 1997, p. 89). The southern Chinese settlement around Campbell Street was seen as the more insalubrious and impoverished end of the city. Since as early as 1876, official reports had recorded that many of the buildings occupied by Chinese in this area were 'unfit for human habitation', and the area became known by the broader community as a slum and 'synonymous with vice and opium smoking' (Fitzgerald 1997, pp. 88, 90). Some of the houses where white women lived were brothels. However, there were also a number of Chinese or 'mixed' families who lived in the area and, while there was certainly a criminal element in this part of town, official reports also identify that there were very functional family households who took great pride in their homes (Fitzgerald 1997). By 1900, this southern settlement had become the biggest concentration of Chinese residents in Sydney city: only 14% of the city's Chinese residents lived in The Rocks and the other 86% in Haymarket and Surry Hills (Fitzgerald 1997, p. 92).

Being surrounded by Chinese compatriots and establishing their own businesses may have been especially important for these early immigrants as they faced significant discrimination and hostility. As Jock Collins and colleagues have noted, the (changing) racialisation of Chinese immigrants has shaped directly or indirectly their experiences in the labour market and host society (Collins et al. 1995, pp. 90–97; see also Collins 2003; Light 1972). Legislation to limit Chinese immigration in the New South Wales (NSW) colony had been introduced as early as 1861 (Fitzgerald 1997, p. 23) and the 'White Australia' policy, introduced with Federation in 1901, as well as discriminatory factory laws further reinforced the position of Chinese immigrants and immigrant entrepreneurs as racialised minorities.[4]

Discriminatory legislation and public opposition to a Chinese presence do not imply that Sydney's Chinese immigrants were passive recipients of victimisation.[5] Some local Chinese became very well acquainted with the immigration laws in order to get around them, and by World War II, some were actively trying to 'undermine and frustrate the system' (Fitzgerald 1997, p. 41). Others were actively complicit in it, with some in the merchant class willing to go along with immigration restrictions while trying to negotiate better conditions, such as voting rights and permanency, for themselves[6] (Fitzgerald 1997, p. 88).

The centre of Sydney's Chinatown moved again in the early twentieth century. Long-standing official concerns about the living conditions around Campbell Street led to 'slum clearance' operations from 1906 that, along with the city's traffic management programmes, forced people to move away. At the same time, Chinese businesses had been voluntarily relocating a few blocks to the east, following the movement of the city's fruit and vegetable markets as they relocated from near Belmore Park to what is now Paddy's Markets (at the northern end of Quay Street). By the 1920s, most Chinese businesses in Sydney had either moved to or set up shop in this area, with many concentrated along Dixon Street.[7] Here, like in the earlier settlements, businesses included lodging houses, cookshops, herbalists and gambling houses as well as a number of fruit and vegetable merchants (Fitzgerald 1997).

As well as becoming a Chinese commercial centre, Dixon Street in the early and mid-1900s was a residential area, housing a number of Chinese immigrants. Many were single men living in boarding houses, but families also came when their Surry Hills houses were demolished by the city council (Fitzgerald 1997, p. 123). According to William Wang, a prominent Chinese immigrant who was very active in Chinese organisations in Dixon Street in the mid-twentieth century, there was a strong sense of community in this period. Most locals then knew 'everybody in Chinatown' (Interview C7). It was also a centre for local social services. Like the earlier Chinese concentrations in Surry Hills and The Rocks, many of the local businesses provided services like banking, mail delivery, travel arrangements, letter writing and even the return of the deceased's remains so that they could 'finally rest on Chinese soil' (Fitzgerald 1997, p. 53).

These services were commonly provided by businesses that catered to particular clan groups. Rex Wong, a well-known figure in Sydney's Chinatown, migrated to Australia from Fiji with his family in 1946. Arriving as a child, he grew up in Chinatown and nearby Ultimo and continued to work in Chinatown through his adulthood. He describes the presence of clan-based businesses in Dixon Street in the early 1900s:

> When Dixon Street was created... most of the Chinese businesses there were linked up with Chinese counties, or what we call clan-based associations... the Chung Shan clan, the Go Yiu and Gouming clan, the Dong Guan, the Jung Sing, the Sze Yup. They were the big five and they still... play a great influence in Dixon Street. (Interview C2)

In this newer centre of Chinese settlement around Dixon Street and up towards Surry Hills, other cultural institutions were also established, including the Chinese Masonic Society, the Kuomintang and the Chinese Youth League. The New South Wales Chinese Chamber of Commerce, with links to the Chinese republican movement, had begun operating in Campbell Street in the early 1900s but by 1915 had established monthly meetings in Dixon Street. It remained there until it closed in the mid-1970s (Interview C2).

By the end of World War II, Sydney's Chinese numbered just under 3500, approximately the same number as at the turn of the twentieth century. While the Chinese population across the country had declined, Sydney's numbers were propped up only by migrations from rural and regional New South Wales. Moreover, the Chinese that were in Sydney were ageing and had become increasingly marginalised in the affairs of the city (Fitzgerald 1997, pp. 2–3). Immediately after the war, new immigrants, particularly Italians, moved into fruit and vegetable retailing in Australia (Collins et al. 1995). The Chinese, who had had a significant presence in this industry, responded to this challenge with flexibility: many turned their business activities to running cafés and restaurants, not only in the cities but also in rural and regional areas. While many Chinese had already settled away from the main urban concentrations, Chinese restaurants now became a common feature of the Australian landscape, spreading to virtually every suburb and country town (Collins et al. 1995; Collins 2003). Chinese entrepreneurs thus exhibited both patterns of clustering in the ethnic market niche of Chinatown and other suburban centres and patterns of dispersal and breaking out into the mainstream market.

The war also saw a limited renewal of Asian immigration in Australia, with Chinese seamen deserting their ships as they came into Sydney Harbour and other Australian ports and almost 800 ethnic Chinese evacuees arriving from Pacific islands such as New Guinea, the Solomons and the New Hebrides[8] (Fitzgerald 1997, pp. 41–44; Yuan 2001, p. 205). These wartime arrivals were followed by several hundred ethnic Chinese students from places such as Malaysia, Singapore and Hong Kong who arrived under the Colombo Plan of the 1950s and 1960s. While many students under the Colombo Plan eventually returned to their home countries, others stayed on. Still others returned to Asia temporarily before settling in Australian in the 1970s (Fitzgerald 1997, p. 49).

The post-war period had signalled the beginning of a significant shift. By 1958, the English-language dictation test was removed from immigration requirements (Yuan 2001, pp. 205–206). Chinese who had been in Australia for fifteen years or more were permitted to obtain citizenship. In the early 1970s, the end of the White Australia policy recinded the restriction on Chinese immigration, and in the middle of that decade, large numbers of ethnic Chinese immigrants arrived in Australia as refugees from the Vietnam War. Wealthy Chinese immigrants also began to arrive from Hong Kong and Taiwan (Fitzgerald 1997, p. 50). This was the first large-scale ethnic Chinese immigration into Australia in three-quarters of a century.

By the 1970s, Australian attitudes were also changing. While some Anglo-Celtic residents and visitors had long frequented Chinatown's restaurants and gambling houses, 'mainstream' consumers, spurred on by the new official policy of multiculturalism and the emergence of articles about Chinese food in popular women's magazines, began to see the consumption of Chinese goods as enticingly 'exotic'. Shirley Fitzgerald (1997, p. 150) suggests that at this time 'everyone in Sydney, it seemed, was learning to use chopsticks'. The Sydney City Council saw potential in reinvigorating Chinatown as a commercial precinct, a task which had become particularly urgent as the fruit and vegetable markets had moved to Sydney's western suburbs and the Haymarket area had become commercially stagnant.

In the early 1970s, the council established and began working with the Dixon Street Chinese Committee, comprised of local Chinese business owners, to plan the redevelopment of the area as a formal Chinatown. Some local Chinese saw the idea as 'contrived and backward-looking' (Fitzgerald 1997, p. 151), while others disagreed about how the redevelopment should proceed (Anderson 1990). However, when the city invited public comment, many submissions were broadly supportive and donations came in from several Chinese businesses. 'Chinese-themed' street lighting, iconography and rubbish bins were installed, and Chinese arches (Fig. 2.1) were built at both ends of Dixon Street. The street was closed to traffic and established as a pedestrian mall (Fitzgerald 1997).

The redevelopment, explored in more detail in the next section, was commercially very successful.[9] It coincided with exogenous changes that saw investment in Chinatown rapidly increase: federal immigration laws had changed again to attract wealthy business immigrants, and the decision made in 1984 to hand control of Hong Kong from Britain to China led to a rush of investment from Hong Kong in overseas property including Sydney's Chinatown (Fitzgerald 1997). Once dominated by businessmen from Guangdong Province in mainland China, Chinatown's businesses became dominated by Hong Kong Chinese.

Further redevelopments of Chinatown since the 1970s and 1980s had been minimal. Under the local government, now known as the *City of Sydney*, major changes to the streetscape were carried out in the lead-up to the 2000 Olympic Games, including the installation of themed street lighting and a public art sculpture called the Golden Water

Fig. 2.1 Chinese arches, Dixon Street, Chinatown (*Source* Kirrily Jordan)

Mouth (Fig. 2.2). In 2003, a new memorial—the Australian Chinese Ex-servicemen Monument—was unveiled in Dixon Street to commemorate over 500 Australians of Chinese descent who have fought for Australia in every war from the Boer War through to the present day[10] (Tsang 2002).

Fig. 2.2 The Golden Water Mouth Fountain, corner Sussex and Hay Streets (*Source* Kirrily Jordan)

Since the 1970s, Chinese immigrants have featured very prominently in Australian immigration intakes. China is the most common birthplace of Sydneysiders other than Australia and the United Kingdom. The most recent Australian census shows that in 2016 there were just under 225,000 Chinese-born people living in greater Sydney—around 79% of all the Chinese-born in Australia at that time (Australian Bureau of Statistics [ABS] 2019). There is a great diversity in the profile of 'Chinese' immigrants in Sydney. Many were not born in mainland China, but in countries like Malaysia, Indonesia and Vietnam. Among those from mainland China, they are no longer restricted to those from the south. One indication of this is the language people speak at home. The census shows that in 2016 a little over 139,000 Sydneysiders spoke Cantonese at home while almost 229,000 spoke Mandarin (ABS 2019).

Ancestry data are also useful in building a picture of the number of Sydneysiders descended from Chinese immigrants. In 2016, nearly 488,000 people out of the 4,823,991 living in greater Sydney claimed Chinese ancestry. Those with Chinese ancestry were the third biggest ancestry group, after Australian and English[11] (ABS 2019). Some of Sydney's Chinese have roots in Australia dating back more than a century; others first set foot in Sydney quite recently. Some arrived as millionaire businessmen or women under the business migration programme or, more likely, as skilled and professional workers with tertiary education qualifications and good English. Some of Sydney's ethnic Chinese population arrived under the humanitarian programme, often as asylum seekers in the 1970s, while others have foregone such formalities to arrive in Australia through undocumented or illegal channels. There are a number of instances of restaurant owners in Sydney's Chinatown being charged with employing illegal immigrants as dishwashers and cheap, exploited labour (Collins 2007), a practice that dates back to the earliest years of Chinese settlement in Australia. Sydney's Chinese population also includes a large number of people on temporary visas who are in Sydney to study or work. There are also many Chinese international tourists to Sydney, with the city's Chinese New Year Festival one of its key tourist events.

Along with their increased diversity of origin, the settlement patterns of Sydney's Chinese immigrants have also changed considerably over time. Newer Chinese and Asian centres have emerged in many Sydney suburbs, with settlement patterns often reflecting the country or region of birth. For example, Cabramatta has become well known for its association with Indo-Chinese, and particularly Vietnamese, immigrants. Hurstville and Chatswood have become significant centres for immigrants from Hong Kong, while Ashfield has become a centre for immigrants from Shanghai (Interview C2). Settlement patterns may also reflect wealth, with less wealthy Chinese immigrants, like many other immigrant minorities, moving out to the western and south-western suburbs of Sydney and wealthier Chinese immigrants choosing to settle in the more expensive eastern suburbs and North Shore.

In recent years, though, the trend to a declining population in Chinatown has reversed and the Chinese resident population in and around Chinatown has increased considerably. This is a function of the growth in downtown high-rise apartment buildings in the last decade and the changing character of ethnic Chinese migration to Australia. Due to their relatively high incomes, skilled migrants can afford the housing costs of high-rise living in Chinatown, or of the new ‘middle class’ Sydney Chinatown of Chatswood on the North Shore (Collins and Castillo 1998). Anecdotal evidence also suggests that many of those living in the high-rise apartment buildings around Chinatown are students studying at one of the many colleges or higher education institutions nearby, with several students often cramped together in one- or two-bedroom apartments (Interview C2; Interview C12). A member of the local Haymarket Chamber of Commerce in 2008, here called John Teo, believes that the population in many of the high-rise apartment blocks in and around Chinatown is 80–90% Asian, having settled in the area because ‘they feel comfortable’ and can easily access familiar foods, whether it be Chinese, Thai, Indonesian or Malaysian (Interview C12).

At the 2016 Census, there were just over 7353 people living in the suburb of Haymarket, which includes most of today’s Chinatown. Table 2.1 shows that the most common birthplaces of Haymarket residents included Thailand and China and other Asian countries. In this suburb, immigrants outnumbered the Australian born by more than twelve to one.[12] Ancestry data are also instructive (Table 2.2). Looking at the list of birthplace countries of Haymarket residents, we could assume that at least some of those born in countries like Indonesia and Malaysia were ethnic Chinese. This is borne out by the census ancestry data, with over 2556 people reporting that they had Chinese ancestry while none of those born in Indonesia claimed Indonesian ancestry. Similarly, none of those born in Malaysia recorded that their ancestry was Malay (ABS 2019).

Table 2.1 Country of birth of Haymarket residents, top ten countries, 2016

Country of birth	*Persons*
Thailand	1519
China	1385
Indonesia	840
Australia	610
South Korea	368
Vietnam	154
Taiwan	130
India	128
Japan	124
Hong Kong	120
Total residents	7353

Source Author's calculation based on ABS (2019)

Table 2.2 Ancestry of Haymarket residents, selected groups, 2016

Ancestry	*Responses*
Chinese	2556
English	411
Korean	382
Australian	181
Vietnamese	162
Indian	150
Italian	112
Irish	103
French	64
Scottish	60
Total residents	7353

Note This question in the census is multi-response—total responses may not equal total number of persons
Source Author's calculation based on ABS (2019)

It is also interesting to note that 42% of people living in private dwellings in Haymarket were aged 25–34 years and the most common living arrangement was a group household. Nearly 38% of total residents in private dwellings and over 41% of the 25–34 years age group lived in this type of household (ABS 2019). At least 38% of Haymarket residents were attending a tertiary, technical or further education institution[13] (ABS 2019). These figures lend support to the anecdotal reports of a large number of Chinese and other Asian international students living in the area.

There are over 100 ethnic Chinese associations in Sydney. With new Chinese settlements springing up across several Sydney suburbs, many of Sydney's Chinese immigrants and associations may have little, or even nothing, to do with the Chinatown in downtown Sydney. Indeed, even in the early days of Chinese immigration, some Chinese who settled in Sydney's suburbs may have rarely, if ever, come to the Chinatown in the city (Fitzgerald 1997, p. 92). However, the downtown Chinatown still plays a role in the life of many of Sydney's ethnic Chinese. While most do not live in Chinatown, many visit it regularly to shop, to meet, to *yum cha* with their families or to consult with Chinese language health, legal and financial professionals whose offices are often located above street level. A number of Chinese clan associations and other Chinese community organisations are also still located in Chinatown, although others have moved away to newer Chinese centres in the suburbs.

While Dixon Street remains Chinatown's symbolic centre, the precinct has grown considerably. The concentration of Chinese shops and businesses extends at least to Liverpool Street in the north, Quay Street in the south and Harbour Street in the west, and even as far as Belmore Park in the east. It has also become a popular entertainment area for national and intentional tourists, particularly for its dozens of Chinese restaurants. The 1994 International Visitor Survey, for example, ranked Chinatown as the ninth most popular tourist destination in New South Wales, behind the Sydney Opera House and Darling Harbour, but ahead of museums, art galleries and zoos (Bureau of Tourism Research [BTR] 1994). The Chinese Garden of Friendship, built next to Chinatown in 1988, is heavily promoted as a tourist attraction and regularly achieves around 200,000 visitors per year (Sydney Harbour Foreshore Authority 2015). The deliberate development of Sydney's Chinatown as an ethnic precinct and its marketing as a tourist attraction are explored in the next sections.

2.1.2 Chinatown as an Ethnic Precinct

Until the 1970s, the location and character of Sydney's Chinatown grew and changed largely as a result of the day-to-day activities of local Chinese residents and entrepreneurs. Of course, this development was significantly influenced by exogenous factors such as the hostility of many non-Chinese, the restrictive legislative framework and the planning decisions of the local government. These influences were occasionally much more direct, such as the forced relocation of many Chinatown residents and entrepreneurs when their homes and businesses were demolished during the slum clearance and traffic management programmes of the early 1900s. However, it wasn't until the 1970s and the demise of the White Australia policy that the local government took a more overt role in the planning, design and promotion of Chinatown.

The motivations were at least twofold. During the mid-twentieth century, the area had attracted little investment and, when the city's main fruit and vegetable markets moved from the southern end of Dixon Street to Flemington in Sydney's western suburbs in 1975, Chinatown lost its principal source of commercial activity. In addition, the new federal policy of multiculturalism encouraged all levels of government to embrace cultural diversity and 'mainstream' popular culture was beginning to accept some aspects of cultural difference as not only acceptable but interesting. As early as 1971, with the closure of the Chinatown markets approaching, the local council began floating ideas for the area's redevelopment.

At the same time, Chinatown's business owners were approaching the city council for help in revitalising the area to attract more customers and new sources of income. One of the men involved in this process was Rex Wong. He recalls that the idea to revitalise Chinatown came from both the business owners and the city council:

> It was the initiative from both sides because we felt that something had to be done, and moving the whole of [the markets] they'd left a vacuum in Chinatown. Before, the markets were an attraction to Chinatown, because Chinese overseas wanted to congregate their businesses, establish very close to the market because they feel that it a good relationship to develop. (Interview C2)

The city council, supported by the Chinese Consul (Taiwan), established the Dixon Street Chinese Committee to work towards the area's redevelopment (Fitzgerald 1997, p. 151). The committee was made up of Chinese traders with businesses in Dixon Street. Rex Wong, who was the committee's secretary, remembers that at that time most of the business owners in Dixon Street were Cantonese-speaking and that the new committee had around 20 members (Interview C2). The chair of the

Dixon Street Chinese Committee was Henry Ming Lai, who, according to Fitzgerald, told the council that 'no-one considered narrow and tawdry Dixon Street to be 'Chinatown'' and that he hoped 'a more extensive precinct could be created once the market buildings became obsolete' (Fitzgerald 1997, p. 151).

Nonetheless, the plans for the redevelopment did centre on Dixon Street, and the first plans were advanced by the Chinatown Redevelopment Company of local Chinese man Gus Homeming. The redevelopment began with the addition of 'Chinese'-themed street lights and rubbish bins and there were plans to build a Chinese arch (*paifang* or *pailou*) in Dixon Street, but activities stalled when an agreement could not be reached over funding.[14] By 1977, the plans to redevelop Chinatown had regained momentum. The council converted Dixon Street to 'shared use', at first in a trial and then permanently in 1979. This decision limited vehicle access to certain times so that for most of the day the street became a pedestrian mall. Architect Henry Tsang, partner in the firm Tsang and Lee and himself an ethnic Chinese immigrant from Malaysia, volunteered his services to work with the Dixon Street Chinese Committee on the new streetscape design. Rex Wong recalls some of the design processes, with temporary wooden arches in Dixon Street later replaced with permanent arches.

Other features like guardian lions and Chinese lanterns were also added (Fig. 2.3). Decisions about layout and design drew on the advice of a Chinese fortune-teller:

> We managed to get a new recruit straight from his architecture degree at UNSW [University of New South Wales]—Henry Tsang ... He and his new partner George Lee put in some design plans, I think they even traveled to China and got some good ideas about archways and lions and beautification. They started to talk to the council, and in 1978 we had a temporary archway built—it was a timber one... And we experimented with closing off the street to traffic. After one or two years, eighteen months, it showed signs of improvement so we installed permanent archways at either end of Dixon Street. They were all completed, along with the lions, Chinese lanterns and trees. And we consulted a Chinese fortune teller, and together with his compass he gave us an indication of where we should do certain things. (Interview C10)

The Dixon Street Chinese Committee and the city council came to an agreement that the Sydney City council would pay for the street-level

Fig. 2.3 Guardian lion under *paifang*, southern end of Dixon Street (*Source* Kirrily Jordan)

changes, including paving the street to make it suitable for pedestrians, while funds would have to be raised by the Chinese community for the rest of the changes (Interview C11). Chinese businesses and associations from the local area and other Sydney suburbs donated money for the revitalisation, often through large fundraising dinners. One man involved in the design process, here called Thomas Low, also helped with the fundraising effort. He remembers that most of the funds were raised from the business community 'because the whole thing is a business proposition. The arch was supposed to revitalise the business in the street' (Interview C11). The money was raised through auctions at organised functions in Chinatown's restaurants:

> [It was] very simple, all the business people, you know, dinner is easy—fundraise dinner because the Chinese restaurant is there. So you fundraise, you invite the Mayor to come, and the people put their hand up, you know to auction. They auction anything… big money… there a lot of money auctioned off, and people who's got a few dollars, they want to be acknowledged, so they would want to be the chairman of this, called Dixon Street [Chinese] Committee. So, you want to be the chairman? How you going to do it? One hundred thousand. Deputy Chairman? Fifty thousand. So everyone who holds a position, actually not just by election, but on how much support you can lend to the project. (Interview C11)

For those involved in the design process, the Chinese arches and guardian lions (sometimes called *fu* lions or *fu* dogs) were important elements. The *paifang* represents the archways found throughout China that first appeared thousands of years ago as markers of the entrance to a town or building. In China, they were erected at crossroads, at the entrance to shrines and temples, on bridges, in parks, on tombs or outside government offices. The guardian lions have also been a traditional Chinese symbol, marking the entrance to important sites and buildings such as imperial palaces, emperors' tombs and government offices from as early as the Han Dynasty that reined from 206 BC to 220 AD. These symbols are also common in modern China and countries of contemporary Chinese immigration, with guardian lions often been incorporated into people's homes.

According to Low, the guardian lions in Dixon Street would 'drive away the evils' (Interview C11; also Interview C10 on the symbolism of the *fu* dogs). Like Rex Wong, he suggests that the archways were designed after the architects had seen other Chinatowns in London and the United States, but he also suggests that 'they are traditional architecture' (Interview C11). The arches are decorated with lucky animals and slogans in Chinese and English, and Low notes that:

> the wording selected on the archways is very symbolic … One side as I remember is… 'among the four seas we are all brothers' … yes, we travel all the way here, but the Chinese and the other people travel around the

> four seas and come to Australia we are all brothers. And the other one is to say that 'do not forget history and heritage as we move to the new era'. It's a very old Chinese saying ... For the Chinese community... we are now in a new land, a new culture, but we should not completely forget [our Chinese culture]... you should not forget, you should not be ashamed. (Interview C11)

For Low, the most important design features were actually those that are buried beneath one of the arches in a time capsule and so invisible to passers-by. According to Low, the capsule contains four elements that 'embody' what the Chinese community was 'feeling towards Australia' at the time. These are 'an old Chinese newspaper' called the *China Southern News* that had been published in Australia for over a century, demonstrating that 'the Chinese is a civilised, cultured community [that] has been in Australia more than a hundred years'. The second element is 'some old Chinese coins... from China'. These:

> symbolise that the Chinese community has always seemed to be branded by the mainstream community as a group of migrants who is not interested in Australia, all they interested is to make their money and bring their gold back to China... So they now reverse, to say that no, the Chinese people are not take their money away from Australia to go to China, in fact the business migrants bring their money to come to Australia. (Interview C11)

The third element is a 'golden tortoise', a lucky symbol to 'say that we will bring luck and fortune, we will bring the money, investment, but we will [also] bring luck into Australia' (Interview C11). And the final element is 'some pebbles and sand' from Guangdong. As Low explains, for many decades, most Chinese immigrants who had died in Australia had their bones sent back to China. He suggests that this was 'because they feel they not wanted in Australia' and couldn't bring their wives or children to Australia to be with them. So, since Australia's quarantine regulations prevent the importation of soil, the pebbles and sand were brought back to symbolise that 'sons and children of the descendants of Chinese migrants can now feel comfortable to be buried in Australia because the soil from China is now in Australia' (Interview C11).

When the plans for the redevelopment were submitted to council and made available for public comment, many people were enthusiastic about the proposal. Shirley Fitzgerald (1997) records some of the positive responses, including some from local Chinese businesses and some from Chinese residents in the Sydney suburbs. On the other hand, some people—both Chinese and non-Chinese—feared that the plans would create a Chinese 'ghetto' (Interview C10, Interview C11). Still others supported the idea of a more formal Chinatown but disagreed over the details of the design (Anderson 1990). However, there was enough support for the plans to go ahead and the finished redevelopment was officially opened in August 1980. The opening celebration was attended by Sydney's Lord Mayor, city councillors, the Dixon Street Chinese Committee and members of the public. It was at the opening celebration that the time capsule was ceremoniously buried. As Rex Wong recalls:

> We had a great whole day of celebration... the whole street was closed down ... We had roast pig, burnt incense, and underneath the male lion we buried Chinese coins for good luck and other artifacts... it was advertised as an open day—there were thousands of people there lining the streets watching it. There was no ticket, no entry fee, it was free for all. And we had a big lunch with the committee and councillors. (Interview C10)

Low remembers that the redevelopment gave Chinatown a new lease on life, with restaurants renovated, and a 'new enthusiasm' from business owners (Interview C11). He argues that the changes have also had long-standing economic effects, playing a part in attracting Asian investment in real estate development projects as well as increasing the attraction of Sydney for Asian students because it is a place where they can 'feel comfortable and diverse' (Interview C11). For the same reason, Low suggests that the Chinatown redevelopment has been a cultural success, citing the example of the Olympic Games in Sydney in 2000:

> Some people can say 'look you create this Chinatown, how do you show your loyalty? I mean you create your own environment, you are not part of mainstream.' Well, a good example is in that... when we were bidding for the Olympic Games for the year 2000 we were competing with Beijing... [there was a] 'support Sydney' rally in Dixon Street... and it so happens CNN [Cable News Network] was in Sydney... So it's interesting for CNN to see that the Chinese community supporting Sydney rather than Beijing... and some people say that we won the games because we demonstrated it's a harmonious multicultural society, and it happened in Chinatown... in the heart of Chinatown, the Chinese supporting Sydney for the Olympic Games. So I think... no doubt Chinatown, archway is a good thing. (Interview C11)

However, the redevelopment of Sydney's Chinatown has been subject to significant academic critique. In particular, Anderson's critique of the 1970s redevelopment suggests that she sees in it a continuity with earlier representations of Sydney's Chinese as an exotic spectacle rather than a break with the racialised past. Ana-Lisa Mak (2003) argues that in drawing on what she sees as stereotypical symbols of 'Chineseness' the redevelopment made Chinatown nothing more than a groundless copy of Chinatowns elsewhere. These perspectives do not sit easily with the recollections of those involved in the design process, including Wong and Low.

For example, while Low notes that the development was, first and foremost, a business proposition, both he and Wong believe that the symbolism reflects aspects of traditional Chinese culture. While they may have been drawing on those features that they felt were most likely to appeal to Western visitors, for them the design was not simply empty cultural clichés. For example, for Low, the most important symbols used in the redevelopment were those buried underground and hence invisible to passers-by. It would be difficult to argue that these features were designed to appeal to Western notions of an exotic 'Chineseness'. In addition, both Wong and Low argue that the redevelopment was not only a commercial project but also important in developing pride among local Chinese who, under the White Australia policy, had been ostracised and isolated. Low suggests that some Chinese who were opposed to the redevelopment were motivated by a desire to avoid drawing attention to cultural differences because of a fear of discrimination, explaining that:

> You've got to understand that at that time, the Chinese after a hundred years of discrimination, they feel comfortable... to become non-Chinese. No-one wants to learn Chinese, everybody's trying to be 'Aussie.' By being non-descriptive you would not attract attention, that was the feeling of a lot of people. (Interview C11)

For Low, building the arches in Chinatown was part of the process of claiming a positive Chinese identity and rebuilding community pride. He sees this as intertwined with the process of commercial development, with pride in being Chinese helping to facilitate business and community relations with non-Chinese Australians (Interview C11). His arguments not only echo those made by Dunn (1998) in relation to Sydney's

Cabramatta, but also suggest there may not be a neat divide between commercial and other community development goals.[15]

Similarly, in Wong's estimation, the redevelopment of Chinatown has given local Chinese status. While Sydney's Chinese were once largely excluded from political decision-making, Sydney's Chinatown has become a place 'where people feel they have that… status to say 'oh let's go to Chinatown and meet the prime minister' or, you know, immigration minister' (Interview C2). In addition, Wong argues that the redevelopment of Chinatown has helped to challenge old racist stereotypes:

> the development of Sydney's Chinatown has… generated progress for us, the image of the Chinese community is no longer the old days of 'ching chong chinaman', you know, the White Australia Policy, no longer. We're part of the multicultural cultural diverse society. (Interview C2)

In this way, according to Wong and Low, the redevelopment of Chinatown was one strategy in resisting negative stigmatisation and social and political marginalisation. It was also a way in which stereotypical portrayals of Chinatown as dangerous and crime-ridden could be challenged. Of course, these arguments draw attention to debates about identity politics. But the valid desire to challenge exclusion through identity politics and the equally valid concerns that static representations of ethnic difference can perpetuate processes of racialisation presents us with a difficult impasse. As British political theorist David Miller has eloquently put it, an interesting project is to 'press those who adopt a non-essentialist hybrid conception of identity to explain how one can institutionalize group recognition without also reifying group identities' (Miller 2002, pp. 268–269). Indeed, the strategic adoption of ethnic representations is often likely to *both* essentialise difference *and* provide opportunities for group recognition. As Tseen Khoo (2009) has argued of Chinatowns in general:

> while critique often centres on Chinatowns and how they function in terms of representation for external stakeholders, they should also be considered as vernacular zones of diverse cultural maintenance for the various communities under the umbrella of 'Chinese,' and a site for economic and intra-communal dynamics. Chinatowns are indeed manufactured zones, yet this manufacturing does not empty the space of meaning for local communities, nor should activities held there be automatically dismissed as 'inauthentic.' Chinatowns have multiple, contested meanings for different sectors of the community, and no single function eclipses others.

Wong and Low's recollections about the redevelopment of Sydney's Chinatown also raise questions about the role of the local council in this process. While Anderson focuses much of her critique on the part played by the local council in making Chinatown look more stereotypically Chinese, Wong and Low (like Ana-Lisa Mak 2003) both highlight the crucial role of Chinese entrepreneurs in designing and fundraising for the redevelopment. Wong also recalls that city councillors actually scaled back the Chinese theming of the site, with the Chinese lanterns in the original design eventually removed by the council because they were 'too Chinesey' (Interview C2). For Wong, Dixon Street is 'a bit too westernised now'[16] (Interview C2).

'Ownership' of the design process is not a trivial issue. In her research on Brixton in south London, Caroline Howarth (2002) has noted that the negative representation of racialised urban spaces as associated with crime, poverty or dysfunction can have a significant impact on the self-esteem and self-perception of local residents. She suggests that an appropriate strategy to reclaim positive recognition and esteem is to seek 'access to, and ownership of, the representational resources to develop alternative, oppositional versions of one's community and, therefore, of oneself' (Howarth 2002, p. 256).

Significantly, representatives from the local Chinese associations the Chinese Masonic Society and Chinese Youth League—both long-standing Chinatown institutions—see the streetscape in Dixon Street as appropriate (Interview C12, C7). Members of the Chinese Youth League donated money for the development and thought that it was 'very good' (Interview C7). The current Grand Master (GM) of the Chinese Masonic Society sees it as a positive development and suggests that the better marketing of the area as a commercial district helped to 'clean it up':

> before it's really dirty, Dixon Street, but now it's clean and tidy down there, there's a difference with about say 1960, 1970. Now it's more better— because it's commercial they put up a lot of cleaning job. (Interview C13)

Another member, the Life Honourable President (LHP) suggests that the arches and lions are representative of Chinese culture, saying that 'Chinese villages does look like that' (Interview C13). The Chinese Masonic Society participated in the 1980 opening ceremony for the redeveloped Dixon Street mall, performing the lion dance 'to bring good luck and prosperity and chase the evil spirit away and thing like that' (LHP, Interview C13). The Grand Master and the Life Honourable President also note the responsiveness of the local council to concerns about images incorporated into the streetscape, with local Chinese associations applying to the council to remove a yin and yang symbol set into the pavement in the mid-1990s. The symbol was seen as inappropriate because 'we must respect this one, the yin yang, so can't put it on the ground to let everybody step on it' (GM, Interview C13). In response to community concerns, the symbol was removed. All of these examples highlight local Chinese agency in the redevelopment of Sydney's Chinatown, suggestive of a 'creative authenticity' in ethnic representation. This is not, of course, to deny the very significant role of the state.

2.1.3 Visitors' Voices

The different perspectives of Anderson, Low, Wong and others suggest that there are very different responses to Chinatown's marketing and symbolism. Of course, the debate conjures up notions of authenticity and legitimacy (Collins 2007, pp. 74–79), including both how 'authentic' visitors perceive a built environment to be and who has the 'legitimacy' to direct the design process. In a 2005 study, Patrick Kunz began to explore the responses of visitors to Chinatown as they walked through its main streets, attempting to discern whether visitors perceived it to be an authentic representation of Chinese culture. He conducted 50 face-to-face surveys of pedestrians in Dixon Street and divided the survey respondents into three categories—'ethnic' (Chinese), 'co-ethnic' (other Asian) and 'others'. He found that ethnic and co-ethnic consumers were more likely to experience Chinatown's built environment as 'fake' and 'kitschy', while those in the other category were more likely to experience it as 'authentically Chinese'. He argued that this confirmed Anderson's critique of Chinatown's redevelopment as exoticising Chinese culture, but that the experiences of non-Asian visitors highlighted the potential of Chinatown as a tourist destination (Kunz 2005).

In April 2007, we conducted a similar random survey of 100 passers-by in Dixon Street to examine further both people's perceptions of the streetscape and the precinct's tourism potential. Like Kunz's earlier study, the survey revealed a range of responses to Chinatown's built environment, from those who felt it was 'very authentic' (Visitor QNO6) to those who felt it was 'a bit kitsch' (QNO40). However, contrary to the findings of Kunz (2005), in the 2007 survey, there was no clear pattern between people's response to the built environment and their ethnicity. When asked what they disliked about the architecture and physical features of Chinatown, only two respondents in the 2007 survey expressed that the streetscape was 'kitsch' or 'tacky'. One identified as being Australian Chinese (QNO40) and the other as White British (QNO60). The mixed responses across ethnicity mirror findings of earlier research by Helen Armstrong (1998, p. 296) on expressions of Greek cultural identity in the Australian built environment, with some Greek immigrants seeing the almost ubiquitous Greek cafés in country towns as 'important elements in the cultural landscape' and others seeing them as examples of 'high kitsch'.

While Kunz's survey asked people to choose descriptors from predetermined options, the 2007 survey asked people about their perceptions of Chinatown with a number of open-ended questions. These included questions about Chinatown's streetscape (*'What do you like most about the architecture and physical features of Chinatown?'*; and *'Are there things you don't like about the architecture and physical features of Chinatown?'*) and atmosphere (*'What do you like most about the general atmosphere of Chinatown?'*; and *'Are there things you don't like about the general atmosphere of Chinatown?'*).

Since the 2007 survey uses a different method to Kunz's, it is not surprising that it produced a different result. The choice of method reflects both the authors' epistemological perspective and the desire to let the respondents speak for themselves rather than guiding and limiting their answers. This allowed unexpected answers to emerge and demonstrated that some respondents were deeply engaged in the issues being explored. The responses to the open-ended questions—which ranged between brief, one-word answers to long, reflective replies—were written down by the interviewer either in full or in paraphrased notes. This allowed a thematic analysis of responses and lends itself to a qualitative, rather than quantitative, study of the results. It demonstrates the range and complexity of people's perceptions rather than trying to establish the proportion of people who responded in a particular way.

In the 2007 survey, those who did not like the streetscape held this position for a range of reasons and came from a range of ethnic backgrounds: ethnicity was not a predictor for people's response. For example, one young man who identified his ethnicity as Taiwanese did not like anything about Chinatown's architecture or physical features not because he thought it was kitsch but because, to him, it wasn't big or grand enough: 'in my country it's better than this—to be a Chinatown you have to build a whole street like a Chinatown (*uses hand gestures to say 'it has to be bigger', 'it's not enough'*)' (QNO2). While this man would prefer a bigger Chinatown, another respondent, who saw himself as a 'normal Australian', did not like the architecture because 'it is a dump' and, like the whole of Sydney, 'should be bulldozed' (QNO13). Many others shared the view that the problem with Chinatown's architecture and physical features was that the area was too dirty, old or in need of renovation. Still others thought it was too alien to them, like one young woman who identified her ethnicity as 'Australian' who particularly disliked the signs being written in Chinese, 'or whatever language it is' (QNO26).

Respondents who liked the architecture and atmosphere in Chinatown were also motivated by a diverse range of considerations. Some liked the architecture because they felt it was 'oriental' (QNO14, QNO64, QNO68) while another liked the atmosphere because it had an 'oriental flavour' (QNO52). These responses may lend some weight to Anderson's argument that such places can perpetuate racialisation. However, in contrast to Kunz's (2005) findings in which 'Chinese' and 'Asian' respondents were more likely to think Chinatown's streetscape was 'fake' or inauthentic, many people in the 2007 survey who identified as having an Asian or Chinese background liked the architecture and physical features and thought they were typically Chinese.

For example, one young woman visiting Australia from China, who identified her ethnicity as 'multicultural', liked Chinatown's architecture and physical features because 'it's pretty Chinese. It's a familiar feel' (QNO5). Similarly, a man who identified his ethnicity as Chinese and who lived in northern Sydney thought that the architecture made Chinatown 'really feel like China' (QNO36). Another young man who identified as 'Australian with an Asian background' said that he 'just loved' the Chinese décor and signs and liked that the architecture was similar to other Chinatowns around the world (QNO7). A young woman from Sydney's inner west who identified her ethnicity as being 'from Shanghai' liked the architecture because it was 'old' and 'classic' but wanted to 'add some western feeling without changing the Chinese traditional design' (QNO21). She would prefer 'a combination of western and eastern, because it's Australia, not China' (QNO21).

While some respondents who identified as having Asian or Chinese ancestry or ethnicity valued Chinatown's 'traditional Chinese' design, others valued its familiar atmosphere. For example, one young man liked Chinatown 'because there are so many Chinese and I am Chinese too—I can feel like I'm in China' (QNO16). A Taiwanese man felt 'at home' in Chinatown (QNO2) while a South-East Asian man living in Sydney's eastern suburbs liked Chinatown because it 'reminds me of home' and is a place where 'I don't feel like an outsider', noting that 'at times it's difficult to mingle with other cultural groups, so you tend to yearn for something familiar' (QNO53).

Interestingly, some respondents stated that they had never noticed the architecture or physical features of Chinatown. For example, one man who identified his ethnicity as 'Australian' said 'I don't think about it because they're just old buildings and facade, but it is the people and activities and ambience that are important' (QNO3). Another, who identified as being Chinese from Hong Kong, said that he had 'never noticed' Chinatown's architecture and physical features (QNO12), while a woman who was 'just white, English' hadn't noticed the architecture because she was 'too busy looking in shop windows' (QNO24).

Survey respondents were also asked a number of other questions about things like whether they felt safe in Chinatown and what, if any, impact they thought Chinatown had on the community. While these questions are complex, people's responses gave important insights into the various ways people react to public space and the interactions between public space, ethnic representation, racialisation and identity. Some people made broad generalisations—both positive and negative—about Chinese people or culture. For example, one respondent who identified her ethnicity as 'Irish, German, English and Scottish' said that she felt safe in Chinatown 'because we know the Chinese respect people' (QNO4). Another cautioned his wife as soon as they entered Chinatown to 'hold on to her bag' because there might be pickpockets and they were entering the 'unknown' (QNO44).

Many respondents felt that Chinatown created a positive opportunity for mixing with people from other cultures or learning about Chinese culture, including some people who identified their ethnicity as Chinese. One of these, a young woman from China, thought Chinatown helped Australian people 'see and know more about China, meet more Chinese, enjoy Chinese culture' (QNO5). One tourist from China thought Chinatowns were good for tourists because it is 'easy for people [from China] to get involved' (QNO55). Another woman valued the opportunity to give her young son a cultural experience different to that available in their predominantly Anglo-Celtic suburb on Sydney's northern beaches (QNO96).

Of course, seeing Chinatown as an opportunity to learn about 'Chinese culture' may exacerbate concerns that it presents a limited or stereotypical view. Respondents who felt Chinatown gave them 'a broader insight into other cultures' (QNO45) or that things in Chinatown were 'really like in China' (QNO73) may well have a limited understanding of Chinese culture if their visits to Chinatown are their main source of information and they believe this information to be authoritative. Moreover, some people felt out of place or ill-at-ease in this environment. One Sydney man who identified as being Indian felt that the atmosphere was 'too Asian sometimes, so I feel a bit alien' (QNO41), while a woman, born in Australia of English and Irish ancestry, thought that places like Chinatown 'probably [have their] good things, but you can feel a bit of a foreigner yourself, and we live here too'. She felt that she could be 'discriminated against' in Chinatown because she is not Chinese (QNO47). Raising a similar concern to Ghassan Hage (1997), a tourist from Scotland thought that Chinatown could 'lead to a kind of diversity tourism, where you come to places like this for a shot of ethnicity without actually having to accept it as part of your life' (QNO60).

On the other hand, some respondents saw Chinatown as an antidote to what they believed was a prevailing attitude of intolerance. One man, who identified his ethnicity as 'Irish, English and Australian', liked that he felt like a cultural minority in Chinatown because it is 'a reminder I live in a very broad culture' and 'it relativises me and my cultural experiences'. He linked this to Australia's political climate, suggesting that Chinatown demonstrated that 'there's no necessarily dominant Anglo culture. It relativises any absolutes you might have, that [Australian PM] Howard has tried to impose on us' (QNO42). A man who identified as Lebanese Australian took a similar view, suggesting that Chinatown was 'good for tolerance, it breeds tolerance in an intolerant society'. He thought this was particularly important since intolerance was being 'directed down by the Howard government' that had 'gotten rid of multiculturalism' in favour of integration, and 'areas like [Chinatown] go directly against that alarming development' (QNO28). One Caucasian man from Sydney's inner west liked the 'Asian influence' in Chinatown but reflected that 'hopefully, while it points out some of the cultural differences, it shows in essence that we're not so different' (QNO11), while a Colombian man living in Sydney felt that Chinatown showed that Australia 'is an Asian country too' (QNO20).

Other people enjoyed the exposure to a different cultural experience but recognised that it was only 'a bit of a taste' (QNO50). Some wanted to increase their knowledge or experience by visiting China (QNO50), reading more about the history of Sydney's Chinese, learning Mandarin (QNO42) or meeting more Asian people (QNO56). One couple wanted to learn more about Sydney's Chinese history in a museum or library because 'if you buy something or just eat you don't learn much' (QNO61). Of course, others saw the value of Chinatown as purely commercial, being 'just a buy and sell deal' (QNO18), a place where you can buy cheap goods (QNO15) or 'one of the few affordable places to eat in the city' (QNO48).

Like Mohammad Aeson's perspective of visitors to Katanning Mosque later in this book, these many and varied responses highlight the need to differentiate between different types of tourists. Some may, indeed, be Hage's (1997) 'cosmo-multiculturalists', but others may be much more like Cohen's (1996) experiential visitors. In addition, the range of responses demonstrates the need to acknowledge the agency not only of those whose cultures are being represented, but also of the tourists and visitors doing the viewing. It requires us to reflect on what MacCannell (2001) calls the viewer's 'second gaze'—the reflexivity of the consumer in which they recognise when what they are being offered is 'inauthentic'. In Rodanthi Tzanelli's (2004, p. 26) words, it requires giving attention to:

> a combination of structuralism (with an examination of the deep structures of consumption) and hermeneutics (with an exploration of how signs are interpreted in the production/consumption chain).

These survey results also raise another interesting point. While Kunz's 2005 survey categorised people into the three groups of 'ethnic', 'co-ethnic' and 'other', giving respondents the opportunity to state their own ethnicity in the 2007 survey highlighted the complexity and ambiguity of the concept.[17] When asked '*how would you describe your ethnicity or cultural background?*', some people gave concise answers such as 'Anglo', 'Chinese', 'Spanish', 'Celtic', 'Caucasian' or 'Thai'. Some people's answers illustrated the cultural specificity of some ethnic descriptors. For example, a number of visitors from the United Kingdom said that they were 'White British', a common phrase in the United Kingdom that does not have an equivalent ('White Australian') in regular usage in this country. The common Australian phrase 'Anglo-Celtic' made no sense to a visitor from Ireland who had never heard it used before coming to Australia.

At the same time, giving respondents the onus of identifying their own ethnicity also illustrated that many people recognise that ethnic 'boundaries' and cultural distinctions are very blurred. A large number of respondents stated that their ethnicity or cultural background was 'multicultural' or 'mixed'. Several gave long answers such as: 'Irish, German, English and Scottish' (QNO4); 'Arabic and North African but I'm from France' (QNO61); or 'I'm married to Pole born in Lebanon, and my background is English and Irish but I was born in Australia' (QNO47). A small minority gave answers that seem to demonstrate a cultural myopia, such as 'normal Australian' (QNO13) or 'very much Aussie' (QNO59).

The recognition of many survey respondents that 'boundaries' of ethnicity, ancestry and identity can be blurred—a complexity also widely recognised among many social scientists (see, for example, Barth 1969; Giddens 1991; Nederveen Pieterse 1996)—may have some implications for arguments about authenticity and ethnic representation. For example, in arguing that the redevelopment of Sydney's Chinatown was part of a process of racialisation and ethnic stereotyping, Anderson (1990) reflects on the political climate of the late 1970s and early 1980s—a time when multicultural policy was very new and Australia was only just emerging from many decades under the White Australia policy. Arguably, the attitudes of many Australians towards ethnic diversity have come a long way over the last 30 years. If the 2007 survey of visitors to Chinatown demonstrates a new recognition of the complex and overlapping nature of ethnic identities, it also points to the likelihood that representations of ethnicity in the built environment will be interpreted differently over time. While the survey is certainly not proof of such a change, it does suggest the possibility that, in a very different political and cultural climate, many visitors to Chinatown today may experience and understand the site in a more nuanced way than those attracted by its new exoticism some three decades ago.

2.1.4 *Regulating Chinatown*

Understanding ethnic representation in Chinatown also requires a focus on regulation. While 'authenticity' can be understood in relation to the perception of visitors, the question of 'legitimacy' concerns who has the authority to make the decisions about how, or if, ethnicity is represented (Collins 2007, pp. 74–79). Regulation is also central to the social and commercial use of space. The key players in the regulation of Sydney's Chinatown include the local (City of Sydney) and state governments, Chinese entrepreneurs and ethnic Chinese associations. A number of important questions arise: What formal and informal structures operate to shape Chinatown's development? In decisions about these processes who is consulted and who is not? What is the nature of the relationships among and between Chinatown's entrepreneurs, Chinese community organisations and local and state government authorities? The roles of the major players, and the relationships between them, are explored in this section.

2.1.4.1 *City of Sydney*

As noted above, the role of Sydney's local government in Chinatown has changed dramatically over time. From the earliest days of the development of Chinatown in The Rocks through to the first decades of the twentieth century, the city council's most conspicuous role in Chinatown was as watchdog and inquirer into the living conditions of Sydney's Chinese. From the 1970s, the city council's role in Chinatown changed from being primarily a controller and enforcer to actively encouraging the precinct's growth. In promoting the redevelopment of Chinatown, the council's main point of contact with local Chinese was the Dixon Street Chinese Committee. Rex Wong recalls that, in the 1970s, a survey showed that around 90% of properties in Dixon Street (between Hay and Goulburn Streets) were either owned or occupied by Chinese 'so it was quite appropriate that we had a talk with the city council and set up a committee' (Interview C2).

While the Dixon Street Chinese Committee was initially involved only in the plans to redevelop Chinatown, Thomas Low suggests that its legacy was much greater in that it established, for the first time, an ongoing working relationship between a Chinese association and the local and state governments. According to Low, this had a lasting effect not only on cooperation on issues such as health and hygiene, but also on the ability of Sydney's Chinese to mobilise in response to other issues like the anti-Asian campaigning of right-wing politician Pauline Hanson in the 1990s. He argues that once the redevelopment was complete:

> people start to work closer to the council about standard of health and so on… it also formalise a group of people that deals with the council and the state government and so… it can respond to things like Pauline Hanson. (Interview C11)

The mobilisation of Sydney's Chinese in response to anti-Chinese sentiment or legislation did predate the establishment of the Dixon Street Chinese Committee. Nonetheless, Low's observation highlights the importance of the new relationship between the Dixon Street Chinese Committee and the city council. This is particularly significant in considering the legitimacy of ethnic representation since the Dixon Street Chinese Committee was limited to a select group of people arguably with a particular class interest. The committee was not only limited to business owners but, as we have seen, the executive positions were allocated to those willing to donate the most money towards the redevelopment (Interview C11). Hence, in the 1970s, wealthy business owners became the de facto representatives of Sydney's Chinese in planning Chinatown's redevelopment with the city council. This reflected a long history of class distinction among Sydney's Chinese, with early associations such as the New South Wales Chinese Merchants Society actively supporting merchant's rights but not those of 'lower class Chinese' (Fitzgerald 1997, p. 88).

With the redevelopment of Sydney's Chinatown complete, the Dixon Street Chinese Committee scaled back its activities.[18] In the mid-1990s, the city council established a new committee, the Chinatown Cultural Advisory Committee, to: advise the council on the development and implementation of projects in Chinatown; assist council to raise funds for events and public works in the precinct; and give advice about cultural events and activities such as Chinese New Year celebrations and public art. The Chinatown Cultural Advisory Committee became the only ethno-specific committee under the auspices of the city council.[19] A Chinese New Year subcommittee, comprising twelve members of the larger committee as well as non-members seconded for their specialist skills, worked closely with council over the course of a year to plan the city's Chinese New Year events.

In 2007, the Chinatown Cultural Advisory Committee and Chinese New Year subcommittee were reformulated as one committee, the Chinese New Year Festival Advisory Group.[20] This group has remained the main point of contact between the city council and Sydney's Chinese community. According to the executive officer of the group in 2007, Stuart Gill, its main purpose is to advise on the Chinese New Year Festival. However, like the previous Chinatown Cultural Advisory Committee, it is able to informally assist with advice on other Chinatown issues (Interview C6). Each year the members are appointed by council on recommendation of the existing members of the Advisory Group. The group can have up to 15 members, and as of December 2007, it had 12 Chinese members plus the executive officer, who was also the City of Sydney's Program Manager for the Chinese New Year Festival at the time.[21]

Like the Chinatown Cultural Advisory Committee, the Chinese New Year Festival Advisory Group is comprised of members of the Chinese community who have expertise in areas such as media, business or the arts. In 2007, the members included prominent figures in Chinese businesses and associations such as the Chinese Australian Services Society (CASS), the Asia-Australia Arts Centre, the Chinese Youth League and the Haymarket Chamber of Commerce. Stuart Gill explains the rationale for selecting committee members:

> basically it is made up of Chinese community leaders, from community groups, sporting organisations, business organisations, individuals, not necessarily people from within organisations, people from arts, that sort of thing. We aim to get as broad a cross section of the Chinese community as we can. A lot of them have been with us for a very long time... and they have an awful lot of experience, amazing expertise within the committee... it is all voluntary [so] we are very lucky to actually get them to participate so wholeheartedly. (Interview C6)

Gill also notes that the council is 'always trying to get new people so we don't have the same people again and again', and that there is some 'kudos' attached to being a committee member (Interview C6).

2.1.4.2 Local Action Plans

While the Chinatown Cultural Advisory Committee and, now, the Chinese New Year Festival Advisory Group have focused most of their activities on the Chinese New Year celebrations, they have also had input into council planning processes. The main avenue for this input is via the council's Local Action Plans (LAPs) which have drawn on community consultation to develop priority lists for improvement projects in each of eight zones in the city. Chinatown falls in the Central Business District (CBD) zone along with Haymarket, The Rocks, Dawes Point, Millers Point and Walsh Bay.

The City of Sydney views its LAP process as a 'bottom-up' approach to city planning (Field notes C29.05.06) and it has recently won the 'RH Dougherty Reporting to your Community Award' from the Local Government and Shires Associations of NSW for its Local Action Plans booklet. The booklet is designed to provide the community with a snapshot of projects under the Local Action Plan Strategy 2007–2010. The award judges noted the 'comprehensive community engagement' in the LAP process (City of Sydney n.d.). Community consultation in developing the LAPs has included the 'biggest program of public consultation ever undertaken in the 169 year history of the City' (City of Sydney 2007a, p. 5). Consultation began in 2006 and has included a city-wide household survey, public forums for each of the eight zones, workshops of community groups, workshops of city councillors, focus groups of randomly selected participants from each area and a street survey designed to capture the views of both workers and tourists (City of Sydney n.d.; Field notes C29.05.06).

At the third public forum for the CBD zone, held on 26 February 2007, of the seven local residents and business people representing the Haymarket/Chinatown area, only two were Chinese. One left early and so did not contribute to the discussion and the other, Kong Sang, raised concerns about inadequate lighting and a feeling among some local Chinese business owners that the Golden Water Mouth sculpture in Chinatown is inappropriate. At the end of discussions, the two priority areas identified by the group were improved lighting and graffiti removal, although the group as a whole did not prioritise concerns about the public art (Field notes C26.02.07). The former Chinatown Cultural Advisory Committee also made an independent submission to the LAP process in the form of a letter to council highlighting a number of key concerns:

> *Kong Sang*: at the beginning of [2007]... we did put forth the issues around Chinatown whereby, as community leaders, we know about this via our contact with the Chinese community, what the issues were and all that, so we put forth a letter to council... [saying] these are the types of things to look at, or to consider during the LAP...

Interviewer: From your perspective, or from what you have heard in the advisory group, what are the most important issues that you see for Chinatown in terms of redevelopment?

Kong Sang: The most important one, in everyone's concern, would be lighting and security... lighting because... of Chinese belief, idea that lights attract more wealth at night... you know, Chinese don't like places that are dark, you know business, trading places that are dark... so what they [business owners] are asking for is brighter street lighting around Dixon Street and Dixon Mall... and improved security. (Interview C5)

He suggests that security is still a concern, particularly in the northern end of Dixon Street where there are fewer shops and less lighting. Kong Sang also suggests that the Chinatown Cultural Advisory Committee has played a role in informing other Chinese groups and associations about council forums which they may have an interest in attending (Interview C5). However, he says that Chinese people can often be reluctant to raise their concerns with council because they do not like to make official complaints (Field notes C29.05.06). Rex Wong, the long-time Chinatown resident introduced earlier, also notes that community forums in the evenings may not be the best way of engaging some Chinese community groups, particularly clan associations, because the members are often elderly, may have poor English, and do not like to go out at night (Interview C2).

The priorities identified in the Local Action Plan process have fed into a number of short- and long-term plans, including a 'Chinatown Improvement Plan', with some actions already included in forward budgets. The actions identified for the Chinatown improvements include a physical upgrade of the precinct, with a focus on Dixon Street. The city's budget has allocated $5 million over three years for the upgrade, and while the plans stress ongoing community consultation, suggestions include changes to 'reflect the contemporary culture of Chinatown' such as lighting, tree planting and paving that incorporates 'heritage messaging', as well as street furniture that supports festivals and art to reflect both 'Chinatown's heritage' and 'contemporary Chinese culture' (City of Sydney 2007b, p. 25).

Suggested changes also include improvements to the public space around the entrances to Market City (a large shopping mall) and surrounding streets to 'reinforce the forecourt of Market City as a meeting place' (City of Sydney 2007b, p. 25). The LAP recommends that these improvements 're-enforce Chinatown's characteristic theme using planting themes, lighting, paving and street furniture to add to the area's identity' (City of Sydney 2007b, p. 25). Concept drawings for the northern end of Dixon Street include public art, flowers and *al fresco* dining. Concept drawings for the streets around Market City pick up on a similar theme of red flowers, with the City of Sydney noting that 'Chinatown's community suggested improvements to the walking streets of the area capturing the spirit, culture and gardens of China' (City of Sydney 2007a, p. 13).

The LAP for the Sydney CBD also includes provisions to: provide a suitable meeting place for Sydney's Chinese community; make Harbour Street more 'pedestrian friendly' while incorporating *al fresco* dining and elements of Chinese theming in the streetscape; improve lighting in Belmore Park; and improve pedestrian access to the Powerhouse Museum in Ultimo and the Chinese Gardens in Darling Harbour (City of Sydney 2007b, pp. 25–26, 40).

In improving the amenity of Chinatown, there is also a focus on safety and security. The issue of tourist safety is central to any government tourist strategy. Few people would want to go to a place where their or their family's safety is put at risk. Control and surveillance are thus embedded in the development of tourism in general as well as in ethnic precincts. Judd (Hoffman et al. 2003, p. 23) points out that building tourist places as fortress spaces is one response to managing issues of tourist safety. Chinatowns the world over have always had a criminal aspect (Kinkead 1993, pp. 4–5), whether real or imagined. Indeed, it is this edgy image of Chinatown that, to some, has been the main attraction[22] (see Kinkead 1993, p. 47). Citing concerns about some people in Chinatown 'pinching bags', Rex Wong notes that the Dixon Street Chinese Committee began working with the council and the local police in the 1990s in a programme he calls 'Sydney business watch' (Interview C2). He suggests that under this programme closed-circuit television (CCTV) cameras, regular police patrols and private security guards have decreased the incidence of crime (Interview C2).

The NSW police continue to work with the community, including in Chinatown, under their Community Safety Precinct Committees. However, Kong Sang notes that some business owners in Chinatown still have concerns about safety, particularly in dark areas like northern Dixon Street (Interview C5). This reflects the findings of Patrick Kunz's (2005) survey of business owners in Dixon Street, where Chinese entrepreneurs reported what they saw as an increasing level of crime within the precinct.

This was attributed to growing numbers of individuals dealing, and using, heroin or other illicit drugs. The Chinese entrepreneurs were highly critical of the response by local police, particularly because of slow police response times to criminal incidents. They felt the CCTV monitoring systems spread throughout Chinatown to be of little use (Kunz 2005).

Despite these concerns of business owners in Chinatown, in the 2007 survey of 100 passers-by in Dixon Street, 91% of respondents reported that they felt safe in Chinatown, the most common reason being that it was very busy and there were always a lot of people around. Among those who did not feel safe, most reported that they only felt unsafe at night and that the biggest threat they felt was from drunk people in the street. As of 2007, the City of Sydney has a new 'street drinking strategy' in which council works with local businesses and police when particular problems are identified (City of Sydney 2007b, p. 33).

2.1.4.3 State Government Agencies

While the City of Sydney is responsible for planning and development in Chinatown, the area borders on to land that is managed by the NSW State Government through the Sydney Harbour Foreshore Authority (SHFA). In 1988, the Chinese city of Guangzhou gifted Sydney a Chinese garden to celebrate their sister city relationship.[23] The result, the Chinese Garden of Friendship, is intended to be a replica of a Zhang dynasty Chinese garden. Built on land adjacent to Chinatown that was reclaimed from industrial use, it was designed both as a tourist attraction and to serve the local community (Field notes C01.08.06).

The Chinese garden is involved in the City of Sydney's Chinese New Year Festival, engaging lion dancers and entertainers for the event (Field notes C01.08.06). This is particularly important as one of the key events in the festival, the dragon boat races, occurs at Darling Harbour and the Chinese garden provides a link between the harbour and Chinatown. However, while the city and SHFA cooperate on the Chinese New Year Festival, historically there has been a distinct lack of coordination between the two bodies on questions of city planning.

Being part of the Darling Harbour precinct which is under SHFA's control, the Chinese garden faces on to the walkway to Darling Harbour but with its back to Chinatown. The back of the garden is surrounded by a high brick wall so that, although it is less than 100 metres from Chinatown, when standing in Dixon Street there is no indication that the garden is there. There is no pedestrian overpass to conveniently connect pedestrians from Chinatown to the Chinese garden, with people moving between the two sites having to navigate through traffic lights across at least two major roads.

As noted above, the lack of a convenient pedestrian connection between the two sites has recently been raised in the City of Sydney's Local Action Plan process, and under its Local Action Plan for the Sydney CBD, the city has now committed to improving the pedestrian connections between the sites and better promoting awareness of the Chinese garden, although it has not specified how this is to be done. The city has also pledged to advocate to SHFA to improve public space within SHFA boundaries that borders on to Chinatown (City of Sydney 2007b, pp. 25–26).

While the City of Sydney's relationship with SHFA has at times been strained, the city does work closely with another state government agency, Tourism New South Wales (TNSW). TNSW does not promote Sydney's ethnic diversity as a driver for long-haul tourism. According to Michelle Hughes, a senior staff member in Sydney Destination Services at TNSW in 2007, the agency's international tourist campaigns focus on what is unique to Australia or NSW (iconic animals such as kangaroos and iconic landmarks like Sydney's beaches and opera house, or other features that research indicates are relevant and appealing to a particular market). However, Sydney's cultural mix is promoted as a supporting message in overseas markets, with the more uniquely 'Australian' imagery used to attract visitors but experiences of cultural diversity presented as adding depth once they arrive. In addition, ethnic and cultural diversity is presented as 'reassurance imagery' in particular international markets where research has shown tourists want familiar foods and experiences to be available when they are away from home (Interview C1). As Hughes explains:

> Italians don't necessarily want to... have Italian food when they get here, they might need reassurance that they can get it if they want to, but it's not the reason they come to Australia. (Interview C1)

Further, she notes that 'some Asian markets will require familiar meals during their visit, particularly during their first visit to Australia' (Hughes personal communication 15.06.09).

The ethnic and cultural diversity of Sydney—including 'precinct experiences' like Chinatown and Leichhardt (Little Italy)—is also promoted by

TNSW for domestic tourism. TNSW also works with the City of Sydney on the marketing and promotion of the Chinese New Year Festival. According to Hughes, it is events and experiences like the Chinese New Year Festival that can make 'ethnicity' or ethnic diversity a selling point to visitors[24] (Interview C1).

The city also works with the state government agency Events NSW on the Chinese New Year Festival. In 2007 Events, NSW had pledged $100,000 per year for three years to the city to assist in planning and developing the festival. However, Stuart Gill notes that much of this funding is then paid to other state government agencies such as the NSW police.[25]

2.1.4.4 *Ethnic Entrepreneurs*

Chinese business owners in Sydney have long organised to represent their interests. As noted previously, the NSW Chinese Merchants Society was established as early as 1903. There are currently two chambers of commerce that are localised in the Chinatown area: the Sydney Chinatown Chamber of Commerce and the Haymarket Chamber of Commerce. The Sydney Chinatown Chamber of Commerce emerged in 1988 and, according to Rex Wong, was particularly important in its earlier years when Chinese business owners in Chinatown could not speak English and needed help in interpreting immigration and commercial laws. While the Sydney Chinatown Chamber of Commerce is still listed in business directories, Wong notes that it is no longer very active[26] as improved relations between Chinese entrepreneurs and the state have limited the need for its activities (Interview C2).

The Haymarket Chamber of Commerce was founded in 2005. Its objectives are focused on this small inner-city area. They include: promoting business and tourism interests and community welfare in Haymarket and Chinatown; supporting or opposing government measures that may influence commerce and community welfare in the precinct; encouraging 'friendly relations' and trade between members; promoting 'interactive projects' with the City of Sydney; and promoting a code of best business practice (Haymarket Chamber of Commerce n.d.). One member of the chamber, here called John Teo, suggests that along with the broader goal of business development, a specific focus of the chamber is to improve the branding and marketing of Sydney's Chinatown to 'make it stand out' from other Chinatowns so that images of the precinct will be instantly recognisable:

> basically, the business people in Haymarket Chinatown, they felt that we have to do something so that we can co-ordinate all the business people... with the single objective of making Haymarket or Chinatown in Sydney some sort of a well known icon in international sort of tourism... where people can... look at the picture at the entrance of Chinatown and they say 'this is Sydney Chinatown'... when tourists come, when people come, once they see this picture, they know this is Sydney. (Interview C12)

While Sydney's Chinatown is clearly identifiable as a 'Chinatown' with its arches and lions at the entrance, Teo believes that 'for a few years it hasn't have any impact' because when members of the chamber ask people overseas:

> what is the image of Sydney Chinatown, nobody could tell them. But for instance if you look at the Harbour Bridge you say 'ah, that one's Sydney'... then when you look at San Francisco Chinatown you 'ah, that's San Francisco Chinatown'. So, hopefully that sort of image will conjure up... an icon to people to say 'ah, we must go to Sydney to visit this place, to visit Sydney' and this is the objective of the Chamber. (Interview C12)

For Teo, this objective involves finding a way to differentiate Sydney's Chinatown from other Chinatowns, like those in San Francisco and New York. He notes that the chamber is working with the City of Sydney on this objective through the Local Action Plan process, with the council having told the chamber to 'go ahead, you guys think of something' (Interview C12). In 2007, the City of Sydney gave the chamber a grant to help with running costs and Teo notes that some of that grant might be able to be spared to fund the development of a conceptual design. Ideas already floated include a covered walkway for shoppers (drawing on design elements from arcades in Japan) as well as improving tourist amenity by converting the existing Chinese pagoda into a small information centre. That would be staffed by volunteers from the chamber who could hand out maps and give advice to tourists about where to go to find restaurants and shops (Interview C12).

The chamber has a close relationship with the city council, with representatives being invited to public meetings. A representative of the chamber also sits on the council's Chinese New Year Festival Advisory Group (and formerly on the Chinatown Cultural Advisory Committee). However, Teo notes that the chamber's role in discussions with the council is usually an advisory one, with the council being the 'driving force' in any decisions about planning and public space (Interview C2). In designing a new look for Chinatown, Teo sees the chamber and council as involved in a 'joint effort', but notes that the original idea for a change came from the council, with the council being 'quite interested to do something about improving Chinatown, whether it's the lighting or landscape, you know, the streetscape' for the last few years. The council approached the chamber to assist with that task (Interview C2).

In December 2007, there were about 50 members of the Haymarket Chamber of Commerce. Many are Chinese, with Teo noting that the chamber has a 'very strong Chinese characteristic', although some of its founding members are not Chinese. Most of the members are in professional services such as accounting, law, medicine and real estate and many offer their services in Chinese languages. The chamber has very few members in retail or restaurant businesses (Interview C12). This raises important questions about representation: with most members of the Haymarket Chamber of Commerce representing professional businesses rather than retail shops or restaurants, the voices of these latter entrepreneurs have less opportunity to be heard.[27] Today, there are more businesses (1798) in Haymarket than people living there (1715), according to the Haymarket Chamber of Commerce (https://www.chamberofcommerce.com/united-states/virginia/haymarket/ Accessed 2 March 2020).

The uneven influence of different groups on council decisions about public space raises questions of legitimacy. This is perhaps best demonstrated with one of the most recent changes to the built landscape of Chinatown, the piece of public art called the 'Golden Water Mouth' that is shown in Fig. 2.2. Erected in 2000, it was designed by Chinese artist Lin Li, using a 200-year-old dead gum tree reinforced with steel on the inside and lined externally in gold in its top half, with recycled water flowing out of the one remaining branch at the top and trickling down the tree. The plaque on the sculpture states that it:

> celebrates contemporary life and the historic character of Chinatown. Australian and Chinese cultures are signalled in the combination of materials creating a Ying-yang harmony using traditional Chinese principles of 'Feng Shui'.

The sculpture was the winning design in a public competition held by the City of Sydney to design a 'gift' from the council to the people of Sydney for the 2000 Olympic Games. Both Rex Wong and Thomas Low were on the judging panel. Rex Wong explains that the materials used, and the placement of the sculpture, are significant:

> Water means life and money to the Chinese, and it's coated in gold leaf, the gold represents the Chinese in Australia from the gold rush era, and the gum tree represents Australians... And it's right opposite the bank of China, which is also good luck. (Interview C10)

In addition, Wong notes that the placement in Chinatown was important because Dixon Street was a thoroughfare for people moving between Sydney's Central Railway Station and Olympic events in Darling Harbour. He also suggests that the sculpture fit the brief because it wasn't 'too Chinese' and was appropriate for a multicultural community (Field notes C23.05.06).

However, some Chinese entrepreneurs in Chinatown argue that a dead tree with water flowing out is bad *feng shui*, particularly for a commercial precinct, because it symbolises the loss of money. This is a position argued strongly by Kong Sang. He notes that *feng shui* is important to business owners in Chinatown, with some shops that face oncoming traffic placing mirrors outside their shops to ward off approaching evil spirits. Wong's response to these concerns is that 'the fortune tellers tell it differently—the dripping of water means it's still alive and still coming out and life is still there—because of the water... without that, it'd be lifeless' (Interview C10).

In reference to the Golden Water Mouth, the Life Honourable President—introduced earlier from the Chinese Masonic Society—suggests that while 'whoever wanted to put that there probably listened to one of them *feng shui* people', that does not settle the dispute: 'even *feng shui* expert they got different opinion, you know' (Interview C12). The controversy over the Golden Water Mouth not only confirms Meethan's (2001, p. 27) argument about the multivocal, ambiguous and contradictory meanings that symbols of ethnicity can carry, but also highlights the significant influence of those that have input into the council decisions of the day. With the complexity and diversity within Chinatown's business community, let alone its other stakeholders, these decisions can rarely claim to represent the majority of constituent's views.

2.1.5 Cosmopolitan Monuments in Chinatown

2.1.5.1 The Chinese Masonic Society Hall

Shirley Fitzgerald, historian at the City of Sydney, describes the Chinese Masonic Society as 'one of the oldest and most respectable Chinese organisations in Sydney' (Fitzgerald 1997, p. 38). It retains a reputation as a significant power within Sydney's Chinese community and its members include some of the city's wealthiest Chinese. The society grew out of the anti-Manchu movement—known as the Yee Hings—that comprised branches of 'centuries-old Triad Societies' and other secret societies that had been present in Australia since the first gold rushes[28] (Fitzgerald 1997, p. 112). The society's Grand Master explains that the organisation emerged in the 1600s when Ming rule was overthrown and the new Qing dynasty was formed: 'we want to turn it back to the Ming [so] we set up a society' (Interview C13). The Life Honourable President elaborates that:

> Qing is actually the Manchurian, from North East China... they control China for 260 years... after the Ming Dynasty, that mean the Masonic, us, they set up, try to depose the Qing government and been struggling like that for years... to protect the Chinese nation. (Interview C13)

While the movement changed names many times, the Grand Master notes that 'at the last what we can remember [it was called] Yee Hing' (Interview C13). The organisation had branches both in China and overseas, with Chinese travelling to the gold rushes of America and Australia setting up branches when they arrived. The Life Honourable President explains that the organisation's anti-Qing activities had forced it to go 'underground as a secret society', and 'because a lot of our people died' overseas branches were a kind of insurance strategy, able to carry on even if people in China 'think that we been defeated' (Interview C13). In the end though, it was Dr Su Yat Sen who 'really defeat the Qing' (LHP, Interview C13). Having joined the Chinese Masonics in Hawaii, 'we appoint him as... commander in chief... and he lead our brothers to depose the Qing government' (LHP, Interview C13). According to the Grand Master, this was done with the help of the Chinese Masonics worldwide:

> all the world ask all other Masonics to donate money, and us, we donate a lot because the Chinese Masonic Society throughout the world donate money to help Dr Sun Yat Sen for his... revolution. (Interview C13)

While it had traditionally been an underground organisation, in 1908 the Sydney society 'went public' by establishing a headquarters in Blackburn Street Surry Hills, moving to nearby Mary Street in 1912 (Fitzgerald 1997, p. 112). The block in Mary Street and the construction of the new building were paid for with donations from member of the society (Interview C13). With the creation of the Chinese republic in 1911, support for Sun Yat Sen grew, and in 1912, the Sydney Yee Hing became the headquarters for all the Yee Hings around the country. When the Mary Street building was opened, the Yee Hing took on the new name of the Chinese Masonic Society. Although it has no association with freemasonry, it has some similarities in that there are branches in many countries, members can identify each other with secret codes (Fitzgerald 1997, p. 113), and the leader is called the 'grand master'. Members refer to the society as the 'brotherhood' and to each other as 'brothers' (Interview C13). The reliance on secret codes is a reflection of the society's history as an underground organisation, with the Grand Master noting that for the Masonics in China, 'if they get caught, they'd be executed by the Qing government' (Interview C13). With its emergence into public life, historian CF Yong suggests the association might have taken the new name of the Chinese Masonic Society to 'make known to the Australian public that the Yee Hing was no more secret and mystical than its Australian counterpart' (Fitzgerald 1997, p. 113). However, since its inception, there have been recurrent allegations that the Chinese Masonic Society is linked to triads and gambling syndicates—allegations that have formed 'part of the baggage of this organisation' (Fitzgerald 1997, p. 113).

The history of the early Chinese associations in Sydney is complex, with changing allegiances and alliances creating a constantly changing institutional landscape. In its early years, the Chinese Masonic Society worked closely with other republican sympathisers, together establishing the *Chinese Republic News* in 1914. But internal tensions led to a split between the Yee Hing and non-Yee Hing elements, with the latter pulling out of the partnership and establishing a branch of the United Chinese National Association in 1916. In 1917, the United Chinese National Association (Chinese Nationalists) opened their own headquarters nearby in Haymarket's Thomas Street, just around the corner from where they would later establish the Asia–Pacific headquarters of the Kuomintang in 1921 (Fitzgerald 1997, pp. 113–114).

While more nationalist organisations were emerging, the Chinese Masonic Society retained a central role. From 1920, it published the weekly *Chinese World News* (Fitzgerald 1997, pp. 38, 113). Working towards a similar cause, the society sometimes worked with the Chinese Nationalists 'to raise funds for the armies, schools and hospitals of Southern China' (Fitzgerald 1997, p. 113). From 1916 through to 1921, the Chinese Masonics held an annual interstate convention in their Mary Street headquarters (Fitzgerald 1997, p. 113). Following World War II, the Chinese Masonic Society was actively involved in supporting Chinese who had arrived during the war as evacuees from Pacific islands. When then Immigration Minister Arthur Calwell sought to deport the evacuees after the war and many evacuees were jailed, the president of the Chinese Masonics provided the surety to secure bail (Fitzgerald 1997, p. 45). The society was also heavily involved in other welfare works. For example, during the prolonged dispute over Chinese seamen following the World War II (discussed in more detail below), the Chinese Masonics helped to pay the expenses for a barrister to prevent the seamen being deported. Funds were also used to support local Chinese and Australian charities and causes. As the Life Honourable President explains, while the Masonics have 'never been a rich society', in the 1950s money donated by the members and raised through Chinese opera performances was used to support the Sydney children's hospital, the Red Cross and the Police Boys Club. The Sydney branch also performed Chinese opera in Melbourne to help that city's Masonics refurbish the local Guan Ti temple (Interview C13).

The fundraising and charity work of the society have continued to the present day. In 1990, they raised money for bushfire relief in NSW, and at around the same time, they raised more than $10,000 through lion dances in Sydney's Chinatown for the forest fire relief effort in northeast China. In early 2008, the Sydney branches together raised around $6000 to help those in China cope with the country's extreme cold snap (Interview C13). According to the Grand Master:

> We do anything's to help, not only lion dance or opera, anything, where we can do it we do it... We have no moneys, but yeah, all the brothers they do have some money there to support fundraising. (Interview C13)

As well as member contributions, the main way of raising money is through lion dances in Chinatown. As the Life Honourable President explains:

> As you can see we are not running a business here, we haven't got a bar and a poker machine, so it's at times we're struggling for fund. And that's why… every year we got this special occasion like Chinese New Year, Chinese New Year Festival and August Moon Festival, those two occasions we do the lion dances around Chinatown try to collect some fund to help the everyday expenditure of this Society. (Interview C13)[29]

Membership of the society is for life, but members are asked to pay an annual membership fee. The Life Honourable President notes that these annual fees are not always forthcoming:

> A lot of member sort of ah, pay membership sort of on a donation base, you know, not forcible. If they pay we collect, if they don't pay they still member [laughs]. (Interview C13)

In the early years of the Chinese Masonics in Sydney, the Grand Master and the Life Honourable President estimate that around 80% of local Chinese were members. As the LHP explains, at that time 'there only one association in Sydney' and because 'we are [the] only one building' in Chinatown most Chinese joined (Interview C13). According to the Grand Master, the Chinese branch of the organisation—headquartered in Beijing—now has around many thousands of members (Interview C13). Current members of the Sydney society live all around Australia and overseas, but the LHP estimates that across Australia there are now over 300 members. Most are men, but although the organisation is still referred to as a brotherhood there are now some women members—with the ratio of men to women 'fifty to one'. The Grand Master adds that the female members are still called brothers. At times, there have also been non-Chinese members.

The contemporary objectives of the Chinese Masonics in Australia are to wholeheartedly serve the public, promote a harmonious society and care for the welfare of the people (Chinese Masonic Society 2004, p. 3). As well as fundraising activities and charity work, the society provides free classes at its Sydney office. Classes have included dancing, opera, lion dance, martial arts, English and Chinese language lessons and sewing, although current classes only include lion dance. The teachers and office bearers are all volunteers and contribute what they can. For example, the Grand Master notes that one member who is a retired ambulance officer has taught first aid. Classes are open to all members but also to the general public, and they have always been free. People from a range of backgrounds—including Australian, Vietnamese, Italian, Singaporean and first- and second-generation Chinese—have accessed these free classes (Interview C13). According to the Grand Master, the non-Chinese participants 'love it... because we treat here like our home, and then we like the people to be our guest to come in our home too, so it's good' (Interview C13). Australian-born Chinese have accessed services like the free Chinese language classes (Interview C13).

The Sydney Chinese Masonic Society remains an important cultural institution. The Life Honourable President notes that since Australia recognised China in the 1970s:

> every ambassador that comes to Australia visit our premises... Some of them pay their very first visit to us—first, [before] any other organisation. Because ours is the oldest so they want to sort of pay respect. (Interview C13)

Membership is highly prized, with the LHP noting that joining the Masonics is not as simple as paying a fee, with a committee carefully considering each application:

> if someone they want to join us it's not easy, it's not easy, not everybody can join us... a lot of people we don't accept to be a member. If they have been a criminal before we don't accept to be member... if somebody introduce to be here... we think about the people character, culture, and background and then we accept it to be member, to be brotherhood, that's very important. So... maybe two... or three [times] every year we open up to new members... not anytime when you pay the fee and then you can be brotherhood, no not like that. (Interview C13)

The Grand Master adds that there are 'a few application here... in the office there for over a year' (Interview C13). The Life Honourable President suggests that the reasoning behind such a rigorous process is the allegations that the society has engaged in criminal activity:

> We really want to find out whether this person... got a clean record or not... some people they blame our society like an underworld or black society, actually we are not, you know, we all... not illegal, never been in trouble with the law... So that's why you gotta be careful to accept the new member. (Interview C13)

However, while the members today shrug off suggestions of a 'secret society', they also make it clear that not everything is open for comment, with the Life Honourable President noting that 'something we can't tell you about that... Not the secret society, I'm not that, not like that, but just... our rules, we can't tell you' (Interview C13).

2.1.5.2 The Chinese Youth League

The Chinese Youth League (CYL) emerged as a splinter group from the Kuomintang (KMT), with many of the young founders of the league having been closely tied with the KMT's Sydney headquarters. Dissatisfied with the leadership, activities and 'political outlook' of the KMT, seven young men began to meet regularly at Sydney's Shanghai Café on Campbell Street, Surry Hills. They established the Chinese Youth Dramatic Association on 1 July 1939, later renamed the Chinese Youth League in 1942. First operating from the Chinese Masonic Association hall in Surry Hills (Interview C7), the CYL began staging musical and dramatic performances to raise money for the anti-Japanese resistance in China and a newly established China Famine Fund. Before long, they began renting their own premises in Dixon Street where they were 'right among the market garden people' (Interview C7).

One of the first performances—*Rather Die Than Surrender*—celebrated the anti-Japanese resistance. A Cantonese opera jointly staged with the seamen of the ship the *Japanese Empress* the following year was called *Make Havoc With Magistrate Mei* (Cottle and Keys 2006, p. 1). One of the early members of the Chinese Youth League, William Wang, recalls that since there were so few Chinese women in Sydney, when they staged Cantonese operas 'they had to use boys to impersonate female roles and sing' (Interview C7). With little in the way of cultural organisations, Arthur remembers that the CYL's operas became 'quite famous' to local Chinese 'who were craving for entertainment' (Interview C7). The hall was full even during rehearsals and these would sometimes go late into the night. Arthur recalls that when the rehearsals went late, one member was teased by his father that 'Mao Tse-tung has gone to sleep already and you still doing that' (Interview C7). The performances were designed to 'build [the audience] with patriotism', and it worked: people were 'throwing money and donations [to] help Chinese fight Japan' (Interview C7). Social scientists Drew Cottle and Angela Keys (2006, p. 1) argue that the enthusiasm of the group 'within months... helped to unite the small and fractured Chinese community within Chinatown'. The emblem of the league—a torch with linked rings—represented 'the flame of youth and the unity of the Chinese people in the motherland and overseas' (Cottle and Keys 2006, p. 1). According to Arthur, while the emerging Chinese associations in Chinatown often had their differences, during this period 'all these people united together in one single common object to resist Japan' (Interview C7).

World War II presented an opportunity to local Chinese in Sydney who sought to 'undermine and frustrate' the White Australia policy and accompanying restrictions on trade and migration. Prior to the war, William Wang had been an indentured labourer in rural NSW, but with the outbreak of war and the ceasing of communications between China and Australia, he was able to leave his work and move to Sydney without fear of deportation (Interview C7). On a grander scale, with China at war with Japan, Chinese seamen on ships bound for Japan that docked in Sydney harbour and nearby ports began deserting[30] (Fitzgerald 1997, p. 41). A coalition among local Chinese associations, trade unions and the Communist Party of Australia emerged in support of the deserters, with members of the CYL having earlier worked with the trade union movement by supporting the Port Kembla pig iron strike in 1939.[31] Supporters of the deserting seamen worked to transport them away from the ports and hide them from the authorities (Fitzgerald 1997, p. 41). In 1942, the CYL helped to establish the Chinese Seamen's Union after Chinese seamen in several Australian ports held a series of 'mass sit-down strikes' (Cottle and Keys 2006, p. 1). Highlighting the significant changes since the anti-Chinese riots led by trade unions in the late nineteenth and early twentieth centuries, the Australian Seamen's Union helped the CYL to form the Chinese Seaman's Union. William Wang was a founding member. He recalls the early days of the new union:

> We had over 2,000 Chinese seaman around and they all looked to the Chinese Youth League, so [we started to organise] the Chinese Seaman's Union, with the help of the Australian Seaman's Union. The Australian Seaman's Union and wharfies were very progressive... you know, anti-fascist and anti-Japanese. They were the first ones to raise their hand to fight the fascists and the Japanese invaders... [they] help us to form the Chinese Seaman's Union, the Malayan Seaman's Union, the Indonesians Seaman's Union... and so on. (Interview C7)

The new Chinese Seamen's Union worked with the Australian Seamen's Union to improve conditions onboard Chinese ships (Fitzgerald 1997, p. 42). Both the Chinese Youth League and the Chinese Seamen's Union also helped to hide deserters:

> False papers or unobtrusive jobs were found. When failure to sign up was followed by arrests and jailings, assistance was forthcoming, not only from these organisations (according to irate shipowners) but also from a wide section of the Chinese community, including the Consular representatives. (Fitzgerald 1997, p. 42)

The Chinese seamen complained of poor conditions and low wages. Poorer treatment and pay for Chinese seamen compared to British and Australian crews were long-standing, but now 'wartime conditions and an emerging organisation across racial divides' were 'providing Chinese seamen with some negotiating strengths' (Fitzgerald 1997, p. 42). Labour shortages caused by the war meant that Chinese seamen who came ashore could find work at Australian award wages. A report in 1943 found that there were around 500 of these seamen in NSW, most of them in Sydney (Fitzgerald 1997, p. 44). Many more had come ashore in Brisbane and Melbourne's ports, with the Chinese Youth League establishing branches in both cities to offer them support. They organised for the seamen to board with local Chinese families, arranged interpreters to help the seamen in reading and writing English, and helped to find them work (Cottle and Keys 2006, p. 1). Meetings of the Chinese Seamen's Union were held at the Chinese Youth League headquarters in Dixon Street. These were really 'worthwhile years and very meaningful and doing very good work for the war effort' (Interview C7). By 1942, Chinese seamen were being recruited for major infrastructure projects. At the request of the Curtin government, the Chinese Youth League organised hundreds of seamen to work at what was to become the Warragamba Dam in NSW. The following year the CYL and Chinese Seamen's Union organised a group of the same size to construct landing craft for the United States army at Bulimba, Queensland (Cottle and Keys 2006, p. 1).

In 1943, the federal government introduced the *National Security (Chinese Seamen) Regulations* to ensure that Australian shipping companies paid Chinese seamen an award wage plus wartime bonuses. When shipping firms tried to reduce wages and conditions after the war, the Chinese were the first to suffer and Chinese seamen continued to desert.

Again, the Chinese Seamen's Union was supported by the Australian Seamen's Union, and this time by the Waterside Workers' Union as well, angry that 'any lowly paid seamen' was a threat to Australian standards (Fitzgerald 1997, p. 44). In 1946, the Chinese Youth League headquarters in Sydney became host to a strike meeting of nearly three hundred Chinese seamen from three ships, protesting at the attempt to reinstate pre-war wages and conditions (Cottle and Keys 2006, p. 1).

According to Fitzgerald (1997, p. 44), the challenge posed by these Chinese seamen had far-reaching consequences. Along with the arrival of Chinese wartime evacuees, it was the beginning of 'turning the tide' in breaking down immigration restrictions. Where 'genuine cause' to be ashore had been established, seamen who had deserted were registered as 'resident aliens' and granted Certificates of Exemption (Fitzgerald 1997, p. 44). Wartime labour shortages had meant that these new arrivals could work in a much broader range of occupations than the local Chinese still restricted by the 1901 immigration act[32] (Fitzgerald 1997, p. 44). Following the war, media criticism was increasingly directed at government policies rather than at Chinese immigrants themselves (Fitzgerald 1997, p. 45).

In addition, Cottle and Keys (2006, p. 1) suggest that the process of assisting the Chinese seamen transformed the Chinese Youth League: it was 'no longer simply an organisation for patriotic Chinese youth', but an active and well-connected organisation working to improve the conditions of Chinese both in Australia and overseas. As well as its work for the Chinese seamen, the CYL had played an active role in the Chinese resistance. From 1942, they published regular periodicals to inform Chinese Australians about the state of the war in China. In 1944, they had organised a week of Cantonese and Hainanese operas in the Haymarket and at the nearby Sydney Town Hall to raise funds for medical aid for the Chinese guerillas behind enemy lines. The events received widespread support, with speakers at the Town Hall including several trade union leaders, the federal minister for transport and a Labor senator (Cottle and Keys 2006, p. 1). William Wang remembers that as these guests spoke on the stage, members of the CYL ran:

> through the audience to [collect] money... [to] help the guerrillas to send medical aid to fight the Japanese behind the line, in the occupied territory, including my village. Money just flew in like anything... money just flew

in, parcels wrapped in newspaper were also thrown in, holding notes and [in one] newspaper parcel, 3000 pounds. Tremendous. (Interview C7)

The money raised helped to build the International Peace Hospital in Yunnan (Cottle and Keys 2006, p. 1).

When Japan surrendered in 1945, the Chinese Youth League organised a victory march through the streets of Sydney: from Dixon Street to the ports at Circular Quay and then returning to the CYL headquarters. They were joined by many Sydneysiders who showed their support, even helping to carry the lion drums. Members of the Chinese Youth League also marched in the May Day parade in 1945, performed an opera to raise money for the Red Cross and encouraged local Chinese to buy Chinese Victory Bonds from the KMT and Liberty and Victory Bonds from the Australian government (Cottle and Keys 2006, p. 1). While the Brisbane and Melbourne branches of the CYL closed after the war, the efforts of the Sydney branch in the war's aftermath were not over. When Arthur Calwell sought to deport Chinese wartime evacuees, the Chinese Youth League took the issue to the courts, arguing that the deportation order was invalid because the dictation test could not be used where a person had lived in Australia for five years. The CYL assisted in hiring a legal defence and the case was won by the defendants, a victory that is seen by some as 'a crucial step in ending the White Australia Policy'[33] (Cottle and Keys 2006, p. 1).

Spurred on by Sun Yat Sen's call to 'struggle together with all the oppressed peoples of the world', the Chinese Youth League also turned their attention to the plight of the neighbours in the Indonesian archipelago (Cottle and Keys 2006, p. 1). With The Netherlands seeking to re-establish Dutch rule over Indonesia in the wake of the Japanese withdrawal, the CYL worked with Indonesian seamen, Australian waterfront unions and shipping crews to boycott the Dutch-chartered ships in Australian ports on their way to assert Dutch rule in Indonesia. The league assisted hundreds of Indonesian Chinese, Malayan, Vietnamese and Indian seamen who had boycotted the Dutch ships, provided food and accommodation at their Sydney offices or billeting the seamen with Chinese families in Chinatown. They also raised funds for a film documenting the Indonesian independence movement in Australia[34] (Cottle and Keys 2006, p. 1).

The Chinese Youth League also continued to work to support China free from 'domination, division and ruin' (Cottle and Keys 2006, p. 1).

From 1948 through the 1950s and 1960s, they held regular screenings of documentaries about China, a popular pastime and important source of news about events in China for the Chinese in Chinatown and other Sydney suburbs. These films had often been banned by the federal government.[35] At the screenings, appeals were also made for donations to support the victims of famine and those orphaned during the war. When the People's Republic of China was proclaimed in 1949, the CYL hoisted the first five-star flag of the 'New China' out a window of their Sydney headquarters. Their support of the new republic raised the ire of some local Chinese, with the Sydney KMT pressuring the owners of the CYL building to have the league evicted. As the Cold War in Asia took hold, Australian security forces also began to see the CYL as a threat, judging it to be serving communist China. While the CYL continued to endorse 'an open progressive form of politics', promote Chinese culture and work towards unity and friendship both among local Chinese and with Australians, fewer people joined the league. William Wang recalls that during the war period members of the CYL had been 'victimised' by the federal government and the Australian Security Intelligence Organisation (ASIO) (Interview C7), and Cottle and Keys suggest that after the war official surveillance of the league's leaders intensified (Cottle and Keys 2006, p. 1). While the number of members had reached as high as 3000 (Interview C7), numbers now dwindled.

However, the few remaining members stayed active throughout the 1950s and 1960s, working with the Chinese Seamen's Union to organise Cantonese language classes at the Sydney CYL offices, continuing to perform plays and participating in the 1950 Melbourne World Peace Conference and 1951 Sydney May Day march. They also helped to organise an international youth festival in Sydney and, in a time when most Chinese in Australia had no contact with the homeland, assisted an Australian Peace Tour Delegation to China and hosted a Chinese Workers' Delegation, a Peace Delegation and a Friendship Delegation in Sydney. Sponsoring sporting teams—including table tennis, badminton and volleyball—among local Chinese, the CYL also organised a welcoming committee and official receptions for a touring Chinese table tennis delegation in 1972 (Cottle and Keys 2006, p. 1).

In the 1950s, the league also rallied again to support the plight of Chinese in Australia, this time focusing their efforts on Chinese indentured labourers brought to Australia after the war by Chinese firms and forced to work for pay and conditions far below those provided to

Australian workers. Their activities again brought them into a collaboration with trade unions, including the Waterside Workers' Federation, the Australian Seamen's Union, the Restaurant Workers Union and the newly formed NSW Chinese Workers' Association. Strikes and 'go-slows' forced several large Chinese businesses—including restaurants and warehouses in Chinatown and Haymarket and market gardens in the southern suburbs—to negotiate with workers and commit to better pay. Meanwhile, with many of the workers only having accommodation provided by their employers, the CYL again helped those on strike to find temporary housing in Chinatown (Cottle and Keys 2006, p. 1). During the same period, the CYL hosted a Chinese theatre group who had travelled from China, taking them on a performing tour of Australia's capital cities. William Wang suggests that this helped in changing public attitudes towards Chinese. For example, the theatre group played in Melbourne when the city was flooded with visitors for the 1956 Olympic Games. Chang recalls that:

> all our sessions there were filled and filled and filled. Tremendous. You see, even the Chinese community were so impressed with it because in those days, anti-communist propaganda was raging everywhere, even the Chinese believed that the communist would share your wife in the village, they confiscated your wife, and... your wife become common ownership. You know, all that type of thing. And when they saw this group of artist, so gentle, so friendly, it changed all their thinking. (Interview C7)

Following the 'normalising' of diplomatic relations between Australia and China in 1973, the political significance of the CYL declined. According to Cottle and Keys (2006, p. 1), as the Cold War receded and China was politically and economically transformed, 'the radical past of the Chinese Youth League faded into the background' and sporting, cultural and welfare concerns became pre-eminent in the minds of local Chinese. The main focus of the Chinese Youth League shifted to reflect these concerns. In 1986, prompted by the state government's 'call for multiculturalism', the CYL held the first-ever Chinatown Carnivale (Chinese Youth League of Australia [CYL] 2007). In 1988, as part of the national bicentennial celebrations the league performed a 'song and dance epic' called *Dragon Down Under* at the Sydney Opera House and in other capital cities, with the final performance in Canberra's Parliament House attended by the prime ministers of Australia and China (CYL 2007). In

2000, the CYL also participated in the opening ceremony of the Sydney Olympic Games. Two years later, it was awarded the Premier's Award for Community Service for raising $45,000 in twenty-four hours for the NSW Bushfire Appeal (CYL 2007). Today, the Chinese Youth League is still located in Dixon Street, just a few blocks from its original premises. Its five objectives are to:

> promote Chinese cultural activities, foster friendship and goodwill between Australia and China, undertake welfare and charitable work, organise recreational and sports activities, [and] participate in community activities to promote multiculturalism. (CYL 2007)

The welfare activities of the CYL include a volunteer youth group and a counselling service for problem gamblers, while its sporting activities include basketball, dragon boat racing, tai chi, table tennis and wushu. The Chinese Youth League dragon boat team was one of the teams in the first-ever dragon boat races in Sydney, held in 1984. In the 1990s, the team twice represented Australia in international races. As well as its welfare and sporting activities, the Chinese Youth League also runs an annual five-week youth tour to China 'to allow Chinese Australians to learn more about their roots and their ancestry whilst having the opportunity to meet other people in their same age group' (CYL 2007). Cultural activities organised in Sydney include Cantonese opera, dragon and lion dances and traditional Chinese dance (CYL 2007).

The CYL lion dancers have become 'the foremost lion dance troupe in Australia', performing in the opening ceremony of the Sydney 2000 Olympic Games and representing Australia at the 2006 Lion Dancing World Championships in Malaysia (CYL 2007). As well as teaching skills and techniques to members, the lion and dragon dance group sees its main objective as educating the general public about lion and dragon dance through 'performances, presentations and interaction', trying to achieve 'knowledge and understanding' and appreciation of Asian arts and traditions by providing information about lion and dragon dance and 'being visible to the community as much as possible' (CYL 2007). Similarly, the popular and successful CYL dragon boat team 'aims to bring Chinese Culture to the wider Australian Community'. The Chinese Youth League has become a large non-profit community organisation. As of 2007, it had around 7000 members (CYL 2007). The clubhouse is still in Dixon Street, although it has moved from its original location at number

66 to number 10, and now houses a small office upstairs and room for table tennis and other activities at street level.

For William Wang, one remaining wish is to establish a monument or other commemorative site for the Chinese Seamen's Union and its important role in local, national and even international history during World War II. He laments that, at the moment, the only public memorial to the union is one photograph of the Chinese seamen in 1943 in the foyer of the Sydney Trades Hall on Goulburn Street. According to Chang, this is particularly pressing as the seamen's union has long since been transformed into the maritime union and 'now all my old comrades are dying off… and the young people don't seem to take much notice' (Interview C7). What happens inside buildings is perhaps more important than the buildings themselves.

2.2 Minority Immigrants and the Built Environment in Port Kembla

Port Kembla is a small suburb in the regional city of Wollongong on the coast of New South Wales (NSW). It is seven kilometres south of Wollongong's city centre and around 80 kilometres south of Sydney. The region has been a significant industrial centre, with Port Kembla hosting the BlueScope Steel steelworks (formerly owned by the Broken Hill Propriety Company Ltd [BHP]) and a major working port. The steelworks are particularly important to Port Kembla's immigrant history, having provided jobs for many immigrants in the region. The maximum number of people employed there at any one time was almost 22,000 in 1979 (Vasos 2008), but in 2011 production was halved as the Steelworks effectively exited the export market and reduced operations to one Blast Furnace only (BlueScope Illawarra 2020). In 2015, the steelworks provided jobs to around 5000 people (Power 2015).

Many non-Anglo-Celtic immigrants were attracted to the employment opportunities at the steelworks, particularly in the post-World War II period. Workers included immigrants from what is now the Republic of Macedonia as well as Greece and Italy. Later, the steelworks also employed immigrants from Vietnam and the Middle East. Many of these immigrants and their families settled in Port Kembla and the neighbouring suburbs of Cringila and Warrawong. Port Kembla and the surrounding suburbs have constituted one of the largest centres of Macedonian immigrants in

Australia, after the major cities of Sydney, Melbourne and Perth (see Hill 1989, pp. 124–125).

2.2.1 Port Kembla's Immigration History

From the late 1920s, a few Macedonian men began to arrive in Port Kembla. Having been employed at the steelworks in Lithgow (to the west of the Great Dividing Range), they moved with the steelworks when it relocated to Port Kembla. The first Macedonian to settle in the area was Riste Sazdanoff who used his truck to transport materials from the Lithgow steelworks to the new coastal site (Trajcevski 2005, p. 9). He then became the 'link' between Macedonians and Port Kembla when the new steelworks became operational in 1928 (Interview PK1). One Macedonian immigrant who works in Port Kembla and has been heavily involved in the local Macedonian community since the 1980s is Antonio T of the Macedonian Welfare Association. Antonio T explains Riste Sazdanoff's role in Macedonian settlement in Port Kembla, with Macedonians from Newcastle and elsewhere first coming to stay at Sazdanoff's home:

> He would be the first one… to come to Port Kembla and eventually establish in Port Kembla, he built himself a little shack, on Flinders Street, next to coke ovens. And as the industry started here more people wanted to come and work, and he was their link you could say. He had sort of like a boarding house… they all gathered there, people from Newcastle was working [in the] steel industry… so when there was [no work] there they would come here. And a lot of people from same village. So a lot of people stayed at that particular house. No electricity, no water, just a tank on the top. Mainly they, what accommodation they could find, they stayed in the shed, if not they put tents outside. So, and the numbers drifted, varied. When there was a job they would stick around here, when there was no job they would go elsewhere. (Interview PK1)

Riste Sazdanoff's son, Alek, also recounts the importance of his father's house to the early Macedonian men in Port Kembla:

> My father was a very resourceful man and his house was like a 'café.' He was able to have a constant supply of beer at a time when there was a beer shortage. The men would gather there every Sunday with some travelling

> all the way from Newcastle to be with other Macedonians and to replenish their beer supplies. (in Trajcevski 2005, p. 9)

Eventually, some of these men built their own houses in Port Kembla. One estimate puts the number of Macedonians living in Port Kembla in the late 1930s at about 120, with numbers dropping to around 40 during World War II[36] (Interview PK1).

The original intention of many early Macedonian immigrants in Australia was to make their fortunes and return home, following the Macedonian tradition of *pečalba*—young, recently married men going away to work before returning to invest their earnings in establishing their new married life (Hill 1989, 2001, p. 572). However, after arrival, many of the men decided to stay, encouraged to settle by their own success in purchasing land and businesses, or deterred from returning home because of the outbreak of World War II, the rise of the authoritarian Metaxas regime in Greece or the failure of popular resistance in the Greek Civil War (Hill 1989). Once they had settled in Port Kembla, some men brought out their families from home, and others who were single married local Australian-born women (see Trajcevski 2005, p. 9).

Understanding Macedonian immigration to Australia requires a brief reflection on the complex history of the Balkans region as the notion of a distinct Macedonian ethnic group has been contested. The modern nation state of the Republic of Macedonia came into being only recently, in 1991. Its history dates back thousands of years, when the word 'Macedonian' was used to refer to an ethnic group who inhabited part of present-day Europe around the southern Balkan peninsula (Floudas 2002, p. 1). Peter Hill, an Australian Professor of Slavonic Studies, suggests that while they were related to the Greeks, Macedonians were considered as foreigners by the latter group[37] (Hill 1989, p. 1). The Kingdom of Macedonia reached its zenith in the fourth century BC when Alexander the Great created a vast Macedonian Empire that extended into Asia and Africa. Soon conquered by the Romans, over the next centuries, 'Macedonia' came to refer to a geographic area in the southern Balkans that corresponded to Roman administrative regions (Floudas 2002). This Macedonia was occupied by many different ethnic groups (Floudas 2002) but was 'overrun' by Slavic peoples from the sixth century AD and has remained predominantly Slavic since (Hill 1989, p. 2). For periods of time, it came under Roman, Byzantine, Bulgarian, Serbian and Ottoman rule (Floudas 2002; Hill 1989).

Under Ottoman rule from the fourteenth century, the term 'Macedonia' was outlawed 'because of its nationalistic connotations', but the area was understood to include the three administrative districts (*vilâyets*) of Skopje, Bitola and Salonika (Hill 1989, p. 4). The Ottoman Empire did not recognise distinct nationalities, only religions, and most people of the 'three *vilâyets*' were distinguished from the ruling Muslim elite by their Orthodox Christianity. For a time, the people of the three *vilâyets* were treated as 'effectively part of the Greek cultural sphere' so that, for example, 'Christian children in Macedonia could attend only Greek schools' (Hill 1989, p. 5). By the late 1800s, Macedonian nationalism was on the rise: the Internal Macedonian Revolutionary Organization (IMRO) was formed to 'weld Macedonian villages into a conscious nation' (Brailsford in Hill 1989, p. 5). Here, the term 'Macedonian' was used to refer to all the inhabitants of the three *vilâyets*. IMRO staged an unsuccessful revolutionary campaign in 1903 which was quickly put down by the Turks (Hill 1989, p. 6).

With the collapse of Ottoman control of the Balkans during the Balkan Wars of 1912–1913, the Macedonian region was partitioned among Greece (Aegean Macedonia), Bulgaria (Pirin Macedonia) and Serbia (Vardar Macedonia), with some western villages ceded to Albania in 1920 (Hill 1989, p. 6). Having gained command of these territories, the controlling powers sought to stamp their own identities on them. In Serbia, Vardar Macedonia was called 'South Serbia' and its inhabitants referred to as Serbs. Schools provided instruction only in the Serbian language. In Greece, the Slavic population of Aegean Macedonia was 'diluted' with Greeks, place names were Hellenised and 'only Greek surnames were officially recognized' (Hill 1989, p. 7). From 1935, under the Greek leader Metaxas, conditions for many Aegean Macedonians 'became intolerable', with 'their native speech... prohibited even in their own homes' (Hill 1989, p. 7, see also Tamis 1994, p. 5). Many Macedonians in Greece and Serbia fled to Bulgaria, although Macedonians there were not officially recognised as a distinct ethnic group (Hill 1989).

Macedonia as currently constituted was further defined under Tito's Yugoslavia (which included Serbia and, hence, Vardar Macedonia). In 1944, Tito declared the People's Republic of Macedonia as one of six republics under a new federal Yugoslav state (Floudas 2002). It was later renamed the Socialist Republic of Macedonia. The 'vernacular speech' of the Slav Macedonians became an official language of the Federal People's

Republic of Yugoslavia (Hill 1989, p. 7). In 1991, the Socialist Republic of Macedonia declared its independence from Yugoslavia and adopted the new name of Republic of Macedonia. Greece strongly objected to this name and expressed concerns that the new country had territorial ambitions to expand into Aegean Macedonia. In a provisional reference that sought to accommodate Greece's concerns, the new country was admitted to the United Nations in 1993 as 'the former Yugoslav Republic of Macedonia' (FYROM) (Floudas 2002), the reference still used officially in Australia.[38]

Corresponding to this complex geopolitical history, the Macedonian diaspora around the world has diverse origins and immigration histories. Some have their origins in what is now the Republic of Macedonia (FYROM), others in Greece, Bulgaria or Albania. Some left Aegean Macedonia for Yugoslavia after the Greek Civil War of 1946–1949, only to later resettle elsewhere abroad. While in ancient times the term 'Macedonian' referred to a non-Greek, non-Slavic ethnic group, in more modern usage it has been used (particularly by Greeks) to refer to any inhabitants of the Macedonian region as it has been variously constituted (see, for example, Tamis 1994). Today, it is also used (particularly by Macedonians) to reflect ethnicity, although it now usually refers to Macedonians, as defined by ancestry, language and customs, within the South Slavic peoples and 'any connexion between the present population and the ancient Macedonians is tenuous, at best' (Hill 1989, p. 2).

To complicate matters, some institutions that claim to represent the Macedonian diaspora only include Greek Macedonians (Hill 1989, p. 8). The existence of a legitimate and distinct Macedonian ethnicity and language is not universally accepted (see, for example, Floudas 2002; see also Tamis 1994). In addition, some people who speak a South Slavic dialect that could identify them as Macedonian feel a stronger affiliation to Greece or Bulgaria (Hill 1989, p. 8). Since the 1990s, some Greek nationalists have argued that there is an 'unbroken line of racial and cultural continuity' between the ancient Macedonians and modern Greeks, and that the 'Republic of Skopje' (as they call the Republic of Macedonia) lies almost wholly outside the territory of ancient Macedonia (Danforth 1995, pp. 31–32). Hence, they argue that the only true Macedonians are Greeks.[39] In his detailed analysis of Macedonian identities, Loring Danforth (1995, p. 182) summarises these complexities, suggesting that there are 'two separate groups of people both of whom identify themselves as Macedonians: Macedonians (in a national sense) who are *not* Greek and Macedonians (in a regional sense) who *are* Greek'.

Most Macedonian immigrants to Australia are from the region now known as the Republic of Macedonia and strongly dispute Greece's claims to exclusive use of the title. A significant number of Macedonians in Australia are from Greece and a smaller number from Bulgaria (Hill 1989, p. 8). Most are Orthodox Christians, although some Protestant Macedonians and Muslim Macedonians have settled in Melbourne and some Romany Macedonians (ethnic Romanies from the former Socialist Republic of Macedonia) have settled in Perth (Hill 1989, p. 9). Most of the Macedonian immigrants who settled in Port Kembla in the 1920s and 1930s were from Vardar Macedonia, especially the town of Bitola (Field notes PK06.09.06). It is likely that many of these men were from a peasant background, with little education or experience in a trade. According to Peter Hill (1989, p. 18), most of the early Macedonian *pečalbari* in Australia were 'itinerant labourers' who travelled around the country in small groups 'taking whatever work they could get'. Those who found work in the two BHP steelworks at Port Kembla (Fig. 2.4)

Fig. 2.4 Port Kembla steelworks, view from Cringila (formerly 'Steeltown') (*Source* Kirrily Jordan)

and Newcastle were lucky—in many urban centres Macedonians were excluded from factory work as a result of union opposition to employing 'dagoes', a racist term applied to Southern European immigrants in the 1950s–1970s (Hill 1989, p. 18).

As noted above, Port Kembla became an important centre for Macedonian immigrants, growing through chain migration.[40] Although the outbreak of World War II interrupted immigration, the Macedonian population in and around Port Kembla in the mid-twentieth century was big enough to sustain a number of Macedonian shops, cafes and cultural institutions. The first Macedonian café in the Illawarra was opened in 1943 (Hill 1989, p. 50), and in around 1950, Port Kembla became home to a Macedonian organisation affiliated with the Macedonian-Australian People's League (Tamis 1994, p. 272). Betty Kris has noted the particular importance of cafés for the early Macedonian immigrants:

> Original settlers... arrived on their own, without their wives and children and found the *cafeneia* a great meeting place. Here they discussed current events, played cards and even conducted their business. It was here that the migrant found himself in an environment similar to that back home. This explains why many of the migrants spent most of their spare time in these (exclusively male) coffee shops. (in Hill 1989, p. 49)

Trajcevski also emphasises the importance of the early cafés, where Macedonians would socialise and play cards:

> Café shops of this period [the mid-twentieth century] played a vital role in assisting the early settlers. They were the place where you would go to socialise with people of your own background, communicate in your language, catch up with friends, make new friends and contacts, find out about other Macedonians in other parts of Australia, find out about what is happening back home from new arrival, who is going back so that you can pass on a message and a gift for loved ones back home, and generally feel comfortable amongst your people. For some, owning and operating a coffee shop became a way of life that they found hard to give up while others found it hard to stay away from cafes. (Trajcevski 2005, p. 10)

Following World War II, Macedonian emigration to Australia picked up again. While the first Macedonian immigrants had been peasants with little education, later groups were more likely to be better educated and have had classes in the Macedonian language (see Hill 1989, p. 33). Like the earlier Macedonian immigrants, on coming to Australia they tended to settle in concentrated groups through networks of chain migration. As Peter Hill (1989, p. 41) describes:

> In the old country, almost all the Macedonians lived in villages... village-type settlement patterns carried over into Australia: concentrations in small towns or in particular suburbs of capital cities... Typically, particular villages move in small groups, then family by family, to one place in Australia... Many villages are now stronger in terms of numbers in Australia than in the old country and exist here in the form of village societies which organise dances, picnics, etc.

The number of new Macedonian arrivals in Australia peaked in the late 1950s and 1960s, although the greatest number of Macedonians from Vardar Macedonia arrived in the late 1960s and early 1970s. From 1969 to 1973, more than half of all immigrants from Yugoslavia were from Macedonia. Many were from the south-western region around Bitola and Ohrid (Hill 1989, pp. 32–33). By 1986, most of the Macedonians in the Illawarra were from Yugoslavia and most had arrived after World War II: just over 18% had arrived in the period 1960 to 1969; 33% had arrived from 1970 to 1979; and 43% had been born in Australia (Hill 1989, p. 42). The growth of the Macedonian community in Port Kembla and surrounds had led to even more Macedonian shops and businesses. A guest house, known as the *Kafeto* (coffee house), was established in Port Kembla to accommodate new immigrant arrivals. It also served a social function as a place where Macedonian men could meet, gamble and drink together (Interview PK1). In the late 1970s, Cringila became home to a Macedonian theatre which showed films that people brought from overseas (Field notes PK06.09.06). Macedonian cafes, such as the now-closed Star Café (Fig. 2.5), retained their importance not only as commercial enterprises but also as places to socialise and express political views (Field notes PK06.09.06).

From the 1960s, Macedonians in the Illawarra also started their own religious and sporting institutions. The Macedonian Orthodox Community of the City of Greater Wollongong was established in the 1960s and led to the formation of the first Macedonian Orthodox Church in the Illawarra, the Church of Saint Dimitrija of Solun. The church was opened in Wollongong in 1972 and its founding body, the Macedonian Orthodox Community of the City of Greater Wollongong then sponsored

Fig. 2.5 Detail from the Star Café window showing support for a free Macedonia (*Source* Kirrily Jordan)

the establishment of a Macedonian soccer club called Wollongong United (Interview PK1). Also known as Wollongong Macedonia, the club began operating in 1976 at the purpose-built football complex called Macedonia Park (Fig. 2.6) (WUFC 2008). Several other Macedonian soccer clubs were also established, including Warrawong United and the Cringila Lions (Hill 1989, p. 99).

During this period, Macedonian immigrants in the Illawarra also began organising traditional celebrations and festivals, including celebrations for Orthodox Christmas, Easter and New Year, celebrations for the patron days of people's home villages in Macedonia, and the well-attended *sredselo* festivities at Cringila's football field. Cringila's *sredselo* (literally 'market place'), which still runs annually, involves three days of Macedonian music and dancing as well as food and drinks. Antonio T, introduced earlier, explains that these celebrations in Cringila are based on the idea of a Macedonian village festival, where everyone would get together in the village centre.[41] The festival falls in mid-January and is followed by celebrations for the Christening of Christ, where a small cross is thrown in the water and children dive for it, with the winner given a small cross

Fig. 2.6 Macedonia Park, home of Wollongong United FC (*Source* Kirrily Jordan)

to wear around their neck (Field notes PK06.09.06). Large Macedonian picnics, attended by Macedonians from Sydney, Newcastle and the Illawarra, have also been held for many decades in nearby National Parks such as the Royal National Park on Sydney's southern outskirts (see Hill 1989; Thomas 2001; Field notes PK06.09.06).

In the 1980s, the Macedonian population of Port Kembla and the surrounding suburbs began to decline. Writing in 1989, Peter Hill suggested that most Macedonians in Australia still clung to the 'dream of the *pečalbar*, to return home with a small fortune' (Hill 1989, p. 33). However, among Macedonians in Port Kembla, those who had made money in the steelworks began to move to more pleasant or prestigious areas further south along the NSW coast. Widespread retrenchments at the steelworks in later years have slowed that process a little (Field notes

PK06.09.06), and Port Kembla retains a significant Macedonian population (ABS 2019). Having arrived in Australia in their peak working age in the 1960s, most of these residents are now in their 50s and 60s or have retired. According to Antonio T, over half of these residents were receiving some kind of welfare support. He believes this is a higher proportion than among many other groups in the area (Field notes PK06.09.06).

While Port Kembla is still a manufacturing and industrial centre for Wollongong and a key site for industrial exports, its town centre has deteriorated badly as jobs at the steelworks have been lost and many people have moved away amid fears of industrial pollution (Power 2015; Fogarty and Appel 2019). Many of the old shops and businesses in Port Kembla's main streets had long been boarded up. But a 'vibrant cast of characters' including migrants and Indigenous people are 'seeking to rejuvenate the area', now a suburb of Wollongong, and 29 new businesses have opened up in the last six years (Fogarty and Appel 2019). The Macedonian Welfare Association of NSW, established in 1984 and based in Port Kembla, seeks to cater for the needs of 'people of Macedonian background and others of all ages, long term residents and recent arrivals and those with disability and their carers so that they become self assertive, capable, independent and valued members of society and active participants in community life' (MWA of NSW 2020).

Today, immigrants from the Republic of Macedonia (FYROM) are counted separately in the Australian Census.[42] Macedonians still constitute the largest immigrant group in Port Kembla and the largest non-Anglo-Celtic group according to ancestry (Tables 2.3 and 2.4). At the 2016 Census, close to 708 of Port Kembla's residents (just over 7%[43]) were born in FYROM. Just over 1300 people claimed Macedonian ancestry. In the Wollongong local government area, which includes Port Kembla as well as neighbouring suburbs such as Cringila, there were almost 2900 immigrants from FYROM and over 6594 with Macedonian ancestry (ABS 2019). Alongside Macedonians, sizeable non-Anglo-Celtic immigrant groups in Port Kembla also included Italians and Greeks. The 2016 Census also showed that a small number of Aboriginal Australians live in Port Kembla.

Mirroring the history of both Griffith and Katanning, discussed later in this and other chapters, Port Kembla was previously home to a significant Aboriginal population. As more of their traditional food gathering areas were alienated by the expansion of Anglo-Celtic and other immigrant

Table 2.3 Country of birth of Port Kembla residents, top ten countries, 2016

Country of birth	*Persons*
Australia	5982
Macedonia (FYROM)	708
Italy	403
England	188
New Zealand	152
Philippines	98
Greece	78
Vietnam	58
Malta	57
Germany	50
Total residents	9749

Source Author's calculation based on ABS (2019)

Table 2.4 Ancestry of Port Kembla residents, selected groups, 2016

Ancestry	*Responses*
Australian	2684
English	2321
Macedonian	1356
Italian	978
Irish	681
Scottish	503
German	296
Greek	203
Maltese	171
Australian Aboriginal	86
Total responses	9749

Note This question in the census is multi-response—Total responses may not equal total number of persons
Source Author's calculation based on ABS (2019)

settlement and widespread industrial land use, they retreated to small creeks and along the shores of water bodies like Tom Thumb Lagoon, where they continued to live until 1928 when forced to shift for harbour works for Port Kembla (Kass 2010, p. 13). Aboriginal people continued to use traditional food sources such as Coomaditchy Lagoon, and many settled on Hill 60, where they could spot schools of fish up and down the coast. In 1942, they were compulsorily moved due to the construction of major defence works on the hill, to the Official Camp, or 'Mission', near Coomaditchy Lagoon (Kass 2010, pp. 13–15). They lived in 'sugar bag shacks and in any kind of shelter they could create' until eventually weatherboard and later (in 1989) brick mission houses were built (Coomaditchie United Aboriginal Corporation 2020).

The Macedonian influence in Port Kembla and surrounds remains clearly visible in the region's buildings and shopfronts, including a number of *burek* shops. Antonio T also notes that many of the Macedonian houses in the Illawarra are distinct, describing them as 'box shape, squarish' buildings with stone lions at the front and a small vegetable garden and kitchen at the back (Field notes PK06.09.06). The region also now has two Macedonian Orthodox Churches—Saint Dimitrija of Solun in Wollongong and the newer Saint Kliment of Ohrid in Port Kembla—as well as a Macedonian Orthodox monastery, Saint Petka, in Kembla Grange. The Churches of Saint Dimitrija of Solun and Saint Kliment of Ohrid and the Saint Petka monastery are explored in more detail below.

2.2.2 Cosmopolitan Monuments in Port Kembla

2.2.2.1 Saint Dimitrija of Solun and Saint Kliment of Ohrid Macedonian Orthodox Churches

Drawing on influential demographer, the late Charles Price, Peter Hill (1989, p. 40) suggests that when wives and children began to join the early Macedonian immigrants in Australia, 'customs of the old country' became 'more entrenched' and religious communities and weekend schools began to appear. In Port Kembla and the surrounding suburbs, Macedonian immigrants began the process of setting up religious institutions in the early 1960s, and the first Macedonian Orthodox Church—Saint Dimitrija of Solun—was built in Wollongong in 1972. This was followed by a second church, Saint Kliment of Ohrid—a former Christian church that was purchased in 1982, rebuilt and then consecrated in 1983. The architecture and interior design of both churches are significant. The four domes on the roof form a cross and the interiors are decorated with religious icons, emulating the traditional style of churches in Macedonia (Field notes PK06.09.06; Interview PK1). Construction of an elaborate Macedonian Orthodox monastery, Saint Petka, began in Kembla Grange, just outside Port Kembla, in 2000.

Like the history of Macedonia itself, the history of the Macedonian Orthodox Church is far from smooth. Both in Australia and overseas it has struggled for official recognition and been plagued by tensions over independence and control. Byzantine or Chalcedonian Orthodox Churches[44] have traditionally been organised along national lines: over time the delineation of national churches has changed as geopolitical boundaries and power structures have been repeatedly redrawn. Special authority is held by the Ecumenical Patriarch of Constantinople who is 'first among equals' among Orthodox bishops and is traditionally a Greek.[45] In the nineteenth century, the Serbian Orthodox Church was granted autonomy from the Greek Church and the Ottoman Sultan agreed to the creation of an independent Bulgarian Orthodox Church or Exarchate.[46] Orthodox Macedonians were able to choose between the Bulgarian Exarchate, the Greek Orthodox Church and the Serbian Church. Pro-Bulgarian, pro-Serbian and pro-Greek armed bands 'terrorized villages' that sympathised with an alternate group, but most Macedonian churches chose to join the Bulgarian Exarchate (Hill 1989, p. 5). After the partition in 1913, the Macedonian churches in Aegean Macedonia remained within the Greek Orthodox Church under the patriarch in Constantinople (Istanbul) and those in Yugoslavia came under the jurisdiction of the Serbian Orthodox Church (Hill 1989, p. 85; 2001, p. 574). The Macedonian Orthodox Church did not come into being until the creation of the People's Republic of Macedonia in the Yugoslav federation. It gained administrative autonomy from the Serbian Church in 1959 and full independence in 1967. Although recognised by the Yugoslav government at the time, the independence of the Macedonian Orthodox Church has not been recognised by any other Orthodox Church[47] (Hill 1989, p. 86; 2001, p. 574; see also Binns 2002, p. 10).

The relationship of Orthodox Macedonians to their churches and the changing position of the church itself has had significant repercussions in Australia. There have been opportunities for both unity and division. Peter Hill (2001, p. 574) has argued that despite political tensions back home, it was in countries like Australia where Macedonian immigrants could enjoy 'relative freedom of organization' that 'Macedonian unity and a sense of nationhood' could be observed. However, he also notes the potential for division, such as when village rivalries carried over from the home country have led to 'unnecessary splits within Macedonian communities' (Hill 1989, p. 4). Indeed, in some Australian towns, 'different villages have set up different churches' (Hill 1989, p. 4). Churches have also, at times, become focal points for broader political tensions. John Shea (1997) has noted that when Australia recognised the former Yugoslav Republic of Macedonia in 1994 resentment spilled over into a number of arson attacks and incidents of vandalism on Macedonian and Greek institutions and Orthodox churches in Melbourne (see also Hill 2001, p. 576). Tensions have also caused splits within the Macedonian Orthodox Church in Australia: in 1997, a separate Macedonian Orthodox Independent Church was established in Adelaide; in 2001, a number of Macedonian Orthodox groups joined together as the Australian Macedonian Orthodox Church (Hill 2001, p. 575). Writing in 2001, Peter Hill suggested that the Macedonian Orthodox Church in Australia has played an increasingly political role in the dispute between Greece and the Republic of Macedonia, becoming an overt key player 'in the struggle to control the Macedonian diaspora', although he also argues that divisions between 'Vardar Macedonians' and 'Aegean Macedonians' in Australia had declined (Hill 2001, pp. 574–576).

For the early Macedonian immigrants in Australia, there were no churches of their own and they often attended other Christian churches including Greek, Serbian, Russian, Syrian or even Anglican or Methodist. The first Macedonian church—Saints Cyril and Methodius—was established in Melbourne in 1950 under a Bulgarian bishop. Priests were sent from the Bulgarian Orthodox Church in the People's Republic of Bulgaria, although parishioners at the time still feared the 'interference' of 'Greek consular authorities' in the church (Hill 1989, p. 86). The church quickly became a key religious, social and cultural centre for Macedonians in Melbourne, to the ire of some Macedonian activists who wanted an independent Macedonian church rather than one tied to Bulgaria (Hill 1989; see also Tamis 1994). The desire for religious independence spurred a small group into action and led to the creation of a new, independent Macedonian church in Melbourne, the Church of Saint George. Despite the local council rejecting the application to establish a Macedonian Orthodox Church in Melbourne 'apparently on the grounds that no such church organisation existed', in 1959 Saint George became the first parish outside Macedonia to be recognised as a Macedonian Orthodox Church when that institution was granted administrative autonomy from the Serbian Church in Yugoslavia (Hill 1989, p. 89). Over the next decades, other Macedonian churches in Australia were also established and recognised by the Macedonian Orthodoxy in Yugoslavia, including the first Macedonian church in the Illawarra, Wollongong's Saint Dimitrija of Solun (Hill 1989, p. 92).

Saint Dimitrija of Solun was built with the donations and voluntary labour of the local Macedonian community under the leadership of the

Macedonian Orthodox Community of the City of Greater Wollongong, the latter having grown out of an earlier committee established to raise money for the victims of the devastating 1961 earthquake in Skopje. As Antonio T explains, there was a need for a Macedonian church:

> where the people can come together and the ceremonies can be carried out in the Macedonian language... and the fact that more and more Macedonian families were now coming to the region, [so there were] more births, christenings, marriages... Having a working party already established through fundraising for the 1961 Skopje earthquake was advantageous in that they then turned their attention to raising funds for the church. (Antonio T personal communication, 29.06.09)

The constitution of the church was formed in the late 1960s and it was officially opened in 1972 (Interview PK1).

Disputes over formal control over Macedonian Orthodox Churches in Australia did not end with the granting of administrative autonomy to the church in Yugoslavia. Melbourne's Church of Saint George, and others such as Wollongong's Saint Dimitrija of Solun that followed its lead, adopted a democratic constitution in which decisions were made by an elected church committee. The committee could hire and fire the priest without the support of a bishop. This put the early Macedonian Orthodox Churches in Australia at odds with the diocesan constitution, under which the Macedonian Orthodox Bishop of Australia and Canada would normally have 'influence over the membership of the church committee' and title to the church's real estate (Hill 1989, p. 94). In the 1960s and early 1970s, the bishop sought to restrict membership of church committees to Yugoslavian citizens (Hill 1989, p. 95). By the mid-1970s, with the conflict between the Church of Saint George and the Macedonian Orthodox diocese unresolved, in most centres around Australia where a church in the 'Saint George model' had been established, a second church with a diocesan constitution was set up 'in opposition to the original Macedonian Orthodox Church' (Hill 1989, p. 95; see also Popov and Radin 1995, p. 42).

In the Illawarra, a new Macedonian Orthodox Church, Saint Kliment of Ohrid, was established in Port Kembla in 1982. However, Antonio T suggests that the creation of this new church stemmed more from divisions among Macedonians in the Illawarra than from disputes about diocesan constitutions. In particular, he notes that when Saint Kliment of

Ohrid was first built, it was associated more with immigrants from the Ohrid region, while the Church of Saint Dimitrija of Solun was associated more with people from Bitola, and these groups had 'different views' (Interview PK1). Peter Hill (1989, p. 99) has also noted the old village rivalries played out between the two churches. According to Antonio T, more personal tensions may have also played a part in the creation of the two separate churches. While the number of Macedonian organisations in the region has now declined, he questions the need for two Macedonian churches when they are 'only full once or twice a year'[48] (Field notes PK06.09.06). Although the two churches assist each other in raising funds and people are now more likely to 'pick and choose' their church irrespective of the village where they or their families emigrated from (Interview PK1), there is an ongoing lack of cooperation between them (Field notes PK06.09.06).

Nonetheless, both the Church of Saint Kliment and the Church of Saint Dimitrija have played an important role in the local area. In his study of Southern Europeans in Australia, Charles Price (1963) suggested that the Macedonian Orthodox Church had played a broader role among the Macedonian diaspora than their primary religious function. For example, he argued that the Orthodox Church played a 'prominent part in furthering Folk-nationalist interests' and 'welding migrants into communities that have strong Folk loyalties, as distinct from regional or district loyalties' (in Hill 1989, p. 85). Similarly, in a study of Macedonians in Australia, Mato Tkalcevic (1980, p. 17) described the Macedonian Orthodox Church as 'a guardian of… traditions and culture'. A survey of Macedonian-speaking residents of the Canberra region carried out in the 1980s by the then Department of Immigration and Ethnic Affairs (DIEA) also found that respondents saw the Macedonian Orthodox Church as important not only for its spiritual and moral functions but also 'as a unifying force and as a central Macedonian identity symbol' (in Hill 1989, p. 85).[49]

Of course, the primary functions of both the Church of Saint Kliment and the Church of Saint Dimitrija are religious ones, with regular services (as well as special services for Christenings, weddings and funerals) held in the Macedonian language (Interview PK1). However, while the creation of two churches may have in some ways reinforced divisions among Macedonian immigrants as a result of personal politics or regional loyalties, both churches have also played a part in developing a Macedonian consciousness and maintaining cultural traditions. Echoing both Price's sentiments and the findings of the DIEA, Antonio T suggests that the Macedonian Orthodox Church in Wollongong, in particular, has been important for cultural, and even political organisation, especially as it was the first Macedonian church in the region:

> An additional purpose of the church was to bring the people together, through events such as dances and celebrations. Dances were held just about every month and the church hall was packed. The church started off the dancing groups and language school and gave support for the formation of the Macedonian Soccer Club Wollongong United. The church was also fighting against bodies opposing its formation and registration in Australia as well as for the rights of the Macedonian minorities in neighbouring countries of Macedonia. It was like a governing body you could say, that was catering for all your needs including spiritual needs. (Antonio T personal communication, 29.06.09)

Local people supported the activities of the church by making donations:

> Australia was booming. Everyone was working their roster day, working doubler or even a tripler [shift]. There was lots of work and lots of money made. Everyone was supporting the church and the functions were well attended. The church was making good money which is used to expand and improve the church and purchase property at Berkeley where the Macedonian Park is now built. (Antonio T personal communication, 29.06.09)

In the 1970s, the regular dances at the Church of Saint Dimitrija were particularly important since at that time many of the new immigrants found they were 'not welcomed anywhere else' (Field notes PK06.09.06). The church hall also allowed large groups of Macedonians to get together for weddings and other significant events, while the funds raised through the church supported both the development of dancing groups and Macedonian football in the Illawarra. The Macedonian football team Wollongong United was established through the organising committee of the Church of Saint Dimitrija and parishioners also raised the funds for the club's home ground at Macedonia Park (Field notes PK06.09.06). Today, while the Illawarra's five Macedonian football teams often have strong connections to a particular Macedonian village,[50] they meet annually for a Macedonian football tournament and become a way of 'bringing people together' (Field notes PK06.09.06).

The churches also bring people together for regular festivals and events. The Church of Saint Dimitrija raises money to finance a Macedonian dance group. Macedonian folk dancing is an important cultural tradition, and Hill (1989, p. 102) notes that 'every Macedonian, whether 8 or 80 years old, dances different *ora* (singular *oro* 'folk dance') whenever there is a social gathering'. Traditional music is played to accompany the dancers, using the Macedonian drum (*tapan*) and bagpipe (*gajda*) (Hill 1989, p. 105). The Church of Saint Dimitrija has celebrated the day of St. Demetrius with an 'extravagant folkloric festival' since 1984 (Hill 1989, p. 43), and both churches still hold celebrations for their patron saint days. Both churches have also supported language schools for the children. In 1992, the Church of Saint Kliment opened the Saint Kliment of Ohrid Macedonian Cultural and Educational Centre in a small hall next to the church.

While the cultural and sporting activities sponsored through the churches provide opportunities for developing and maintaining bonds among Macedonian immigrants, like many such institutions they are increasingly struggling to retain the younger generations. Antonio T notes that the number of young people at Macedonian festivals and patron days is dropping off, and when confronted by political disputes within the church, the younger generations 'vote with their feet and leave' (Field notes PK06.09.06). Peter Hill (2001, p. 576) suggests that divisions within the Macedonian Orthodoxy in Australia are now more likely to be played out between first-generation immigrants and the younger generations, rather than being based on old national or village rivalries. According to Antonio T, the main way of engaging younger Macedonians in church communities in the Illawarra has been through dancing groups, but even there the numbers are 'faltering' (Field notes PK06.09.06). He suggests there are a number of factors involved in this decline: the busyness of people's lives; their rejection of church politics; the reluctance of the 'old guard' to vacate the positions they have occupied for many years; the inability of traditional cultural heritage to compete with new multimedia attractions; and the greater acceptance of Macedonians within the broader community, reducing the need for in-group support. Hill (2001, p. 576) also argues that in some Macedonian churches in Australia, the older generations have been unwilling to cede control to the younger members and the churches have continued to be dominated by older immigrant men. Popov and Radin (1995, pp. 48–49) have identified the 'conservative and patriarchal values' promulgated by those on most church boards as one reason for younger generations turning away.

There are some concerns for the sustainability of the two churches in the Illawarra, particularly as they are supported financially by a relatively small community. For example, Antonio T notes the significant investment of community resources over recent years as the large hall at the Church of Saint Dimitrija has undergone a one million dollar renovation and the Church of Saint Kliment has embarked on a multimillion dollar project to build the Saint Petka monastery (Field notes PK06.09.06). However, the monastery project has succeeded in garnering much community support through both donations and voluntary labour. The estimated value of the project if it were completed at full cost is around ten million dollars, but the expenditure saved by volunteer workers and discounted rates on materials have kept the costs to about a third of that amount (Field notes PK18.10.07). Recent fundraising activities for the monastery suggest that the Macedonian Orthodox Community in the Illawarra is still dedicated and can inspire the participation of a cross-section of its members, even if the younger generations are not actively involved in the churches on a regular basis. For example, the decision to build the monastery was made by the small group of mostly 'mature age' men of the Church of Saint Kliment of Ohrid's committee, and some members of the Macedonian Orthodox Community of the Illawarra have questioned the need for a monastery when other community facilities, such as a Macedonian club or nursing home, might have a more practical use (Interview PK1). However, fundraising functions have demonstrated broader community support. In late 2007, a group of second-generation women organised a fundraising function for the monastery that raised around $40,000. Over 550 people turned up to the event, a number that Antonio T says is the largest at any Macedonian function for 'a couple of decades' (Interview PK1).

Like the Churches of Saint Dimitrija and Kliment, the Saint Petka monastery incorporates traditional symbolism and design. The builders have worked with specialist artisans in the construction process, with the latter working on traditional features such as the large domes and the stained glass windows that adorn the church building. As well as the church itself, the monastery includes a large, separate building that provides accommodation for the Macedonian nuns, a large dining hall and kitchen that can cater for special functions, and accommodation for visitors in hotel-style rooms. As of late 2007, there was some suggestion that a future development of the site may include a retirement village next to the monastery (Field notes PK18.10.07).

While the Church of Saint Kliment of Ohrid has committed itself to the monastery project, the Church of Saint Dimitrija of Solun also holds considerable assets. The large, recently renovated hall next to the church is available for hire. The land at Macedonia Park is increasingly valuable and, as of late 2007, the church committee was in discussions with a developer who proposed to rent the site for the purpose of building a retirement village. As well as rental receipts, if the project went ahead the developers would provide the church with more modern sports club facilities (Interview PK1).

2.3 Minority Immigrants and the Built Environment in Griffith

Griffith (Fig. 2.7) has grown from a rural town to a regional city in south-western NSW. With a population of around 19,144 people it is employment in farming and related industries that has attracted many

Fig. 2.7 Griffith, a 'tidy town' (*Source* Kirrily Jordan)

of Griffith's non-Anglo-Celtic immigrants. While the large majority of Griffith residents are Australian born, the local population includes an increasing number of immigrants from almost 45 countries. The 2016 census shows that around one-fifth of the population have Italian ancestry (ABS 2019). The cultural diversity of Griffith makes it unusual for a regional city, with immigrants in Australia (particularly those from outside the main English-speaking countries of the United Kingdom, New Zealand, Canada and the United States) having tended to settle in the large cities along the eastern coast (see Burnley 2001). With federal government immigration policy having shifted in recent years to encourage 'regionalisation'—the settlement of immigrants in regional and rural areas—Griffith provides an interesting case study in which to examine the experiences of immigrants in multicultural place making in the regional context.

Ethnic diversity in rural areas has been recently signposted by a considerable debate examining the intersection of 'Otherness', marginalisation and rurality, particularly in the United Kingdom. There has been a strong suggestion that rurality is a signifier of an exclusive and white national identity. For instance, Julian Agyeman and Rachel Spooner (1997) have addressed the nature of racism in the English countryside, referring to a series of reports of the 1990s that found a significant amount of racial violence, harassment and resistance to the arrival of incomers into rural communities. Similarly, Sarah Holloway (2007), Sarah Neal (2002), Charlotte Williams (2007) and others have investigated the experience of non-white ethnic groups in rural areas in the United Kingdom, highlighting the tensions associated with increasing ethnic diversity in these predominantly white areas (see also Garland and Chakraborti 2007; Knowles 2008; Ray and Reed 2005). The authors point to the need to look beyond idyllic and static representations of the rural environment to the reality of ethnic exclusivity.

In Australia, there has been comparatively little research on immigration and ethnic diversity outside the major cities, or on the relationship between immigrants and place making in these settings. However, research by James Forrest and Kevin Dunn (2006) that draws on a survey of over 5000 respondents in Queensland and New South Wales suggests that the degree of racism and intolerance to ethnic diversity in Australia does not coincide with a neat urban/regional/rural divide. For example, in Queensland, the most tolerant areas were the regional cities of MacKay,

Townsville and Cairns, the largely rural and remote Far North Queensland, and some areas of Brisbane city. The least tolerant included the regional city of Bundaberg, some Brisbane suburbs and the rural areas surrounding Townsville. In New South Wales, the patterns of racism and intolerance were similarly mixed across urban, regional and rural areas. Notably, though, the most intolerant parts of the state included rural regions in the southwest (Forrest and Dunn 2006).

This section explores the patterns of immigration and ethnic diversity in Griffith, then turning to an examination of multicultural place making and a number of 'multicultural monuments' built and occupied by immigrant groups over the last 80 years. The case study develops the themes of belonging, inter-ethnic interaction and cultural tourism introduced in part one.

2.3.1 Griffith's Immigration History

Griffith (in the NSW Riverina) is a regional centre in a rural area dominated by farming industries based on irrigation. With a population of over 19,000 people (ABS 2019), it shares a degree of cultural diversity usually associated with Australia's major cities. Griffith sits in the traditional lands of the Wiradjuri people—the largest Aboriginal language group in New South Wales.[51] The Wiradjuri are the 'people of three rivers'—the Macquarie, Lachlan and Murrumbidgee. Around Griffith, the Wiradjuri lived on both sides of the Murrumbidgee (NSW DECC 2008), setting up small kinship-based camps as well as larger 'village-like, community camps' (Kabaila 2005, p. 10). There were permanent pathways along the rivers, with many years of repeated use making them like 'well-trodden roads' (Sturt in Kabaila 2005, p. 10).

Anglo-Celtic immigrants began to arrive in Wiradjuri country in the early nineteenth century. During the 1830s, the expansion of the pastoral industry saw sheep and cattle graziers moving 'rapidly down the river corridors' (Kabaila 2005, p. 11). The land along the rivers, so important for Wiradjuri livelihoods, was taken over for large pastoral stations. The competition for land created a 'moving frontier' with both armed resistance from the Wiradjuri and massacres, murders and reprisals from the new arrivals. The 'Wiradjuri Wars' went on throughout the 1830s in the Riverina area, with the Wiradjuri eventually restricted to towns and missions such as at Darlington Point and Three Ways, the latter still existing as a largely Aboriginal settlement near central Griffith (Kabaila 2005).

From 1912, the new Murrumbidgee Irrigation Scheme brought a population boom to the Riverina. Soldier settlers, city folk and farmers from selections elsewhere all came to 'cash in' on the expected prosperity. New immigrants also arrived, beginning with British but also including Italians, Spanish and Germans in the first wave (Kabaila 2005, p. 53). Of these new immigrants, the Italians 'constituted the most distinct group' (Kabaila 2005, p. 53). The first Italian immigrants to arrive in Griffith came via Broken Hill between 1913 and 1915 (Kelly 2001). They were soon followed by those who came directly from Italy: these were mainly Trevisani from the Veneto region in Italy's north (Huber 1977).

Subsequent immigrants came from many other regions of Italy: prior to World War II, they were mostly from the northern provinces, especially from the north-east of Veneto and Friuli (including the Friulani, Veronesi, Vicentini and Bellunesi) (Piazza 2005, pp. 10, 19). Following World War II, a new wave of Italian immigrants arrived, this time mostly from the southern regions, particularly Calabria and Sicilia (Piazza 2005, pp. 10, 19). Those from the south eventually came to equal or even outnumber those from the north (Kabaila 2005, p. 53; Kelly 2001, p. 497). Other Italian immigrants came from Abruzzo, Toscana, Piemonte, Marche and Campania (Piazza 2005, pp. 10, 19).

The first Italians to arrive in Griffith came with few personal belongings and found a region with little industrial development. The early Italian immigrants took up farming and trades, bringing valuable skills as builders, tailors and small-scale farmers with them from home. With skills and experience in a 'mixed economy'—working for cash as well as producing their own food in small plots and vegetable gardens—the Italians found success while many of the soldier settlers failed (Kabaila 2005, p. 55). Where Anglo-Celtic Australians had abandoned farms that had been damaged by salt intrusion or waterlogging, Italian farmers were able to repair them and 'bring them back to full productivity' (Kelly 2001, p. 497). Italian immigrants became central to the region's economic growth, dominating the fruit and vegetable farming industry and introducing new industries such as wine production that remain central to Griffith's prosperity today. By the 1930s, the relative success of the Italian farmers had contributed to an 'increasing hostility towards Italian settlers' in the region (Heritage Branch NSW 2006).

While they worked hard to develop their economic resources, Italian immigrants also developed a strong cultural life. In the early days, 'they played favourite folk songs at social gatherings, cooked traditional foods and visited friends and family on weekends' (Kabaila 2005, p. 55). Over time, numerous Italian regional associations, music clubs and social clubs were born, some of them with affiliations overseas. Many Italian families carried over customs and traditions from their homelands, including seasonal religious festivals, regional dialects and recipes for traditional Italian foods handed down over generations (Kabaila 2005, p. 56). The importance of family and community was strongly impressed on the younger generations. Huber (1977) and Kelly (1984) analysed the social interaction and integration of Italian migrants to Griffith. They found that Italian immigrants formed close-knit communities which had a strong capacity for internal social and economic support. The importance of family commitments and relationships is still a strong feature of Griffith's Italian community.[52]

Today, many Italian immigrants and their descendants—the second generation—are well-respected professionals and business people in Griffith and several have become key players in local politics. Over the last 20 years, there has been only one non-Italian mayor of Griffith City Council, with Italian immigrants holding the position for all but approximately three years. By 2009, four of the twelve councillors were first- or second-generation Italian immigrants.

Following the Italians, the next largest immigrant group in Griffith are Indians. Sikhs began arriving in Griffith in the mid-1970s, with the first group coming via Melbourne to work as fruit pickers on local farms. As word spread about the available work, another wave of immigrants followed. In the mid-1980s, a new wave of Sikh immigrants arrived, many with formal qualifications. The last three decades have seen further immigration to Griffith from South and Central Asia (India, Pakistan and Afghanistan), the Middle East and Southern Europe (Iraq, Turkey, Lebanon) and, most recently, Africa (Zimbabwe) (ABS 2019). Many immigrants from these regions have formed sizeable communities and have often taken up work in fruit picking, farming or agricultural processing. The Aboriginal community in Griffith is also a relatively large group, with many local Aboriginal families living close to Griffith's city centre at the former reserve known as Three Ways. The diverse cultural mix of Griffith, evident in the 2016 census and outlined in Tables 2.5 and 2.6, makes it quite unusual for a rural area.

Table 2.5 Country of birth of Griffith residents, top ten countries, 2016

Country of birth	*Persons*
Australia	13067
India	902
Italy	842
New Zealand	347
Philippines	197
England	174
Fiji	165
Taiwan	145
Pakistan	117
Afghanistan	111
Total residents	19,144

Source Author's calculation based on ABS (2019)

Table 2.6 Ancestry of Griffith residents, selected groups, 2016

Ancestry[a]	*Responses*
Australian	5604
English	5042
Italian	4405
Irish	1573
Scottish	1245
Indian	899
German	582
Chinese	303
Filipino	215
Australian Aboriginal	131
Total residents	19,144

Note [a]This question in the Census is multi-response. Total responses may not equal total number of persons
Source Author's calculation based on ABS (2019)

While the census data put the proportion of Griffith residents claiming Italian ancestry at around 23%,[53] some locals estimate that the proportion is much higher. It is commonly estimated that up to 60% of Griffith's population has Italian ancestry,[54] with some 'Italian' families now into their fifth generation in Australia (Field notes G20.07.06).

Griffith has often been seen as a 'success story' of multiculturalism. For example, Kabaila (2005) argues that the early arrival of Italians to the region has meant that more recent waves of immigrants have been well accepted, with local people being accustomed to cultural diversity and the more established Italian immigrants knowing well the difficulties of adjusting to a new country as a cultural minority. However, it has not all been 'smooth sailing'. Certainly, there was significant tension early on in Griffith's history. For example, while never coming close to the violence of the Wiradjuri Wars of the 1830s, there were early points of tension between the Anglo-Celtic and Italian communities. In 1928, the same year that the Griffith Shire Council was proclaimed, several of the local Anglo-Celtic residents formed the Jondaryan Club. Local historian Peter Kabaila (2005, p. 172) describes it as 'a partnership of the Anglo-Australian power brokers in the town'. The fifteen original men in the club carefully scrutinised membership applications to ensure that only the town's most influential men—either property owners or professionals—could join. High membership fees and a limit of 100 members also helped to reserve the club for the wealthy and powerful.[55] Italians were specifically excluded from joining this influential club until 1959 (Kabaila 2005, p. 172).

Even though the Jondaryan Club ceased operating in 1998, with the club building transformed into the less exclusive 'Exies on Burrell', the history of the club denying entry to Italians has remained a sore spot for some of Griffith's Italian residents. In 2006, attempts by some of Griffith's community to have the club building listed on the city's municipal heritage register were thwarted by developers. Many local Italians sided with developers, having little sentiment for the heritage of a club with racist origins. After a long dispute, the club building was demolished to make way for a supermarket (see Drape 2006).

As well as historical tensions between Griffith's Italian and Anglo-Celtic communities, there have also been significant tensions among Griffith's Italian immigrants, particularly along regional lines. This is described by Kabaila (2008):

> Following the end of the Second World War, a marked division between those more established Italians who had settled in the interwar years and the more recent settlers quickly emerged. At the top of the scale were the wealthy Veneti farmers. Italian vegetable growers were the lowest on the social and economic rung. Further tension existed between different regional groups, notably the Veneti's disdain for southern Italians, particularly the Calabresi whom they considered socially inferior and clannish. Even within the Veneti community the religious/anti-cleric divide shaped

> relations. These divisions manifest themselves most markedly in the formation of rival clubs which became the focus of social interaction within the Italian community.

While Kabaila may exaggerate the extent of regional divisions, animosity and distrust have certainly been long-standing features of relations between some of Griffith's northern Italians and some southerners. There are also some ongoing tensions between other Griffith residents that have tended to play out along 'ethnic' lines. In early 2007, relatively isolated incidents of violence among youth threatened to boil over into racialised conflicts. In particular, following the death of a young Maltese-Australian man early on new years' day, for which two Aboriginal boys were charged, racist graffiti was painted around Three Ways and rumours of planned reprisals surfaced in the local media. There is also a long history of exploitation of newly arrived immigrants in employment and some hostility among local unionised workers over the belief that cheap, non-unionised immigrant labour is being recruited in some industries to reduce the power of unions and keep wages low (Interview G6).

2.3.2 Cosmopolitan Monuments in Griffith

The successive waves of immigration to Griffith have had a clear impact on the city's built environment. Some immigrant groups, such as the Italians, have had more of an impact than others. The influence of Italian immigrants on Griffith's built environment is evident in, among other things, the four 'Italian' clubs (the Coro Club, Yoogali Club, Yoogali Catholic Club and Hanwood Sports Club), the Italian Museum and Cultural Centre, the Scalabrini retirement village and the Our Lady of Pompeii Catholic Church. In addition, many of the town's public buildings were built by Italian immigrants and their descendants.

While the evidence is subtle, several Italian immigrants have also expressed their heritage through 'ethnic nostalgia' in their homes (Kabaila 2005, p. 127). For example, several of the homes in Kookora Street adopted Italian elements such as elaborate metalwork fences or arched verandahs (see Fig. 2.8). On the outskirts of town, the Italian influence on some farming houses is also apparent, incorporating Italian-style columns or statues of lions, the latter a symbol of Venice. Other immigrant groups

Fig. 2.8 Italian homes in Kookora Street, Griffith (*Source* Kirrily Jordan)

have also had a noticeable impact on Griffith's built environment, especially the Sikh community—through the Sikh Gurdwara in Yoogali—and the Muslim community through the small mosque in central Griffith.

2.3.2.1 The 'Italian' Clubs

When the early Italian immigrants arrived in Griffith, they met for social gatherings at their friend's houses, on the banks of the Murrumbidgee River or on local farms. With music, makeshift bocce courts, home-cooked meals and home-made grappa, these were lively affairs (Kabaila 2005). As noted earlier, the first waves of Italian immigrants were not welcome at the Jondaryan Club and they soon established their own clubs where they could speak Italian and enjoy each others' company. As one early Italian immigrant—here called Angelo De Luca—recalls, in the 1930s and 1940s, Italians were sometimes turned away at the Jondaryan Club's door:

> I was playing football for Griffith, and all the team went in after the game and I was stopped at the door. So I then took on board the Italian clubs and patronised them. (Interview G1)

The first of these clubs was the Italo-Australian Club (now the Coro Club). It was soon followed by the Yoogali Club, the Yoogali Catholic Club and the Hanwood Catholic Club (now the Hanwood Sports Club). Today, while the clubs may seem less 'Italian' and have mixed membership, some still continue the traditions of bocce and cards and regularly host meetings of local Italian associations such as the Alpini and Trevisani nel Mondo.

2.3.2.2 Coro Club

The Italo-Australian Club was the first Italian social club in the area (established in 1937 in Yoogali, two kilometres east of Griffith) and was immediately popular (Ceccato n.d.). The clubhouse resembled the men's social centres—or *osteria*—in the villages of Veneto, with its two fibro and corrugated iron rooms used for drinking, socialising and gambling.[56] Outside the clubhouse were bocce courts and the Coronation Hall, the latter often used for social dances and wedding receptions.

Unlike Griffith's Jondaryan Club, which was open only to the region's distinguished Anglo-Celtic gentlemen, the Italo-Australian club was always open to members of any ethnic background. Original members were mostly Italian, Irish or Anglo- or Irish-Australian. However, like most clubs of its day, it was originally closed to women (Field notes 23.01.07). Women and children were allowed to attend the club only on Sunday afternoons, which became the busiest time for the clubhouse. Women would serve food they had earlier prepared while the children played together and the men played bocce (Kabaila 2008).

The Italo-Australian club was thriving until Italy's entry into World War II in 1940 when it was closed down.[57] When the war ended, the club premises were rented by the new Yoogali Club (see below). In 1954, the Yoogali Club moved to nearby Mackay Avenue and the Coronation Club was formed in the now mostly vacant Coronation Hall and clubhouse. The club soon took on its abbreviated name as the Coro Club.[58]

The Coro Club carried on the traditions of gambling, bocce and socialising that had been central to the earlier Italo-Australian Club. According to a resident of Griffith whose father was heavily involved in the Coro Club, it was common practice for the members to stomp on the floor of the club if they saw police approaching, and the gamblers would quickly exit through the back door (Field notes 23.01.07). Neville Mitchell, a long-term resident of Griffith who was born there in the 1950s and has been mayor of the city, recalls the Coro Club's reputation:

> Most people feel that as a bit of a dodgy type of club... after the six o'clock close type of stuff, people used to go to the Coro Club. And it was an old hall that was basically converted into a drink shop... and I should say it certainly wasn't just Italian cultural background people that utilised it, there was certainly quite a number of people that used to skip out there including some of the constabulary over the years... It used to be a bit of a haunt for people who kind of enjoyed a bit of a risqué... look at the world [who] got together and talked crap and drank and gambled and whatever. (Interview G3)

In 1978, the Coro Club moved to new premises in Harward Road, Griffith (Fig. 2.9). Since its move to Harward Road, the Coro Club has continued to grow. Today, it is Griffith's third largest club, after the Ex-Serviceman's Club and the Leagues Club. While some club members still remember its strong Italian origins, the club now appears very similar to the other sports clubs in the region.

The primary functions of the club are still as a place for socialising, organised social events and sporting activities. Sporting facilities have changed dramatically since the days of the Italo-Australian Club in Yoogali. The new premises do not have bocce courts, but have a large sports oval next door. The Coro Club sponsors darts, rugby union, rugby league, cricket, football (soccer), freshwater fishing, game

Fig. 2.9 The Coro Club, 20–26 Harward Rd, Griffith (*Source* Kirrily Jordan)

fishing and basketball clubs. It also hosts a poker tournament and regular bingo nights and houses snooker tables, an outdoor barbecue area, poker machines and Keno and TAB (Totalisator Agency Board) facilities (Coro Club n.d.).

The ethnic mix of club members is now very diverse, reflecting the changing ethnic mix of Griffith's residents. Different users make use of different club facilities. For example, according to club staff, Pacific Islanders use the club as a function space, bringing their grass mats to sit on. Islanders also join the rugby clubs and so become Coro Club members. People from northern and southern Italian backgrounds and Anglo-Celtic backgrounds use the bar on a regular basis, although staff report that while the northern and southern Italians are friendly to each other and may say hello, they often sit separately. On some reports, there is one table of Calabrians who sometimes drink at the club 'who you wouldn't want to offend' (Field notes 22.01.07). The club's in-house Chinese restaurant is run by a local Chinese family.

The club is actively involved in fundraising activities and is a member of the Community Development Support Expenditure Scheme which provides funding to charity organisations through donating a percentage of poker machine takings to charity. Donations are also made from bingo nights. For example, in 2007, $6000 was donated to support Cystic Fibrosis Australia and $6000 to the Griffith branch of Diabetes Australia (Coro Club n.d.).

2.3.2.3 Yoogali Club

The Yoogali Club also had its genesis in the Italo-Australian Club's Coronation Hall and clubhouse. The Italo-Australian Club had been closed during World War II, and when peace was declared in 1945, it was decided that the time had come to establish a new club (see Ceccato n.d.). Following a public meeting in 1946, the new club was established.[59] Carrying on the traditions of the Italo-Australian club, the Yoogali Club hosted bocce on Sunday afternoons and regular Saturday night dances and wedding receptions[60] (Ceccato n.d.). The Coronation Hall had become an important institution.[61] One of the early members of the Yoogali Club, an Italian-born man now in his eighties who will be referred to here as Tony, suggests that without places such as the Coronation Hall, some of the Italian immigrants to Griffith would not have stayed:

> There was a dance there [at the Coronation Hall] on a Saturday night and that's how we met, yes, even that was something that was lovely to newcomer. If it wasn't for those places there, I would not stay here in Australia, no, I would go back to Italy. Otherwise live here like animals, you know, you got nothing. So, we started to build things... and enlarging them and started to build up here a good community until we felt you know it was good to live here. (Interview G5)

The Yoogali Club had a clear policy from its very early days that membership was open to all men. It was non-sectarian and non-racial, with all men, 'regardless of political affiliation, religious beliefs or cultural background' allowed to join (Kabaila 2008). However, in the early days, its membership was predominantly northern Italian (especially Veneti) and Anglo-Celtic Australian. The first president and secretary of the club were of Irish descent (Kabaila 2008). While women were not allowed to become members in the club's early days, the club held a regular ladies night dance and the policy of excluding women from membership soon changed (Kabaila 2008). The club 'is thought to be the first club in NSW to admit women' (Kabaila 2005, p. 171), with women allowed to join from 1959. Tony remembers that the membership grew significantly when this change was made—from around 1000 members to more than 3000 (Interview G5).

In 1954, the Club bought land and built a new premise, only a few hundred metres away from the Coronation Hall on Mackay Avenue[62] (Ceccato n.d.). The new club building was much bigger and had more modern facilities than the original clubhouse (see Fig. 2.10). The new Yoogali Club building included bocce courts and a large function room that could seat up to 1000 people and, until similar-sized halls were built in the late 1970s, was the key site for large weddings and other large functions in the region. That meant that it hosted events whenever 'big names' (including performers and politicians) came to town.[63] As Tony, a club member since 1949, recalls:

> Certainly, if those walls could talk there, they'd say, oh, they seen a lot, a lot of big people go through those doors. (Interview G5)

Like most of the Italian clubs in Griffith, the popularity of the Yoogali Club has declined since those animated days. In the late 1970s, the development of new venues for large functions removed the Yoogali Club's

Fig. 2.10 The Yoogali Club, 647 Mackay Avenue, Yoogali (*Source* Kirrily Jordan)

monopoly. With competition from other clubs already having eaten into the Yoogali Club's profits, it began to struggle financially (Interview G5). While its financial position has fluctuated since then, Tony suggests that with competition from other clubs its current position is still a concern: 'it's not making much money, just keeps the head above water, put it that way' (Interview G5).

While the club sponsors a popular and successful local football team through which it gains some new and younger members, membership has declined to around 850 people (Frank Bruno personal communication, 25.05.09). Interestingly, while it was originally popular among mostly northern Italians, it is now known by many as the 'Calabresi' club, with many of its members having either been born in Calabria or having Calabrian ancestry.

2.3.2.4 Catholic Club Yoogali

Like the Yoogali Club, the Catholic Club Yoogali was established in 1946. With the support of the Catholic Archbishop of Wagga, a local group of immigrants from northern Italy attempted to buy out the Italo-Australian Club to establish their own Catholic club. While they failed in their bid to buy the old premises, they established their club in a new building behind the Our Lady of Pompeii Catholic Church in Yoogali (Kabaila 2005). They also built bocce courts which were later built over with a convent (Kabaila 2008). The church, which is still in use today, is directly across the road from the original Coronation Hall.

Reflecting the tensions between northern and southern Italians in and around Griffith at the time, the Catholic Club was originally closed both to non-Catholics and to Calabresi (Kabaila 2005, p. 171). One local Italian who was involved in the early days of the club suggests that the Catholic Club was established by those who felt the Yoogali Club's activities were too irreligious (Field notes 21.07.06). In its temporary location behind the Catholic Church, the club was a social venue for the parishioners.

The Catholic Club Yoogali hosted many of the same activities as the Coro Club and Yoogali Club. According to one of the early presidents of the Catholic Club, introduced earlier as Angelo De Luca, a key focus was time spent with the family:

> It was a meeting place for the families to get together ... By law, the men only could go to the bar, and the children were kept separate from the bar, that's by law. But our tradition was that we all as a family get-together, mainly on weekends. (Interview G1)

In 1954, the Catholic Club Yoogali moved to a new premise in Hebden Street, just around the corner from the church (Piazza 2005, p. 39) (see Fig. 2.11). Several renovations have occurred since, with the clubhouse expanded and bocce courts added out the back in 1957. More recently, a further extension of the club building in October 2003 has allowed a bigger function room and tennis courts have been added to improve the facilities and increase revenue and membership (Field notes 04.02.07).

Today, the Hebden Street premises house a bar, poker machines, a large kitchen and large dining and function room. While club membership is not as strong as the Coro Club, the Catholic Club Yoogali has many regular members including many elderly Italian immigrants, mostly from the north. While the club also hosts dance parties and has attracted some young and new members through the construction of tennis courts, most of the club's members are middle aged or elderly. Italian men still use the club regularly to play Italian card games, many of them speaking their regional Italian dialects. Both men and women play in the weekly bocce

Fig. 2.11 The Catholic Club Yoogali, 2 Hebden Street, Yoogali (*Source* Kirrily Jordan)

competition against the other local clubs, although, again, most players are elderly.

2.3.2.5 Hanwood Sports Club

In 1955, a fourth Italian club was established. The Hanwood Catholic Club (Fig. 2.12) was opened as a venue for parishioners at the local Catholic Church (many of whom were Italian immigrants) and other residents of Hanwood, around five kilometres south of Griffith. Angelo De Luca joined the new club soon after it opened. He recalls that at that time transport was not always readily available to newly arrived immigrants so the commute to a club in Griffith or Yoogali was often too far. In its first few years, the Hanwood Catholic Club suffered from regional divisions. As De Luca recalls:

> The Hanwood Club was in trouble and it looked like closing down... There was disenchantment with the board of directors or committee at the time ... [there were] Italian factions from different regions of Italy. At the time the different factions wouldn't fratonise. (Interview G1)

But De Luca remembers that a new president of the club, John Toscan, established improved relations by starting football (soccer) games among the children:

Fig. 2.12 Hanwood Sports Club, 21–27 Yarran Street, Hanwood (*Source* Kirrily Jordan)

> The kids didn't recognise factions, and the parents following the kids began to fratonise. That created the unity… it became mixed and it remained that way, it was just a gathering of all factions, including the Australian faction. I think the club… helped to integrate all of them, through membership and through sporting activities and socialising. (Interview G1)

Activities at the Hanwood Catholic Club were similar to the other Italian clubs. Bocce courts were built and the club hosted social dances. Sponsoring football remained an important feature of the Hanwood club, with the teams from Hanwood and the Yoogali Club becoming keen rivals. With the focus shifting to sports and the introduction of poker machines, the name of the club has now officially changed to the Hanwood Sports Club. The membership of the club became mixed, being roughly balanced among Italian and Australian born and among those over and under 50 years of age (Frank Bruno personal communication, 15.05.09). However, like the Yoogali Club and, to a lesser extent the

Yoogali Catholic Club, membership today is on the decline. The club is in a poor position financially, although it continues to sponsor its successful football team and is still used regularly for bocce.

2.3.2.6 *Griffith Italian Museum and Cultural Centre*

The Griffith Italian Museum and Cultural Centre is a relatively new building, with construction completed in 2003. The museum grew out of a desire among local Italian immigrants to record the history of Italian settlement in the region and the contribution of Italian pioneers in the region.[64] For example, the first treasurer of the committee established to build the museum, Giovanni (John) Piazza, suggests that:

> We built our museum to create a tangible witness to the contribution made by the Italian immigrants to the vast development of Griffith over the past decades. The Italian immigrants and their younger generations are proud of their contribution to the development and prosperity of the City of Griffith. (Piazza 2005, p. 49)

Similarly, one of those involved in the very early stages, Italo Codemo, suggests that there was a desire for a permanent public record of what Italians had contributed to the Griffith area (Kelly 2001, p. 498). Some of those involved in the development of the museum also saw it as a means of passing on Italian traditions and heritage to the younger generations, with ideas floated that the museum would offer demonstrations of traditional pasta and salami making and record family histories that could be accessed by future generations (Interview G2).

The idea of building a museum received popular support among Griffith's Italian immigrants. The inaugural 16-member committee for the museum was established in 1994[65] (Piazza 2005, p. 49; Interview G7). In planning the initial stages, key advocates of the museum had wanted a representative from each of the Italian regions on the committee to avoid political division among immigrants from the north and south. However, in the end, most of the committee members were from Veneto and, of those who were not, some have since resigned. As of 2007, members of the museum committee included only three from outside Veneto: one from Calabria, one from the central-east province of Marche and one from neighbouring Abruzzo[66] (Interview G7). Several committee members suggest that this reflects the large number of Venetian immigrants and the difficulty of finding willing participants among the populations from other regions (Interview G5; Interview G7). As committee member Francesco (Frank) Bruno explains:

> Initially we started with the idea that there should be a representative of each region of Italy, which of course is a good idea, but then... it wasn't quite practical because... there are 20 regions in Italy, and possibly just about every region was represented [in Griffith] but there might be two from one region and 3,000 from another. (Interview G7)

Soon after the museum committee was elected, fundraising efforts began. A dinner was held for local builders, contractors, tradespeople and Italian community groups and donations were called for. John Piazza notes that 'a considerable sum of money was offered immediately, while contractors and tradesmen promised contributions in kind' (Piazza 2005, p. 50). The initial response was enthusiastic: according to Piazza, 'All of this was well beyond our expectation. It showed that the whole of Griffith accepted and approved of the project' (Piazza 2005, p. 50).

By the end of financial year 2002–2003, donations from local social groups and clubs totalled just over $81,000. Many donations had come from the various Italian groups in the area, including regional groups such as the Abruzzo, Calabria group, Trevisani, Veronesi, Vicentini and Fogolar Furlan; armed forces groups such as the Alpini and Marinai D'Italia; and sports and social groups such as the Hanwood and Yoogali Bocce Clubs, Italian Sports Club and Italian Republic Day Committee. Donations also came from the broader Griffith community, including from the Griffith East Rotary Club and Griffith Social Dancers and fundraising events such as the Australia Day Dinner Dance (Piazza 2005, p. 53). The largest donation, of $10,000 per year for five years, came from the corporate group Prime Life who run one of the local retirement villages (Piazza 2005, pp. 53–54). The NSW government—through the Ethnic Affairs Commission and Ministry for the Arts (Kelly 2001, p. 498)—and the Italian Consul General also contributed funds. Among the local clubs and associations, the largest donations were from the Trevisani and Alpini clubs (Piazza 2005, pp. 53–54). This probably reflects the high proportion of Italian immigrants in Griffith who came from Treviso and other northern villages (where the Alpini also originated), but may also reflect the high proportion of northern Italians in the museum committee.

Initial enthusiasm for the museum project was checked with disagreements over the location of the museum, its size and architectural design. After a long period of debate, the committee decided on a design by local architect Steven Murray. The design was for a large museum, with the committee deciding to locate it in the Council-owned Pioneer Park on Griffith's outskirts. Alternative plans to build the museum in the city centre were set aside because by locating it in Pioneer Park the museum would receive the support of Council caretakers and park staff. The majority opinion was that building the museum in town would have meant it needed to be staffed entirely by community volunteers and, consequently, may not have been able to open full time (Interview G7; Field notes G20.07.06).

The design for the museum is intended to reflect both Griffith's Italian heritage and Australian rurality, with the front of the building consisting of Italian columns and arches with a *torre*, or bell tower, that is reminiscent of building designs in Italian villages (Kabaila 2005, p. 151). The back of the building, with its corrugated iron roof, represents a common rural Australian shed (see Fig. 2.13). One of the members of the original museum committee, a middle-aged man with Italian heritage, here called Lorenzo Rossi, talks about the significance of the design:

> This was meant to mould the two communities together, the Anglo-Saxon and the Italian... Steven Murray—whose mother is Italian, from the North—came up with this design... the building had the arches and the tiled roof at the entrance as a portico, and that's typically Italian, and then the rest of the building is in zinc alum iron, which is styled like... an early Riverina shearing shed, so that the two came together... Rather than build a typically Italian building we just wanted to show the community that... we weren't being divisive, and here it is, a building that it achieved, that the two cultures could meet and live together. (Interview G2)

The land in Pioneer Park was made available by Griffith City Council (Field notes G20.07.06), with the Council also providing the museum committee with a $50,000 interest-free loan that was to be paid off over five years. As well as the substantial money already raised, much of the labour and materials needed for the project were donated or provided at less-than-usual cost by local businesses[67] (Piazza 2005). Voluntary labourers on the project included scores of men of Italian descent as well as a dozen or so other workers (see Piazza 2005, pp. 55–56).

Fig. 2.13 The Griffith Italian Museum and Cultural Centre, Pioneer Park (*Source* Kirrily Jordan)

Of the Italians, Frank Bruno recalls that they had come from 'all over the place, you know not just northerners', with around eight of the twenty Italian regions represented (Interview G7; Frank Bruno personal communication, 25.05.09). Many others helped with the building and fit-out, including women who assisted by providing lunches. Such displays of volunteerism are often taken as evidence of building social capital (see, for example, Atherley 2006).

Nonetheless, while so many people helped at the building site, significant disagreements arose within the museum committee over the size and style of the internal display. Some committee members wanted a large display, and others preferred to limit the number of items displayed in order to keep the quality very high. The latter view prevailed, with the professional curator hired for the task advocating a contemporary, minimalist style (Interview G2; Field notes G20.07.06). The aim was to avoid the perceived problem of many rural and regional museums that display a lot of material but include many badly damaged items or things that are of little interest to visitors (Field notes G20.07.06).

The museum was officially opened on 28 October 2004 by the then NSW Premier Bob Carr. The Federal Minister for Citizenship and Multicultural Affairs Gary Hargrave and other local and state government representatives also attended the opening ceremony, along with around 200 local residents and many of the volunteer tradespeople and representatives of firms that helped with the construction. Traditional Italian food was prepared and served (Piazza 2005, p. 64; Frank Bruno personal communication, 28.05.09). As of December 2004, the final cost of the museum had been just over $314,000, although Piazza suggests that:

> many thousands of dollars should be added to this sum to record the many hours of voluntary work given by [local] tradesmen and the value of rebate on cost of building material granted us by local suppliers. (Piazza 2005, p. 54)

Frank Bruno estimates that, including voluntary contributions, the cost of the building and fit-out was closer to $500,000 (Field notes G20.07.06).

While the museum's opening ceremony was well attended, the construction of the museum had not enjoyed universal support. Neville Mitchell suggests that there was some envy among non-Italians, although from his perspective the initial 'ripple' soon faded and 'people have generally let it go' (Interview G3). Rossi also remembers some initial (although fairly limited) reaction against the museum, with someone vandalising the museum's wall with a reference to the Italian involvement in the 'mafia-like' activities (see Bottom 2008) surrounding the 1970s disappearance of politician Donald MacKay[68]:

> someone got pretty keen and actually painted some graffiti on the wall but it was only once... it was a bit of a throw back from the Donald MacKay days... I just forget what they put on now, but anyway, it wasn't nice. (Interview G2)

According to Rossi, such initial opposition 'eventually died down and we got on with the job' (Interview G2).

With the building completed, the museum was handed over to Griffith City Council to manage through the Pioneer Park. However, the museum committee retained a fundraising role and control over decisions about the exhibit (Interview G2; Interview G5). Handing the museum to the Council was seen as a gift to the community, as Rossi explains:

> we've just said 'well here it is, it's completed, we've got exhibitions'... and so we handed it back to the community of Griffith... the committee at the time, and the Italian community in general, were very proud to hand that over to the community of Griffith. (Interview G2)

At the opening of the museum, the display consisted of a number of large glass cabinets housing materials including photographs of early Italian settlers, coffee grinders and pasta ladles brought out from Italy in suitcases, early building and sewing equipment, and even items of furniture that the early immigrants had fashioned out of wooden crates. Larger pieces of equipment and furniture—including an early wine press—circled the display cases around the walls (see Fig. 2.14). A computer had also been installed to allow public access to historical records of the first 200 or so Italian immigrant families, including their place of birth, date of arrival in Griffith, activities on arrival, subsequent progress and family photographs (Piazza 2005, p. 52). The computer also included a record

Fig. 2.14 Permanent display, Griffith Italian Museum & Cultural Centre (*Source* Kirrily Jordan)

of all donations of cash, labour and materials that went into the museum's construction, including a list of the names of volunteer workers (Piazza 2005, p. 52).

However, the minimalist display remained controversial. In particular, with a large number of items donated to the museum by the local community being retained in storage, many people were upset that their cherished belongings had not been put on display for the public. To counter this concern, the original plan was to rotate the exhibits so that more of the materials could be put on public view. As Piazza suggested in 2005:

> The exhibit does not include all of the items donated. These will be exhibited in turn when the original display will be changed periodically... Present storage does not allow receival [sic] of other contributions. City council is expected to approve new storage area and this will permit the acceptance of new items for storage. Furthermore, future plans are to have an area specifically set apart for Cultural Centre, in which landscapes, maps, historical items and such will be exhibited. (Piazza 2005, p. 51)

By January 2007, none of these plans had been realised. Importantly, the displays had not been rotated and a large amount of material remained in storage. This created significant tension, with many people feeling left out. In particular, the old division between northern and southern Italian immigrants was brought into play since much of the material on display was donated by those from the north. Hence, some saw the museum as a predominantly northern Italian project. As Frank Bruno explains:

> There was some truth in the fact that they [the broader Italian community in Griffith] thought that there was an overbearance of northerners in the committee, or not only on the committee, but also what was going to be displayed... so that alienated the groups from the south, who thought 'this is a northern thing'. And I don't think that's waned yet, I think that's still there. They feel that the committee, that it's mainly the northerners that want to... establish it and therefore put their ideas which is a bit of a shame. (Interview G7)

Others share this view. For example, Brenda Walker, a young third-generation Italian-Australian woman who is actively involved in the City's youth services, recalls her first impressions:

> It was a lot different from what I was expecting... I was expecting there to be a lot more stuff. And, it just seems to be like one kind of family's perspective on it... when I saw it, it was like 'that's not really all the Italian community in Griffith, it's just like one certain [region]'. (Interview G8)

Similarly, one entry in the museum's visitor book, dated April 2006, suggests that 'It would be nice to see the other regions represented—Not everyone is from Treviso'.

In all, the result of the disagreements over the display was that the initial enthusiasm for the project waned and was replaced by widespread attitudes of disappointment, resentment and apathy. Frank Bruno sums up his perception of the community's view of the museum:

> There were a lot of people disappointed with, not by the building, but by the fact that they didn't have... enough exhibits in there. You know that's a... common view, of all the Italians, I think of the majority, is that you know all that money and what have we done? (Interview G7)

In defence of the curatorial decisions, some members of the museum committee have argued that the dominance of materials from northern Italian immigrants reflects the earlier arrival of northern Italians in Griffith: since the museum represents the earliest days of Italian immigration, the predominance of northern Italian materials is only to be expected (Field notes G20.07.06; Interview G7). In addition, some committee members have expressed that they are conscious of the perception of northern Italian 'bias' and are 'endeavouring to give as much exposure as possible to non-Veneti if cooperation and assistance is offered' (Frank Bruno personal communication, 25.05.09).

Indeed, the museum committee still plans to extend the display and is attempting to reignite community support for the museum. In particular, in 2007, the committee began making plans to significantly develop the exhibit, adding extra display cabinets and allocating the new display space for each of the different regional Italian groups that had active local associations. The expectation was that each group would fundraise to contribute to the cost of a half or a whole cabinet. As of early 2009, new displays for the Calabrian, Abruzzo and Sicilian regional organisations (as well as displays for other Italian associations such as the Alpini) were at, or nearing, completion. The committee has also developed a plaque listing the names of all the individuals and groups that have donated to the building and fit-out of the museum, with the plaque now on display. The museum committee is optimistic that the new display has made 'everyone happy' (Tony personal communication, 25.05.09).

While the addition of the new cabinets may have taken the museum away from its original idea of showcasing the early Italian pioneers, members of the museum committee see this as a pragmatic approach. For Frank Bruno, it is a way forward even if it has moved away from being a 'traditional' museum:

> At least that might get things moving... we want the Calabrians to say 'right, this is what you've got'... the Sicilians, 'right this is what you got'... it's getting away from what the original thought [of displaying] purely old things, cause I can see that it's going to be exhibits which are more recent than pioneering days... but then again... if it's only recent now, in 50 years time it will be old... Is that the museum idea? I suppose it is in a way. (Interview G7)

While the opening of the museum was well attended, visitor numbers since that time have been relatively low. The museum's visitor book shows that visitors include school groups from Griffith and surrounding areas such as Leeton. They also include visiting Italians, with interviews suggesting that local Italian-Australian residents commonly show the museum to family members visiting from overseas (Interview G2). Other entries listed in the museum's visitor book appear to be from national tourists, including visitors from Victoria, New South Wales and Western Australia.[69] Rossi, who has served on Griffith City Council, notes that the museum has also been used for civic functions:

> At the council sometimes we may, if we have an Italian... consul turn up or somebody, some dignitary, we like to have a civic welcome and we usually have it up there [at the Italian museum], it's a nice venue... just to show 'em what we've done. (Interview G2)

The peak periods for visitation of the museum appear to be the Australia Day celebrations held in Pioneer Park each year and the annual *Festa Delle Salsicce* (Festival of the Sausage, or Salami Festival). *Festa Delle Salsicce* has been organised by the Italian museum committee each year since 2003, with the first festival being held inside the museum before the display was installed. The festival involves Italian food (cooked by the local women), wine (donated by local wineries) and Italian music (played by local men). Festival-goers can also join in traditional Italian dances, songs and games. The highlight of the festival is the announcement of the winner of the salami competition, with the top three salamis awarded cash prizes and the other entries to the competition sliced up for everyone to share.

On the day of the festival, while Italian women prepare the food, Anglo-Celtic and Italian men work together to set up the marquee and tables and chairs. Here, whoever arrives first pitches in. A similarly mixed group of volunteers stays behind after the days' events to pack up. During the 2006 festival, families from Anglo-Celtic and Italian backgrounds shared long communal tables and, as the drinking and dancing continued, shouts of 'Viva Italia' were interspersed with friendly cries of 'Aussie Aussie Aussie', to both much shared laughter and applause (Field notes G20.08.06). In the survey of ten festival participants in 2006, festival-goers were asked if the festival was meaningful to them and, if so, why. A number of respondents noted the festival was meaningful to them because it brings people from different cultural backgrounds together: 'it's all the different nationalities...it's nice and harmonious, there's no hate' (QNOG8), 'everybody amalgamates' (QNOG3) and 'for integration it's really great' (QNOG8).

The salami festival is billed as a fun-filled and one-of-a-kind experience in Australia but behind the scenes the salami competition is taken very seriously. Salami judging is carried out under the watchful eye of independent scrutineers, knives are cleaned between cutting each salami so as not to mix the tastes, and efforts are made to ensure that each of the four tables of four judges has at least one southern Italian on board so that claims of northern Italian bias will not wash (Field notes G.19.08.06).[70] The prizes, too, are serious, with the top salami in 2008 bringing in a cash prize of $1400 and second and third places respectively awarded $400 and $200 (Pattison 2008a).

While no longer held inside the museum, the salami festival now takes places on the lawn just outside. Whiling away the hours, many festival-goers also wander through the museum. The profit made through the festival (with tickets costing $40 each in 2008) is retained by the museum committee for ongoing development of the building and displays and exhibits (Field notes G23.01.07).[71] The festival has grown steadily since 2003, with 300 people attending in 2006 (Field notes G20.08.06), 450 in 2007 (Pattison 2008b) and 600 in 2008 (Griffith City Council 2008; Pattison 2008c). These included locals of both Italian and Anglo-Celtic heritage as well as some groups from interstate.[72] With prizes and much of the food and wine donated by local businesses, a significant proportion of the money raised through annual ticket sales has been invested back into the museum. These funds helped the museum committee to pay off the last instalment on the loan from Griffith City Council in 2008.

The popularity of the festival has led to growing media interest and has been noted by tourism staff at Griffith City Council. One employee, here called Sandra Manning, notes that while 'it's pretty low profile at the moment', it is 'starting to build as far as popularity goes... it's starting to get to the stage where it could become a major festival in itself' (Interview G13). Organisers, though, have been keen to maintain independent control over the festival, being nervous that Council involvement would weigh the organisation down in 'red tape', particularly in relation to food safety standards concerning the dozens of home-made salamis entered into the competition (Field notes G19.08.06).

As noted earlier, one aim for developing the museum was to remind the younger generations of Italian Australians in Griffith about their cultural backgrounds (Interview G5). However, interviews suggest that at least some of this target audience remain uninterested. For example, although Walker has Italian heritage, and she is actively engaged in arts and cultural services in Griffith and generally enjoys visiting museums, she only visited the Italian Museum in 2007—three years after it opened:

> I was kind of interested I guess when it first opened—there was a lot of hype around the idea—and then never sort of got out there and kind of forgot about it...I don't know many young people that would go up [to Pioneer Park] just for the museum, unless you're showing Italian tourists around [laughs]... I've got a few friends that are Italian, that are from Italian descent as well, and I don't know if they've even been up there to have a look... not unless they were up there for something in particular, like an event or something like that. (Interview G8)

Tony, introduced earlier, expressed some concern at the lack of young people on the committee. He suggested that extensions of the museum's display should be done quickly before too many of the committee members pass away:

> We're going to push forward... before we getting too old... if we, two or three of us go, it's not going to be done anymore, so pushing now to have it done as quick as possible, so we still healthy. (Interview G5)

While the members of the museum committee are middle aged or elderly, plans for the future of the museum aim to attract interest from the younger generations, including hands-on demonstrations of traditional salami, pasta and tomato sauce making and a larger archive of family histories so that 'as generations come along... they can learn about the history of their Italian parents... or grandparents, or even great grand-parents' (Interview G2). The committee has also tried to actively engage younger generations in the *Festa Della Salsicce*. For example, in 2006, the organisers of the salami judging deliberately invited three younger men to be judges, with some of the older generation expressing concern that without more involvement from youth the Italian traditions may be lost. The same spirit of inclusivity did not extend to women: the salami making and salami judging processes are an almost exclusively male affair.[73]

The Italian Museum is still less than two decades old. However, a 2005 study of local history recommended that it be listed on local and state heritage registers for its 'high significance to the Italian community' (Kabaila 2005, p. 194). The ongoing efforts of many members of the local Italian community in developing the museum and the many donations and hours of voluntary labour that have gone into its construction highlight the importance of the project for some residents. However, the significance attached to the museum varies considerably among Italian immigrants and their descendants.

2.3.2.7 Gurdwara Singh Saba

With the large numbers of Sikh immigrants arriving from the 1970s, the Griffith area has become home to a Sikh Gurdwara, with the Gurdwara Singh Saba opening in Yoogali in 1993. The Gurdwara Singh Saba is one of only approximately twenty Sikh temples in Australia and one of only around six that are outside the capital cities. In the late 1980s, the Sikh community—then comprising about 15 families—had no formal place of worship but met for communal prayers once a month in a rented hall. By the early 1990s, the decision had been made to build a gurdwara. After around six months of fundraising, the chosen site—the old Coronation Hall in Yoogali—was purchased outright. The fundraising had been well organised, first collecting money from Sikh families in Griffith and then sending delegations to Sikh communities around Australia to collect more funds. One member of Griffith's Sikh community, a young father who arrived from India in his teens who is here referred to as Harpreet, describes the process as follows:

Harpreet: We collected the money from Griffith first, then we went to Melbourne and Brisbane and all the places, so collected all the required money, and we came back, so we didn't borrow any money, so it just was done and bought it for cash… And, that's a pretty common practice, like if Melbourne wants to do something, or Sydney or whatever, they go other places and collect it…

Interviewer: So, it means physically travelling… you go to Melbourne and talk to people there?

Harpreet: That's right, physical, like what happened four or five people, depend sort of on networks and everything too, like you might have three or four people that they have good friends in Melbourne… they are either committee members or whatever, so then you know that they would take you around to different people's places and just help you to raise that funds. So, yeah, it's like when people from Melbourne coming, they will come and see the committee members here, and they will take them down [to collect from] peoples 1,000 bucks, 500, 200, whatever they can. (Interview G11)

Once the building was purchased, the community set about converting it into a temple. While the outer structure was untouched at first—save a new paint job and the addition of a flag and signage to indicate its new purpose (see Fig. 2.15)—the inside was converted into a prayer hall and separate lunchroom (*langar*) with the addition of an internal partition. The existing kitchen was also renovated. Over time, the building was extended with a new section on the side that became the formal langar (Interview G11; Field notes G19.08.06).

The Gurdwara Singh Saba is in continual use by a full-time priest. When the temple first opened, the community could not afford to pay a priest so the position was filled by local men who had full-time farming jobs but would stay in a small room at the back of the gurdwara rent free. As the community grew, funds were raised to pay a full-time priest, with three-year contracts offered to bring trained priests out from India. As Harpreet describes, the 'guru' in the Sikh religion is the holy book, the Guru Granth Sahib, but the priest is relied on to 'bring the community together' (Interview G11). In Griffith, Harpreet suggests, this has been effective, with the prayer meetings that at first occurred only monthly, now being held twice a week and some people attending daily evening prayers:

Fig. 2.15 The Gurdwara Singh Saba, 11 Edon Street, Yoogali (*Source* Kirrily Jordan)

> We started from doing once a month, ok, then every weekend, now we doing it every weekend, plus also one of the week days. So you can see how the gradually sort of building up. And not only that now, in the evening you will see people go every day too, because when they are, we call it Rehras Sahib [evening prayers where the Guru Granth Sahib is ceremoniously put to rest]. What happens is that… every evening, they all sort of do a prayer and then they will, fold [the holy book] up and take it… and then in the morning they would do the same thing, bring it back and open it, so then it can be left open all day.

People of all ages attend the gurdwara, particularly for the large gatherings that occur regularly on Saturday nights. The temple can only be used for religious activities, including not only regular prayers and recitations from the Guru Granth Sahib but also the serving of meals and tea that are prepared by the women in the on-site kitchen (Interview G11). Meetings can also be held at the temple—in the small room at the back—but only if they relate to the gurdwara. Other functions are not allowed, as Harpreet explains:

Under the nature of it we can't use it for anything else, other than for religious purposes... you can't just hire for something else or nothing. No, it's purely for the temple only, so is everything has to be correctly. If you want to hold function or something, you can't do it there, you have to go hire something else, like we do sometimes hire the St Mary's hall next door, if it's to do with some religious function. But if you are going to do anything else in the town then you hire something in the town.

The gathering of the community at the gurdwara does, though, also serve a social function. Harpreet suggests that this might be the main way the temple is used by the younger generation:

Interviewer: And are the younger generation interested in the temple?

Harpreet: Yeah, it becomes a place to go and meet people so... although they may not, like, some of them just sit outside and have a chat, but still it's a communal place, they can actually go and talk. Then you know that everyone will be there, so it becomes, it does that part, bringing the community together in that way.

Interviewer: And is there any other place that does that, in Griffith?

Harpreet: No, no, there's no place to do that... so that's the only place we do... you might [have] five or six guys all standing like talking and say 'oh what you doing weekend?' That's when you start planning things and doing things and goes from there. (Interview G11)

While the gurdwara is not used for non-religious events, the number of users does swell when special events bring more Sikhs to town. For example, Griffith is host to the annual Sikh sports carnival. This event attracts competitors from all around Australia to participate in mainstream sports such as athletics as well as traditional Indian games such as kabaddi, a team sport which Harpreet likens to wrestling. The carnival, held over the June long weekend, brings about 600 competitors to Griffith, with the local Sikh community fundraising to pay for their full accommodation and food expenses during their visit. Motel accommodation is booked well in advance and food and drinks are provided at no cost to everyone who attends the sporting events, including non-Sikh spectators who 'come in and have a look and see what's going on' (Interview G11). In the evenings, while many of the young visitors to town go out for a night of music and dancing, the older generations attend a ceremony at the gurdwara (Interview G11).

Like Griffith's Italian community with its complex internal politics, the Sikh community has some intra-group rivalries. Rivalries are played out within the management committee of the Gurdwara Singh Saba (itself comprised only of men), with two groups of roughly equal numbers jostling for power at the committee's elections for office-holders (Field notes G19.08.06). However, these divisions do not interfere with the community's efforts at fundraising, whether for the Sikh community's own purposes or for the broader needs of Griffith. For example, if there is a need for funds, the Sikh community will mobilise just as they did when raising money for the temple, with individuals making the rounds of each house to ask for a contribution. As Harpreet explains:

> It could like hospital may need some money for some sort of fundraising like they may need an extra bed or some machine… [or] there were bush-fires, some things like that. What happens is the member of the community they say 'OK, you should do something', so then we say 'OK', four or five of us go and collect the funds for that sort of thing. So, they do that sort of thing quite a lot. (Interview G11)

Harpreet believes that the presence of the gurdwara may assist in that fundraising:

> When you got 20, 30 guys standing together in an area, then ideas develop and then they said one: 'Why don't we do this?' Alright let's think, OK, let's pass it on. It become, it gives him a formal direction. I think if you didn't have a place like the temple or anything like that, you will not have what we doing here. (Interview G11)

With the Sikh community in and around Griffith continuing to grow, plans are currently well underway to build a much larger temple. This will house not only a prayer hall that can seat up to 1000 people and langar that can cater for up to 600, but also a library, small language school and temporary accommodation for travellers. Depending on the amount of money raised, the complex may also include a sporting oval and community hall that would be available for external hire. The building will be more in keeping with the traditional design of a Sikh temple than the current gurdwara, with an instantly recognisable domed roof. Harpreet believes that is important:

> Because that's... how do you differentiate from building to building. So the building has to have some sort of architectural character that makes you different, so the domes are the ones that makes things different... that's what they're for... If the current building the way it is, if you don't read the sign on the door, you don't know—it's a building. But if you put the domes on that building, straight away you will see it, so that's the integrity of the building, so yeah, so that's what we looking at... like the temple of Woolgoolga and you go on the Pacific Highway you see that, yeah. (Interview G11)

The new gurdwara is expected to cost upwards of $2 million, with donations being sought from Sikh families in the Griffith area and around Australia. As with other fundraisings in the community, each Griffith household is expected to contribute, with families making an annual donation of $1000 and single people asked to donate $500 per year. Sikh families around Australia are asked to contribute what they can. As of August 2006, around $40,000 had been collected from Sikh households in Griffith and Queensland. While the 1000 person capacity is larger than required for Sikh families in Griffith today, the plans are being developed with a view to the future and to cater for visitors to town for special events like the annual Sikh sporting carnival.

2.3.2.8 Riaz Mosque

As well as having a Sikh temple, the Griffith area has a local mosque. The Riaz Mosque is very near the centre of Griffith but remains quite inconspicuous. Located in a largely commercial area, the mosque is architecturally unremarkable and set some way back from the street—only the sign above the door gives its presence away (Fig. 2.16). Prior to founding the mosque, Griffith's Muslim community first established regular prayer meetings at the local showgrounds, coming to an agreement with the showground's administration that they could use the venue every Friday for prayers and a short lecture (Interview G4). In 2000, the group decided to hire their own premises, renting a former service station (Interview G3) near the Council Chambers on Benerembah Street. The hall was bought outright in approximately 2005, but unlike the relatively formal process of collecting donations employed to purchase the Sikh temple, the Riaz Mosque was purchased with a large, single, anonymous donation.

Fig. 2.16 Riaz Mosque, 58 Benerembah Street, Griffith (*Source* Kirrily Jordan)

The running costs of the mosque and any repairs are funded by voluntary donations that the congregation can place in a box as they enter the mosque (Interview G4).

While Griffith's Sikh community is relatively homogenous as an ethnic and religious group—notwithstanding their own intra-group politics—the Riaz Mosque, like the Italian clubs, shows a complex reality about what is often thought to be a homogenous group. The mosque is used by a number of different ethnic and national groups, including Turks, Fijians, Pakistanis, Iraqis and Egyptians (Field notes G.22.08.06). The users are predominantly Sunni, with most of the Afghan immigrants in Griffith—who are Hazara refugees from the Shia sect of Islam—preferring to use a public park and a rented school hall as places to gather and conduct Friday prayers (Interview G3). One Afghan resident of the area noted that there are no plans to build a Shia mosque in Griffith because the community is too small (Field notes G01.02.07), but plans are underway to raise funds for their own community centre (Interview G3).

Like the Sikh gurdwara, the Riaz Mosque is used primarily for religious purposes. It also plays a social role, being a place where people can get together both on a regular basis and for special occasions like feast days. On some occasions, non-Muslims have been specifically invited to attend the celebrations, including a member of the local city council and a member of parliament (Interview G4). As in Katanning in WA, local Shia Muslims (predominantly Afghan refugees) choose not to use the mosque. However, a senior member of the mosque, Dr M, stresses that the mosque is open to anyone who wishes to attend at any time, provided they observe rules about appropriate dress and respectful behaviour. This invitation extends to both non-Muslims and Shia Muslims, and Dr M says he has challenged anyone to come to the mosque and see if anyone asks them to leave. He stresses in particular that Shia Muslims are welcome to attend the mosque or even to lead the Friday lecture:

> The Mosque is actually not belonged for one, no. Anyone can come whatever—Sunni, Shia, no problem for anyone to come... I have some Shia, they come to have the prayer with us, and I was very clear with every and each one, I told them there is no difference at all because all of us at the end, we pray for one God and all of us we go for pilgrimage in Mecca in the same place... and this was my even dialogue with someone, um, if you bring the holy Koran, it is... say printed in Saudi Arabia and then another one from Egypt, another one from Pakistan, another one in a foreign country... Please open any page in, and start to read, is there a difference?... No difference, ok, so no fighting, no... I will be happy if some of the Shia is going to lead [the lecture at the mosque], because he will not recite different religion, no, if he is going to recite something it will be the same, it's in the same holy book. (Interview G4)

Dr M suggests that the reason some Shia Muslims choose not to attend the Riaz Mosque is a misunderstanding that happened some years ago. As he describes:

> In the past there was something maybe happened... there was some group [of Shia Muslims] actually, coming to have celebration for the feast, and... they celebrate in a noisy way... Let me say that now we are praying, and this even in Christianity, is it allowed inside the church? While the Pope or the priest is giving the speech, and the prayer is going on, that someone is going to be clapping or going to make some noise or talking or something else? No.... [So then when I moved to Griffith] I see some group is not coming [to the mosque] a lot, they just come one or two and not a lot, so I was wondering. Then I had learned the story [of this misunderstanding in the past]... But what is supposed to be, when you enter [the mosque],

all the respect while the prayer is going on… So it was a matter of the misunderstandings. (Interview G4)

Since his arrival in Griffith, Dr M has worked to improve relations between local Sunni and Shia Muslims, speaking at the mosque about what he sees as the fundamental similarities between the two branches of Islam. He has also attempted to build understanding between Muslim and non-Muslim residents. For example, while the Riaz Mosque does not have official 'open days', in 2006 Dr M gave a lecture at the local public library where non-Muslims could ask questions about Islam, and he has written in the local newspaper, the *Area News*, 'giving a call… to have peace [among] the nations' (Interview G4). Indeed, he suggests that improving community relations is a crucial function of the mosque. According to Dr M, since the word Islam means peace, it is the mosque's role to contribute to peace and harmony in the community. That means encouraging local Muslims to have good relations in their family, neighbourhood and workplace:

Dr M: This word itself—Islam—it means peace, this means to be peace with yourself, to be peace with the others, to be peace with the nature, to be peace with the plant, to be peace with the animals. So in this way, the message comes from the mosque… to be in peace with yourself, to be having harmony, harmonisation for the whole community, this is our intention… [One] verse has been mentioned by the Prophet that ah, spread peace among the people. This is an order, it is an order to spread peace… he didn't say just to be peaceful, no, he asked us to spread this peace, that means that we must have an effort to be done, that we have some duties to spread peace.

Interviewer: And is there guidance as to how… people might do that?

Dr M: Spreading peace actually even by having a good relation with your neighbour, support your family, do your work in honesty, smile and give nice words… because even to hurt someone in his feelings sometimes it is bad and worse than using the stick, if you hurt someone in his feelings he may be affected by this maybe a long time. … go in depression from the words. (Interview G4)

As well as encouraging those attending thecha the mosque to be neighbourly, lectures at the mosque promote active participation in the local community. For example, Dr M recalls lectures on the value of work, encouraging people to feel proud of even 'very, very small work' as a gardener or farmer rather than relying on social security payments that give someone else the 'upper hand' (Interview G4). In this way, he suggests, people can help to 'build up the community. But if we come to say that the government is paying through Centrelink, what is our role? What our building is going to be? Nothing' (Interview G4). The mosque also provides an avenue for local Muslims to contribute to charities or other local community needs. For example, at various times, the donations collected at the door of the mosque have been presented to organisations such as the Heart Foundation and a suicide prevention group. And without the mosque, Dr M argues, the Muslim community in Griffith would lose its way, with Griffith more likely to suffer religious tensions under the influence of events elsewhere:

> If there was no mosque actually... I can see that Griffith was not going to be having a matter of co-operation because it was going to be having actually misunderstanding, and the Muslim group themselves I feel that they are going to be lost... maybe their thoughts would not be arranged in the proper way as the message is to be for peace... [For example,] one factory is called Barters and there is some Muslims working there, they are working very good and hard, and [if] no one is guiding them... some days you may find either lazy or misunderstanding... then if he sees something happening overseas or something on television he may come on the second day not feeling well towards another one which is not correct—you are Sunni, you are Shia, you are Christian, all are human beings. So if there is no mosque actually, there will be a big gap in the community... Because, without the mosque who is going to say for this... Muslims ones be in harmony with others?... The mosque is important for the [Muslim] community... to guide them. Not a person, not the person, because if I am here from this day I am dead on another day... life is not like that, OK, but the mosque or the place itself it will guide the whole group. (Interview G4)

Notes

1. A small number of Chinese had settled in the New South Wales (NSW) colony in the late eighteenth and early nineteenth centuries, including Chinese sailors who had unofficially discharged themselves when they reached Sydney and others who had been brought out as labourers. However, Chinese migration to Australia began in earnest in the late 1840s and the discovery of gold in the eastern colonies in the 1850s triggered a rapid increase in immigration (Rolls 1992). By 1861, there were nearly 13,000 Chinese in NSW (Fitzgerald 1997, pp. 18–23). Most

of these early Chinese immigrants were men and most had come from the poor southern provinces of China, particularly Guangdong. While most came seeking their fortunes in the gold rushes, some decided it would be more profitable to stay in Sydney and establish businesses like cook shops, produce stores or boarding houses that catered to those passing through the ports. Several of these businesses sprung up in The Rocks, particularly around George Street North (Fitzgerald 1997, pp. 67–68).

2. Fitzgerald (1997, p. 68) notes that 'the term 'Chinatown' was not widely used until the twentieth century'.
3. While Chinese opium smoking and gambling joints were often referred to as dens, in Sydney they were often in the top story of buildings so that the smoke could escape through the roof undetected (Field notes C23.05.06).
4. Discriminatory federal immigration gave official imprimatur to the popular anti-Chinese racist sentiment of the time. Violent attacks on Chinese immigrants and their business had been occurring since at least 1878, often spurred on by trade union campaigns that sought to stamp out Chinese immigration (Fitzgerald 1997, p. 75). Perhaps ironically, the tendency of early Chinese immigrants to settle in concentrated pockets within the city may have fuelled anti-Chinese sentiment, with the high visibility of Chinese in those areas adding to undue concern about Sydney being 'swamped' by Chinese (see Fitzgerald 1997, p. 28).
5. Chinese immigrants may have noted the racist stereotyping of their own people but evidence from the early Chinese language press indicates that they sometimes held strong beliefs about their own racial superiority over the British (see Fitzgerald 1997, pp. 7, 86; see also Rolls 1992).
6. Through the late 1800s, many Chinese arrived in NSW under an illegal system of contract labour whereby wealthy Chinese would pay the poll tax for poor, newly arrived Chinese men but then exploit them as indentured labourers. Later, Chinese who arrived in the country illegally were sometimes employed by Chinese entrepreneurs under poor working conditions and for little pay (Fitzgerald 1997, p. 32).
7. Surry Hills also remained important as a centre of Chinese settlement.
8. Following World War II, the then immigration minister, Arthur Calwell, sought to deport the Chinese evacuees and seamen who had arrived during the war. In the end, a change of government meant the pressure to remove the wartime evacuees or seamen was eased (Fitzgerald 1997, pp. 44–45; Yuan 2001, p. 205), but local Chinese support for the evacuees and seamen meant that Chinatown had become a hub of Chinese political activity, particularly through the Chinese Youth League (Cottle and Keys 2006, 2007).
9. At the same time, some saw this period as a troubled one for Sydney's Chinatown, with new immigrants and refugees from China, Malaysia,

Singapore and Vietnam establishing criminal rackets demanding protection money from local entrepreneurs (Interview C7).

10. The monument was initiated by the Australian Chinese Ex-services National Reunion and built with the assistance of several Chinese and non-Chinese community associations and corporations and financial support from the NSW government and the federal Department of Veteran's Affairs.
11. This question in the Census is multi-response, so the same people could have identified as having Australian and Chinese ancestry, for example.
12. After non-responses were excluded.
13. A further 16% of total residents stated that they were attending an educational institution but did not specify the type of institution (ABS 2019).
14. While the city council and Taiwanese government had originally planned to share the costs of building the arch, the agreement broke down when Australia recognised the government of the People's Republic of China in 1972 (Fitzgerald 1997, p. 151).
15. Low suggests that the redevelopment also incorporated some community development objectives. In the late 1970s, there were dozens of elderly Chinese men living in basic accommodation above the shops in Dixon Street and the decision to reduce traffic in the street had these men in mind since it meant they could sit outside. As Low notes, 'it's their front garden' (Interview C11).
16. Others, too, argue for increasing the Chinese theming of today's Chinatown. While the Dixon Street Chinese Committee is no longer very active, the local council's main point of contact in decisions about Chinatown is the Chinese New Year Festival Advisory Group. One member of the advisory group in 2008, here called Kong Sang, has argued for the reintroduction of Chinese lanterns not only in Dixon Street but in the surrounding streets both to inform people they are in Chinatown and to encourage the expansion of Chinese businesses (Interview C5). For Sang, like Low and Wong, the Chinese arches in Dixon Street are traditional Chinese architecture. While he recognises that Chinese culture is incredibly diverse, he suggests that the arches are unifying since 'you can look at the arches and see something 'distinctly Chinese'' (Interview C5).
17. In this survey, the avoidance of categories such as 'ethnic', 'co-ethnic' and 'other' seeks to avoid the no-doubt unintentional essentialising of ethnic difference. As social anthropologist Thomas Hylland Eriksen has argued, in ethnicity studies 'there is a real danger that scholars, usually against their own intentions, end up confirming a view of the world as essentially made up of competing ethnic groups' (Eriksen 2001, p. 19).
18. The Dixon Street Chinese Committee continues to participate in local affairs, particularly in assisting the City of Sydney with the lion dance

programs for the annual Chinese New Year festival and Chinese Moon Festival.

19. It met at least four times each year and was comprised of up to ten members selected by the council who the council deemed to be leaders or 'experts' in media, business, the arts, sport or Chinese community associations. The committee also included one member of council staff who acted as executive officer and liaised with council officers. All appointments were made by the council's Lord Mayor. There had previously been a Spanish community committee to assist with the city's Spanish Quarter Street Festival for two years in the early 2000s.
20. Kong Sang, who was a member of both the Chinatown Cultural Advisory Committee and the Advisory Group, explains that the changed committee structure was to make participation easier for committee members who were all volunteers and found it hard to attend meetings for both the Chinatown Cultural Advisory Committee and the Chinese New Year subcommittee (Interview C5).
21. Stuart Gill no longer works for the City of Sydney.
22. Kinkead (1993, p. 47) notes that in the first decades of the twentieth century New York tourists 'went to Chinatown to ogle vice: guidebooks warned of the immorality and filth of the quarters. The sightseers hired guides to show them opium dens, slave girls, and sites of lurid tong murders'.
23. The gift from Guangzhou included the plans and artisans, while the conceptual design was completed by a Chinese-Australian architect and the construction was paid for from NSW public funds.
24. The main responsibility for marketing and promotion of the festival is taken by the City of Sydney, in 2007 spending an estimated $120,000 on producing and distributing brochures, postcards, street banners, posters and advertisements for Chinese language print and radio. TNSW works at distributing the brochures and other advertising interstate and internationally (Interview C6; Stuart Gill, personal communication, 20.09.07).
25. According to Gill, the city is applying for 'Hallmark Event' status from the NSW Department of Premier and Cabinet's Office of Protocol and Special Events (OPSE) which would then exempt them from these costs (Interview C6). 'Hallmark events' are those with complex logistics that require coordination between a number of agencies and that are deemed to 'enhance awareness, appeal and profitability of a destination at a particular time' and have 'an international and/or national audience and provide significant economic and social benefits' (OPSE 2008).
26. Stuart Gill from the City of Sydney notes that the council does not have much to do with the Sydney Chinatown Chamber of Commerce (Interview C6).

27. In his research in Chinatown in 2005, Patrick Kunz interviewed 10 Chinese entrepreneurs who owned retail shops and restaurants in Dixon Street (see Kunz 2005; Collins and Kunz 2007). He found that there was a lack of communication between them (which was explained by business time constraints) and none of his respondents were members of local organisations or enterprise associations. Relations between them were more likely to be competitive than cooperative, and while their shops and restaurants form a large part of the visitor experience in Chinatown, they were not actively involved in the processes that shape its development.
28. The organisation has been active in Australia since at least 1854 (Chinese Masonic Society 2004).
29. The Life Honourable President notes that in June 2008 the Chinese Masonic Society raised over $10,000 for the Sichuan earthquake appeal in China. In February 2009, they raised over $6000 for the Victoria bush fire appeal. In both cases, the money was raised through lion dances in Chinatown (Mar personal communication, 12.06.09).
30. Chinese seamen had been coming ashore in Australian ports for some years, disembarking from their ships when their contracts ended and waiting to be deployed with a new crew. The CYL also provided support to these seamen, helping them fulfil tax requirements and organising crews for deployment (Interview C7).
31. The pig iron dispute lasted from November 1938 to February 1939. Waterside workers at Port Kembla refused to load pig iron onto ships bound for Japan, believing the iron would be used to make armaments. William Wang notes that founding members of the Chinese Youth League supported the strikers by bringing them fruit and vegetables from the market (Interview C7).
32. Nonetheless, many of the seamen found work running cafes and restaurants, including in Dixon Street where they served chop suey to American soldiers (Interview C7).
33. The government then brought in the War Time Refugee Removal Act to attempt to deport the seamen. As noted previously, when Chinese were arrested under the new Act, the Chinese Masonics provided surety to keep the evacuees out of jail. The CYL assisted with a challenge in the High Court, but the Act was eventually repealed in 1956 when the change of government gave Chinese seamen, wartime evacuees and indentured workers residency (Cottle and Keys 2006, p. 1).
34. While working in support of the new Indonesian republic in 1948, the long-time president of the CYL, Fred Wong, died in mysterious circumstances (Cottle and Keys 2006, p. 1). His death is still a matter of concern and controversy today.
35. While these films—imported from Hong Kong and southern China—were often delayed by Australian Customs, the CYL used its connections with

the Chinese Seamen's Union to have films brought in surreptitiously by sea. ASIO raids on the CYL headquarters in Sydney uncovered literature and films brought in from China, proof to them that the organisation was acting as a spy for the People's Republic (Cottle and Keys 2006, p. 1).

36. The exact number of Macedonians in the Illawarra region at this time is not known—official records did not identify them as Macedonian and until recent years many Macedonian immigrants preferred that their Macedonian heritage was not advertised beyond their own communities. In addition, it has been difficult to trace Macedonian families by name. Many Macedonians changed their names either by necessity (such as after the partition of Macedonia) or by choice. Members on one nuclear family may have different surnames if they emigrated at different times. For example, a Macedonian family in Australia may include a father who emigrated prior to World War II with the surname *Chadevich* (a typically Serbian name) and a son who emigrated after the creation of the Republic of Macedonia with the more typically Macedonian surname *Čadevski* (Hill 1989).
37. There is currently no consensus on the 'ethnicity' of the ancient Macedonians. Many Greeks argue that they were a Greek people but this is disputed by some contemporary Macedonians (Danforth 1995, Chapter 11).
38. Greece argues that the country's name should make no reference to 'Macedonia' as the term is 'an inalienable and eternal possession of Hellenism, a piece of its soul' (Papathemelis in Danforth 1995, p. 30). Most international institutions, including the UN, the WTO, the IMF, NATO and the EU, refer to the former Yugoslav Republic of Macedonia or FYROM. This term is resented by some Macedonians who see it as 'a foreign imposition' (Thomas 2001, p. 56; see also Balalovski 1995). While few countries initially recognised the constitutional name Republic of Macedonia, as of 2008 over 120 countries have accepted it, including the United States, China, Turkey and Bulgaria (Macedonian News 2008). Australia still uses the term FYROM and it did not allow a Macedonian embassy in Australia until 2004.
39. The Greek nationalist argument is that a Slavic 'Macedonian' identity is a fiction created by the Yugoslav state. Many Macedonians living in Greece who identify as Macedonian (and not Greek) are denied cultural and linguistic rights (see Danforth 1995, Chapter 11).
40. Spase Karoski (1983) describes in detail the chain migration process of early Macedonian immigrants, in which it was common for the person sponsoring their newly arrived friend or relative to rent rooms of their own houses to them. He suggests that 'it was not unusual in the late 60s and early 70s to find more than ten men living in overcrowded conditions in the home of another' (Karoski 1983, p. 31).

41. Thomas (2001, p. 61) notes that in Macedonia *sredselo* could occur in nearby fields.
42. Thomas (2001, p. 56) notes that Census figures can be misleading as some people who are ethnically Macedonian can be counted as Greek.
43. Calculated after non-responses excluded from total.
44. These are the Orthodox churches with their origins in the Byzantine or Eastern Roman Empire that are mostly 'in communion with' the Patriarch of Constantinople (Binns 2002, p. 9).
45. Today, the Ecumenical Patriarch has direct jurisdiction only over the Patriarchate of Constantinople but has a broader oversight role for the whole Orthodox Church and presides at Orthodox synods. He also has authority over some Orthodox Christians who live outside of the territory of national churches, including some Orthodox Christians in America and Australia. Under modern Turkish law, the Patriarch must be a Turkish citizen (Binns 2002, Chapter 2).
46. In their study of the Macedonian Orthodox Church in Australia, Christopher Popov and Michael Radin (1995, p. 39) suggest that prior to these developments, the Greek Patriarch of Constantinople attempted to 'hellenize' the Macedonian population by sending Greek bishops and priests to 'educate' Macedonian parishes.
47. There are two levels of independence among Chalcedonian Orthodox Churches: 'autocephalous' churches, which are fully self-governing and can select and consecrate their own leaders, and 'autonomous' churches which must receive the blessing of the 'Mother Church' to consecrate their leaders. Binns (2002, p. 10) notes that 'the movement towards independence may be erratic, with a Church recognised by one Church and not by another'. Some churches within the Chalcedonian Orthodox tradition, including the Macedonian Orthodox Church, are not recognised by the other Churches as they are considered 'uncanonical or irregularly established', although they 'may become recognised in due course if their status is accepted by the other Churches' (Binns 2002, p. 10).
48. It is significant that when the Church of Saint Kliment of Ohrid was built the Macedonian population of the Illawarra was in decline. In 2016, there were 1,183 Port Kembla residents whose religion was listed by the ABS as 'Eastern Orthodox' (ABS 2019).
49. Popov and Radin (1995, p. 36) note that the link between the Macedonian church, Macedonian cultural development and a developing Macedonian 'national psyche' dates back to medieval and late feudal times. Considering the long-standing political tensions in the Balkans, this is perhaps not surprising. Interestingly, they also argue that the influence between the Macedonian Orthodox Church and the diaspora goes both ways, suggesting that the campaign to develop a Macedonian church in Melbourne in the 1950s was a significant influence on the 'mother

Church' in Macedonia's proclamation of its autocephalous status in 1967 (Popov and Radin 1995, pp. 51–52).

50. The different Macedonian football teams in the Illawarra have historically been associated with different Macedonian villages. For example, Wollongong United (established by the Macedonian Orthodox Community of the City of Greater Wollongong, which also established the Church of Saint Dimitrija of Solun) has been closely associated with players from the Bitola region. Warrawong United has been more closely tied to the Mariovo region and the Cringila Lions has been associated with Ohrid (see Hill 1989, p. 99).
51. The Wiradjuri language group actually consists of several dialects (Kabaila 2005, p. 8).
52. In fact, one interview respondent suggested that traditional family ties and obligations within Griffith's Italian community are stronger and more restrictive than those in today's Italian villages, with the older generations in Griffith preserving the traditional family system while families in Italy have modernised and liberalised (see Interview G3).
53. Percentage calculated after non-responses excluded.
54. While this may be an overestimate, the reality probably lies somewhere in between this figure and the official census count.
55. The club also received close support from the Shire Council. With the help of the Shire's engineer and gardener, it had established a club house (including billiard tables), bowling green, tennis court and garden by 1932. In 1935, a second wing was added that included a bar and locker room for storing members' own provisions of alcohol (Kabaila 2005).
56. Since the club was not licensed to serve alcohol, members had to bring their own liquor and give it to the club's manager to be stored in a private locker behind the bar. Each member had their own locker and purchased drink tokens—with each token costing the price of a bottle of beer—that could be exchanged at the bar for their liquor. This 'locker system' allowed the club to work around the alcohol prohibition that denied alcohol licences to all local clubs until after World War II (Kabaila 2008).
57. With Mussolini siding with Nazi Germany, Italian immigrants in many parts of Australia were interned. While the Italo-Australian club was closed down, the Coronation Hall continued to be hired out for wedding receptions and dances. The dances were often fundraising events for the war effort, including for the Spitfire Fund and the Sheepskins for Russia Fund (Ceccato n.d.).
58. As well as reflecting the name of the hall, the Coronation Club was named in honour of the coronation of Queen Elizabeth II who visited Australia in 1954. The name soon had to be changed as a club in Sydney's Burwood

had already been registered by the same name. Members settled on the abbreviated 'Coro Club'.

59. Pompeo Vardanega, who had established the Italo-Australian Club, joined with compatriot Angelo Salvestro to provide the start-up capital and the new club leased the old Italo-Australian club house and Coronation Hall (Kabaila 2005, p. 171).
60. Beer was still served through the locker system that had been used earlier by the Italo-Australian club until the Yoogali Club was able to obtain a liquor licence in 1951 (Kabaila 2008).
61. For example, among the Ceccato family alone, six of Antonio Ceccato's children and seven of his grandchildren had their wedding receptions in the hall (Ceccato n.d.). One of the early members of the Yoogali Club, an Italian-born man now in his eighties, met his wife at the Coronation Hall. He remembers that the men would stand around talking and 'as soon as the music start and everybody rushes, three or four rushing to one girl' (Interview G5).
62. When the Yoogali Club moved, the old club house remained vacant until it was taken over by the newlyformed Coronation Club later that year, although in the interim the Coronation Hall remained in use when it was hired out for wedding receptions and other functions, including Saturday night dances held by the Continental Music Club (Ceccato n.d.). The Continental Music Club was formed by local second-generation immigrants in 1951 to celebrate continental music, assist newly-arrived immigrants to meet the locals and become part of the community (Piazza 2005, p. 30) and help to bridge the gap between Italian and Anglo-Australians (Kelly 2001, p. 497). The club held regular dances and picnics as well as establishing an informal 'night school' to educate recent immigrants about local customs and the practicalities of Australian life (Piazza 2005, p. 30). It also regularly brought high-profile Italian singers and performers to Griffith and broadcast the first non-English language radio program in the country—a two-hour program of Italian music on local station 2RG.
63. One of those 'big' people was the well-known English journalist David Frost who came to Griffith to cover the 1977 murder of Donald Mackay. Frost interviewed federal Commissioner for Community Relations, and former member for the Riverina and federal immigration minister, Al Grassby, with the event attracting an audience of over 2500 people. Tony recalls the scale of the event, with the crowd so large that many people had to stand outside and listen to the interview played over the PA system (Interview G5).
64. The idea for the museum was inspired by the Italian Museum in Lismore on the north coast of New South Wales. Some members of the Griffith

Alpini Club—a group of Italian immigrants who had served in the mountain companies of the Italian Army—had visited the Lismore museum on a trip and felt that a similar museum could be built in Griffith.

65. The committee was elected at a public meeting at the Yoogali Club. The initial enthusiasm for the project was reflected in the large turnout (around 300 people) at the public meeting (Interview G7).
66. Some members are Australian born with Italian ancestry.
67. Including building materials as well as food and wine to feed the workers (Piazza 2005, pp. 56–57).
68. Unfortunately, Griffith is perhaps best known outside the region for its alleged connections to the Italian mafia and the drugs trade. Most infamously, it was the site of the 1977 murder of local anti-drugs campaigner and businessman Donald Mackay. A local cell of the Calabrian-based organised crime syndicate *'Ndrangheta* (or *L'Onorata*, The Honoured Society) was found to be responsible for the murder. In the ensuing investigation, Griffith was named as the 'centre' of the marijuana industry in New South Wales (Bottom 2008). Today, while there is some local acknowledgement that organised criminal activity still occurs in Griffith, most members of the community are anxious to put that 'chapter' of Griffith's history behind them. However, the recent arrest of four Griffith residents, including at least two with Italian ancestry, for the importation of 4.4 tonnes of ecstasy (with a street value of $440 million) has likely reinforced the public perception of Griffith as one of Australia's organised crime capitals and reignited concerns about a local mafia (see Bottom 2008; Madden 2008; Murphy et al. 2008). Of course, of the many thousands of Griffith residents with Italian ancestry, only a very small handful have criminal connections.
69. It should be noted that many visitors may choose not to sign the visitor book.
70. The traditional northern Italian recipes for salami are quite different from those from the south. Pattison (2008c) reports that the first *Festa Delle Salsicce* in 2003 was inspired by 'an age-old Italian argument' over whether northerners or southerners make the best salami.
71. One member of the museum committee estimated that the 2006 festival raised around $7000 for the museum's funds (Interview G5).
72. In 2006, festival-goers included families and organised tour groups from Melbourne, Cobram and Geelong (Field notes G20.08.06).
73. Field notes G19.08.06. As a young woman who had been invited to the 2006 salami judging on the day preceding the festival, I was informed that I had been bestowed a privilege in being allowed to attend this gathering of men. Certainly, my presence was noticed, with gifts of wine and salami showered on me over the two days.

References

Agyeman, J., & Spooner, R. (1997). Ethnicity and Rural Environment. In P. Cloke & J. Little (Eds.), *Contested Countryside Cultures* (pp. 197–218). London: Routledge.

Anderson, K. (1990, October). 'Chinatown Re-oriented': A Critical Analysis of Recent Redevelopment Schemes in a Melbourne and Sydney Enclave. *Australian Geographical Studies, 28*(2), 137–154.

Anderson, K. (1991). *Vancouver's Chinatown: Racial Discourse in Canada, 1875–1980.* Montreal: McGill–Queens University Press.

Armstrong, H. B. (1998). Migrant Placemaking: A Mode of Communication. In G. Gumpert & S. J. Drucker (Eds.), *The Huddled Masses: Communication and Immigration.* Cresskill, NJ: Hampton Press.

Atherley, K. (2006). Sport, Localism and Social Capital in Rural Western Australia. *Geographical Research, 44*(4), 348–360.

Australian Bureau of Statistics (ABS). (2019). *Community Profiles.* https://www.abs.gov.au/websitedbs/D3310114.nsf/Home/2016%20Census%20Community%20Profiles. Accessed 12 March 2020.

Balalovski, R. (1995). Australian Law, International Treaties and the Government's "Slav" Prefixes. In V. Bivell (Ed.), *Macedonian Agenda: 16 Essays on the Development of Macedonian Culture in Australia.* Includes Cultural Values, Language, Religion, Arts, Identity, Women's Issues, the Elderly, Immigration, Politics, the "Child Refugees," Human Rights and More. Five Dock, NSW: Pollitecon Publications.

Barth, F. (Ed.). (1969). *Ethnic Groups and Boundaries.* Oslo: Scandinavian University Press.

Binns, J. (2002). *An Introduction to the Christian Orthodox Churches.* Cambridge: Cambridge University Press.

BlueScope Illawarra. (2020). *Our History.* https://www.bluescopeillawarra.com.au/about-us/our-history/. Accessed 23 March 2020.

Bottom, B. (2008, August 14). Drug Bust Reveals That Mafia Still Casts a Shadow over Griffith. *The Australian.* http://www.theaustralian.news.com.au/story/0,25197,24178158-5013404,00.html. Accessed 20 August 2008.

Boyle, D. (2003). *Authenticity: Brands, Fakes, Spin and the Lust For Real Life.* London: Harper Perennial.

Bureau of Tourism Research (BTR). (1994). *Annual Results of the International Visitor Survey 1994: International Visitors in Australia.* Canberra: Bureau of Tourism Research.

Burnley, I. H. (2001). *The Impact of Immigration on Australia: A Demographic Approach.* South Melbourne and Oxford: Oxford University Press.

Ceccato, G. (n.d.). *The Coronation Hall.* Unpublished notes.

Chinese Masonic Society. (2004). *150th Anniversary of the Chinese Masonic Society of Australia.* Sydney: Chinese Masonic Society.

Chinese Youth League (CYL). (2007). *Chinese Youth League of Australia Inc.* http://www.cyl.org.au/about.html. Accessed 2 February 2009.

City of Sydney. (2007a). *Preserving and Enhancing Sydney's City of Villages: A Snapshot of Projects, Local Action Plan Strategy 2007–2010*. http://www.cityofsydney.nsw.gov.au/Development/LocalActionPlans/Default.asp. Accessed 1 January 2009.

City of Sydney. (2007b). *2007 Local Action Plan Sydney CBD and Its Neighbourhoods*. http://www.cityofsydney.nsw.gov.au/Development/LocalActionPlans/CentralBusiness.asp. Accessed 1 January 2009.

City of Sydney. (n.d.). *Local Action Plans*. http://www.cityofsydney.nsw.gov.au/Development/LocalActionPlans/Default.asp. Accessed 1 January 2009.

Cohen, E. (1996). A Phenomenology of Tourist Experiences. In Y. Apostolopoulos, S. Leivadi, & A. Yiannakis (Eds.), *The Sociology of Tourism: Theoretical and Empirical Investigations* (pp. 90–114). London and New York: Routledge.

Collins, J. (2002). Chinese Entrepreneurs: The Chinese Diaspora in Australia. *International Journal of Entrepreneurial Behaviour & Research.*, *8*(1/2), 113–133.

Collins, J. (2003). Australia: Cosmopolitan Capitalists Down Under. In R. Kloosterman & J. Rath (Eds.), *Immigrant Entrepreneurs: Venturing Abroad in the Age of Globalization*. Oxford and New York: Berg.

Collins, J. (2007). Ethnic Precincts as Contradictory Tourist Spaces. In J. Rath (Ed.), *Tourism, Ethnic Diversity and the City* (pp. 67–86). New York: Routledge.

Collins, J., & Castillo, A. (1998). *Cosmopolitan Sydney: Explore the World in One City*. Sydney: Pluto Press.

Collins, J., & Kunz, P. (2005, May 26–28). *Spatial Dimensions of the Commodification of Ethnicity in the City: Producers, Consumers and the Critical Infrastructure in Four Sydney Ethnic Precincts*. Paper to IMISCOE Cluster B6 Workshop on Ethnic, Cultural, and Religious Diversity, Amsterdam.

Collins, J., & Kunz, P. (2006). *Ethnic Entrepreneurs, Ethnic Precincts and Tourism: The Case of Sydney, Australia* (Unpublished).

Collins, J., & Kunz, P. (2007). Ethnic Entrepreneurs, Ethnic Precincts and Tourism: The Case of Sydney, Australia. In G. Richards & J. Wilson (Eds.), *Tourism, Creativity and Development* (pp. 201–214). New York and London: Routledge.

Collins, J., Gibson, K., Alcorso, C., Castles, S., & Tait, D. (1995). *A Shop Full of Dreams: Ethnic Small Business in Australia*. Leichhardt: Pluto Press.

Coomaditchie United Aboriginal Corporation. (2020). https://www.coomaditchie.org.au/our-history. Accessed 23 March 2020.

Coro Club. (n.d.). *Coro Club*. http://www.coroclub.com.au/whatson.html. Accessed 17 July 2008.

Cottle, D., & Keys, A. (2006). Building the Bridge of Solidarity: The Politics of the Chinese Youth League in Australia, 1939–73. *Journal of Chinese Australia, 2*. http://131.172.16.7/jca/index.html. Accessed 2 February 2009.

Cottle, D., & Keys, A. (2007). Red-hunting in Sydney's Chinatown. *Journal of Australian Studies, 91*, 25–31.

Danforth, L. M. (1995). *The Macedonian Conflict: Ethnic Nationalism in a Transnational World*. Princeton, NJ: Princeton University Press.

Drape, J. (2006, June 5). Tears as Last Days of Jondo Loom. *The Area News*, p. 1.

Dunn, K. M. (1998). Rethinking Ethnic Concentration: The Case of Cabramatta, Sydney. *Urban Studies, 35*(3), 503–527.

Eriksen, T. H. (2001). Some Current Priorities for Ethnicity Studies. *Ethnicities, 1*(1), 17–19.

Fainstein, S. S., Hoffman, L. M., & Judd, D. R. (2003). Making Theoretical Sense of Tourism. In L. M. Hoffman, S. S. Fainstein, & D. R. Judd (Eds.), *Cities and Visitors: Regulating People, Markets, and City Space*. Oxford: Blackwell.

Fitzgerald, S. (1997). *Red Tape, Gold Scissors: The story of Sydney's Chinese*. Sydney: State Library of New South Wales Press.

Floudas, D. A. (2002). Pardon? A Name for a Conflict? FYROM's Dispute with Greece Revisited. In G. Kourvetaris, V. Roudometof, K. Koutsoukis, & A. Kourvetaris (Eds.), *The New Balkans: Disintegration and Reconstruction* (pp. 85–113) (No. 600). Boulder, CO: East European Monographs.

Fogarty, N., & Appel, G. (2019). *'It's Got Its Ghosts and It's Got Its Future': The Rise, Fall and Rebirth of Port Kembla*. https://www.abc.net.au/news/2019-06-29/the-rise-fall-and-reinvention-of-port-kembla/11107216. Accessed 23 March 2020.

Fong, T. P. (1994). *The First Suburban Chinatown. The Remaking of Monterey Park, California*. Philadelphia: Temple University Press.

Forrest, J., & Dunn, K. M. (2006). Racism and Intolerance in Eastern Australia: A Geographic Perspective. *The Australian Geographer, 37*(2), 167–186.

Garland, J., & Chakraborti, N. (2007). 'Protean Times?': Exploring the Relationships Between Policing, Community and 'Race' in Rural England. *Criminology & Criminal Justice, 7*, 347–365.

Giddens, A. (1991). *Modernity and Self-Identity*. Cambridge: Polity.

Griffith City Council. (2008). *Calendar of Events: All Special Events from August 2008*. http://www.griffith.nsw.gov.au/calendar/Calendar.asp?Special=Yes. Accessed 29 August 2008.

Hage, G. (1997). At Home in the Entrails of the West: Multiculturalism, 'Ethnic Food' and Migrant Home Building. In H. Grace, G. Hage, L. Johnson,

J. Langsworth, & M. Symonds (Eds.), *Home/World: Space, Community and Marginality in Sydney's West* (pp. 99–153). Sydney: Pluto Press.

Haymarket Chamber of Commerce. (n.d.). *Haymarket Chamber of Commerce*. http://www.haymarketchamber.org.au/hcc/?page_id=2. Accessed 4 January 2009.

Heritage Branch NSW. (2006). *Our Lady of Pompeii Roman Catholic Church, Heritage Database Listing*. http://www.heritage.nsw.gov.au/07_subnav_01_2.cfm?itemid=5052102. Accessed 10 September 2008.

Hill, P. (1989). *The Macedonians in Australia*. Carlisle, WA: Hesperian Press.

Hill, P. (2001). Macedonians. In J. Jupp (Ed.), *The Australian People. An Encyclopaedia of the Nation, Its People and Their Origins*. Australia: Cambridge University Press.

Hoffman, L., Fainstein, S., & Judd, D. (Eds.). (2003). *Cities and Visitors: Regulating People, Markets, and City Space*. Oxford: Blackwell.

Holloway, S. (2007). Burning Issues: Whiteness, Rurality and the Politics of Difference. *Geoforum, 38*, 7–20.

Howarth, C. (2002). 'So, You're from Brixton?': The Struggle for Recognition and Esteem in a Stigmatized Community. *Ethnicities, 2*(2), 237–260.

Huber, R. (1977). *From Pasta to Pavlova: A Comparative Study of Italian Settlers in Sydney and Griffith*. St. Lucia, Qld: University of Queensland Press.

Kabaila, P. (2005). *Griffith Heritage: A Thematic History*. Canberra: Pirion Publishing.

Kabaila, P. (2008). *Drink Tokens. Statement of Significance for Objects Through Time Series of the New South Wales Migration Heritage Centre*. http://www.migrationheritage.nsw.gov.au/exhibitions/objectsthroughtime/objects/tokens/. Accessed 24 July 2008.

Karoski, S. (1983). *The Macedonian Community Profile*. Macedonian Australian Welfare Association of NSW. Sydney: Ethnic Affairs Commission of NSW.

Kass, T. (2010). *A Thematic History of the City of Wollongong—Draft Report*. http://council.wollongong.nsw.gov.au/council/haveyoursay/Documents/Local%20Heritage%20Review/Draft%20Thematic%20History%20of%20Wollongong%20Report.pdf. Accessed 23 March 2020.

Kelly, B. (1984). Ethnic Participation in Australian Political Systems: A Griffith Case Study. In J. Jupp (Ed.), *Ethnic Politics in Australia* (pp. 126–138). Sydney: Allen & Unwin.

Kelly, B. (2001). Italians in the Riverina. In J. Jupp (Ed.), *The Australian People: Encyclopedia of the Nation, Its People and Their Origins* (pp. 497–499). Cambridge: Cambridge University Press.

Khoo, T. (2009). Affirming Cosmopolitanism? Chineseness and the Chinese Museum of Queensland. In E. Y. L. Ho & J. Kuehn (Eds.), *China Abroad: Travels, Subjects, Spaces* (pp. 209–224). Hong Kong: Hong Kong University Press.

Kinkead, G. (1993). *Chinatown: A Portrait of a Closed Society*. New York: Harper Perennial.
Knowles, C. (2008). The Landscape of Post-imperial Whiteness in Rural Britain. *Ethnic and Racial Studies, 31*, 167–184.
Kunz, P. (2005). *Ethnic Entrepreneurs, Ethnic Precincts and Tourism: Missed Opportunities from Sydney* (Unpublished PhD thesis). Sydney: University of Technology.
Light, I. (1972). *Ethnic Enterprises in America*. Berkeley, LA: University of California Press.
Lin, J. (1998). *Reconstructing Chinatown: Ethnic Enclave, Global Change*. Minneapolis: University of Minnesota Press.
MacCannell, D. (2001). Tourist Agency. *Tourist Studies, 1*(1), 23–37.
Macedonian News. (2008). *Macedonia Has No 'Name Issue'*. https://www.vmacedonianews.com/2008/04/. Accessed 23 March 2020.
Madden, J. (2008, August 14). Drugs Again Darken Griffith's Image. *The Australian*. http://www.theaustralian.news.com.au/story/0,25197,24177887-2702,00.html. Accessed 20 August 2008.
Mak, A. (2003). Negotiating Identity: Ethnicity, Tourism and Chinatown. *Journal of Australian Studies, 77*, 93–100.
Meethan, K. (2001). *Tourism in Global Society: Place, Culture, Consumption*. New York: Palgrave.
Miller, D. (2002). Doctrinaire Liberalism Versus Multicultural Democracy. *Ethnicities, 2*(2), 261–287.
Murphy, D., McKenzie, N., Welch, D., & Houston, C. (2008, August 9). World's Biggest Ecstasy Bust. *Sydney Morning Herald*. http://www.smh.com.au/articles/2008/08/08/1218139079745.html. Accessed 20 August 2008.
Neal, S. (2002). Rural Landscapes, Representations and Racism: Examining Multicultural Citizenship and Policy-Making in the English Countryside. *Ethnic and Racial Studies, 25*(3), 442–461.
Nederveen Pieterse, J. (1996). Varieties of Ethnic Politics and Ethnicity Discourse. In E. N. Wilmsen & P. McAllister (Eds.), *The Politics of Difference* (pp. 25–44). Chicago: University of Chicago Press.
New South Wales Department of Environment and Climate Change (NSW DECC). (2008). *South Western Slopes—Regional History*. http://www.environment.nsw.gov.au/bioregions/SouthWesternSlopes-RegionalHistory.htm. Accessed 8 August 2008.
Office of Protocol and Special Events (OPSE). (2008). *User Charges Policy*. http://www.events.nsw.gov.au/event-organising/user-charges-policy/?searchterm=hallmark%20event. Accessed 1 January 2009.
Pattison, T. (2008a, August 15). Griffith's Battle of the Salamis Is Set to Sizzle. *Area News*. http://griffith.yourguide.com.au/news/local/news/general/

griffiths-battle-of-the-salamis-is-set-to-sizzle/1245137.aspx#. Accessed 29 August 2008.

Pattison, T. (2008b, July 9). The Hunt Is on for Griffith's Best Sausage. *Area News*. http://griffith.yourguide.com.au/news/local/news/general/the-hunt-is-on-for-griffiths-best-sausage/807604.aspx#. Accessed 29 August 2008.

Pattison, T. (2008c, August 20). Aussie Salami Snags Top Award at Italian Festival. *Area News*. http://griffith.yourguide.com.au/news/local/news/general/aussie-salami-snags-top-award-at-italian-festival/1249137.aspx. Accessed 29 August 2008.

Piazza, G. B. (2005). *A History of Italian Settlement in Griffith* (Unpublished Local History).

Popov, C., & Radin, M. (1995). The Macedonian Orthodox Church: Its Role in the Moulding and Maintenance of Ethnic Identity in Australia. In V. Bivell (Ed.), *Macedonian Agenda: 16 Essays on the Development of Macedonian Culture in Australia* (pp. 36–52). Includes Cultural Values, Language, Religion, Arts, Identity, Women's Issues, the Elderly, Immigration, Politics, the "Child Refugees," Human Rights and More. Five Dock, NSW: Pollitecon Publications.

Power, J. (2015, September 18). The Do-or-Die Decision Facing Port Kembla's Steelworks. *The Sydney Morning Herald*. https://www.smh.com.au/national/nsw/the-doordie-decision-facing-port-kemblas-steelworks-20150917-gjoxx4.html. Accessed 23 March 2020.

Price, C. (1963). *Southern Europeans in Australia*. Canberra: Australian National University Press.

Rath, J. (Ed.). (2007). *Tourism, Ethnic Diversity and the City*. New York: Routledge.

Rath, J., Bodaar, A., Waagemakers, T., & Yan Wu, P. (2018). Chinatown 2.0: The Difficult Flowering of an Ethnically Themed Shopping Area. *Journal of Ethnic and Migration Studies*, *44*(1), 81–98.

Ray, L., & Reed, K. (2005). Community, Mobility and Racism in a Semi-rural Area: Comparing Minority Experience in East Kent. *Ethnic and Racial Studies*, *28*(2), 212–234.

Rolls, E. (1992). *Sojourners: The Epic Story of China's Centuries-Old Relationship with Australia*. St Lucia: University of Queensland Press.

Shea, J. (1997). *Macedonia and Greece: The Struggle to Define a New Balkan Nation*. Jefferson, NC: McFarland & Company.

Sydney Harbour Foreshore Authority. (2015). *Sydney Harbour Foreshore Authority Annual Report 2014–15*. https://www.property.nsw.gov.au/sites/default/files/SHFA%20Annual%20Report%202014-15.pdf. Accessed 24 March 2020.

Tamis, A. (1994). *The Immigration and Settlement of Macedonian Greeks in Australia*. Bundoora: La Trobe University Press.

The Macedonian Welfare Association of NSW (MWA of NSW). (2020). https://www.facebook.com/pg/mwansw/about/?ref=page_internal. Accessed 23 March 2020.

Thomas, M. E. (2001). *A Multicultural Landscape: National Parks and the Macedonian Experience*. Hurstville and Annandale, NSW: NSW National Parks and Wildlife Service and Pluto Press Australia.

Tkalcevic, M. (1980). *Macedonians in the Australian Society*. Melbourne: Gov. Print.

Trajcevski, M. (2005, Spring). The First Macedonian Family in the Illawarra. *KOMPAS*, pp. 8–11. Port Kembla, NSW: Macedonian Welfare Association Inc. Media Group.

Tsang, H. (2002). *Australian Chinese Ex-Servicemen Monument*. Hansard of the NSW Legislative Council. http://www.parliament.nsw.gov.au/prod/parlment/hansart.nsf/V3Key/LC20021112041. Accessed 12 February 2009.

Tzanelli, R. (2004). Constructing the 'Cinematic Tourist': The 'Sign Industry' of The Lord of the Rings. *Tourist Studies, 4*(21), 21–42.

Vasos, C. (2008, October 22). *Personal Email Communication, Customer Consultant BlueScope Steel Direct*.

Williams, C. (2007). Revisiting the Rural/Race Debates: A View from the Welsh Countryside. *Ethnic and Racial Studies, 30*, 741–765.

Wollongong United Football Club (WUFC). (2008). *Wollongong United FC*. http://www.wufc.com.au/index.php?option=com_frontpage&Itemid=1. Accessed 22 October 2008.

Yuan, C. M. (2001). Chinese in White Australia 1901–1950. In *The Australian People: Encyclopedia of the Nation, Its People and Their Origins* (pp. 204–206). Cambridge: Cambridge University Press.

Zhou, M. (1992). *Chinatown: The Socioeconomic Potential of an Urban Enclave*. Philadelphia: Temple University Press.

Zukin, S. (1995). *The Cultures of Cities*. Cambridge, MA and Oxford: Blackwell.

CHAPTER 3

Immigrant Minorities and the Built Environment in Queensland

Queensland, like most of Australia, is a culturally and linguistically diverse state, but has a higher non-metropolitan population than other states. Settled after the colonies of New South Wales (NSW) and Victoria, Queensland was reluctant to join the Australian Federation in 1901 because it meant that the state had to end the practice of *Blackbirding*, a form of slavery whereby south Pacific Islanders—through deception and/or kidnapping—were forced to work as unpaid or poorly paid labourers, particularly in the sugar cane industry (Evans et al. 1975). The adoption of the White Australia policy as the cornerstone of the new Australian nation helped Queenslanders to come to the party. This is important to note because the focus of this book is immigrant minorities, including the ancestors of Kanakas, as the blackbirded south Pacific Islanders were called. While it is half a century since the White Australia policy was officially abandoned, racist practices and attitudes towards Indigenous and immigrant minorities persist at individual and institutional levels. In this way, the changing processes of racialisation are an important backdrop to our understanding of minority immigrant settlement patterns and settlement outcomes, including their impact on the Queensland built environment.

The contribution of migrants to Queensland's economic, social and cultural life is well documented (DLGRMA 2019). Their contribution to the built environment, however, has not received adequate attention in research and documentation. The contribution of the culturally

J. Collins et al., *Cosmopolitan Place Making in Australia*,
https://doi.org/10.1007/978-981-15-8041-3_3

diverse communities to the built environment has been enormous. It has transformed the physical layout of the environment not only in claiming space for their cultural heritage but changing the dynamics of what we all can share and do in this built public space together. Landscapes and cultures of Queensland have been transformed with influences of particular migrant communities such as Italians in Cairns, South Sea Islanders in Mackay and Rockhampton, Chinese in Fortitude Valley and Sunnybank, Pacific Islanders in Inala, Darra and Caboolture, Vietnamese in Darra and Goodna, Arabic-speaking communities in Woodridge, Greeks in West End, Sudanese in Yeronga and Nundah, and Turkish in Gold Coast to name just a few.

This chapter outlines the contributions of ethnic communities to the built environment in Queensland. The cosmopolitan framework of this book means that we are interested in the Indigenous history of the places and spaces that immigrant minorities settle in, as well as exploring the diversity and difference within and between minority immigrant communities themselves. Firstly, a brief history of Aboriginal and Torres Strait Islanders and migration patterns into Queensland is outlined. The diversity of contemporary Queensland is then presented. In-depth reflections on how immigrants impact the built environment are provided in three case studies across urban, regional and rural Queensland. These case study areas are Fortitude Valley, Cairns and Caboolture. Each of these areas is distinct in their histories of immigrant settlement and their contribution to the built environment. The chapter concludes with an outline of the findings from the stocktake that was undertaken across Queensland of the immigrant impact on the built environment.

3.1 Indigenous History of Queensland

Queensland has one of the largest populations of indigenous people in Australia, second only to New South Wales. The different communities that make up the indigenous groups of Queensland encompass a range of languages and cultures, with over 80 languages being spoken at the time of colonisation. The different Aboriginal groups indigenous to Queensland are also known as the Murri or the Goorie people (Fesl 2001). It is estimated that in 1770, when Captain Cook annexed Eastern Australia for the British Crown, 120,000 of the estimated total of 300,000 Australian Aborigines as well as several thousand Torres Strait Islanders lived on what is now Queensland territory (MAQ 2001).

The expansion of European settlers fuelled by the establishment of the penal colonies and the discovery of rich agricultural land in the Darling Downs led to the removal of the Aboriginal people from their land, and the attendant loss of lifestyle and social networks. The Indigenous population was also severely impacted on by disease and drugs such as opium and alcohol brought in by the European settlers, lending support to the widespread adoption of the theory that the Indigenous people would die out if they were not protected. The Queensland Government passed the Aboriginal Protection and Restriction of the Sale of Opium Act in 1897, a very oppressive law that enabled the removal of Aboriginal people to Reserves, ostensibly to protect them from extinction. What the law did, in effect, was to dispossess entire communities of their traditional lands, remove them from all links with their traditional way of life and culture, and marginalise them further. The removal of children to missions, in what is now referred to as the 'Stolen Generation', was particularly devastating in terms of loss of culture and family as well as ongoing alienation from the general population (Hollinsworth 2006).

Torres Strait Islanders are another group of Indigenous Australians. They have a distinct identity, origin and history that is separate from that of mainland Aboriginal Australians. In terms of language and cultural identity, the Islander population belong to five distinct groups: The Saibailgal (Top Western Islanders), the Maluilgal (Mid-Western Islanders), the Kaurareg (Lower-Western Islanders), the Kulkalgal (Central Islanders) and the Meriam Le (Eastern Islanders) (Shnukal 2001).

The first European settlement in the Torres Strait Islands was on Albany Island off Cape York in 1863. The pearl-shell industry for the production of buttons from mother-of-pearl began in the Torres Strait from 1868. People following the pearl rush quickly inundated the islands, and this led to numerous abuses of the indigenous people and/or their land. Subsequently and ostensibly in response to these problems, the Queensland Government annexed the Torres Strait Islands between 1872 and 1879. Initially, the Torres Strait Islander communities were spared from the impacts of the 1897 Aboriginal Protection and Restriction of the Sale of Opium Act but by 1904 began to be subject to its provisions.

Both Aboriginal communities and Torres Strait Islander communities continued to resist the restrictions of the Act and the protection regime through the first half of the twentieth century. Through a series of new legislations culminating in the National Referendum in 1967, the indigenous people of Australia were finally able to come into their own as citizens of Australia and be able to determine their own destiny.

The struggle for indigenous rights and for a process of reconciliation between non-indigenous and indigenous Australians continues, with landmark decisions in the 'Wik' and 'Mabo' cases providing the legal framework for ongoing negotiations. A number of issues such as the 'Stolen Generation', the 'Stolen Wages', health, education, land and sea rights as well as identity remain critical to the process of reconciliation. Indigenous Australians continue to be core contributors to the social, cultural, economic and political progress of Queensland.

3.2 Immigrant History of Queensland

European contact with the land that was to become Queensland began with the Dutchman, Willem Jansz, who explored the western coast of Cape York Peninsula in 1606 followed by the Spaniard Torres who sailed through the Torres Straits in the same year.

Captain Cook's annexation of Eastern Australia for Britain in 1770 was the precursor to the first British exploration of Queensland. In 1799, Mathew Flinders was the first of the British explorers to sail into Moreton Bay and climb Mt. Beerburrum. The explorations led on to settlements and the establishment of penal colonies in Redcliffe, Moreton Bay and on the north Bank of the Brisbane River. The penal colony on the Brisbane River came to be known as Brisbane Town. The new colony of Queensland was established on the 10th of December 1859.

The first migrants were largely from the United Kingdom. The 'Potato Famine' in Ireland had a great impact on migration, and in the 1860s large numbers of Irish migrants making their way to the Queensland, which became the 'most Irish State' of Australia (MAQ 2001). The new colony had a major issue in terms of the lack of sufficient labour to run the new industries such as agriculture and mother-of-pearl collection, especially since manual labour in the tropics was perceived to be too much for the white settlers. Accordingly, the problem was resolved through the importation of labour from across Asia, the Pacific Islands and parts of Europe.

The first non-British were the Germans, Danes, Swedes and other North Europeans, who were encouraged to come to Australia as part of the process of assimilation. But the Gold Rush as well as the nascent sugar cane industry ensured that numbers of Chinese and Indian people also made their way to Queensland from 1848 onwards. They worked as cheap labour in an environment where they were paid less than European workers, denied social and political rights and remained on the fringes of mainstream society. The Chinese were a significant proportion of Queensland society, forming an estimated 6% of the total population in 1876. The demise of the gold rush moved many of these Chinese immigrants to the Coast, where they were major drivers of the agricultural and fishing industries.

The Pearl Rush in the Torres Straits was the focus of Japanese migrants who controlled the industry by 1890. They also worked in the sugar industry of North Queensland, mostly as indentured labour. The number of Japanese in Colonial Queensland peaked at 3247 in 1898 (MAQ 2001).

The years between 1863 and 1904 saw widespread practise of 'Blackbirding', the colloquial term used to refer to the recruiting and trafficking of Pacific Island labourers. Over 62,000 Pacific Islanders or 'Kanakas' were brought to Queensland in this period as indentured labour. Though they were brought in under legal contracts, many of them were subject to exploitation, abuse and slavery. Most of these Islanders were deported back by 1908, with just 1654 being allowed to stay by reason of marriage or length of stay. It is estimated that over 15,000 Queenslanders are of South Pacific Islander descent (Mercer 1995).

The 1900s saw fresh waves of immigration of Sikhs, Germans, Italians, Yugoslavs, among others, coming into work in the rapidly expanding agricultural sector, especially the sugar cane fields of Northern Queensland. Many of these migrants began as labourers and went on to become owners of the plantations themselves. However, through all this, there continued to be a focus on the attraction of British immigrants, or in their absence, European migrants, in line with a White Australia policy.

The Great Depression of 1929 and the lead up to World War II considerably reduced the movements of people into Australia and into Queensland. The end of World War II heralded a sea change in immigration policies, leading to the great ethnic mix that is Australian society today. With changing economic and political priorities and geopolitical alliances, the proportion of migrants coming in diverse cultures increased drastically, with people from different parts of the world including the Asian sub-continent, South-East Asia, Eastern Europe, Africa, and South and North America. The immigration flows have also been impacted on by the flows of refugees from countries like Vietnam, Laos, Cambodia, Afghanistan, Iraq, Palestine, former Yugoslavia and African countries like Ethiopia, Eritrea and the Sudan.

Over the last decade, the demographics of Queensland's population are also changing due to the large numbers of people moving in from the southern States, mainly Victoria and New South Wales. Internal migration, fuelled by a booming economy and lifestyle aspirations, continues to be an important factor in the multicultural society that is Queensland.

Within the context of the contribution of non-British migrants to Northern Queensland, the Queensland Museum (QM) states:

> The heritage of these peoples and their contributions to the sugar and pearling industries and commerce of North Queensland is evident in family names, place and business names, architectural styles, festivals, pastimes, and carefully preserved artefacts. Their dedication to hard work, their love of family, their teamwork, their adoption of their new country and sharing of their traditions, customs, food, arts and crafts continue to enrich the local culture of North Queensland. (QM 2006)

These words encapsulate the heritage of migrants to all of Queensland, especially given their struggles to survive and prosper in an environment that was harsh and demanding, where the laws were often discriminatory and where they were often marginalised from the larger community. Yet they persevered and established themselves and their families while also establishing the flourishing State that is Queensland.

3.3 Multiculturalism in Contemporary Queensland

The make-up of Australia's population has changed dramatically during the past 232 years since white settlement, from an almost total Aboriginal population to predominantly Anglo-Celtic by 1900. Subsequent immigration policy and attitudes and practices to Australia's First Peoples have meant that at the 2016 national census about 74% of the population had Anglo-Celtic ancestry, 19% other European and 4.5% Asian ancestry (Australian Bureau of Statistics [ABS] 2019).

Indigenous Australians form 4% of the total population of Queensland with 186,482 people identifying in the 2016 Census as Aboriginal or as Torres Strait Islander.

According to the 2016 Census, the Queensland population demonstrates a rich mosaic of diversity: 30% of the population are born overseas, and 37% of the population are either born overseas or have one or both parents born overseas. Over 19% of the population speak a language other than English at home. While these figures are lower than the overall Australian figures, the rapidly changing demographics of the State will probably reflect dramatic change in the future as may be demonstrated in the new Census data. In terms of overseas birthplace groups, the largest cohort continues to be those from New Zealand (4.3%) followed by England (3.8%), India (1%), China (1%), South Africa (.9%), Philippines (.8%) and Scotland (.5%), followed by Germany, Vietnam, South Korea and the United States at .4%, and a number of other countries with smaller proportions of the population (Australian Bureau of Statistics [ABS] 2019).

The ethnic and cultural mix of Queensland is spread across the State. Historically, the rural areas, collectively referred to as the 'Bush', were the strongest driver of the State's prosperity, and as such attracted the majority of migrants to work on industries such as agriculture, grazing, mining and fisheries. As such, the lives of culturally and linguistically diverse groups have impacted on society across the State. However, the end of World War II began a gradual trend of movements of people towards the coast where new secondary and tertiary industries were attracting labour. The trend has continued till the present, with larger numbers of migrants tending to settle in towns and cities along the coastal belt.

As Queensland's diversity has grown and changed, there has been a parallel development of the recognition of this diversity in government policy. The current Queensland Government Policy recognises multiculturalism as a strength in terms of communities, trade, business and workforce. The Queensland Government policy commitment, ***Multicultural Queensland—Making a World of Difference*** sets out a blue print for cultural diversity in the state. It states that the Queensland Government will promote equal rights, responsibilities and opportunities for all Queenslanders, regardless of their cultural, ethnic, religious background or gender. It will continue to foster an inclusive, cohesive and open society so that everyone is: given opportunities to share their knowledge, values and cultural heritage to contribute to building the State; offered a fair go and equitable access to services; able to exercise their civic rights and responsibilities; and protected from discrimination (Queensland Government 2006).

The Queensland Government funds a significant range of activities that support cultural diversity in the state including cultural officers based in local government, community development officers, special development projects and funding for cultural festivals. The Policy also requires all Queensland Government departments to produce multicultural action plans and report against the stated achievements. While the government policy to the super-diversity of Queensland is one of multiculturalism, the nature of Queensland society itself increasingly cosmopolitan, as the following case studies attest.

3.4 Minority Immigrants and the Built Environment in Fortitude Valley

Fortitude Valley (Fig. 3.1) is a suburb in inner city Brisbane. Brisbane covers an area of approximately 76 square kilometres from Everton Park and Stafford in the north to the Brisbane River in the east and south and to Ferny Grove and Upper Kedron in the west. As well as Fortitude Valley, the main suburbs include Alderley, Ashgrove, Bowen Hills, Brisbane City, Enoggera, Ferny Grove, Gaythorne, Grange, Herston, Kelvin Grove, Keperra, Milton, Mitchelton, New Farm, Newmarket, Newstead, Red Hill, Spring Hill, Upper Kedron, Wilston, Windsor and parts of Bardon, Everton Park, Paddington, Stafford. The area is mostly residential but contains some light industry. It includes the Queensland Parliament House and Brisbane City Council Chambers. The Enoggera Military Camp and many Commonwealth Government, State Government and business administrative offices are found in the area (Australian Electoral Commission 2007).

3.4.1 Indigenous History

The Brisbane region, including the larger islands of Moreton Bay, has been the domain of Aboriginal people for as long as 40,000 years before European settlement. Tribes followed seasonal pathways, determined by the fruits and foods available in different areas at different times of the year. Many of Brisbane's suburbs draw on the names by the original inhabitants such as Toowong (gootcha or tu-wong, meaning a name for honey or call of koel cuckoo), Woolloongabba (woolloon-capemm, meaning whirling waters or place of the whip-tailed wallaby).

Land, language and people are linked together in three important elements of Aboriginal culture: family, clan and language. In the Brisbane area, the Yaggera language group was used and the clans associated with this group of languages were the Jagera and the Turrbal (Our Brisbane 2006). Brisbane was known as 'Mian-jin', which means 'place shaped like a spike'. The Turrbal and the Jagera had numerous campsites, including those at Woolloongabba, Toowong, Bowen Hills, Newstead, Nundah and Nudgee, and many pathways that allowed them access to different parts of Brisbane. The Turrbal clan, also called the 'Duke of York's clan' by the whites, had its main encampment in 'Yorks Hollow'. This gully passed through Victoria Park and the Royal National Association Showgrounds at Bowen Hills.

Fig. 3.1 Fortitude Valley precinct (*Source* H. Babacan and N. Gopalkrishnan)

3.4.2 Immigrant History

European exploration of the region began with John Oxley in 1832. The first settlement was located at Redcliffe but was later transferred upstream to the site of today's city of Brisbane, named after the Governor of New South Wales (NSW). The new colony was initially a penal settlement, notorious for its harsh treatment of convicts under the command of Captain Logan. In 1837, free settlers, led by Andrew Petrie, pushed for the end of the convict settlement and the opening up of the area.

Originally, the area was dense bush and swampland, home to Aboriginal people and native fauna. The population increased considerably on 20 January 1849 when the ship 'Fortitude' brought Presbyterian Minister Dr. John Dunmore Lang and 256 free British immigrants to Moreton Bay. The area developed as a village with dairies and farms and rough timber houses. To commemorate their arrival, the area was named Fortitude Valley (Brisbane City Council [BCC] 2003).

Gold rushes in Queensland led to the growth of the region with Queensland becoming a separate colony in 1859 with Brisbane as its capital. The original inhabitants were steadily displaced from the area with increased European occupation and by the 1860s the remnants of the 'Duke of York's clan' had been forced to camp at Breakfast Creek or Enoggera (ValleyNet 2006).

Between 1850 and 1880, the land around Fortitude Valley was cleared and sub-divided. Some allotments were purchased by traders, foreshadowing The Valley's future development as a commercial centre. The first brick building, the 'Lamb Inn', was erected on the present site of the Royal George Hotel in 1854. There were about 150 dwellings in the Fortitude Valley stretching as far as Breakfast Creek (ValleyNet 2006).

The first cutting of the formidable Duncan's Hill in Ann Street in 1865 facilitated further development. Fortitude Valley experienced a building boom. By the 1880s the area was densely settled. The tram and train line were extended to Fortitude Valley from the City. An urban village was gradually created with hotels, stores, churches and a school. The wealth and optimism of the decade were reflected in the buildings constructed. Among these were Apothecaries Hall & Bragg's Bakery, Empire Hotel & Prince Consort Hotel, Shamrock Irish Pub, the Forester's Hall, Swift and Grice Building, Holy Trinity Church, Presbyterian Church, Valley Methodist Church and Fortitude Valley Post Office (BCC 2003).

The establishment of the competitive commercial emporiums of T. C. Beirne, McWhirters and Overrells in the 1890s added life and bustle to Fortitude Valley. The Valley became one of the major shopping venues for Brisbane and a popular residential area being close to centres of employment. To cater for the influx of working-class families, new housing was built on the tiny allotments in the streets beyond the commercial centre concentrated in Ann, Brunswick and Wickham Streets. As more people of different cultural backgrounds lived in the suburb, social and religious institutions were built to meet their needs. These developmental trends explain the super-diversity of The Valley, characterised by commercial buildings, hotels and churches side by side with residential buildings (ValleyNet 2006).

In the 1920s, another boom prompted a renewed wave of development in Fortitude Valley. Fortitude Valley expanded further with retail premises expanding and new community and industrial buildings being constructed. Many buildings still exist from this period including Tranberg House and The Valley Baths that were built on the site of an earlier swimming pool called the Booroodabin Baths in 1925 (BCC 2003).

The Chinese community is chosen for discussion here as it represents the largest ethnic group in Fortitude Valley (ABS 2019) and Chinese have a high level of community involvement and business development that have a significant impact on the built environment. As written on one of the storyboards in Chinatown Mall, Fortitude Valley, 'Pioneers in a new land, the Chinese people have made an outstanding contribution to Queensland prosperity, using their knowledge, skill and culture to enrich their adopted land' (BCC 2004a).

The history of Chinese migration dates to 1848 when the first boatload of Chinese labourers arrived in Moreton Bay to alleviate the severe labour shortage in the district. The North Queensland Gold Rush, particularly the discovery of the wealthy Palmer Goldfield in 1873, saw the greatest influx of Chinese immigrants to labour for money to send to their family back in China. By 1877, there were 18,000 Chinese prospectors on the Palmer—over 80% of the goldfield population. However, they were victimised and oppressed by increasing restrictions on mining rights and immigration legislation (Evans et al. 1975; Markus 1994). As a result, many returned to China. A few drifted to new settlements including Fortitude Valley, seeking their fortune in commerce, services industries and agriculture (BCC 2004a).

3.4.3 *Cosmopolitanism in Fortitude Valley*

According to the ABS 2016 Census, Indigenous people comprised 1.5% of Brisbane Local Government Area population. West End, Woolloongabba and New Farm had the significant Indigenous communities but the highest proportion was in Fortitude Valley. The Census further shows that 31% of the Brisbane Local Government Area population was born overseas. Fortitude Valley had 41% of its residents from non-English speaking countries, which was higher than the 28% of non-English speaking residents of Brisbane as a whole. The top non-English languages spoken at home in Brisbane Local Government Area were Chinese (20.8% of all people speaking another language) and Vietnamese (5.8%) (ABS 2019).

These figures illustrate that Fortitude Valley has a culturally diverse population with European and Asian communities supporting ethnic small business, turning the place into a buzzing multicultural community. The unique suburb's culture is reflected in the various foods, lively music scene and vibrant arts. A walk into the commercial village places Italian, Greek, Irish, English and French style coffee shops and restaurants maintaining a link with the original ethnic influences. Further along, the Chinatown mall is dominated by Asian businesses.

Restaurants expanded markedly in number and variety over the years in Fortitude Valley. International fast-food chains, elite cafés and sidewalk cafés made their appearance during the 1990s competing with existing coffee shops. Today, spread along Duncan Street and Brunswick Street (Fig. 3.2), are captivating cafés and coffee shops, displaying a wide range of multicultural cuisines, various exotic bars, hotels, night clubs and gift shops for tourists and locals alike.

Many immigrants are entrepreneurs operating a wide range of trades such as cafés, restaurants, bakery, grocery, fashion and florist stores, herbal acupuncture stores and salon shops for tourists and residents of different cultural backgrounds. Many stores and restaurants have culturally-specific stocks. These include Korean supermarkets, Indonesian and Thai grocery stores, Asian/Chinese supermarkets and Thai, Korean, Japanese, Vietnamese, Chinese & Italian restaurants and stores for video rental and magazines in many languages as also Chinese herbal medicine practitioners and shops. Fortitude Valley is clearly a cosmopolitan place, reflected not only in the built environment of immigrant entrepreneurs but also in the people who live, work, eat and shop there.

Fig. 3.2 Brunswick Street Mall (*Source* H. Babacan and N. Gopalkrishnan)

Multiculturalism and comsopolitanism is captured through the Valley Market along Duncan Street and Brunswick Street. The open-air shopping precincts provide an opportunity for people of diverse backgrounds to set up shop on the weekend, trading and sharing unique products and services such as fabulous handmade accessories, cultural custom and artwork, a massage or clairvoyants and card readings.

Although the Valley Market is largely catering for shoppers, Fortitude Valley is also recognised as a significant place for entertainment and social gathering, characterising the cultural diversity of Brisbane. Various events such as the Valley Fiesta, Music festival, Moon Festival & Chinese New Year celebrations have been enabling individuals and ethnic groups to learn about other cultures, enjoy and celebrate cultural diversity.

3.4.4 Ethnic Minorities and the Built Environment in Fortitude Valley

According to a Councillor of Brisbane City Council, 'population density and diversity is what The Valley is all about. This is what makes it unique'.

The present discussion on ethnicity and the built environment comprises two aspects. One is the impact of migration/ethnicity on the built environment, in particular relating to business/services. The other is the linkage between migration/ethnicity and the social use of space.

It is important to understand that many facets have contributed to the transformation of Fortitude Valley. While the built environment has been shaped by migrant settlement in the area under study, it is also largely determined by government policy on town planning and land use and redevelopment in the Brisbane Inner City.

Commerce has been central in the history of the Fortitude Valley, which is only about 1 km from Brisbane Central Business District. When Fortitude Valley celebrated its centenary of settlement in 1949, its enthusiastic retailers boasted The Valley was '…one of the greatest commercial centres in Queensland'. Indeed, up until the 1960s Fortitude Valley was a major retail centre (Bailey 1992). However changing shopping patterns, more widespread use of private transport and increased competition from suburban shopping centres resulted in a decline in its status as a major retail centre.

According to Maria H., a Vietnamese migrant who was a local resident of The Valley for more than 30 years, there were not many shops in Fortitude Valley in the 1970s. Most of the shops were owned by Anglo-Australians. The only Asian grocery shop 'Far East' was on Wickham Street owned by a Chinese family from Hong Kong.

About two years later the shop 'Far East' was relocated to the opposite side of the road. In addition to retailing business on the ground level, 'Far East' started video rental and had its second level for 'Yum Cha'. 'It was probably the first Chinese restaurant with "Yum Cha" on Wickham Street during that time'. In recollection, Maria thinks Fortitude Valley was referred as 'Chinatown' ever since and had become a place of significant to Chinese migrants. Another two years later, the Chung Shan restaurant with a similar set up was opened along Brunswick Street. The biggest and most popular 'New Chung Shan' Chinese restaurant was later opened in Chermside, in the north side of Brisbane.

The Fortitude Valley, now officially named as Brisbane's Chinatown, opened in 1987 as the cultural and recreational heartland of Brisbane's Chinese community, Chinatown Mall. The major streets in Brisbane Chinatown are Duncan Street and Brunswick Street, which are parallel to each other, whereas Wickham Street and Ann Street are the main roads linking the Valley to The City. The main streets have their names written both in English and Chinese languages.

Brisbane Chinatown, Fortitude Valley, reflects unique Chinese culture and the iconography and architecture seen in Chinatowns around the world. The Brisbane Chinatown project was achieved with the cooperation of the State Government, Brisbane City Council and the Community. The Architects and Engineers from Guangzhou, People's Republic of China specially designed the Chinatown Mall and the two magnificent Lions dominating the Mall's entrance were a gift from the Chinese Government (Chinese Club of Queensland [CCQ] 2005).

According to focus group participants, 'It was after Brisbane Expo in 1988 that business started to boom in Fortitude Valley'. In addition, the opening of Chinatown Mall (Fig. 3.3) and the relocation of CCQ from

Fig. 3.3 Duncan Street, Brisbane Chinatown Mall entrance. Among an array of Chinese restaurants, people enter Duncan Street Mall between two lions (*Source* H. Babacan and N. Gopalkrishnan)

Deagon to Chinatown after 1989 had gradually attracted more people to 'Chinatown' for social gathering, shopping and for business.

Chinese and other immigrant settlement followed. Fortitude Valley experienced the fastest growth rate of the Brisbane Inner City Region (56.1% a year) in the period 1996–2001. More than half of the Fortitude Valley population was born overseas. The biggest non-English speaking community is Chinese (including Cantonese, Mandarin and other Chinese languages), followed by Spanish, Korean and Hindi (ABS 2019).

The wave of Chinese migration in 1990s was partly due to the aftermath of 1989 Tiananmen Square Massacre in China when the Australian government granted special permission for Chinese overseas students to stay in Australia. Further, owing to the fear of losing personal and political freedom under the Chinese government, many Chinese people migrated from Hong Kong, Macau and Taiwan. Scholars, professionals and wealthy people in China also took up the opportunities to live in overseas when the Chinese government adopted a more open-door policy for visiting, study, business and migration. Chinese immigration has increased in the past two decades, with Chinese (and Indian) immigrants at the top of both permanent and temporary immigration lists, and with international students increasingly prominent among the latter (Wang et al. 2018).

Chinese migrants are often concerned with the necessities of life including clothing, food, shelter and transportation. The choice of living in close proximity to all amenities and low maintenance is on their top priorities. As such, many Chinese settlers choose to reside in the Valley, a place close to the City, to transport and to culturally specific food and other business.

In addition to lifestyle choices, the significant changes to the Fortitude Valley landscape, both physical and socio-economic, are an outcome of a range of market and policy interventions. Like all Chinatowns, Fortitude Valley transforms not only as a consequence of changing immigrant populations and the impact on the built environment of Chinese immigrant entrepreneurs and community groups but also when local and state government regulators and planners change the face of the neighbourhood (Collins and Kunz 2009). The Valley has been pushed by the concept of 'urban consolidation' as a policy to boost renewal plans for degraded areas, attract people back to live in the inner city suburbs, to stem the tide of urban sprawl and to more effectively use existing urban infrastructure (Stimson et al. 2000).

Fortitude Valley was once dominated by commercial and warehouse activity. The wave of urban renewal in Fortitude Valley has driven manufacturing industry out and created new opportunities to build large mixed-use developments on derelict sites. The whole Valley district now provides a more vibrant mix of small business, renovated warehouse lofts, new apartments as well as older apartment blocks and restored historic buildings.

The Central Brunswick development is a prime example with residential, retail and commercial uses on the 2.6 hectare Carlton and United Breweries site. Another large mixed-use project in the same area is the Cathedral Place development of 519 units of affordable accommodation for people seeking a quality residential lifestyle near the City (Stimson et al. 2000). The number of stand-alone houses in Fortitude Valley has continued to fall. Flats, units and apartments increased substantially and by 2001 accounted for 86% of private dwellings (ABS 2001).

It is the promoted intention of urban renewal planners to ensure the Valley can enjoy the best of both worlds—sustainable development and cultural and social diversity (BCC 2004b). Like Sydney's Chinatown, Fortitude Valley has been 'remade' a number of times. Brunswick Street Mall (Fig. 3.4) was upgraded in 1995 to create a people-orientated envi-

Fig. 3.4 T.C. Bernie building, Brunswick Street Mall (*Source* H. Babacan and N. Gopalkrishnan)

ronment with more opportunities for outdoor dining and entertainment. Improvements included a new stage, landscaping, trees and lighting. The central feature of the pavement artwork is a patterned watercourse, reflecting the Valley's multicultural heritage, and a carpet snake, which is an important local Aboriginal symbol (Our Brisbane 2006).

Brisbane Chinatown also had another major refurbishment in 1996 (Fig. 3.5). Improvements included a larger stage, a traditional Chinese water feature, pergolas re-roofed in an ornate Chinese style and a new arch at the Ann Street entry. The roof structures were made in Shandong province by Chinese artisans who came to Brisbane to assemble them on site (Our Brisbane 2006).

Fig. 3.5 Duncan Street, Brisbane Chinatown Mall, Fortitude Valley (*Source* H. Babacan and N. Gopalkrishnan)

3.4.5 Cosmopolitan Monuments in Fortitude Valley

3.4.5.1 Chinese Club of Queensland and Cathay Community Association

The Chinese Club of Queensland (CCQ) and the Cathay Community Association (CCA) are the two well-known Chinese groups in Brisbane Chinatown. These two groups have different interests in mind. The CCQ was conceived to provide cultural, social and recreational pursuits among the fast-growing Chinese Community in Brisbane and to foster closer relationships and goodwill among the Australian Community. The CCA started as a social club, a meeting place for 'wantoks' (people of the same origin) from Papua New Guinea. The Club soon identified itself as a community group for servicing newly arrived Chinese migrants.

3.4.5.2 The Chinese Club of Queensland

The influence of the CCQ on the built environment is evident in the construction of the clubhouse and the building and restoration of Chinese temples. A Chinese citizen, the late Mr Tommy Young, together with a few leading Chinese in Brisbane, convened a series of meetings to establish a Club House for the Chinese Community in Queensland. In 1953, the CCQ bought four allotments of land in Dixon Street, Auchenflower and the first Chinese Club House was built in 1957. Unfortunately, a disastrous flood extensively damaged the Club House in 1974 and the directors decided to sell the property and look for a new building site.

The Club approached the State Government for assistance and five acres of land in Deagon was purchased for a clubhouse. The remaining land was used to build a Chinese temple, known as the Ching Chung Taoist Association.

The Club members were not happy with the second Chinese Club House built in Deagon. They felt it was too far away from the city. The directors soon suggested moving back to the city. During that time, the Suncorp building was up for sale in the Fortitude Valley. Its location is convenient with good bus/rail services linking to surrounding suburbs and a taxi rank and parking station adjoining the building. The Club bought the premises in 1989 and refurbished it for the third Chinese Club House which now has a gaming area for 50 poker machines, TAB (Totalisator Agency Board), Licensed Yum Sing Bar, Bistro, Keno and Administration office (CCQ 2005).

The Chinese impact on the built environment of Brisbane pre-dated these more recent development. The Triad Holy Temple (Sarm Sung Goong) or 'Joss House' was erected in Breakfast Creek in 1864 by voluntary subscription from the Chinese Community residing in Brisbane. Owing to the departure of many elderly Chinese citizens to their native land, the Temple lapsed into inactivity. The Chinese community examined the possibility of restoring the Temple and the difficulty encountered was ownership as the original trustees were no longer living. Through a long and slow negotiation process with the Parliament, the land and tenure of the 'Joss House' was finally returned to the Chinese Temple Society of Brisbane. In cooperation with the CCQ, the Temple has now been restored to its original status as a place of worship and as a historical monument.

3.4.5.3 Cathay Community Association

The CCA's influence is seen through its community services and its inputs to local and state governments. CCA, previously known as Cathay Club, was established in 1980 in Brisbane Chinatown on commercial premises. Cathay Club knew that there were many migrants who were experiencing real hardships settling into Australia. The Club applied for a grant from the Department of Immigration to help newly arrived Chinese migrants. In 1984, the first welfare worker was employed to assist these migrants and their families. Along with community settlement service, Cathay Club held seminars and classes and provided a social space for Chinese people.

The Cathay group had gradually extended its service from helping newly arrived Chinese migrants with settlement to providing Home & Aged Care services for fragile seniors. Commencing with six clients in 1989, today CCA services nearly 400 clients requiring the assistance of 45 part-time Home Care Providers (CCA 2020).

According to the President, the change of Cathay Community Settlement Service from direct assistance by worker/volunteers to information provision is related to the level of English proficiency of migrants arrived in the recent years. CCA offers settlement information in Chinese, Korean and Japanese languages. These groups of immigrants are often from the business or professional categories and their settlement needs are often information and direction. Moreover, the Chinese community is considered as an established community in Brisbane. Many newly arrived migrants may also have friends/relatives from whom they can seek help to settle in Brisbane.

CCA has been working together with Brisbane City Council, expanding its community services to the wider community including people of Anglo-Saxon/Celtic as well as diverse ethnic backgrounds. It plays an important role in representing the Chinese community to provide inputs to governments, council and business groups for improving welfare, infrastructure and the built environment for the community users in the Brisbane Inner City.

One of the examples is the joint project with the Papua New Guinea Volunteer Rifles Association and Queensland Chinese Forum to obtain funding from the Department of Veteran Affairs to erect a war Memorial Bell in Brisbane Chinatown. This was to acknowledge and honour those service persons of Chinese heritage who had taken part in defence of Australia. Becoming the focal point in Brisbane for the Australian Chinese community during Anzac Day, Remembrance Day and other special occasions, the bell was unveiled on 10 March 2007 (Malloy 2007).

3.5 Minority Immigrants and the Built Environment in Cairns

3.5.1 Indigenous History

Settlement and colonisation in the Cairns area was mainly on the traditional lands of the Gimuy Walabara Yidinji people and the Yirrigandji people, while the areas around Kuranda were those of the Djabugai people. The first settlers began to arrive in Cairns in the 1870s. The period of first contact was one characterised by conflict and mistrust. The Aboriginal people found the Europeans hard to deal with, firstly because of the settler attitudes of fear and hatred, and also because of the breaking of Aboriginal law and traditional practices. Some of the mother-of-pearl fisherman began to kidnap Indigenous people to work for them, almost as slaves. Many of the activities undertaken by the settlers and the government were disruptive to Aboriginal life. In one case, the development of the Cairns to Herberton railway along a traditional walking track led to violent attacks by the Djabugai people, and the attendant violent response from the settlers.

These incidents and the incursions onto traditional lands led to escalated violence and killings on both sides. The Native Mounted Police were then brought into deal with the issue, on behalf of the settler populations of Cairns. Being Aboriginal people themselves, the Native Police were very successful in tracking the local Aborigines and killing or 'dispersing' them. These activities were also exacerbated by the ravages of disease as the Indigenous populations had little or no resistance to diseases brought in by the Europeans. By 1898, only around 500 of the original Aboriginal population remained in Cairns and the surrounding districts (Cairns Museum 2006).

The passing of the Aboriginal Protection and Restriction of the Sale of Opium Act in 1897, added to the restrictions on the way of live of local Aboriginal people. By this time, they had started 'coming in' and becoming fringe-dwellers, finding work wherever they could. Two missions had been set up by this time, one at Yarrabah and the other at Mona Mona, near Kuranda. While the missions were set up for altruistic purposes, Aboriginal people from different parts of Queensland were sent to them, often against their will. By 1910, only 60 of the 300 people at Yarrabah were actually from the area. At Mona Mona, there were people from as far away as Normanton (Cairns Museum 2006). The move into the missions and other reserves played a major role in the separation of Aboriginal people from their land and their spiritual and cultural roots. The Referendum in 1967 and the final amendments to the Opium Act by 1971 enabled Indigenous Australians to finally be able to have equal rights as all other Australians (Anti-Discrimination Commission Queensland 2018).

In terms of present-day Cairns, the 2016 Census shows that Indigenous people account for 8.9% of the population (12,876 people) (ABS 2019). Over 10% of the Indigenous population of Queensland has been reported to live in Cairns, a population that is characterised by a younger age profile than the non-indigenous one and one showing a rate of growth, over the previous decade, of over 5 times the annual growth rate of the overall population (Cairns City Council 2004).

3.5.2 *Immigrant History*

The first British settlers came to the Cairns area in the 1870s and Cairns soon became the centre of the North with the establishment of the Kuranda railway and the opening up of mining. Agriculture soon became an important industry, leading to the importation of different groups of people to feed the great demand for labour in the area (Jones 1976).

Since 1860 thousands of South Sea Islanders were brought to Australia as cheap labour to work in the emerging sugar cane industry of Queensland. The majority of the South Sea Islanders came from Melanesia, Vanuatu, the Solomon Islands and the New Hebrides. During forty years from the early 1860s, over sixty thousand were brought to Queensland. The recruiting ceased in 1904—part of Queensland's deal to become included in the new nation of Australia in 1901—and between 1906 and 1908 most of the workers were deported. About 2000 were allowed to stay due to long residency in Australia, inter-marriage or land ownership. The South Sea Islanders of North Queensland are one of the oldest migrant groups in all Australia to have preserved a distinctive identity down to the present day (Mercer 1995).

In the 1870s, Chinese immigrants arrived in search of gold on the Palmer River. By 1877, the Chinese had settled in Cairns and land was leased to them for banana growing. They also experimented with crops such as cotton, tobacco, coffee, rice and sugar, which contributed to the economic growth of Cairns. During 1876–1920 Chinese migrants played a key role in the development of Cairns' agricultural industry. Many also were market gardeners that grew fruit and vegetables for the new and emerging community.

Chinese migrants settled in Grafton Street, which at that time was called Sach Street and became known as Chinatown. This area of town consisted of eating houses like soup kitchens, lodging houses or recreational places. Lodging houses were popular and provided budget accommodation for lodgers when they arrived into Cairns. Work on Sunday was forbidden so many farmers came to Sash St and spent their weekends socialising, catching up with friends, smoking opium or visiting the numerous brothels.

Chinatown was a culturally diverse community consisting of Japanese, Malay, Afghan, South Sea Islanders and European men, women and children. Here are the historical roots of the super-diversity of Queensland's Chinatowns. It was also the largest and longest running Chinatown outside Brisbane lasting into the 1950s. Today Grafton Street is important to the Chinese community due to its direct connection to early Chinese settlers in Cairns and because many Chinese residents today have family links to early Chinese immigrants. Cairns has many Chinese restaurants and takeaways, local farmers and Chinese Herbalists. The Chinese New Year is a multicultural event in Cairns and is celebrated by members of the broader community and tourists (May 1984; Robb 2004).

The first Sikhs came to North Queensland in the 1890s along with the Melanesians to work as canecutters on the sugar cane plantations. The early migrants began to cluster in two distinct groups in northern New South Wales mainly in the Clarence District and the Atherton Tableland in Queensland. They moved between these two locations depending on seasonal work and ventured into surrounding areas. During this time records indicated that there were approximately 250 Sikhs working in the Cairns area on sugar cane farms. The Sikhs worked in very harsh conditions and lived in straw huts and were segregated from whites. In 1901, there were approximately 800 Indians, including Sikhs and Muslims in NSW and Qld (Queensland).

Most of the Sikhs were men who had left behind their women and families. Many returned back to India after a few years but some stayed on and brought their families and relatives into Australia when it became possible. The Sikhs that stayed saved up enough money to purchase farms along the north coast of NSW and Cairns. In 1918, the government passed legislation forbidding migrants from leasing crown land. Many Sikh families moved to NSW but a few stayed on and after 1946 Sikhs were again permitted to work and own sugar cane farms in Qld. The early Sikhs in Qld have made significant contributions to the success of Australia's sugar and banana industry. The Indian community continues to grow in Cairns and the Hinterland.

The first shipload of 335 Italians arrived in Townsville in December 1891. Most of the immigrants were single men between the ages of twenty-two to forty-five years except for a few women and families. Many entered the sugar industry as canecutters and lived in the barracks on the farms where they were supplied with food. These new immigrants worked hard in the tropical climate in extremely difficult conditions. Many cleared scrubland for cultivation in exchange for food and accommodation and would only be paid if the farmer were successful in the growing of his crops the following year. Italian migrants were known for their determination to accept hardship and poor working conditions. Eventually these Italian immigrants became cane farmers and settled and raised their families in Far North Qld, mainly in Innisfail, Mareeba and Cairns.

The number of Italian migrants arriving in North Queensland peaked again in the years following World War II. The Italians were the largest ethnic group to be employed in the sugar industry and have made a significant contribution to the sugar growing communities of North Queensland, including Innisfail.

The migration patterns of the early Greek community were very similar to those of the Italians, with single men who came to Innisfail in the early 1900s to work as canecutters on the sugar cane farms. When they saved up enough money, they would then marry and set up businesses such as milk bars, sweets shop, fish shops and boarding houses. In 1916, when the South Johnstone Mill began crushing, there were 41 Greek immigrants in Innisfail and 11 in Cairns. There are approximately between 200 to 250 people from Greek backgrounds currently living in Cairns. The majority of the Greek community here are elderly, as the younger Greek-Australian generation tend to move to Brisbane or Townsville for more opportunities for study and work.

Many German immigrants came to Australia at the same time as the Italians and the Greeks in the early 1900s to work in the cane fields. This was followed by another wave of migration following World War II.

The first Serbian immigrants came from the Former Yugoslavia and arrived in far North Queensland in the 1930s to work on the tobacco and sugar cane farms. Following World War II, many Serbian refugees arrived from displaced persons' camps in Germany. They also mainly worked on the sugar cane farms and by the 1950s had settled in Queensland and sent for their families to come and live in Australia. There are currently approximately 100 Serbian people in the community in Cairns.

Like the Greeks, Italians and Germans, the first Spanish-speaking migrants came to North Queensland in the early 1900s. They were mainly Basque and Catalans and worked on the farms when some of them went on to own the farms. There is a small Spanish community in Cairns. The Latin American community in Cairns consists of migrants from Brazil, Puerto Rico, Chile, Uruguay, Ecuador, Peru, Columbia, Venezuela, Mexico, El Salvador, Honduras, Argentina, Dominican Republic and Cuba. Within each of these groups there are from one to thirty persons.

The decades after World War II were a period of dramatic change in the Cairns region. Immigrants came in from across Europe, including Germany, Austria, the Former Yugoslavia, Greece, Poland and Hungary among others. Migrant communities made up more than 25% of the population and the region became one of the most culturally diverse in Australia at the time.

The diversity of Cairns and its surrounding areas is also changing with the impact of settlement of communities coming in through the humanitarian programmes. The Vietnam War and its aftermath saw the arrival of refugees from South East Asia. The Hmong people are an ethnic minority from Laos and started to leave their homeland in 1975 after many years of dislocation as a result of the Vietnam War. The Hmong came as refugees to Cairns from 1987 and are currently one of the largest refugee groups in Cairns. Initially they had settled in NSW, Victoria and Tasmania; however, they were not used to the cold climate and so many migrated to North Qld. By 2000, there were approximately 600 Hmong people living in North Qld. Most Hmong people in Cairns work either on banana farms, run small businesses or work in hotels and restaurants (SPK Housing 2001). There are also families from Vietnam and Northern Thailand. Currently there are also approximately 100 families from Thailand living in Cairns. Other refugee groups that are growing in the region are the African communities such as groups from Sierra Leone, Burundi, Sudan, Liberia and Ethiopia. There are also communities formed from refugee groups from the Former Yugoslavia.

The tropical climate of Cairns has also been instrumental in attracting migration from many of the Melanesian and Polynesian Islands. Communities from Papua New Guinea, the Cook Islands and Samoa are significant groups in society, and their numbers are increasing through internal migration from the other states of Australia. The expanding tourist and hospitality industries continue to play a major role in the demographics of the local area. Japanese tourists form a significant majority of the tourist trade to Cairns accompanied by significant numbers of Japanese language speakers employed in the industry. Chinese tourism has increased significantly in the past decade.

3.5.3 Cosmopolitanism in Cairns

The 2016 census shows figures for Cairns that are reflective of the overall figures for Queensland. 22% of the population is born overseas and if added to the figure for people with one or more parents born overseas, these would add up to more than 40% of the population. The largest group of people born overseas are from the United Kingdom (18%) followed by New Zealand (14%), Papua New Guinea (7%) and the Philippines (5%) (ABS 2019).

In terms of language, 23% of the people living in Cairns spoke a language other than English at home. The most common languages other than English were Japanese (7%), Australian Indigenous languages (3.5%) and Mandarin (3.4%) (ABS 2019).

3.5.4 *Ethnicity and the Built Environment in Cairns*

The impact of the different waves of migration on the built environment of Cairns is clearly defined but not as widely visible as in the case of large cities like Brisbane and Sydney. The different structures are scattered across the suburbs of Cairns and do not present a unified whole at any place such as Fortitude Valley in Brisbane.

However, there are distinct expressions of cultural traditions in the built environment that are influenced by the ethnic communities that built them. The places of worship are a clear example of such diverse influences on the built environment. The two Sikh temples or Gurudwaras, in Cairns and in Gordonvale, are very distinct structures built in the traditional style with arches, pillars and onion-shaped domes. They fly the traditional flag, which was used to guide worshippers travelling long distances by foot along the flat plains of the Punjab in India. The Chinese Temple in Innisfail is another example of traditional architecture and ornamentation used to create an important site in the built environment. Many of the artefacts in the temple were imported from China and date back to the late 1800s. The temple is also important in the fact that many Ah Buks, or elderly Chinese men from the Gold Rush days, used to stay at the temple to be supported by the community.

The Greek Orthodox communities support the Church of the Parish of St. John the Baptist in Cairns and the Greek Orthodox Church in Innisfail. These two churches are of significance in the area as they provide services to several orthodox communities such as the Serbian, Croatian and other East European Communities. The Church of the Good Counsel Parish of Innisfail is supported by the Italian community and has been in its present form since 1928.

Ethnic communities have also made their mark in terms of distinctive memorials. The canecutters memorial in Innisfail is built to demonstrate the contribution of Italian migrants to the sugar industry. The memorial was constructed in 1959 in Italy and then brought into its present location on the Esplanade. It is a life-size statue of a canecutter and reflects the importance of the industry to the development of the district's economy. The Spanish Castle at Mena Creek, Paronella Park, is a vivid memorial to the life of a Spanish migrant, who lived the proverbial rags to riches life and built this amazing Moorish style castle in memory of the land he left behind.

Cairns' ethnic communities are also visible in the number of distinct business establishments in Cairns and suburbs. Italian, Greek, Indian, Chinese, Japanese and other cafes and restaurants compete for space in the central areas of Cairns and in lesser numbers in the suburbs. Many of these businesses are relatively new while others can trace historical links back many decades. The Asian Food Store in Innisfail is an example of a traditional Chinese Food Store established in a building that has had Chinese businesses since the early 1900s.

3.5.5 Cosmopolitan Monuments in Cairns

3.5.5.1 Paronella Park: Mena Creek

José Paronella migrated to Australia in 1913 decided to migrate to Australia. He worked for many years as a canecutter until eventually he saved enough money to buy his own sugar cane farms. He went on to make a significant fortune through buying rundown farms, upgrading them and then selling them.

José had a dream of building a Spanish castle, with the architecture he had so much admired in his native Catalonia. In 1929, José Paronella acquired some land on the banks of Mena Creek for £120 where he planned to build his castle for his family and other visitors to enjoy. He built the house they would live in first, followed by the actual castle. Although the house was made of stone, all of the other structures were constructed of poured, reinforced concrete. The concrete was covered with a plaster made from clay and cement, which they put on by hand, leaving behind the prints of their fingers as a reminder of the work they had done.

His work showed Moorish influence from Spain, especially in the castellated rooflines, the balustrade fencing, with square planter pots at the corners. He built a cafe near the pool, which was inspired during his visit to the botanical gardens in Madrid. On the second level of the cafe was a roof garden where visitors could enjoy the gardens and cool breezes. Later he added a pavilion to the cafe area where musicians played for dances or at other times used it as a spectator stand for the tennis tournaments they often held. Next was a Spanish-style castle tower, a cinema, ballroom and tennis courts.

In 1935, all the major building work was completed costing over 20,000 pounds. José had created a romantic fairytale castle set against the deep green of the tropical jungle. The park became a retreat from the everyday world and provided an oasis from the acres and acres of sugar cane that surrounded his gardens. His creation blended Spanish architecture with the Queensland bush. Paronella Park was described as the 'cultural and social centre for the Innisfail and south Johnstone shire community'.

During this time there were approximately thirty other Spanish families that the Paronella family formed close friendships with, and they all enjoyed getting together listening to Spanish music and dancing. The local primary school consisted of children from a range of backgrounds—Italian, Spanish, Greek, Maltese, Yugoslav, German and Chinese.

In 1948, José died of cancer and in 1977 Paronella Park was sold out of the family. Afterwards the park was damaged and closed due to a fire. Cyclone Winifred in 1986 and a flood in January 1994 also caused a lot of damage (Leighton 1997).

Mark and Judy Evans, the current owners purchased the Park in 1993 and since then have worked on maintaining and preserving the park with many restoration projects. The Park gained National Trust listing in 1997, and has been recognised by a total of 11 Tourism Awards in the period from 1998 till April 2000.

Paronella Park's life as a pleasure gardens continues as José intended, for visitors and tourists and with social gatherings, particularly weddings, continuing to make use of this unique location.

3.5.5.2 The Germania Club: Cairns

The German, Austrian and Swiss Association Inc. was formed in 1971 to promote cultural activities for the community. During this time, the German, Austrian and Swiss community used to gather at each other's houses for social functions and celebrations. They also did a lot of fundraising through dances, raffles and functions and over the next ten years had raised a significant amount of money.

In 1981, a member drove past an old church that was for sale and brought it to the attention of the association as a possible site for the club. After much discussion it was decided that the old church would become the 'Germania' Club, as it is known today. Everyone came together and helped out in any way they could whether financially or by volunteering their time. It took many months of hard work to transform the little old church to the new centre for the German, Austrian and Swiss Association.

The 'Germania' club is open to the public every Friday night from 6 p.m. and has a restaurant and a licensed bar. This is a popular time for the community to get together and socialise and the gathering often includes Australians of various cultural backgrounds as well as some tourists. There is a musician that plays German music as well as rock n roll and other popular English songs for entertainment. The inside of the club is like a little Germany as it has been carefully decorated with many cultural artefacts.

The Centre is available for functions to any other communities and is often used for celebrations such as birthdays, weddings and monthly dances as it can hold up to 100 people. The Polish community use the Centre to celebrate their National Day, while the Italian community uses it for parties and dances. The Dutch community also uses the Centre for various functions. The German, Austrian and Swiss Association Inc has German language classes held every week for anyone that wants to learn. The Annual Oktoberfest is also held on the club's premises.

The focus group raised a number of key points in terms of the value of the club to the community and the users. One participant felt that without the club, Polish culture in Cairns would have been lost, as the community had nowhere to gather prior to the Germanic Club. Others reiterated the common statement that the club has helped them to learn so much about each other's cultures and to heal much of the conflict left over from wars. The older people from the different communities benefit particularly as it helps to deal with social isolation in the community. One participant commented that the club was more of a multicultural club than focused on particular ethnic communities. As such it had enabled people to learn the skills to communicate with others of different cultures, as well as overcoming the shyness and reluctance to do so.

There are issues in terms of the long-term sustainability of the club, with a large proportion of the members being of the older generation. The younger generation, below 30, are not showing much interest in visiting the club or participating in its activities and it was felt that the club would suffer from attrition as the members became older. The building is still maintained by the members putting in the time and work.

3.6 Minority Immigrants and the Built Environment in Caboolture

3.6.1 Indigenous History

Caboolture is 44 kilometres north of Brisbane. Caboolture's traditional landowners are the Kabi people. The name 'Caboolture' is derived from Kabi words meaning 'Place of the Carpet Snake'. The Kabi people lived nomadically harvesting bush food, freshwater mussels, oysters, fish and few game animals (Caboolture Shire Council [CSC] 2006). The majority of the Kabi indigenous people were removed from their traditional land as European pioneers settled on newly acquired titles of land in the area.

3.6.2 Migrant History

Caboolture has a rich, yet largely unknown migrant history. Being close in proximity to Brisbane, Queensland's capital, it was one of the first areas of European settlement in the State. The European settlement of the land that became Caboolture Shire commenced in 1770 as HMS Endeavour sailed along her shores in Moreton Bay (CSC 1979). Before 1842, few Europeans settled in Caboolture due to limited transport options to cross the Caboolture River and waterways of Pumicestone Passage. Up to the 1860s the principal industry driving the development of Caboolture was timber, followed by agriculture. The Gympie gold rush days developed railway link around the 1890s (Tutt 1974) with local government starting in the area on 11 November 1879 with the establishment of the Caboolture Divisional Board (PIFU 2003).

Though Caboolture hails from a strong European history of migration and settlement, the cultural diversity was predominantly of Anglo-Saxon/Celtic origin. A recent interview with Caboolture Shire Central Library's Local History Officer revealed that very little historical account has been recorded about the shire and its people especially from a cross-cultural perspective. The only formal account outside of colonial settlement from 1770 to the 1920s is the brief photographic journal cited on the Library's website of Congeau House at Bribie Island.

3.6.3 Cosmopolitanism in Caboolture

In Caboolture, people hail from approximately 129 different nationalities with many of these reflected in historical European settlement. More than a quarter of Caboolture residents are first- or second-generation migrants from countries where English is not the primary language. The most established migrant communities include those from a German, Italian and Dutch background, while new and emerging communities include Samoan, Filipino, Fijian, Malaysian and Vietnamese groupings (CSC 2004).

ABS Census data does not always distinguish adequately one of the largest cultural groups in the Shire—the Samoan community. The reason for this is that many Samoans arrived in Australia from New Zealand and have been included as New Zealanders, rather than being shown separately by cultural identity; moreover, respondents do not always state their country of birth. Drawing statistics from Census data using the category of Languages Spoken at Home rather than the Country of Birth identifier, the 2001 Census showed that 3.4% of residents claimed to speak a language other than English at home, and that the language other than English spoken most at home in the Caboolture Shire was Samoan (10.8%) (ABS 2001).

From 2000 through to early 2002 Council's Multicultural Planner and a newly appointed Multicultural Liaison Officer, a Samoan Chief, identified the Samoan population throughout Caboolture Shire as being substantially higher than that indicated in the ABS 2001 Census. After conducting a number of community survey processes, Council was able to formally recognise the Samoan community as the largest group in the Shire from a non-English speaking background. The estimated population size then ranged between 2000 and 3000.

In 2002, the local Multicultural Association of Caboolture Shire Inc. partnered with local culturally and linguistically diverse (CALD) peoples to host their first Multicultural Festival. From these early days, where small beginnings were made, the Caboolture community still celebrate their Multicultural Festival, now known as the Moreton Bay Multicultural Fiesta (MACS Inc. 2020). The festival enjoys an ever-increasing representation of local multicultural people performing and trading there. Each year sees the festival grow in size with increasing government, business and community support participating at each event. According to the most recent census (2016), 83% of people in Caboolture spoke English at home whereas 17% of residents claimed to speak a language other than English at home. The top five languages other than English spoken at home in Caboolture were Mandarin (6.3%), Tagalog (3.9%), Samoan (3.2%), Korean (2.5%) and Vietnamese (2.1%) (ABS 2019).

3.6.4 Cosmopolitan Monuments in Caboolture

The diversity in the Caboolture community is largely of very recent origin, with significant migration from the Pacific Islands as well as increased internal migration leading to the changing demographics. The Council's Multicultural Planner and Library History Officer both confirmed that very few buildings or landmarks of ethnic significance existed in the shire. As such, the main impacts on the built environment are the establishment of numerous ethnic businesses, especially restaurants and take-away establishments. These are visible across the Shire especially in the town area of Caboolture as well as on Bribie Island. The two significant landmarks that were identified were Congeau House on Bribie Island and the Samoan Maota Fono at Deception Bay.

3.6.4.1 Congeau House: Bribie Island

Congeau House was built in the early 1920s by an Albanian wine and spirit merchant named Mr Congeau. Together he and his English wife resided in the home until she took ill and was hospitalised. Mr Congeau, unable to fetch a reasonable market bid for the sale of the property, donated it to the Church of England. It then became a holiday home for Anglican clergy. During the war years, high-ranking American and Australian service personnel often used Congeau House. After the war, it continued to be used by the Anglican clergy until 1968 when it was offered for sale to a local Queensland community organisation, Toc H Brisbane, and managed by the Bribie Island Project committee. Today Congeau House is both a local community group's meeting venue and a holiday home for those who are handicapped or are in need. Members of Toc H donated extra funds in the early 1970s enabling the building to be raised into a double storey dwelling. This has increased its capacity to accommodate up to twenty-eight people at any one time—sixteen in a dormitory arrangement downstairs and twelve in bedrooms upstairs. In 1981, the house was further renovated to cater for disabled people, i.e. front ramp, special toilets and bathrooms.

3.6.4.2 Maota Fono—Deception Bay, Queensland

With the Samoan community formally recognised by CSC, the Department of Housing's Community Renewal Program partnered with Caboolture Council to build the community a Samoan meeting place, a Maota Fono. Further funding was obtained from Jupiter's Casino and the Gambling Community Benefit Fund. During an interview held on 31 May 2006 with CSC's Multicultural Planner, he confirmed that a number of government and community consultations ensued from January 2002 through to the official opening in November 2003, bringing about the successful development of the first-ever Maota Fono built outside of Samoa.

Council provided significant support to plan, develop and build the Maota Fono. Resources such as the allocation of government land, design and building costs including all labour and building materials, hosting community consultations, negotiating partnerships for further funding support, building a toilet block and providing electricity to the venue without charge to the community highlights the level of commitment this agency gave to this initiative and the Samoan community.

In Samoa, the Maota Fono or Meeting House is one of the most sacred edifices in the village. It is a building specially built and set aside for very special occasions and ceremonies. The design is usually oval shaped and in most cases is situated in the middle of the village where people can have easy access. Having the Maota Fono here is very special and unique for Deception Bay, Caboolture Shire and beyond as it helps to re-connect Samoan people with their cultural values and customs.

The building (Fig. 3.6) is for use by all people irrespective of cultural background for special occasions such as:

- Welcoming visitors from another community, district or government
- A meeting place to discuss community issues
- A place for ceremonies such as: weddings, funerals, birthdays, reconciliation activities
- Training chiefs and other non-titled members of the community
- Community education sessions and events
- Community group meetings and other activities generally.

Fig. 3.6 Maota Fono (*Source* H. Babacan and N. Gopalkrishnan)

Aiga Samoa Association manages the Maota Fono and will help the Islander and the Anglo Australian populations enjoy and celebrate each other's culture under its roof.

In its short history, the Maota Fono has already proven its unique function in building the capacity of the Samoan community in Deception Bay and throughout the shire. Tafai, the President of Aiga Samoa Association, Brisbane North Incorporated, shared of the numerous Samoan meetings that occur under its roof, for instance monthly Council of Chiefs meetings, children's playgroup, women's support meetings, and the association's monthly executive meetings. He added that this was not the case before the Maota Fono was built; Samoan people simply would not come together for Samoan community specific meetings in neighbourhood centres, community halls and so forth.

Similarly Samoan young people meet in the Maota Fono for debriefing sessions after school camps. These meetings comprise Samoan leaders and school staff. The wider community also use the facility to run their dance classes. Other community groups book the venue to host family and community programs for all people regardless of cultural background.

Following several strategic planning workshops hosted in the Maota Fono in 2004–2005, the Chiefs and elders are developing traditional workshop programs for their people and too as a product to market in time, as a tourist attraction at the site. Samoan language and culture classes have been operating from the Maota Fono since it opened. These initiatives serve to strengthen the sustainability of the Maota Fono into the future and to encourage ongoing involvement by the Samoan and wider communities also.

This unique venue has set a standard of wider community participation under its large roof. To date the Maota Fono has housed many events for people from all cultural backgrounds. In an interview with the High Chief Orator on 15 May 2006, he outlined some of the events conducted therein, such as, Queensland State Library's multicultural website launch, Department of Immigration and Multicultural Affairs, Department of Employment and Training, Education Queensland, Queensland Police Services and Queensland Health, to name only a few, have each conducted community workshops at the Maota Fono. The region's largest multicultural peak body Caboolture and Redcliffe Multicultural (CARM) Forum have hosted many special events and meetings at Maota Fono. In effect thousands of people have participated in varying events hosted at this site.

These events culminate in strengthening relationships between the Samoan community, the wider community, the three tiers of government and community agencies. This has been observed through the ongoing support and participation of people from all cultures attending various functions and workshops since the Maota Fono was officially opened. There are a number of positive outcomes to the local community because of the activities that occur directly from the Maota Fono. These are the Samoan culture being more widely shared among non-Samoan people; a comfortable breezy and relaxed venue where government consultations to address serious social issues have been explored and projects developed which have brought about support and assistance for local residents and multicultural communities generally; the Samoan community has been able to accumulate culturally traditional materials from income generated by Maota Fono hiring fees earned; Samoan young people are learning more of their cultural identity which is helping to develop their leadership skills.

Participants of the Samoan focus group confirmed that relatives, friends and visitors generally travel from all areas of Brisbane, other states of

Australia and abroad—from New Zealand, Samoa and beyond—all to visit the Maota Fono. Increasingly more and more of the traditional ceremonies are being planned here at the Maota Fono. This has helped to develop confidence in local Samoan people as pride and respect in the Samoan culture increases. This is another example of how the Maota Fono continues to empower the Samoan and broader cultural communities throughout Deception Bay.

3.7 Stocktake of Immigrant Minorities Contributions to Queensland's Built Environment

3.7.1 Religious Institutions

3.7.1.1 Parish of St John the Baptist Cairns, Greek Orthodox Archdiocese of Australia

In 1993, the Greek Orthodox Archdiocese Property Trust purchased land in Redlynch as it was more affordable than the preferred Cairns Central Business District. After the purchase, the Greek community came together and spent the next few months fundraising through raffles, cake stalls and organising social functions. Donations for the building of the Parish came from parishioners, other parishes and donors throughout Australia as well as a large amount from an anonymous donor in Cairns. The new parish was named 'St John the Baptist' and the first service was held in the church (Fig. 3.7) on the 5th of June 1993. His Eminence Archbishop Stylianos officially opened the Parish on the 25th September 1994.

A day care centre and house for the priest was built in 1996 to keep the church going. Then in 1999 a respite centre was built which is now St John's Community Care. Today many people from all backgrounds including indigenous Australians use the centre. Service is held every Sunday and many people stay on after the service for a coffee and to socialise with other Greek people. The church is the centre of the Greek community and supports those in need financially and otherwise.

Many other ethnic communities in Cairns, without a common precinct of their own, meet at St John's Community Care. Some of these include the Polish, Italian, Russian, Romanian, Bulgarian, Serbian and as well as Indigenous communities. St John's Greek Orthodox Parish being the only Orthodox Church in Cairns, other Orthodox religions such as the Serbian community attend the church.

Fig. 3.7 St John the Baptist Church, Cairns (*Source* H. Babacan and N. Gopalkrishnan)

3.7.1.2 Greek Orthodox Church, Innisfail

The Greek community in Innisfail purchased a house in 1928 to use as a Greek club. The Association called itself the Hellenic Society of North Queensland and was one of the first Greek Associations formed outside a metropolitan area. In 1935, the Association was changed to the Greek Orthodox Community and a Greek church was built.

The church was the first Orthodox Church in Far North Queensland and the second in the whole of Qld. The Church was built on Owen Street in the centre of town and nine Greek families raised the money with J. Fardoulys as the president. Father Sideris, who had originally come to Australia to cut cane, was the priest of the Greek Orthodox Church in Innisfail from 1945 to 1972.

In the 1970s, the site of the original church was sold and a new church was built on Ernest Street (Fig. 3.8). The Greek community all contributed towards the building of the new church and a small house

Fig. 3.8 Greek Orthodox Church, Innisfail (*Source* H. Babacan and N. Gopalkrishnan)

was built for the priest to live in. The original altar and holy table were placed in the new church and is still used today.

The Greek Orthodox Church in Innisfail is an important place for young people as it gives them an opportunity to attend religious services, learn about their culture and socialise with other young Australian—Greeks. There is a Greek school, currently attended by about 10 children on a weekly basis. The Greek community also gets together for barbecues and other functions organised by the Association.

The Church is open every Sunday for the community to attend, however Greek services are only held monthly, as they have no resident priest in Innisfail. The association has approximately 150–170 members and services are attended by people of all Orthodox cultures including Greeks, Serbians and Croatians.

3.7.1.3 Good Counsel Parish of Innisfail

Father Martin Michael Clancy OSA built the Good Counsel Parish of Innisfail Church in 1928 (Fig. 3.9). It replaced the previous wooden church that was destroyed by a cyclone in 1918. It is used by the Italian community in Innisfail as they have Italian masses on the 3rd Sunday of each month.

Fig. 3.9 Good Counsel Parish of Innisfail Church (*Source* H. Babacan and N. Gopalkrishnan)

3.7.1.4 Sikh Temples, Cairns

Prior to Sikh temples being built, the Cairns community used the Masonic hall in Edmonton and each other's houses for celebrations. In 1979, there were discussions to form an Association for the Sikh community. Some members were content to continue meeting at houses and the hall and so they continued to do so. However, the other group formed the Sikh Association of Queensland and commenced looking at purchasing a suitable site to build their temple. The majority of the Sikh community lived around Edmonton and the land for the temple was donated by Gordanvale farmer, Mr. Gian Singh, a member of the Sikh Association of Queensland. Each member of the Sikh Association of Queensland contributed towards the building of the temple and some members went to Woolgoolga, NSW, where there was a large Sikh community, to raise more funds.

The Guru Nanak Sikh Temple (Fig. 3.10) was designed and built by

Fig. 3.10 Guru Nanak Sikh Temple, Cairns (*Source* H. Babacan and N. Gopalkrishnan)

Mr. Ken Chappell who was shown pictures of temples in India. It was built in three stages: temple, hall and kitchen. Cr Tom Pyne, chairman of the Mulgrave Shire, officially opened the temple in November 1993. It was the first Sikh temple to be built in Queensland. The temple as it stands today is a masonry complex with three domes. There is a flag at the temple that is significant because it can be seen from a distance and is reflective of the practice in India where the flag would guide the path of worshippers who travelled long distances on foot to get to the temple.

Three years after the temple was built in Edmonton, the Sikh community in Gordonvale decided to build a temple close to where they lived and so another temple, the Guru Gobind Singh Sikh Gurdwara Temple (Fig. 3.11), is located in Gordonvale.

The temples are important to young people as they get to learn about and really experience their religion. They hold language and religion classes and also celebrate weddings at the temples. The temples are not used by any other groups for functions, although all people are welcome

Fig. 3.11 Guru Gobind Singh Sikh Gurdwara Temple, Gordonvale (*Source* H. Babacan and N. Gopalkrishnan)

to visit. Occasionally school groups go to the temples for a visit to learn about the Sikh religion. The Gurudwara building is a very visible attraction to tourists on the Cairns highway.

3.7.1.5 Islamic Mosque, Cairns

As the number of Muslim families in and around Cairns increased, the community purchased a house in September 2000 to be used as a mosque (Fig. 3.12). Although a house, it was classed as a place of worship by the local council. Donations for the purchase of the house were received from the Islamic community in Cairns and Islamic Associations from all over Australia. The property was accordingly purchased by the Trust of the Islamic Society in Cairns.

This Mosque was open every day for Muslims to pray, and prayers were held five times a day. Each Friday there were approximately 40 community members that came together to pray. During important Muslim events, such as the end of Ramadan, there could be up to 120 people attending.

Fig. 3.12 Islamic Mosque, Cairns (*Source* H. Babacan and N. Gopalkrishnan)

Fulfilling plans to build a new and bigger mosque on the same property, a new mosque, the Abu Bakr As-Siddiq Mosque, was completed in 2010, controlled by trustees and administered by Cairns Imaam, Managing Trustee, Abdul Aziz Mohammed. Although the Cairns Muslim community is almost 100 years old, it is still very small, around 200–250 people, made up of more than 11 different nationalities (Cairns Mosque 2020).

3.7.1.6 Chinese Temple: Innisfail

The first Chinese Temple was built in Innisfail in 1886 on the corner of Owen and Edith Street. It was built of timber and iron and was damaged by a cyclone in 1918, repaired, and remained standing for another twenty years. In 1940, the original temple was demolished, land was purchased with the money, and a new temple was built.

The temple (Fig. 3.13), as it stands today, was built by Romano and Sons. The majority of the temple's artefacts date back to 1886, originally

Fig. 3.13 Chinese Temple: Innisfail (*Source* H. Babacan and N. Gopalkrishnan)

brought from China. Covered in gold leaf they represent deities of the Taoist, Confucian and Buddhist traditions. Until recently the temple was the home to many Ah Buks, elderly Chinese men who were supported by the community. Originally the men came for the gold rush in the 1880s and lived in exile when they failed to make their fortunes and bring good honour to their families. In 1940, there were twelve Ah Buks living in a house behind the temple.

The temple is heritage listed and the trustee custodians are descendants or connected by marriage to one of the two original trustees. It is open every day of the year for people to pray and for the general public to visit. Chinese along with the Hmong community and Western Buddhists in Innisfail all use it to fulfil their spiritual needs.

3.7.1.7 *Chenrezig Institute: Sunshine Coast*

Chenrezig Institute is a centre for Buddhist study, meditation and retreat, nestled in the forested hills of the Sunshine Coast hinterland in South East Queensland, Australia. It is a flourishing community of nuns, monks and lay people. Chenrezig is the name of the Buddha of Compassion who embodies the compassionate wisdom of all the Buddhas. The goal of Chenrezig Institute is to benefit others and realise ultimate happiness.

Chenrezig was one of the first centres of Tibetan Buddhism to be established in the western world. In 1974, a month-long meditation course, the first ever of its kind, was conducted by Lama Thubten Yeshe and Lama Zopa Rinpoche in nearby Diamond Valley, Mooloolah. This now historic course attracted approximately 200 people from all across Australia, many of whom went on to play key roles in establishing and running centres in other states of Australia, and indeed the world. During the course many students decided they wanted the opportunity for ongoing study and so the Eudlo property was donated by four of the Lamas' students so that a meditation centre could be established.

This rather barren plot of land, lying fallow, became what is now the lush subtropical environment of Chenrezig Institute. This transformation from one-time cattle grazing land to thriving centre for Tibetan Buddhist education and practice was made possible by the hard work of countless volunteer students and visitors over many years.

Today programmes at the Institute include meditation retreats, teachings on Buddhism, advanced study courses, art classes and workshops on Buddhist psychology and mental well-being. The centre also has accommodation facilities, a vegetarian cafe, library, meditation hall, art studio, memorial garden and beautiful grounds which are all open to the general public (Chenrezig Institute 2020).

3.7.1.8 Chung Tian Buddhist Temple: Brisbane

Chung Tian Temple was constructed in 1992 using traditional Chinese Buddhist architecture and is situated between Brisbane and Logan. Surrounded by nature, the temple provides a peaceful and culturally beautiful venue for the community to celebrate their multicultural diversity and multi-faith harmony through Humanistic Buddhism. The gardens at the front of Chung Tian have miniature saints and depict stories from the Buddha's life.

Bestowed by Venerable Master Hsing Yun with the name Chung Tian, or literally 'central heaven', and situated in Brisbane's southern suburbs, it is surrounded by parklands and state forest. Chung Tian Temple plays not only the role of exchanging ideas between Eastern and Western cultures, but also of promoting Dharma, spiritual, charitable and various multicultural activities in Australia.

The Temple has become an educational and tourist centre and visitors from overseas, impressed by the well-run organisation, praise Australia for its multicultural approach, as a successful model for the rest of the world.

3.7.1.9 Brisbane Hebrew Congregation: Margaret Street, Brisbane

The Brisbane Synagogue (Fig. 3.14) at 98 Margaret Street was built in 1885 for the Brisbane Hebrew Congregation. Renovations took place in 1965 to celebrate the centenary of the formation of the Brisbane Hebrew Congregation. Many people who had lost family members during the Holocaust donated additional stained glass windows. At this time, the congregation's spiritual name 'Kehilla Kedosha Sha'ari Emun'—the Holy Congregation of the Gates of Faith—was added over the arched entry.

3.7.1.10 Temple Shalom, Gold Coast

As a result of numerous requests by those desirous of practicing Progressive Judaism on the Gold Coast, a handful of enthusiastic people gathered at the home of Mr and Mrs Len Spray in October 1976, thereby realising the humble beginnings of Temple Shalom, Gold Coast. After a tremendous amount of work and fundraising, a historical event took place on Sunday, 23 May 1982, with the opening and consecration of Temple Shalom on the Isle of Capri (Fig. 3.15). The Temple was registered as a Religious Body with the Queensland Government and is affiliated with

Fig. 3.14 Brisbane Synagogue (*Source* H. Babacan and N. Gopalkrishnan)

Fig. 3.15 Temple Shalom, Gold Coast (*Source* H. Babacan and N. Gopalkrishnan)

The Union for Progressive Judaism. The building of a beautiful new sanctuary followed this in 1992. The Temple now comprises the Synagogue, Cheder room, function hall, kitchen and offices, and provides members with all the facilities that one would require.

3.7.2 *Memorials*

3.7.2.1 *Nepalese Pagoda, South Bank, Brisbane*

The Nepalese Pagoda in Brisbane (Fig. 3.16) is a memorial to peace and tolerance and was a gift from Nepal to the people of Brisbane after the World Expo 1988. The Pagoda is entirely made of wood, hand carved by artisans who came from Nepal for the purpose. The Pagoda stands on the redeveloped South Bank, a regular destination for local Brisbane residents as well as tourists.

3.7.2.2 *Canecutters Monument: Innisfail*

The Canecutters Memorial (Fig. 3.17) is an important monument to the community as it demonstrates the contribution of Italian migrants to the sugar industry. The memorial was constructed in 1959 by the Italian community to honour the pioneers of the sugar industry, many of whom were Italian. It is situated on the Esplanade in the centre of Innisfail alongside the Johnstone River. A life-size statue of a canecutter, it was chosen to reflect the importance of the sugar cane industry in the development of the district's economy.

The proposal for the sculpture followed a suggestion by the Queensland Government that communities commemorate the centenary of separation from New South Wales with a permanent structure. A group from the Italian community in Innisfail decided to erect a statue. Old photographs of the sugar industry were used and given to Sydney artist L. Yonna who suggested a statue in the form of a canecutter. The committee formed to oversee construction wrote to the Chamber of Commerce of Carrara, Italy, requesting the submission of designs by suitable sculptors. The design by Renato Beretta, the Instructor at the Carrara Academy of Arts, was selected. The monument was made in Carrara, arriving in 32 cases to be erected by an Italian migrant P. Bertolani who had arrived in Australia two months previously. The Premier of Queensland, the Hon F Nicklin, officially unveiled the monument on 4 October 1959.

Fig. 3.16 Nepalese Pagoda, Brisbane (*Source* H. Babacan and N. Gopalkrishnan)

3.7.2.3 Comino's House, Cairns

George Comino migrated to Australia in the 1900s from the Greek Island of Kythera. He worked in the cane fields until he saved up enough money and went back to Greece to marry. He returned with his wife and family

Fig. 3.17 Canecutters Memorial, Innisfail (*Source* H. Babacan and N. Gopalkrishnan)

in 1926 and later purchased a house, now known as Comino's House (Fig. 3.18), a well-known building in the City of Cairns.

The original high set timber home was built on the corner of Abbott and Florence Streets in the 1800s as indicated by architectural features such as the 'Union Jack' verandah balustrading. It was built by Mr. Alfred Street, a builder and member of the first Cairns Council and, after a few owners, was sold to George Comino in 1927.

Fig. 3.18 Comino's House, Cairns (*Source* H. Babacan and N. Gopalkrishnan)

The Comino family was the first Greek family in Cairns and as other Greek families moved into Cairns they used to get together at Comino's house for Greek food and folk dancing. Eventually a Greek club called 'Acropolis' was formed where the men would go and play cards. George Comino opened a store called Comino's Café, which at that time was the focal point of Cairns and was known as the biggest department store in the North. Comino's café was a landmark in Cairns until the 1950s when it was closed. His son, Peter Comino, took over the family business when George died in 1962 and opened Orchid Plaza in 1990. The Comino family built Orchid Plaza on the same site of Comino's Café.

'Comino's House' remained with the Comino family until 1988, when the land was sold for development. The timber home was offered to the Cairns City Council for relocation, and was moved to its present location to be used as a community centre. It is currently being conserved as authentically as possible and maintained by 'Friends of Comino's House'.

3.7.3 Clubs and Other Community Organisations

3.7.3.1 The Greek Club and Convention Centre, South Brisbane

The Greek Club in South Brisbane (Fig. 3.19) has traditionally played a major role in 'Paniyiri', the popular annual festival celebrating Greek culture, held in Musgrave Park, and is attended by tens of thousands of Australians of every cultural heritage. The Greek Club and Convention Centre has long been an institution with excellent facilities to cater for a number of occasions, such as weddings, corporate events, parties and celebrations as well as special events for New Year, on Melbourne Cup Day and on other significant days.

Today the Club hosts gatherings from small meetings of 10 to large and lavish functions catering for up to 800 guests, and provides a venue for events, seminars, conferences, galas, trade shows and meetings of all sizes in central Brisbane. Featuring sweeping views of Musgrave Park in

Fig. 3.19 Greek Club and Convention Centre, South Brisbane (*Source* H. Babacan and N. Gopalkrishnan)

West End and the Brisbane City skyline it offers both a Greek and Modern Australian menu in its on-site Nostimo Restaurant which is open every day (Greek Club 2020).

References

Anti-Discrimination Commission Queensland. (2018). *Aboriginal People in Queensland: A Brief Human Rights History*. http://www.qhrc.qld.gov.au/__data/assets/pdf_file/0013/10606/Aboriginal-timeline-FINAL-updated-25-July-2018.pdf. Accessed 8 April 2020.

Australian Bureau of Statistics (ABS). (2001). *Census*. http://www.abs.gov.au/AUSSTATS/abs@cpp.nsf/DetailsPage/3050512282001?OpenDocument&tabname=Details&prodno=305051228&issue=2001&num=&view=&. Accessed 23 May 2006.

Australian Bureau of Statistics (ABS). (2019). *Community Profiles*. https://www.abs.gov.au/websitedbs/D3310114.nsf/Home/2016%20Census%20Community%20Profiles. Accessed 12 March 2020.

Australian Electoral Commission. (2007). *Queensland Division—Brisbane*. https://results.aec.gov.au/13745/website/HouseDivisionProfile-13745-156.htm#helpbookmark. Accessed 7 March 2020.

Bailey, D. J. (1992). *Two to the Valley, Fortitude Valley A Portrait in Black and White*. Fortitude Valley and Brisbane: Valley Business Association, Brisbane City Council.

Brisbane City Council (BCC). (2003). *Heritage Experience Guides—The Valley. A Brisbane City Council Heritage Trail*.

Brisbane City Council (BCC). (2004a). *Storyboards in the Chinatown Mall*.

Brisbane City Council (BCC). (2004b, May). *Urban Renewal Newsline* (No. 46). Brisbane: Urban Renewal Task Force.

Caboolture Shire Council (CSC). (1979). *From Spear and Musket 1879–1979: Caboolture Centenary: Stories of the Area Once Controlled by the Caboolture Divisional Board*. Queensland: National Library of Australia.

Caboolture Shire Council (CSC). (2004). *Culturally Caboolture: Enacting Caboolture Shire's Multicultural Policy*. Policy Development and Implementation: An Overview. Caboolture: CSC.

Caboolture Shire Council (CSC). (2006). *Local History*. http://www.caboolture.qld.gov.au/tourism/default.htm. Accessed 8 April 2006.

Cairns City Council. (2004). *Statistical Profile of People from Diverse Cultural and Linguistic Backgrounds and Aboriginal and Torres Strait Islander People*. Cairns: Cairns City Council.

Cairns Mosque. (2020). https://cairnsmosque.com.au/. Accessed 9 March 2020.

Cairns Museum. (2006). *The War for the Land: A Short History of Aboriginal-European Relations in Cairns*. cairnsmuseum.org.au. Accessed 16 August 2006.
Cathay Community Association (CCA). (2020). *History*. http://english.cathay.org.au/history/. Accessed 4 March 2020.
Chenrezig Institute. (2020). https://www.chenrezig.com.au/about/. Accessed 9 March 2020.
Chinese Club of Queensland (CCQ). (2005). *Chinese Club of Queensland*. Brisbane: CCQ.
Collins, J., & Kunz, P. (2009). Ethnicity and Public Space in the City: Ethnic Precincts in Sydney. *Cosmopolitan Civil Societies: An Interdisciplinary Journal, 1*(1), 39–70.
Department of Immigration, Multicultural and Indigenous Affairs (DIMIA). (2005). *Fact Sheet 4*. Canberra: DIMIA.
Department of Local Government, Racing and Multicultural Affairs (DLGRMA). (2019). *First Progress Report on the Queensland Multicultural Policy*. http://www.dlgrma.qld.gov.au/resources/multicultural/policy-governance/first-progress-report-on-qmp.pdf. Accessed 8 April 2020.
Evans, R., Saunders, K., & Cronin, K. (1975). *Exclusion, Exploitation and Extermination*. Sydney: A.N.Z. Books.
Fesl, E. M. D. (2001). *Australian Aborigines in Multicultural Queensland*. Brisbane: Multicultural Affairs Queensland.
Greek Club. (2020). https://www.thegreekclub.com.au/. Accessed 9 March 2020.
Hollinsworth, D. (2006). *Race and Racism in Australia* (3rd ed.). Melbourne: Thomson Social Science Press.
Jones, Dorothy. (1976). *A History of Cairns and District*. Cairns: Cairns Post Pty Ltd.
Leighton, Dena. (1997). *The Spanish Dreamer: A Biography of Jose Paronella*. Wollongong, NSW: Rosemount Press.
MACS Inc. (2020). *Morton Bay Multicultural Fiesta*. http://www.macscaboolture.com.au/moreton-bay-multicultural-fiesta.html. Accessed 14 March 2020.
Malloy, S. (2007, March 11). Bell Rings for Wartime Allies. *Brisbane Times*.
Markus, A. (1994). *Australia's Race Relations 1878–1993*. Sydney: Allen & Unwin.
May, C. (1984). *Topsawyers: The Chinese in Cairns, 1870–1920*. Townsville: James Cook University.
Mercer, P. W. (1995). *White Australia Defied: Pacific Islander Settlement in North Queensland*. Townsville: James Cook University.
Multicultural Affairs Queensland (MAQ). (2001). *Multicultural Queensland*. Brisbane: MAQ.

Multicultural Affairs Queensland (MAQ). (2003). *The People of Queensland: Statistics from the 2001 Census*. Brisbane: MAQ.

Multicultural Affairs Queensland (MAQ). (2005). *Diversity Figures*. Brisbane: MAQ.

Our Brisbane. (2006). http://www.ourbrisbane.com/living/suburbs/fortitude_valley/history/. Accessed 22 May 2006.

Planning Information and Forecasting Unit (PIFU). (2003). *Demographic Profile: Incorporating First Release Data from the 2001 Census*. Queensland: Department of Local Government and Planning.

Queensland Government. (2006). *Multicultural Queensland—Making a World of Difference*. http://www.premiers.qld.gov.au/multicultural/. Accessed 9 October 2006.

Queensland Museum (QM). (2006). www.qm.qld.gov.au. Accessed 24 August 2006.

Robb, S. (2004). *Cairns Chinatown Cultural Heritage Study [CD-ROM]*.

Shnukal, A. (2001). *Torres Strait Islanders in Multicultural Queensland*. Brisbane: Multicultural Affairs Queensland.

SPK Housing. (2001). *Hmong Shamanism Booklet*.

Stimson, R., Mullins, P., Baum, S., Davis, R., Gleeson, S., & Shaw, K. (2000). *Inner-City Renaissance: The Changing Face, Functions & Structure of Brisbane's Inner-City*. Brisbane: Techtrade Australia.

Tutt, S. (1974). *Pioneer Days: Stories and Photographs of European Settlement Between the Pine and Noosa Rivers, Queensland*. Queensland: Caboolture Historical Society.

ValleyNet. (2006). www.valleynet.org.au/abut-history.html. Accessed 1 May 2006.

Wang, S., Sigler, T., Liu, Y., & Corcoran, J. (2018, November). Shifting Dynamics of Chinese Settlement in Australia: An Urban Geographic Perspective. *Geographical Research, 56*(4), 447–464.

CHAPTER 4

Immigrant Minorities and the Built Environment in Western Australia

In 2019, 2,474,410 people lived in Western Australia (WA), while Perth today has a population of just under 2 million (ABS 2019b). The interesting feature of WA relevant to this book is that it has a higher migrant presence—35% were born-overseas or were first-generation immigrants (ABS 2019c)—than any other Australian state. It also has a different immigrant population than NSW and Queensland: Perth and WA have higher proportions of people born in the United Kingdom and fewer people from Southern Europe, the Middle East and Asian countries. WA does replicate the pattern of other states with a key dominant urban population centre surrounded by a large number of regional cities and rural towns: Perth has eighty percent of the state's population. In more than ten Perth suburbs immigrants comprised more than half of the population. In the suburb of Cannington, 12 kilometres south-east of Perth, 62% of the population are immigrants, with Indians being the biggest group. In neighbouring suburb Queens Park, 59% of residents were born overseas (with those from India the largest group), as in Crawley (where Chinese are the biggest group). Glendalough and Bentley have a foreign-born population of 57% led by Indian and Malaysian migrants, respectively (Paddenburg 2017).

Like the previous chapters on NSW and Queensland, in this chapter we take one urban site (Northbridge) and one rural site (Katanning) to investigate the impact of immigrant minorities on the changing built environment but in WA we look at *two* regional sites—Freemantle and

J. Collins et al., *Cosmopolitan Place Making in Australia*,
https://doi.org/10.1007/978-981-15-8041-3_4

Kalgoorlie. The addition of an extra regional site was due to a request by our WA research Industry Partner—The National Trust of Australia (Western Australia). Our interest is twofold: firstly in the changing history of minority immigrants in each area which, to pursue our cosmopolitan framework, is embedded within the Indigenous history; and secondly in the social processes that lay behind—and are at the same time impacted by—the changing built environment of Northbridge, Freemantle, Kalgoorlie and Katanning. The Northbridge case study provides a Chinatown continuity that we saw in Sydney's Haymarket and Brisbane's Fortitude Valley. The difference this time is that the attempts to put the 'Chinatown' tag on Northbridge failed. This was partly a consequence of the decision of the regulators of Perth city and the Northbridge local area, and partly the competing claims on Northbridge that other immigrant minorities and their immigrant entrepreneurs held. We draw heavily on informants to narrate the changing interrelationships between a transforming population and a transforming built landscape of WA.

4.1 Immigrant Minorities and the Built Environment in Northbridge

Northbridge is a cosmopolitan neighbourhood and restaurant precinct in the heart of Perth, the capital city of WA. While only a few hundred metres from Perth's central business district and main railway station, Northbridge is separated from the city by the railway line. WA has the highest proportion of immigrants of any Australian state, with Australia as a whole having relatively more immigrants than most western nations (OECD 2019). Like in other Australian states, most immigrants to WA have settled in the major cities (see Burnley 2001). In Perth, Northbridge has received successive waves of immigrants, with the country of origin changing over time as Australia's immigrant net has selected those from different ethnic backgrounds (Collins 2013; Productivity Commission 2016). Chinese immigrants in the late 1800s were followed by Greeks and Italians in the mid-twentieth century and a more diverse array of immigrants since the 1970s. Just as in Sydney's Chinatown, many of these immigrants have set up their own small retail and hospitality businesses along Northbridge's main streets. They have also established places of worship and ethnic associations that feature prominently in the area's built and social environments.

This section details the historical development of Northbridge as an ethnic precinct and cosmopolitan neighbourhood over more than a hundred years of (changing) immigrant settlement. Over that time Northbridge has had a number of (changing) ethnic faces, and its identity is still in flux as an attempt to re-brand the area as Perth's Chinatown was rejected and local and state government agencies increasingly seek to highlight its multi-ethnic cosmopolitan character. This case study draws on visitor surveys and interviews with local government, ethnic community organisations and ethnic entrepreneurs (see Appendices 1 and 2) in order to explore the complex and sometimes contradictory interactions between them. This enables two central research questions that shaped the fieldwork for this book—'how do visitors experience the built environment and atmosphere of the precinct?' and 'is social value undermined by commercialisation, ethnic theming and the commodification of ethnicity?'—to be carefully unravelled. Furthermore, it explores in depth the precincts' history, social use and changing regulatory environment.

4.1.1 *Northbridge's Immigrant History*

For many years after the European settlement of Perth, Northbridge[1] was isolated from the city by its swampy terrain. Being so protected from rapid development, it remained important for local Aboriginal people who had been displaced from the more accessible land to the south.[2] The Aboriginal people of this area were Yabbaru Bibbulmun and spoke the Illa kuri wongi dialect. Today, as in Katanning, the region's Aboriginal population are most often referred to as Nyoongars.[3]

The first non-Aboriginal settlers in the areas north of Perth were several men who took up large land grants from the 1830s. The area was more heavily settled by Europeans in the 1860s, when convict arrivals meant the Swan River Colony was growing substantially and the demand for food was pushing market gardening further to the north (Town of Vincent 2004, pp. 3–4). Settlers in this period included small landholders, artisans and discharged soldiers (Heritage Council of Western Australia [HCWA] 2002, p. 4). The area also became home to some of the city's poorer residents, including Chinese immigrants (Gregory 2007, p. 3), who were attracted by the prospects in market gardening, the proximity to the city and the relatively cheap cost of accommodation and commercial sites (Stannage 1979; also Interview N25). The area was divided from the city by the railway line in 1881, with road access across the line not re-established until 1903 (Town of Vincent 2004, p. 11). This separation from the city contributed to the further concentration of poorer residents in Northbridge, with the 'north side of the line' attracting 'those who [were] on the margins of society so to speak, especially… new migrants, and in particular those who couldn't speak English' (Interview N25). Through the late 1800s, Northbridge became both a commercial and residential centre and, although the neighbourhood included some middle-class residences, it also became Perth's 'red light' district, housing brothels, Chinese gambling houses and opium dens.

Chinese immigration to Perth had begun in the early years of the Swan River colony, with indentured Chinese labourers brought to the settlement to address labour shortages.[4] These labourers were recruited in Singapore, but were from diverse ethnic and linguistic backgrounds. Anne Atkinson (2001, p. 214) notes that 'just one page' of the list of Chinese arrivals in Western Australia in 1889 'records 33 emigrants from 13 different districts and from five major linguistic groups—Cantonese, Hokkien, Hailam, Teochiu and Huichiu'. This reminds us at the outset that a cosmopolitan framework is required if we are to appreciate the diversity within so-called ethnic groups and if we are to reveal the complex, uneven and often contradictory super-diversity of the relationship between immigrant minorities and the built environment of the places and spaces in the neighbourhoods where they settle.

While the number of Chinese indentured labourers brought to the colony declined during the period of convict transportation from 1850 to 1868, the 1890s saw a doubling of the Chinese population in Western Australia following the discovery of gold in the towns of Coolgardie and Kalgoorlie in the colony's east. Legislation to restrict the immigration and activities of Chinese had been introduced as early as 1874, with the *Imported Labour Registry Act* preventing Chinese workers from bringing their families to the colony (HCWA 2002, p. 3). However, fears that Chinese would 'take over' both the gold mining and pearling industries prompted the introduction of further restrictions in 1886, with the *Goldfields Act* and *Pearl Shell Fishery Act* prohibiting Asians from direct engagement in these activities (Atkinson 2001, p. 214).

The restrictions on pearling and gold mining prompted enterprising Chinese to establish ancillary businesses, with the colony's rapidly growing population after the gold discoveries attracting Chinese to both Perth and Fremantle and providing expanding business opportunities in the south-west of the colony (Atkinson 2001, p. 214). Most of these new Chinese arrivals came from the east coast,[5] particularly Sydney and Melbourne, and brought with them 'capital and expertise they had built up in those cities' (Atkinson 2001, p. 214). Around 50% of the Chinese in Perth found work as market gardeners, growing Chinese vegetables for the Chinese population and European vegetables for Europeans. Perth's Chinese immigrants also established other businesses, including laundries, furniture factories, retail stores and import agencies (Atkinson 2001, p. 215; King 1998; Peters 2007).

As noted previously, Chinese immigrants were a racialised minority in Australia at that time, with Chinese entrepreneurship in part a response to their 'blocked mobility' in the labour market (Collins et al. 1995). As Atkinson described in her 1983 thesis on the socio-economic experience of early Chinese settlers in Perth:

> the ideology of a white society, transported from a closed economy, allowed Chinese only into occupations which were marginal, non-competitive and complementary to those already dominated by members of that society. Retail outlets, import/export agencies and hand laundries were such occupations. Chinese furniture makers, because they were in an industry dominated by white labour, were an exception and experienced constant racial harassment from host labour organisations. (King 1998, p. 36)

By the early 1900s, Chinese entrepreneurs dominated the market gardening industry and, despite restrictive legislation,[6] dominated the laundry industry and held a 'considerable share of the furniture trade' (Atkinson 2001, p. 215).

Chinese market gardens were established in several Perth suburbs (including Northbridge) as well as rural towns (such as Katanning) (Atkinson 2001, p. 215). The swamps made Northbridge and North Perth ideal for gardening (until they were filled in during the 1920s), and Chinese market gardeners established commercial enterprises at several places including Smith's Lake, Stone's Lake and Second Swamp. With fresh produce markets opened between Northbridge's James and Roe Streets in 1906, the area became central to Perth's fruit and vegetable trade. The new markets were 'probably the most important wholesale outlet for Chinese growers' (Atkinson 1984 in King 1998, p. 90) and after visiting the markets the growers would buy goods at nearby Chinese shops or visit opium and gambling dens and 'spend a few hours gambling and talking with friends' (Doug Sue in King 1998, p. 91).

Chinese stores were concentrated in three main metropolitan areas: Fremantle, Murray Street (just to the south of the central railway station) and Northbridge. The latter concentration spread along James and William Streets (William Street cuts across James Street), with shops 'catering almost exclusively to the Chinese community' selling imported Chinese food and clothing as well as gardening equipment and household utensils (Atkinson 2001, p. 215). In 1912, local Chinese shops in James and William streets included a number of laundries, furniture factories, herbalists, grocers, restaurants and retail stores. Hop Hing & Co., like many of the stores in Sydney's Chinatown, also provided banking services. This allowed Chinese market gardeners to cash their cheques at the store and facilitating remittances back to China (King 1998, p. 91). Chinese shops were also important meeting places for local Chinese and those who made the trip to Perth's fruit and vegetable market from the outer suburbs, particularly before the formation of the Chung Wah Association (CWA) (literally the association for Chinese people) in Northbridge in 1909.[7]

Other shops in Northbridge also provided translating and interpreting services. However, according to Atkinson, it was the role of the shops as meeting places that was particularly important since it 'helped to foster a strong sense of community and community spirit' and was instrumental in establishing the CWA (Atkinson 2001, p. 215) that subsequently organised to promote the rights of local Chinese residents and entrepreneurs (King 1998). With the concentration of Chinese businesses and social and political activities in Northbridge, the area soon gained the reputation of being Perth's 'Chinatown' (Atkinson 2001, p. 215; Peters 2007, p. 1).

While the number of Chinese in Sydney stayed roughly the same in the first few years of the White Australia policy (with the numbers boosted by those moving back to the city from regional areas), the Chinese population of Perth declined.[8] Chinese immigration virtually ceased and many ageing immigrants who had arrived in earlier decades returned to China to live out their final years. With the onset of the Great Depression, many Chinese entrepreneurs found continuing their businesses impossible, reducing the incentive for them to stay in Perth. While the CWA managed to survive through this period, Perth's 'Chinatown' all but disappeared (Atkinson 2001, p. 215; King 1998).[9]

At the end of World War I, Greek and Italian immigrants began arriving in Northbridge in significant numbers. The suburb was attractive for its proximity to the city's produce markets and Central Business

District (CBD) while still offering relatively cheap rents. Many of the new immigrants moved into boarding houses and later into existing homes, remodelling these in styles now referred to as 'immigrant nostalgia', reflecting 'the recreation of styles reminiscent of those left behind' (Town of Vincent 2004, p. 27).

Greek and Italian immigrants were seen by many in their new host country as the 'Chinese of Europe', a racialised minority who could replace the Chinese in the least desirable jobs (de Lepervanche 1975, see also Church 2005; Price 1963). Faced with institutional and popular racist hostility, many Greek and Italian immigrants in Australia found work through self-employment. In Northbridge, several Greek and Italian immigrants established small businesses, particularly cafés, greengrocers and delicatessens (EPRA 2000a; Yiannakis 1996). Greeks tended to be concentrated in fruit and vegetable selling, fishmongering and running small cafés or *kafeneon* (Interview N29). Italians opened delicatessens, restaurants, cafés, butchers and specialty stores (Interview N15; Interview N21; Interview N22). Some of the new immigrants also worked in factories in Northbridge, including the Micheledes cigarette factory (Interview N29) and a number of macaroni factories (Interview N22).

A number of these early Greek and Italian stores have become iconic symbols of Northbridge, surviving in the memories of successive waves of immigrants or adapting to a contemporary market and continuing to operate today (Interview N15; Interview N21; Interview N22; Interview N29; Maiorana 1997). The strong Italian character of the neighbourhood was also reflected in the establishment of the Casa d'Italia (or 'home for Italians', now the WA Italian Club) on Fitzgerald Street in 1937[10] (Interview N21; WA Italian Club 2009). The Greek influence was apparent in the construction of the first Greek Orthodox Church in Western Australia, the Church of Saints Constantine and Helene.

The Greek and Italian cafés in Northbridge were the first to be allowed *al fresco* dining, now an institution in the suburb and an important aspect of its contemporary appeal. Over several decades, these cafés were also important centres of socialising and social support for newly arrived immigrants and those struggling to adapt to their new environment. The stores and cafés were sometimes able to offer employment and often able to provide comfort with familiar foods (Interview N20; Interview N27). Evangelia Demetriou, the daughter of Greek immigrants who owned a shop in Northbridge, remembers her mother saying that on arriving in

Northbridge she relied heavily on the few Greek stores like the Kakulas brothers' delicatessen because she:

> just couldn't eat any of the food. She dwindled away to nothing because she was just so used to Greek cheese and olives... and back in those days the Australian cuisine was tasteless, and she just couldn't adjust, so having the Kakulas brothers store was her link to the homeland... and her life line. (Interview N20)

Like the Chinese, many of the early southern European immigrants were single men, and illegal gambling houses replaced the Chinese opium dens (Interview N2). Hostels provided housing and functioned as unofficial welfare and employment agencies. The number of Italian and Greek immigrants in Northbridge increased considerably after World War II (Kringas 2001; Stransky 2001), often via 'chain migration' (Price 1963) with travel costs often paid for by family members already settled in Northbridge or via a state-sponsored assisted migrant scheme (Interview N20).

No longer referred to as Perth's Chinatown, the concentration of Greek and Italian businesses and homes in Northbridge led to the new colloquial names of 'Little Megisti' (reflecting the birthplace of most of the area's Greek residents) and 'Little Italy'[11] (City of Perth 1989, p. 5; Peters 2007). After this string of colloquial names, the whole district was officially named Northbridge in 1981 (Northbridge History Project [NBHP] 2005, p. 2).

Historian and social scientist John Yiannakis has critiqued the tendency of some Australians, particularly before the introduction of the policy of multiculturalism in the 1970s, to group 'peoples from southern Europe as if they are of one entity', noting it is a 'gross generalization' and stressing the importance of ethnic and national differences between Greeks, Italians and others (Yiannakis 1996, p. ix). This tendency was apparent among Perth's Anglo-Celtic residents in the mid-twentieth century. For example, Nicholas Alexiadis, a Greek immigrant who migrated to Northbridge as a young man after World War II, remembers that when he arrived:

> Australians weren't very ah, (nervous laugh)... they weren't very well learned because they couldn't distinguish the difference between Greeks and Italians... They were all 'wogs' you know, so very few Australians were really socially educated to know the difference. (Interview N3)

While the many different immigrant groups in Northbridge throughout the 1950s maintained distinct cultural and religious traditions, Northbridge in this period and through to the 1980s is fondly remembered by many who grew up there as a friendly, family-oriented neighbourhood where these many different cultures happily co-existed. For example, Kay Phua, a woman with Chinese heritage who grew up in Northbridge and has retained a strong connection to the area through her involvement with the Chung Wah Association, remembers the effect of this cultural mix:

> growing up, I was unaware that I was Chinese... because growing up in Northbridge, as much as there weren't a lot of Chinese, there were Greeks, there were Italians, and everyone was talking their own languages and I just thought that was normal. (Interview N25)

Similarly, Robert Conti, who was born out the back of his Italian father's butcher shop in Northbridge, remembers the area as a 'safe haven' from the racism and discrimination he experienced elsewhere. In Northbridge, there was 'freedom of expression, no discrimination, the whole lot... That only existed here. Over the other side of the [railway] line we were the foreigners, we were the outcastes' (Interview N15).

From the 1950s, immigration laws began to be relaxed and, while the number of Chinese living in Perth remained small during the 1950s and early 1960s, the Colombo Plan saw Chinese students begin arriving in Perth from Asian countries like Malaysia and Singapore. By the 1960s, laws were changed to allow non-Europeans to settle permanently in Australia. From the end of the decade, Chinese from Malaysia, Singapore and Burma (some of them former students under the Colombo Plan) took up residency in Perth. In the 1970s, Vietnamese refugees began to settle in Northbridge and the surrounding suburbs.

Like those before them, many of these minority immigrants established their own small businesses. Some of the area's Greek and Italian shops remained but they were now joined by Vietnamese and Chinese restaurants, Asian butchers, and a number of professional services targeting an Asian clientele. The growth of Vietnamese shops and restaurants along north William Street prompted the new nickname for that area of 'Little Saigon' (Peters 2007). From the 1960s, Chinese restaurateurs from Sydney, Melbourne and Brisbane also moved to Perth and established restaurants in Northbridge to take advantage of Western Australia's mining boom. While there had been two Chinese restaurants in Perth in the early 1960s, by the mid-1970s there were nearly 200 (Atkinson and Yee 1986, p. 3).

Today, Northbridge's population continues to evolve. A real estate boom in Perth, and the proximity of Northbridge to the city, have led to a significant increase in housing costs and a gentrification of existing properties. Wealthy urban professionals have displaced many of the earlier immigrants, with immigrant groups such as Italians and Greeks having moved further out into the suburbs in a process of 'upward mobility', only to see Northbridge's inner city housing later become highly sought after and rapidly increase in value (Interview N20).

While Northbridge currently has only a small residential population (with a significant number of houses demolished to make way for freeway developments since the 1960s), the number of residents is set to increase in the short term as a number of new high-density housing projects are completed. According to the 2016 Census, just over 1300 people lived in the suburb at that time, with almost half of them Australian born (see Table 4.1). The largest immigrant group was from South Korea, followed by those from England, Hong Kong and Malaysia. The census recorded that only nineteen Northbridge residents were born in Italy and three were born in Greece. It is interesting to note that in the neighbouring suburbs within the Town of Vincent, Italian, New Zealand and Irish born residents were the largest immigrant groups after the English (Australian Bureau of Statistics [ABS] 2019a).

Table 4.1 Country of birth of Northbridge residents, top ten countries, 2016

Country of birth	*Persons*
Australia	301
South Korea	88
England	48
Hong Kong	43
Malaysia	38
China	35
Taiwan	33
New Zealand	24
Singapore	24
Ireland	19
Total residents	1307

Source Author's calculation based on ABS (2019a)

Ancestry data (Table 4.2) reveal that the number of residents with Italian and Greek ancestry in Northbridge was higher than the numbers in the respective birthplace groups (48 people with Italian ancestry and 7 with Greek). While only 9 people identified that they had been born in China, almost 170 recorded Chinese ancestry. Nonetheless, the data show the predominance of residents from Anglo-Celtic backgrounds in Northbridge (note especially the 344 people claiming English, Irish or Scottish ancestry), again suggesting the relocation of many earlier non-Anglo-Celtic immigrants away from the suburb.

As the residential population of Northbridge has changed, many immigrant entrepreneurs have re-branded their product to appeal to a professional middle class. For example, several of the original immigrant grocery stores now market themselves as gourmet food stores, selling high-quality products and a wider range of European, Asian and Middle Eastern foods. With its diverse restaurants and food stores, Northbridge has become one of the most popular sites in Perth for both locals and tourists to experience a range of ethnic cuisines.

The built environment of Northbridge also remains clearly cosmopolitan or multi-ethnic. As well as being visible in the buildings of its small businesses, the traditional role of Northbridge as immigrant repository is evident in built form in its community buildings, many of which are now important icons. The area is home to Perth's first

Table 4.2 Ancestry of Northbridge residents, selected groups, 2016

Ancestry[a]	*Responses*
English	199
Chinese	170
Australian	126
Korean	87
Irish	85
Scottish	60
Italian	48
German	28
Indian	23
Filipino	21
Total responses	997

Note [a]This question in the Census is multi-response—total responses may not equal total number of persons
Source Author's calculation based on ABS (2019a)

Greek Orthodox Church, first Italian Club, first Vietnamese Buddhist Temple, first Chinese association and Western Australia's first mosque. In addition, it has remained an important meeting place for the Nyoongar community and a key site for Nyoongar political organisation.

4.1.2 Northbridge as an Ethnic Precinct

While Little Megisti, Little Italy and Little Saigon were unofficial titles, they illustrate that even by the early 1900s Northbridge had begun taking on the informal characteristics of an ethnic precinct. As noted earlier, a key feature of ethnic precincts is the changing face of buildings for the provision of ethnic food and ethnic restaurants (Gabaccia 1998; Warde and Martens 2000). In Northbridge, the majority of immigrant entrepreneurs have established restaurants or wholesale and retail food stores. This is a common pattern among immigrant entrepreneurs, perhaps reflecting the relatively low entry costs and qualifications needed for these industries (Collins et al. 1995). While most of Northbridge's early immigrant entrepreneurs catered to a local market, in recent decades the restaurants and food stores have become popular among residents, tourists and visitors. As in Sydney's Chinatown, this reflects changing public attitudes to immigrant minorities and ethnic foods. Also mirroring developments in Sydney, in recent decades local and state governments have recognised Northbridge's ethnic diversity as a potential attraction.

As well as offering a wide variety of ethnic cuisines, goods and services, Northbridge hosts several annual festivals that reflect the area's immigrant history. Chinese and Vietnamese New Year celebrations, the Greek Glendi festival and a world music festival are all held in Northbridge each year. The annual Northbridge Festival highlights contemporary arts and acknowledges Northbridge's ethnic diversity, with the 2007 programme including a Chinese orchestra and history tours pointing out important sites in the area's immigrant heritage. Northbridge is also a key site for other cultural events including the Perth International Arts Festival and annual gay and lesbian Pride Parade, reflecting not only its diverse history but also suggesting a relationship between sites of ethnic diversity and other culture industries. Tourism in Northbridge has also developed around more traditional cultural attractions such as the Western Australian Museum, Art Gallery of Western Australia and Perth Institute of Contemporary Arts that are all situated at Northridge's east side.

With its combination of ethnic diversity and cultural industries, Northbridge closely approximates Michael Keith's (1995) conceptualisation of a cultural quarter. Tourist brochures for Perth advertise Northbridge's mainstream cultural institutions, late-night entertainment and ethnic diversity as a 'package' of attractions, encouraging tourists staying elsewhere in Perth to visit the area during their trip.

Licensing laws have also altered the character of Northbridge, significantly influencing its transformation into a destination for tourists and visitors. That is, Northbridge is one of the few districts in Perth where clubs and pubs remain open into the early morning. As a result, it has become synonymous with late-night entertainment. This is one example of how regimes of regulation help shape not only the tourist experience but also the character of an area (Hoffman et al. 2003), with the presence of many clubs and nightclubs in Northbridge and the late-night service of alcohol both attracting some tourists and visitors and repelling others. Many of the tourists attracted to Northbridge's pubs and clubs are backpackers, and Northbridge has become one of the key sites in Perth for backpackers' accommodation.[12] Backpackers' hostels bring thousands of tourists to the area annually as well as providing a ready source of labour for the local hospitality industry.[13] One local entrepreneur who is active on Northbridge business committees notes that this pool of labour has been significant during Western Australia's mining boom and resultant labour shortage in the cities:

> while we have a growing economy, trying to find staff is very difficult... [but] we actually have this huge pool of workers that can work within the precinct because they live close and they... could be here for twelve months, or two years, or six months and they do have a working visa so they can slot in and earn an income. (Interview N13)

Northbridge is also still Perth's 'red light' district, with the main streets of Northbridge housing a number of sex shops and massage parlours interspersed with restaurants and other shops. Like the licensing laws and nightclubs, this has a mixed effect. As will be shown in the next section, while it brings some visitors to Northbridge, others prefer to eat out in nearby suburbs with a more 'family' atmosphere.

4.1.3 Visitors' Voices

While licensing laws, the development of cultural institutions and the re-orientation of immigrant entrepreneurs to a mainstream market have opened up opportunities for tourism in Northbridge, little is known about its visitor base. A 1989 study of Northbridge found that many shoppers came to the area for the availability of 'ethnic goods' (MEAC and OMA 1989, p. 31). Visitor surveys discussed in this chapter were carried out in November 2006. The majority of respondents (around two thirds) were visitors who lived elsewhere in Perth or in nearby urban centres. A further quarter of respondents were domestic or international tourists. Like in Sydney's Chinatown, the most popular reason for visiting Northbridge was to eat (almost half of all respondents). A small number specified that they came for particular foods such as yum cha (Visitor QNO9), Chinese food (QNO3, QNO27) or bubble tea (QNO42, QNO65). Unlike in Chinatown, however, several respondents specified that they were visiting Northbridge for other cultural attractions such as art galleries and cinemas (QNO5, QNO7, QNO51). A number reported that they were in Northbridge to drink (QNO45, QNO82, QNO100).

These responses reflect Northbridge's diverse cultural attractions, while Chinatown's main attractions are its Asian shops, restaurants and services, as noted in the previous section Northbridge is known for its mix of ethnic enterprises and restaurants as well as bars, nightclubs, galleries, fashion stores and sex shops. This mix was clearly reflected in people's responses to the question '*What, if anything, distinguishes Northbridge from other parts of the city?*' In Chinatown, the large majority of people answered the equivalent question with reference to the area's 'Chinese character'. In Northbridge, many people did point to the area's cultural diversity, whether its diversity of people (QNO14, QNO52, QNO61) or Chinese, Vietnamese or other ethnic enterprises (QNO3, QNO38, QNO53, QNO97). One respondent saw Northbridge as Perth's Chinatown (QNO39). Still more respondents, however, pointed to other features of Northbridge as evidence for its distinctiveness from other parts of the city. Many saw it as distinct because of its 'night life' or late opening hours (QNO4, QNO11, QNO46, QNO62). Others noted its business and vibrant atmosphere (QNO13, QNO37, QNO68, QNO96); the *al fresco* dining (QNO17); the sex shops (QNO57, QNO99), the heritage buildings (QNO5) or the concentration of clubs, pubs and restaurants all in one area (QNO12, QNO28, QNO59).

Like its social and commercial landscape, the architecture of Northbridge's main streets is very varied. Colonial heritage buildings with large verandahs and elaborate metalwork sit side by side with modern, concrete, almost windowless buildings. The Chinese *paifang* on Roe Street (discussed in the next section) and red and green awnings on a number of shops provide the extent of the Chinese theming. Among survey respondents, this architectural variation was sometimes seen as 'too random' (QNO24, also QNO5). Others specified that they liked the heritage buildings or disliked the more modern concrete ones (QNO7, QNO18, QNO28, QNO37). One respondent liked the mix of styles: 'it's good to see Chinese architecture in combination with European style buildings' (QNO8). Just as in Sydney's Chinatown, some respondents said that they did not look at or notice the architecture (QNO11, QNO14, QNO34). While Northbridge provides an example of a 'multiethnic' precinct, the limited use of ethnic theming in its built environment minimises the concerns about racialisation that have been identified in Sydney's Chinatown.[14]

Respondents in Northbridge were significantly more likely than those in Chinatown to report feeling unsafe in the precinct. In Chinatown, 91 of 100 respondents said that they felt safe there, while the equivalent number of Northbridge respondents was 72. Importantly, over half of these indicated that they only felt unsafe at night. As will be discussed below, in recent decades Northbridge has developed a reputation for being unsafe after dark and it is known by police as a major trouble spot. This appears to have significant influence on the way people use the site, with several respondents indicating they avoid Northbridge at night and/or go home early if having an evening meal in the area (QNO64, QNO80). When asked what they did not like about Northbridge's atmosphere, a number of people made reference to violence or other unwelcome behaviour: 'people start fights, angry drunk people late at night' (QNO1); 'at night too many drunk men' (QNO15); or 'at night it's scary' (QNO80). A number of people specifically referred to being approached by people: there are 'lots of drug addicts, you get approached when on your own' (QNO7); 'lots of people come up to you and ask for things' (QNO16); 'junkies hang around hassling for money' (QNO28).

Some people linked their feelings of being unsafe or uncomfortable to the presence of particular groups: 'there's a lot of shady characters, half castes,[15] people that don't have much ethics in their makeup' (QNO3); 'too many Chinese or Japanese' (QNO11); 'too many young trouble makers' (QNO26); and 'at night there are many drunk people, violence, lots of Aboriginal people' (QNO86). One Aboriginal respondent suggested that 'a lot of people here don't like Aboriginals' (QNO100). While several people made reference to Indigenous people, the Western Australian police report that violence and crime in Northbridge are largely alcohol-fuelled rather than related to any one ethnic or Indigenous group (Interview N7).

Like in Sydney's Chinatown, while some survey respondents described their ethnicity or cultural background with fairly standard labels ('Chinese' QNO15; 'Scottish' QNO20; 'Australian' QNO26; or 'Caucasian' QN040), others reflected the 'fuzziness' of the concept. For example, responses included 'multicultural' (QNO8, QNO45), 'mixed' (QNO49), 'Outside White, inside ethnic Chinese and Middle Eastern'(QNO69); 'International, like all Australians' (QNO72); 'a mix of Indian, Burmese, German and Irish' (QNO71); and even 'culturally confused' (QNO19). A small number referred to their own ethnicity as 'normal' (QNO33, QNO52), possibly suggesting a lack of cultural reflexivity.

4.1.4 Regulating Northbridge

Ethnic precincts do not exist in an institutional vacuum. They are shaped by the interaction of producers (including immigrant entrepreneurs), consumers, governments, residents, community organisations and Zukin's (1995) 'critical infrastructure'. While the local government in Sydney promoted the redevelopment of that city's Chinatown in the 1970s, in Perth a mining boom staved off the imperative for state-led redevelopment throughout the 1980s. However, with the onset of economic recession of the early 1990s, much of Perth's office space became empty and the city's economy began to slide.

In Northbridge, the problems were compounded by competition in retail and hospitality from suburban shopping precincts and a new casino development in East Perth that created competition as the city's entertainment centre (Interview N20). In addition, there was longstanding uncertainty over the major freeway development through the suburb's north. As noted above, the reservation of land for the freeway in the 1960s had caused a residential decline. In the 1990s the construction of a cut-and-cover tunnel caused traffic dislocation and a loss of business confidence (NBHP 2005, p. 2). In addition, with Northbridge's immigrant communities moving away, the state government was increasingly concerned that 'Northbridge was losing its special and distinctive qualities' (NBHP 2005, p. 2). At the same time, Northbridge was gaining a growing reputation for crime and violence, at least in part associated with the consumption of alcohol at its many clubs (Interview N20).

In response to these concerns, the local (City of Perth) and state governments embarked on a new programme to attract investors and consumers to the city, believing that the solution was to create a new identity for Perth's central area, including Northbridge. As Iveson (2000, p. 229) describes:

> one of the main roles identified for government was investment in public space improvements which it was hoped would create a 'sense of place' and thus encourage shoppers, tourists, residents and employers back to the Central Area.

The state programme of action has been concerted and ongoing. For at least five years, the 'reinvention' project has attempted to recast Northbridge in its old image of safe, vibrant and culturally diverse entertainment centre. Evangelia Demetriou, introduced above, became a City of Perth councillor. She explains that she:

> just could not comprehend how an area that was just so vibrant, so magical, full of life could suffer such an adverse identity crisis... The City, State Government and other key stakeholders are working together to implement new projects aimed at restoring the Northbridge image. (Interview N20)

Evangelia's sentiments are echoed both elsewhere in the City Perth and across a number of state government agencies. In 2000, the state government statutory authority the East Perth Redevelopment Authority (EPRA) was given control over a large portion of Northbridge, previously governed by the City of Perth.[16] The entry of EPRA into the playing field divides 'greater' Northbridge[17] into three separate local jurisdictions: roughly, the City of Perth between Roe and Aberdeen Streets, EPRA along both sides of Newcastle Street, and the Town of Vincent north of Newcastle Street to Brisbane Street.[18]

The continued revitalisation of Northbridge is coordinated under the Northbridge Board of Management, established in 2005. Chaired by Councillor Evangelia Demetriou, the board includes representatives from the City of Perth, EPRA, the Western Australian Police, the state Department of Premier and Cabinet (DPC) and Tourism Western Australia. It also includes members of the Business Improvement Group of Northbridge (BigN). This group was established by local entrepreneurs in 2002 on the recommendation of the City of Perth and includes local business owners, workers, residents, community groups and even buskers. It has the stated aims of improving the area's physical, aesthetic and community amenities for locals and visitors and improving the area's safety and reputation.

The City of Perth and the BigN approached the relevant agencies to form the Northbridge Board of Management. According to one local entrepreneur and chair of the BigN, Peter Adamos, the board 'meets regularly to identify the projects that we need to work on in Northbridge as well as provide funding for those projects'. Funding comes from the City of Perth, the state government and EPRA. Recommendations of the board are subsequently put into action by a full-time precinct manager. Reflecting the close coordination of the agencies involved, while the precinct manager is funded by the City of Perth, EPRA and the Department of Premier and Cabinet (DPC), she also acts as the full-time representative of the BigN, liaising with local business owners (Interview N20) and reporting back to the Board of Management (Interview N13).

The strategy for creating a 'sense of place' in Northbridge has included major physical redevelopments such as the construction of several multi-storey commercial and residential complexes, some social housing and retail space (Interview N19). EPRA has bought several retail properties on William Street and is developing a rental plan to dictate the types of businesses that can operate there.[19] The City of Perth is planning to develop the 'Northbridge Piazza', a public square in central Northbridge, including space for commercial tenants, community facilities and a gallery, as well as an open area, stage and 24-hour LED screen to allow for performances and special events. The aim is to make the area a 'commercial, cultural and creative hub' for Perth (City of Perth 2007). The plans to create a sense of place to attract consumers to Northbridge have also included two additional elements: a focus on the area's ethnic diversity and strategies to improve safety.

In describing the transformation of cities into centres for cultural consumption, Zukin (1995) emphasises the importance of creating a 'vision' of the city to capture the imagination of tourists and corporate elites. She suggests that this is a contested process, with 'constant political pressures by interest groups and complex interwoven networks of community groups, corporations, and public officials' generating multiple visions that may not be easily reconciled (Zukin 1995, p. 14). In Northbridge, the 'vision' has included a focus on the area's ethnic diversity in at least two distinct ways. The first includes two attempts to market the area as Perth's 'Chinatown'. The second includes a number of approaches that draw on Northbridge's multi-ethnic character.

By the early 1980s, with the influx of Asian immigrants in the area, a small group of Malaysian Chinese businesspeople began to plan a Chinatown for Northbridge. The plan aimed to 'retain and enhance the character and ethos of the Orient within a totally planned modern environment', complete with Chinese arches, awnings and iconography (Chinatown 1982, p. 1). The proposal roughly coincided with the redevelopment of formal Chinatowns in Sydney and Melbourne on Australia's east coast (see Anderson 1990). All three were attempts to market an area on the basis of its ethnic character and were indicative of similar developments in other western cities. However, the motivation for developing a Chinatown in Northbridge had a unique aspect: in promoting the concept, the developers made explicit reference to using the development as a leverage point for securing permanent residency visas for foreign nationals who would be employed in the proposed Chinatown (Chinatown 1982).

The developers purchased land on Northbridge's southern edge (along Roe Street) and constructed Chinese arches leading into two parallel laneways. The original plan was to purchase surrounding properties to also include over 30 specialist Asian food stalls, a Chinese theatre, a 49-bed hotel, entertainment facilities and professional offices (Chinatown 1982, p. 1). However, this broad-ranging plan was never fully implemented because of three key factors: poor positioning, the reluctance of property owners to sell to the developers and the blow-out in interest rates in the late 1980s. The development was limited to the two short laneways that are lined on either side with narrow shops. The Chinese arches mark the entry to the laneways at the Roe Street end (Fig. 4.1).

This small 'Chinatown' has gained limited interest. The two laneways run along a narrow strip of land between a busy main road and railway line

Fig. 4.1 Northbridge's 'Chinatown' on Roe Street has no pedestrian thoroughfare (*Source* Kirrily Jordan)

at the Roe Street end and a small parking lot at the other (it is significant that the laneways extend only half way into the block and do not join up to James Street). While the area is close to the main shopping streets of Northbridge, particularly James and William Streets, there is no visual indication on either of these streets that the Chinatown exists. The arches may provide a clear visual cue, but they are of limited use in attracting visitors as very few pedestrians walk along Roe Street, an area dominated by large industrial and commercial buildings and virtually devoid of retail premises. As of 2008, the shops along Chinatown's two laneways included a handful of Chinese restaurants, a hairdresser and a Chinese tea house. A number of shops remained vacant.

While the plans for this Chinatown were never fully realised, twenty years later a second attempt to create a formal 'China Town' in Northbridge began to gather momentum. This attempt was spearheaded by Town of Vincent Mayor Nick Catania who wanted to develop a 'readily identifiable and popular precinct' that 'for want of a more appropriate name might be called "China Town"'. He suggested that a formally defined and marketed Chinatown was appropriate for any city wanting to be taken seriously on the global stage, with 'almost every major city in the world [boasting] a colourful and culturally diverse "China Town"' (Town of Vincent 2006, p. 1). Here, Catania's argument is very similar to the one made by Brisbane's lord mayor and reported on in David Ip's research (2005, p. 69), with the mayor suggesting that 'every self-respecting city' has to have a Chinatown. It indicates that, at least from the perspective of elected city representatives, just the presence of a Chinatown is seen as a significant card in the stakes to become a 'global city'.

However, following consultation with business owners and residents in upper William Street, it became clear that the proposal had limited support. In particular, many of the businesses were owned by non-Chinese entrepreneurs, including Vietnamese, Thai and Japanese. Even some ethnic Chinese entrepreneurs felt little connection with China, having been born in South-East Asia. The proposal was also opposed by some members of Perth's peak Chinese organisation, the Chung Wah Association, who felt that establishing a formal Chinatown did not accurately reflect the area's history and ran the risk of both alienating members of the non-Chinese community and stereotyping Chinese. Kay Phua, introduced above, explains that, for her, the idea of developing a Chinatown in north William Street:

> is rather puzzling because the Chinese weren't really big at that end of town, and in fact there's a Mosque up there and all sorts of other things... Northbridge has always just reflected migrant history as such so, it's never

> been sort of, Chinese or whatever... it doesn't have the history behind it. (Interview N25)

In addition, Poon suggests that:

> [for] a lot of the Chinese... the word 'Chinatown' makes them cringe, cause there's also these connotations of very, ah, untoward and unsavoury types of going ons... we're not really trying to create that kind of precinct area so to speak because we feel it's just, not going to benefit the community as a whole... the people within the community say they always have this negative feeling about it... for those that don't have [a commercial] interest in it they definitely don't really want to... be promoting it. (Interview N25)

Similarly, Wang Wei, a prominent local Chinese immigrant from Malaysia, thinks the existing 'Chinatown' on Roe Street is 'very artificial' and he does not support the creation of a new Chinatown:

> *Wang Wei*: Personally I don't like the idea just to create... artificial gates that signify the Chinatown...I think it's very artificial... that itself is purely for those non-Chinese to identify this is Chinatown, but it can be very misleading...
> *Interviewer*: And does the symbolism of those arches have any meaning for, say for Chinese from Malaysia?
> *Wang Wei*: Not to me, not to me.
> *Interviewer*: And I've heard some talk of there being an idea for a Chinatown up in William Street. Would you feel the same way about that?
> *Wang Wei*: Yes, I do. I do...I think it is just a marketing strategy and nothing else. And I also don't like the connotations of a Chinatown, because... always it's associated with... gangsters, you know, especially in the North America. Try to specially create it, to create an object to travellers, a 'Chinatown.' That doesn't work well with me. (Interview N4)

Kay Phua and Wang Wei's concerns reflect the common academic critiques of ethnic precincts canvassed earlier. Hence, as we have seen in Sydney's Chinatown, in 'branding' an ethnic precinct, decisions about what symbols are appropriate, who decides, and how, are crucially important. Notably, opposition to the creation of a Chinatown among local Chinese in Northbridge is not universal. For example, another prominent local Chinese immigrant (and former president of the Chung Wah Association), Dr Graham Chen, supports the idea of a Chinatown in William Street as a way to create more colour and interest in the landscape:

> I think we now in this place needs colour, I think it's a dull... so, yeah, the more colour we have the better. But do it not as some symbol of racial symbols but as a way of saying, you know, there are these cultural myths around. I would be just as happy if the French... built a mini Eiffel Tower and the Italians have a Leaning Tower of Pisa... we just need more colour. (Interview N23)

Nonetheless, acknowledging community concerns in Northbridge, Nick Catania backed down on the plans for a China Town, saying that:

> In deference to the area's diversity of cultures, both past and present, we refer to the proposal [for redevelopment] simply as William Street... Whilst the name may be a bit contentious, the philosophy behind the area is not. (Town of Vincent 2006, p. 1)

With the plan to create a formal Chinatown sidelined, the redevelopment of William Street will include public art that incorporates symbols from the area's diversity of ethnic groups.

The second, and more successful, approach to marketing Northbridge's ethnic diversity has involved a greater recognition of its cosmopolitan or multi-ethnic character. Broadly, this has been done in two ways. Drawing on input from public forums and advice from representatives of government, business groups and Greek, Italian, Chinese and Indigenous community organisations, EPRA has constructed public places that recognise some of the area's diverse ethnic groups[20] and 'the contribution that those groups have made to the community' (Interview N19).

For example, 'Piazza Nanni' is a public square that celebrates the first Italian priest to oversee Northbridge's Italian catholic congregation, while 'Plateia Hellas' (Fig. 4.2) is a square that acknowledges Northbridge's Greek community[21] (EPRA 2000b). Calling on public suggestions for street names that recognise prominent Northbridge figures, EPRA has also named several roads in honour of local Italian, Greek and Chinese families. These include Via Torre, Kakulas Crescent and Hoy Poy Street.[22] Along with the inclusion of social and public housing in the Northbridge redevelopment, EPRA see this is part of a strategy to 'try

Fig. 4.2 Plateia Hellas, Lake Street, Northbridge (*Source* Kirrily Jordan)

and maintain… the vibrancy and the diversity of Northbridge' (Interview N19).

The BigN and Northbridge Board of Management have also been conscious to highlight the area's immigrant diversity as an asset. Peter Adamos, the local entrepreneur and chair of the BigN introduced earlier, notes the great diversity of cuisines available in Northbridge and the potential of this diversity to attract tourists and visitors:

> If you have a look around you have a variety of different cuisines, and I'm talking a large variety ok, Greek, Italian, Irish, English, Chinese… Iranian, Lebanese, oh, I can go on, there's much more. I mean that's quite unique. You go to other precincts around Western Australia, it does not possess that… we are quite proud that we have such a diversity of cuisines in Northbridge. (Interview N13)

In addition to the work of EPRA, the BigN and the Northbridge Board of Management in marketing and redeveloping Northbridge, the state

Department of Premier and Cabinet has funded the Northbridge History Project. This project was developed in response to a 2002 report by the state Department of Premier and Cabinet called *Northbridge: Shaping the Future*, which recommended 'understanding and embracing' the history of Northbridge in order to 'create diversity, interest and business and tourism opportunities' (NBHP 2005, p. 2). The project aims to recognise the area's history through public signage, public art, exhibitions and walking tours and to use this heritage not only to create 'a "sense of place and ownership" for residents, business people and visitors' but also to rejuvenate the area in an 'authentic' way and inform decision-making in urban design, business development and tourism and marketing strategies (NBHP 2005, p. 2, see also NBHP 2007).

The Northbridge History Project has involved extensive community consultations over several years. The project is steered by the Northbridge History Reference Panel which (as of 2008) includes 'community leaders' from Chinese, Italian, Greek, Vietnamese, African, Nyoongar and Asian associations, as well as representatives from the Perth Mosque and Perth's Jewish, Roman Catholic and Gay and Lesbian communities, all of which have an important part in Northbridge's diverse history. Members of the panel also include representatives from local and state government organisations (including the mayors of the City of Perth and Town of Vincent and representatives from the Western Australian Police, EPRA, the local TAFE [Technical and Further Education] and the Department of Culture and the Arts) as well as business and community groups with a history or interest in the area (such as the BigN, the Western Australian hotels association, the Cabaret Owners Association and Unions WA) (NBHP 2008). The aim of the reference panel is to 'ensure that the Project reaches community and interest groups' (NBHP 2005, p. 2).

The formal consultation plan, developed in 2005, outlined a five-stage process to gain community input. This included: (1) the creation of the reference panel; (2) a series of public 'Discovery Workshops' with different ethnic or interest groups; (3) individual and online submission of materials; (4) a 'Public Summary Presentation' at the conclusion of the Discovery Workshops; and (5) an ongoing Community Consultation Group of volunteers. A separate 'Research Panel' of relevant academics and experts was also developed to 'ensure the history is as inclusive as possible' (NBHP 2005, p. 4). As of 2008, members of the larger ethnic groups with a history in Northbridge—including Greek, Italian and Chinese—had been consulted, along with other groups and individuals such as those with Irish, Macedonian, Vietnamese or Jewish heritage. The project had also engaged with Perth's Gay and Lesbian community as well as local institutions. While some groups had been consulted more formally through community meetings, others had been involved as individuals.

Throughout the consultation process, a significant degree of creative control has been retained by the contributors, with the consultation plan having stipulated that the project team would be 'guided by how the Community would like the Project findings to be used' and that consultations with the reference panel, community consultation group and other 'key stakeholders' would occur before any decisions were made (NBHP 2005, p. 4). In practice, different groups have decided to display their heritage in different ways. For example, while the Italian contributors developed information panels to be displayed in the windows of Italian-owned shops, other groups decided on temporary photographic displays or simply to contribute to a central archive of documents and photographs. Greek contributors focused on oral history interviews, the collection of photographs and a mapping exercise to record the Greek shops and residences that have existed in Northbridge over time (Interview N29).

The materials contributed to the Northbridge History project have been used in developing an online database and an educational tool for high school local history studies programmes. A new initiative of the Northbridge History Project is the 'Look Up! Northbridge' history tours, which show visitors some of the key ethnic institutions in the area.

While much of the recent effort to market Northbridge's ethnic diversity as an attraction for tourists and visitors has drawn on community consultation, criticisms of this approach remain. For example, some long-standing Anglo-Australian residents have argued that in the effort to revalorise Northbridge's immigrant history the area's Anglo heritage has been overlooked (Interview N5). In addition, while the development of Plateia Hellas has drawn on input from public forums and ethnic community representatives, there is some disagreement over whether its location on Lake Street is appropriate: while the street was home to several Greek residences, it also housed a number of Italian shops. That Italian heritage is not recognised in the Plateia (Field notes N23.11.07). There is also some criticism that the design of the Plateia is not particularly Greek[23] (see Interview N29).

Such concerns have not led to widespread dispute or resentment, with most parties willing to accept the outcomes of the planning process. However, the concerns do reflect the difficulty in finding consensus about symbols of ethnicity in areas with a multi-ethnic or cosmopolitan history. As we have seen in Sydney's Chinatown, even when ethnic precincts take on a 'mono-ethnic' identity, the legitimacy problem becomes one of which among the 100 or so ethnic Chinese community groups in Sydney gets included in decision-making processes (and even which people within those community groups). For multi-ethnic precincts, like Northbridge or Sydney's Cabramatta (Collins and Castillo 1998), the problem of legitimacy becomes more apparent.

Like in Sydney, concerns over the use of ethnic symbols may also reflect the limitations of traditional planning processes such as public forums and key stakeholder consultations in engaging people from ethnic minority groups, effectively limiting the number and range of voices that are heard (Stewart et al. 2003, see also Burayidi 2003; Sandercock and Kliger 1998a, b; Thompson 2003). These problems are compounded where ethnic minority groups are multiple-origin, small or scattered, a condition described by Vertovec (2007) as 'super-diversity'. The political implications are significant. As we have seen, where different ethnic groups, organisations or even individuals have differential access and input into decision-making processes, it reflects a cultural unevenness in urban citizenship, with some denied the full accordance of rights and responsibilities in decision-making about the design and use of public space (see Dunn 2003, p. 154).

'Selling' Northbridge to tourists and visitors has also involved efforts to improve safety. The issue of tourist safety is central to any government tourist strategy. Control and surveillance play an integral part in the development of tourism in general, especially in potential tourist precincts such as ethnic neighbourhoods. Body-Gendrot (2003, p. 39) emphasises the importance of 'techniques of social control and security' that mega-event tourism, such as the Olympic Games or World Cup soccer events require. Borrowing from Foucault, Edensor (1998) notes that in shopping malls there is a 'remorseless surveillance through panopticon visual monitoring'. Shopping is encouraged, but, as Judd (Hoffman et al. 2003, p. 29) argues, 'aimless loitering is discouraged or forbidden'.

There are a number of aspects of control and surveillance that relate to ethnic precincts. The first relates to the historical social construction of minority immigrant and Indigenous communities as criminal (Collins et al. 2000) so that the places and spaces where they concentrate attract a criminal reputation. This is reinforced by the way that racism, prejudice and xenophobia construct immigrant and Indigenous minorities as the criminal 'Other' who are a threat to the safety of the host society (Poynting et al. 2004). Ethnic precincts of minority immigrant groups are thus constructed as places of crime such as gambling, drugs and prostitution and of criminal gangs at the same moment that they are marketed as enticing and exotic attractions.

In Northbridge, safety at night has been an ongoing concern over the last two decades. Media reports have linked crime to the area's ethnic diversity, focusing in particular on crime purportedly committed by Nyoongars and alleged Vietnamese gangs (Mac Arthur 2007; MEAC and OMA 1989; Rayner 2003). While they exaggerate the link between crime and ethnicity, concerns about violence in Northbridge have not been unwarranted. Being one of Perth's main venues for late-night entertainment, alcohol-fuelled violence has been a recurrent problem. Late-night brawls outside Northbridge's pubs and clubs are not uncommon, although the perpetrators are not limited to any one ethnic group and the attacks are rarely racially-motivated (Interview N7). However, the tendency of some Nyoongars to congregate and drink in Northbridge's parks or walk along Northbridge's main streets asking restaurant patrons for money has exacerbated perceptions of a lack of safety. To an extent, this practice may be associated with the continued and systemic socio-economic disadvantage of many Indigenous Australians. However, it also indicates a significant cultural difference in the use of public space, with parallels here to Wise's (2005) research on cross-cultural tensions where there are disjunctures in habitus.

Recognising concerns about personal safety and the potential negative impact on consumer visitation and demand, the Northbridge Board of Management has made safety a key issue. Under their revitalisation programme, regular police patrols now have a more visible presence in Northbridge in order to limit fights erupting outside pubs and clubs. Police work alongside the Nyoongar Patrol, introduced in 1998 in response to concerns about Indigenous people congregating in Northbridge's public spaces. In contrast to trends in places such as the United States that have seen the increasing privatisation of security (see, e.g., Zukin 1995), the Nyoongar Patrol is a publicly funded, community-based programme under which Aboriginal workers with limited formal powers patrol Northbridge and attempt to resolve situations with Nyoongars before police action is needed. The aim is to prevent enmeshment with the criminal justice system (Blagg and Valuri 2004; Government of Western Australia 2008).

The Nyoongar Patrol has been praised by police and other government agencies as a critical early intervention and outreach strategy and effective in reducing public complaints (Government of Western Australia 2008). The presence of young Indigenous people on Northbridge's streets is also controlled through a youth curfew, introduced by the state government in 2003. Under the curfew, any unaccompanied children who are in Northbridge at night can be picked up by police and taken back to their families or to a refuge (Cox 2003).

These approaches to policing in Northbridge highlight the tensions between everyone's rights to use a public space, including young people, and the negative impact that a history or reputation of conflict, violence or 'public nuisance' has on tourism and the profitability of ethnic enterprises. Entrepreneurs in Northbridge, particularly those in hospitality businesses that rely on evening trade, have long expressed concerns that they are losing business due to the reputation of the area as unsafe, and there is no evidence that Northbridge attracts the kinds of 'vice tourists' identified by Kinkead (1993).

While Northbridge's entrepreneurs may therefore applaud the youth curfew and its potential to reduce public nuisance, it has been heavily criticised by lawyers and rights activists for its disproportionate impact on Indigenous youth, with almost 90% of children picked up during the first three months of the curfew being Aboriginal (Rayner 2003). It has also been argued that the curfew reinforces false stereotypes of young and Indigenous people as being disproportionately responsible for crime, while failing to address underlying causes of young people being out alone at night (Cox 2003; Mac Arthur 2007).

In addition, while the state government and police have praised the work of the Nyoongar Patrol, it has been criticised by local business owners who see it as a 'taxi service' taking intoxicated people to sobering centres rather than deterring criminal behaviour (Government of Western Australia 2008). In 2005, the City of Perth withdrew a significant share of its funding for the programme, backing business concerns that it does not act as a deterrent to criminal conduct (*The West Australian* 2005).

The state government's continued support of the youth curfew and the City of Perth's wavering support for the Nyoongar Patrol have led to criticisms of government 'visions' of Northbridge's diversity. For example, it has been argued that in seeking to market the area's cultural diversity, planners have drawn on romantic notions rather than the lived realities of people on the streets, with diversity including 'al fresco dining, shoppers and workers and tourists intermingling, jazz bands and farmers markets' but excluding subgroups such as Indigenous people and youth (Iveson 2000, p. 231).

In addition, while the Northbridge History Project was presented as an opportunity to 'ensure the traditional custodians of the land can tell their stories about their connection to the area' and 'contextualize the longstanding relationship of Noongar people with the area and promote understanding between the Indigenous and wider community through shared histories' (NBHP 2005, p. 3), as of 2008 there was some recognition that 'the Indigenous side [of the project] probably needs a bit more work' (Interview N25). At the same time, though, government efforts to improve the perceptions and realities of safety in Northbridge may enhance the prospects for profitability among local entrepreneurs and the vibrancy and enjoyment of the precinct for the majority of visitors. These are important concerns that must be weighed up against the risks of ethnic stereotyping when determining a suitable approach to policing and place-marketing. To complicate the matter further, Peter Adamos from the BigN has argued that *too much* formal policing in Northbridge is now deterring visitors to the area and 'unfairly' targeting Northbridge when other inner-city areas also have problems with crime (*The West Australian* 2009).

4.1.5 Cosmopolitan Monuments in Northbridge

4.1.5.1 Perth Mosque

Perth Mosque is located on William Street in the inner city suburb of North Perth.[24] Having been built in 1905, it is the second-oldest surviving mosque in Australia (after the Adelaide Mosque), and the oldest mosque that has been in continuous use.[25] It was built by cameleers who had come to Australia from south Asia to run camel trains into the western and central deserts in the mid to late 1800s. Although they have usually been referred to in Australia as Afghans, these cameleers came from the regions now known as Afghanistan, Pakistan and India (Interview N1; Fazal 2001, p. 164). Camel handlers who arrived in this period also included men from Iran, Egypt and Turkey. The term 'Afghan' has been used to refer to all of these men, in effect being adopted to mean 'cameleer' and hence distinguish the camelmen from other immigrants from south Asia who came to Australia as agricultural workers. A descendant of one of these early cameleers who is now closely associated with the Perth Mosque, here called Irfan, explains that:

> back in those days... [the cameleers] in WA were mainly Pakistanis, and they were from the north of Pakistan... near the border of Afghanistan, so they are all sort of lumped in together. But in actual fact... they were predominantly Pakistanis not Afghanis... my grandfather was one of them, one of the guys who actually had one of those camel trains that used to go between [Perth] and the east coast. And anyone who sort of did that was sort of called Afghani in that sense. (Interview N1)

While some of the cameleers were Sikhs and Hindus, most were Muslims. All were expected to return to their countries of origin after their employment contracts ceased (Dunn 1999, p. 227).

The first Muslims in Australia were the Macassans who camped temporarily on Australia's northern and north-western coasts as they hunted for trepang. Hence, the first Islamic places of worship on the continent would likely have been temporary sites used seasonally by these visitors. As Kevin Dunn notes, these sites may only have lasted 'for the four months of their stay' (Dunn 1999, p. 228). While the Macassans visited the coasts periodically, most Afghans stayed in Australia for long periods and many settled permanently. According to Abdul Khaliq Fazal, they were 'the founders of the Islamic religion in Australia' (Fazal 2001, p. 164). As they travelled between the coast and the remote interior, the early Afghans 'were remarkably resilient at maintaining their culture, and particularly their religious faith and practice' (Dunn 1999, p. 229). The rituals of daily prayer were observed even while the cameleers were on treks, 'with each cameleer carrying their own individual prayer mat, often having to settle for a symbolic ablution using dry sand or dirt when water was not readily available' (ibid., p. 229). The Afghans also established camps and settlements both in remote regions and the growing cities, and at these camps (often known as 'Ghantowns') they commonly built mosques.

The earliest mosques were 'mud mosques' or 'bush mosques', often made from wattle-and-daub techniques with thatched roofs. This type of construction was common in Ghantowns that sprung up in outback towns and stations. Many of the bush mosques were later replaced with structures made from wood and iron (ibid., pp. 233–234). They were typically 'small square buildings with a pointed roof, slightly separated from the other Ghantown buildings and sometimes sited on an elevated point of land' (ibid., p. 234). In the capital cities of Perth and Adelaide (SA), the mosques were made from brick and stone (ibid., p. 233). In the bush (rural) mosques, 'unofficial leaders' emerged, often the older men, the leading camel hands or the owners of the camels (ibid., p. 234). Their duties included calling the faithful to prayer, leading the prayers, maintaining the mosque and educating the younger men about Islam (ibid., pp. 232–234). Bush mosques were also visited from time to time by 'professional Imams' who would take over religious leadership and settle any unresolved disputes (ibid., p. 234).

As well as providing a central site for building mosques and practising religious observances, the development of Ghantowns allowed the provision of some welfare services for the Afghan cameleers. For example, 'charity housing' might be offered to those in need, such as older or destitute Afghans (ibid., p. 232). While the Ghantowns were 'fringe settlements' that were poorly serviced by local authorities and suffered with typhoid outbreaks and the threat of bushfires, they provided 'social support' and 'cultural maintenance' in a largely hostile cultural environment (ibid., p. 232). According to Kevin Dunn's extensive research, there were six Ghantowns in Western Australia, in Kalgoorlie, Wiluna, Coolgardie, Marble Bar, Fremantle and Port Hedland (ibid., p. 232). In these towns and cities, as elsewhere in the country, Afghans faced significant prejudice. The Anti-Afghan League (sometimes referred to as the Anti-Asiatic League) was established in the Western Australian goldfields in 1894.[26] The league was established amid fierce resistance from gold miners to the arrival of Afghans and other immigrant groups, particularly Chinese. It had the support of 2000 miners across nine branches and aimed to have Afghans and other Asians removed from the goldfields (Stevens 1989, pp. 144–145). Residents of Kalgoorlie also petitioned the government to prevent further Asian and Afghan immigration, citing 'the serious danger to the health, morality and general wellbeing of the white population, through the presence and continuous influx of Asiatics into this colony' (King 1998, p. 43).

Dunn (1999, p. 232) notes that the Afghans' strong maintenance of cultural and religious traditions set them apart from white settlers and 'enhanced the ridicule, vilification, marginalisation and sometimes violence they suffered'. Resentment towards the cameleers was also exacerbated by their industrial success: the horses and bullocks used by Anglo-Celtic transport teams were no competition for camel trains in the desert regions.[27] Stevens (1989, pp. 139–141) reports that raids on camel camps, verbal attacks on Afghans and even fist fights were common as horse teamsters tried to protect their former monopoly of bulk transport from the threat of competition from the 'Afghan camel invasion'.[28] Despite this 'constant ridicule and religious intolerance', the Afghans 'tenaciously clung to' their religious practices (Stevens 1989, p. 167), with Ghantowns providing a 'short-term escape from vilification and violence' (Dunn 1999, p. 232).

In the capital cities of Perth and Adelaide, the more permanent brick and stone mosques were built with funds from the cameleers, including funds collected from *Zakah*.[29] Adelaide's mosque in Little Gilbert Street took at least ten years to build, from the inception of the project to when building was completed in 1899. The mosque was later extended with anterooms, a madrasa, minarets and accommodation. In Perth, the planning of the mosque also took ten years, with the foundation stone laid in 1905 (Dunn 1999, p. 233). The original mosque consisted of a small prayer room—the interior elaborately hand-painted—and a cottage. Like the Adelaide Mosque, it was later extended with the construction of a madrasa and anterooms. An additional prayer room was built for women (ibid., p. 233). The façade of the original section has a high tripartite parapet, with the upper parapet apparently having functioned 'as a tower, en lieu of a minaret, for the call to prayer' (HCWA 2009a). Construction of the original mosque building was funded by the Afghan cameleers (including the wealthy and renowned camel owner Faiz Mahomet) and was designed and built by Din Mohammed (HCWA 2009a).

In an early annual report, the committee of the Perth Mosque noted their intention to ask the state for a grant of land for building a place of worship, as was given to those of other religious groups: 'We... trust that the government of the state will be pleased to extend a helping hand to us by granting a piece of ground for the use of the Mosque, treating us in the same manner as other Denominations, who have received grants of ground for the use of their respective churches and synagogues'. However, the committee were denied the government grants given to other religious denominations and met with difficulties in obtaining municipal planning permissions (Dunn 1999, p. 233). As well as these frustrations, the mosque committee was beset with ethnic tensions (cf Vertovec's concept of superdiversity). In an agreement about the management and control of the mosque signed on 13 August 1906, reference is made to 'several Mahammedan communities resident in Western Australia', with access to and control of the mosque and its facilities to be shared equally between five groups:

> Afghans of the one part, Indians (including Punjabies, Bengalies, Sindhies and other races of India) of the second part and Syeds of the third part, and Baloochies (including Brohies and Mekranies) of the fourth part, and Arabs and other various Mohammedan races of the fifth part.

Distinctions were also made between 'Pishori' and 'Durranie' Afghans, and a Cingalie, a Malay and two Sikhs are also recorded as having been associated with the mosque in 1905–1906 (Cleland, n.d.). Despite the August agreement, ethnic tensions persisted. In November 1906, a senior Islamic figure, His Holiness Agha Syed Mohammed Padshah, visited the Perth Mosque from Port Hedland over 1500 kilometres up the west coast. He was appointed to conciliate between the different ethnic groups, and a resolution was made by the mosque community that they would manage the mosque more cooperatively. Representatives for the Afghans and Indians were appointed. In 1919, a new set of rules for the mosque was drawn up. Article 7b reinforced the distinctions between Afghans and others, stating that:

> So long as any present member of the mosque of Afghan nationality...shall be residing in Western Australia one of... [the] Trustees shall be elected by the Afghans voting separately for the election of such Trustee. The other Trustee shall be elected by the members of the mosque who are not of Afghan nationality. (Cleland, n.d.)

Even as recently as the mid-twentieth century, the special place of Afghans in the mosque was reinforced. Amendments made to the management rules following World War II excluded non-Afghans from taking on the role of mosque leader, and strictly defined who could claim to be Afghan:

> Whenever the word Afghan is used in these rules it shall mean a person irrespective of his place of birth whose parents, both father and mother, are Afghan of full blood and whose parents resided in Afghanistan or in the North west Frontier Province of Pakistan. (Cleland, n.d.)

The definition excluded the Australian-born where both parents were not Afghan.

While ethnicity remained an important signifier within the mosque, the mosque community were also acutely aware of religious prejudice outside it. In November 1906, a report on the progress of construction of the mosque noted that:

> The Mosque as now built has all necessary conveniences attached to it for ablution, etc., to satisfy the present requirements, and the cottage has enough accommodation for those of our brethren who stay in Perth temporarily and who are unable to find accommodation in public hostels in the city on account of the prejudice at present prevailing amongst the inhabitants of this country against colour and Asiatic races. (Cleland, n.d.)

However, from the earliest days of the mosque's construction the mosque committee were concerned with improving the understanding of Islam among the general public. In 1905, they agreed that any surplus funds after the mosque was built should be used to establish a public library and reading room:

> in order to enlighten all those gentlemen who often want to know whether we belong to the Roman Catholic or Protestant Church, or whether we worship the sun, moon, the stars, fire or other material objects. (Cleland, n.d.)

While the Perth Mosque has remained in continuous use since it was built, for many decades the number of Muslims attending regular prayer meetings was very small. For example, Irfan notes that during the 1960s and '70s the regular gatherings for prayer saw around 30 people attending the mosque, including Pakistani, Afghan, Egyptian, Turkish and Lebanese families. However, during the 1980s the numbers 'soared' as large numbers of Asian students started arriving in Perth (Interview N1). This prompted the renovation and expansion of the mosque complex in the late 1980s and early 1990s (see Fig. 4.3), with the construction of an additional prayer room, a library and a kitchen. The complex now also includes an office, accommodation for the Imam (who lives at the mosque full time) and two rooms for short-term visitor accommodation. The original room is still used as the main prayer hall, and numbers at regular Friday prayers can now reach around 200. On special occasions such as celebrations for Eid, numbers have been as high as 1000. Many

Fig. 4.3 The Perth Mosque, 427-429 William Street Perth, in 2005. The original prayer room is on the right (*Source* Kirrily Jordan)

of the students who now use the mosque are Indonesian, Malaysian and Pakistani, and there are also some people from Iran and Egypt. Mosque users also come from as far as Bunbury and Albany on the southern WA coast. While the mosque used to run a Sunday school for children to learn about Islam, the growth of private Islamic schools in Perth has meant that there is now little demand. Instead, the Imam can tutor children on request (Interview N1).

Today, the complex ethnic make-up of the mosque's congregations is recognised and is celebrated at special events. For example, at the 2005 celebrations for the mosque's 100-year anniversary, the many guests were served meals that deliberately incorporated specialties from the different regions mosque-users come from in order to highlight the mosque's ethnic diversity (Field notes N20.11.05). As of November 2007, mosque leadership was still held by a Pakistani (who would formerly have been known as an 'Afghan'). While some mosques in Perth were subject to significant attacks and displays of violence (including firebombings) post-September 11 2001, the Perth Mosque has so far escaped relatively trouble-free. As Irfan explains, following the terrorist attacks in the United States the local police called the mosque to warn of possible attacks and suggest increased vigilance, but:

> The only thing that we got was graffiti on the wall... [and] we get graffiti anyway. But apart from that no, for some reason the Perth Mosque was actually very lucky... we didn't have a lot of trouble, or nowhere near as much as the some of the other mosques in Perth did. I'm not quite sure why, because the mosque is fairly visible, you can't really miss it. (Interview N1)

At around the same time, some of the students who were attending the mosque approached the mosque's manager about initiating an open day. Irfan explains the rationale:

> especially post 9-11... we just thought that the image of Muslims around the world was fairly bad... so we thought that as, not so much as PR, but to get a bit more awareness in the general public about the mosque and of Muslims in general, it would be a good idea if we start to hold a few open days and things like that... Because the more the general public knows about us, the better informed they will be, so their bias towards Islam, it will hopefully break down the barriers that people do have. (Interview N1)

For Irfan, the task is to increase non-Muslim's exposure to Muslims and to Islam in order to challenge pervasive stereotypes:

> the majority of my friends are actually non-Muslims... they know me, they know what I am like, and if they ask me we talk about religion and things like that... so they generally know what Islam is like in that sense. But the average Joe who doesn't know any Muslims or anything like that has this perception that Islam is out to conquer the world and kill people... I would like to see that view changed, and I don't know how in the near future you are going to do that, apart from holding open days and just generally educating the general public. (Interview N1)

The original intention was to have an open day at the Perth Mosque twice a year. However, since the organisers are often international students who have exam commitments and tend to return home during holidays, the open days have been held less often (Interview N1). Irfan explains that the events have usually been held over a weekend, with the total number of visitors usually around 100:

> It hasn't been huge ... they normally do it over a weekend, over a Saturday and Sunday. I think the total numbers for the last one were maybe about 100 to 150 people. So, it's not small, but it's not huge... the numbers have increased quite significantly... Which is a good thing, you know. (Interview N1)

The Perth Mosque was listed in the local government's Municipal Heritage Inventory in 1995.[30] This means that any works (beyond routine maintenance and refurbishments that do not compromise the heritage significance of the site) are subject to a strict approvals process by the Town of Vincent. In practice, this has been interpreted by the mosque committee to mean they 'cannot touch' the old sections of the mosque complex:

> And that's actually heritage listed... so you can't actually touch the old section of the mosque, which is why we've sort built round it rather than sort of touching that because it's been there for so long. (Interview N1)

However, the mosque committee planned to significantly extend the mosque complex. In 2005, they bought the neighbouring block to make room for new developments. While the proposed extensions have stalled due to difficulties in getting council approval, the plan is well-developed:

> What we would like to do is extend the new sections again, build another prayer hall, to build a proper library—people could come in who want to read or, like you, if you want to find out about the mosque or Muslims or things like that, they can go to the library and do that sort of stuff ... and [we would also build] a bit more accommodation for visiting guests and things like that. (Interview N1)

The plan also includes building three commercial shops at the front of the property on William Street in order to bring in a revenue stream for the mosque. As Irfan explains, most of the existing renovations and extensions to the mosque complex have been paid for by donations and bank loans, often relying on a few major donations by a small number of wealthy individuals. This has been bolstered by revenue from providing certification services for halal meat exporters, but according to Irfan this revenue is unpredictable:

> the main problem the mosque has, and with most churches also I suppose, is the lack of money. Apart from donations and things like that the mosque, up until three or four years ago, didn't have any real source of income, it has a bit now... [with] halal certifications... [but] that was up and down you know, depending on the meat business. So that's why we sort of say 'that's fine' but we need to also generate a steady income... That is why we are looking into building a shop. (Interview N1)

While the mosque could access government grants, particularly as it can get funding related to its heritage listing, Irfan admits that grant funding is an option the committee would rather avoid:

> if we have wanted to do something we have been able to pretty much do it privately... rather than going down that path [of government grants]... I know because it's heritage listed there are different options available to us. But... the less we have to deal with government as such... the better off we are in the long run. (Interview N1)

4.1.5.2 Chung Wah Association Hall

The activities of Chinese in Western Australia were legally restricted as early as 1886, when legislation was passed to restrict Chinese in the pearling and gold mining industries. While the Anti-Afghan (Anti-Asiatic) League vehemently opposed the presence of Afghans in Western Australia, members were equally as convinced that Chinese immigrants were a threat. Anti-Chinese sentiment was promulgated by some of the major publications of the time, with *The Bulletin* in particular running an ongoing campaign to restrict Chinese immigration and deny rights to Chinese. In 1887, the publication proclaimed that 'No nigger, no Chinaman, no lascar, no kanaka, no purveyor of cheap coloured labour, is an Australian' (King 1998, p. 37). By 1891, *The Bulletin* had produced a 'manifesto' that denounced four things: religious interference in politics; foreign titles; imperial federation; and the Chinese (King 1998, p. 37).

The 1901 Immigration Restriction Act, anti-Chinese prejudice and restrictive factory acts had a profound impact on the Chinese who had settled in Perth. At Federation in 1901, Perth's Chinese community were active participants in the city's celebrations, carrying a long

Chinese dragon down St George's Terrace while thousands of spectators looked on (see King 1998, p. 45). But with the first act of the new Australian parliament enshrining the principles of a White Australia, the celebrations were short lived. Informal groups of Chinese 'protested against the harshness' of the new laws and, in 1902, sought to have a Chinese Consul-General 'appointed to Australia to protect Chinese interests' (Atkinson and Yee 1986, p. 1). One descendant of a Chinese furniture maker who worked in Northbridge in this restrictive period recalls the personal impact of the anti-Chinese policies, noting that his father was not allowed 'to go into certain furniture shops in the front door'. Instead, he had to 'go around to the back' to sell them his wares: 'they didn't want him to be seen coming in through the front door. It was quite hard for a lot of them in those days' (Interview N25).

In the face of such ongoing hostility and legal restrictions, community meetings were held among the Chinese in Perth to discuss the idea of forming a united association. At the time, there were just under 850 Chinese living in the city and surrounding suburbs. At a series of informal and official meetings (with the first official meeting held in Wing Sang's business in Murray Street), those in attendance agreed to form the Chung Wah Association (King 1998, p. 56; Atkinson and Yee 1986, p. 1). Members elected to the executive committee included representatives of Chinese market gardeners from each of the main gardening regions (Osborne Park, Guildford, Bayswater and Fremantle) as well as Chinese laundry workers (Atkinson 2001, p. 215; Atkinson and Yee 1986, p. 1).

The Chung Wah Association—which translates from Cantonese as the association for Chinese people (Interview N25)—was officially established in 1909. While at least two Chinese organisations (the Friendly Society and Emperor Reform Society) had been formed in earlier years, the CWA became the first registered ethnic association formed in Perth. At its inception, the association had around 600 members (Atkinson 2001, p. 215) and the monthly meetings, held on Saturday evenings, usually attracted around 60 people (Atkinson and Yee 1986, p. 1). The association aimed to meet 'the social, cultural and political needs of the Chinese in Western Australia' (CWA 1996 in King 1998, p. 57). It became a 'voice for the Chinese people' at a time of widespread anti-Asian discrimination (Interview N25) and committed to 'do its utmost to investigate and examine cases where members are bullied or ill-treated' (CWA minutes, April 1909, in King 1998, p. 57). In its early days, the association:

> not only provided a substitute family for the community (which consisted almost entirely of single men who were forced to leave their families in China), but was also a means through which individual Chinese could find communal protection and voice their protest against laws aimed at restricting the lives of Chinese in Western Australia. (CWA 1996 in King 1998, p. 57)

The forward to the minutes book from the association's meeting in April 1909 noted the importance attached to forming a united Chinese association:

> Unity is strength and an Association is vitally necessary. If there is no Association there is conflict and a feeling of not belonging anywhere. The overseas Chinese living in Western Australia are far away from the several thousand strong community in the other states ...We are like scattered sand, it is no wonder that the Westerners are bullying us, passing stringent legislation aimed to displace us. Our countrymen should consider this situation and not ignore their responsibility to the community ... Solidarity is the best plan. (King 1998, p. 56)

Only one month after the members officially registered the association they made arrangements to buy land and build a new premises at 128 James Street—in the heart of Northbridge and adjacent to several Chinese shops. The site was also 'across the road' from the fruit and vegetable markets where Chinese market gardeners often sold their produce (Interview N25; see also HCWA 2002, p. 4; King 1998, p. 60). The building was to have two storeys, the upper floor providing a hall for meetings and social functions and the ground floor housing two shops that were to be rented out to bring in an income for the association (King 1998, p. 60). The facilities would also include a committee room and 'two large kitchens, and a special kitchen for festival days and other appointments' (*The West Australian* 1910 in HCWA 2002, p. 5). The cost of building the hall was financed through membership fees and fundraisers as well as a mortgage taken out to allow work to get underway, with the foundation stone laid in October 1910.[31] The CWA hall was officially opened at Chinese New Year in 1911, with a celebratory banquet for 260 members held upstairs (King 1998, p. 60). It was the first building built by and for an ethnic group in Perth (Atkinson 2001, p. 215). Designed by non-Chinese architects and adopting characteristics of the established Federation Free style, the building itself had 'little expression' of the ethnicity of the user group (HCWA 2002, p. 2; 2009b). Kay Phua, introduced earlier, suggests that this may have been simply because Perth's Chinese community did not have 'the funds at that time to warrant that type of venture', instead choosing an affordable design in the period style (Interview N25). Kay Phua also notes that with the community's limited numbers and resources building the hall at all was an 'amazing feat' (Interview N25). While Sydney and Melbourne had much larger Chinese populations than Perth, the CWA hall:

> was built even prior to Melbourne and Sydney's Chinese community having a community hall being built... I find it rather an amazing feat because... obviously [Perth's Chinese] were not earning an awful lot of money. (Interview N25)

The significance of the CWA's achievement was duly noted among the Chinese in the eastern states, with a 1910 article reporting on the construction of the hall in the Sydney-based Chinese newspaper the *Tung Wah Times* betraying a competitive spirit:

> Although there are not as many Chinese as we have in Sydney, and commerce and business are not as great, now they have an Association. It is surprising we do not hear about Sydney and other cities doing the same thing. Compared to Perth we should be ashamed ... All the Chinese in Sydney should stand up and not allow WA to claim the praise alone. (*Tung Wah Times* 1910 in HCWA 2002, p. 5)

From its earliest days, the CWA had three main objectives: to provide welfare services, education and cultural activities (CWA 2009). Early forms of welfare activity included giving financial support to elderly or sick Chinese who wanted to return to China. Kay Phua explains that the association:

> would basically follow up any problems that you might have had... so if there was a problem and someone elderly was trying to return to China because they could no longer work, quite often they would not have enough money to return home. So... [the association] would pay the costs for sending someone back home. If anyone needed to go to the courts for whatever reason, they would assist if need be, if they needed translations or representations. (Interview N25)

In its first years, the association held many social functions and fundraising activities, making repayments on the mortgage as well as funding the group's welfare work and the purchase of needed items like tables, tableware and banners. The association also made donations to charities and causes both in Western Australia (the Royal Perth Hospital, the Red Cross, the European War Fighting Fund, the children's hospital and orphanage) and China (to support the victims of floods in Anhui and Guangdong). The association's cultural activities included establishing a library for members, with books from China and newspapers from Hong Kong ordered through local Chinese businesses. By 1923, the association had also established the first Chinese school (King 1998, pp. 62–63).

Like the Chinese Youth League and Chinese Masonic Society in Sydney, the CWA was active in supporting the republican movement in China. Several members were also members of the Kuomintang (KMT). In 1911, the CWA organised members to raise money for Sun Yat-sen and Chiang Kai-shek's Revolutionary Army, with £1200 collected in that year. Following the successful revolution, the relationship between the CWA and the KMT continued, with the first meeting of the KMT's Perth branch held in the Chung Wah hall in 1921 (King 1998, p. 65).

The CWA's links with the revolutionary movement in China meant that it was at the centre of Chinese political activity in Perth. Its location in James Street also placed it at the centre of Chinese commercial activity, with James Street and adjacent William Street forming part of an early 'Chinatown'. While the CWA Hall has been in continuous use by Chinese organisations for 100 years, maintaining the CWA became increasingly difficult during the mid-twentieth century as the White Australia policy saw the number of Chinese in Western Australia rapidly decline. The period from the 1920s to the 1960s saw the CWA kept alive by a 'skeleton committee' (King 1998, p. 94; CWA 2009), with the local Chinese population reduced to only a handful of families (Interview N26).

In 1922, struggling to meet costs with its dwindling membership, the CWA decided to rent out its hall on condition that the tenant would 'hire back' the hall to Chung Wah members when needed (CWA 1996 in King 1998, p. 65). The association's members determined that the hall could only be hired to either the KMT or the Chinese Christian Society, with the KMT eventually taking on the lease. It is believed that the KMT continued operating from the hall into the 1940s (King 1998, p. 65). One early member of the Chung Wah who grew up in Northbridge, here called Hiu Tung, recalls that during this time the association 'went very quiet for a while' and was 'almost closed' for around ten years or more (Interview N26). However, the association did continue some activities including fundraising to support the Chinese during the second Sino-Japanese War and to support the Australian war effort during World War II (Interview N25).

With the relaxation of immigration laws from the 1950s, the CWA was revived. In 1951, the association re-registered after a period in which registration had lapsed and wrote a new constitution along 'similar lines to the first' (Atkinson and Yee 1986, p. 2). The number of members was small, with only ten members required for a quorum at general meetings, and three required for a quorum of the executive committee (Atkinson and Yee 1986, p. 3). From the 1950s to the 1970s, small numbers of Chinese arrived in Perth from several Southeast Asian countries, especially Malaysia, Burma, Vietnam and Singapore. The doors of the CWA were opened to these new immigrants in 1970, and 'immediately, some of them were invited to join the committee and take an active role in the affairs of the Association' (Atkinson and Yee 1986, p. 3). The association also negotiated a lease with a Chinese restaurant to operate on the ground floor, with the revenue allowing the renovation of the now dilapidated hall. Between 1951 and 1972, membership was free, and by 1973 a membership drive saw the number of members increase to almost 200 (Atkinson and Yee 1986, p. 3).

During the 1960s and early 1970s, the activities of the association were focused on the social needs of members. Wang Wei, a past president of the association introduced earlier, explains that during this period 'there was no need for welfare services' since most members of the association were either Australian born Chinese who could access mainstream services or new migrants with professional qualifications who were 'financially... very well off anyway so they can look after themselves' (Interview N4). However, what was needed was 'social contact' so the association organised many social activities including a food fair, picnics and dances (Interview N4).

In 1975, a new constitution was written that expanded the objectives of the association beyond the prevailing emphasis on social activities. By moving away from assimilationist public policy and recognising and affirming the 'diverse cultural, linguistic and religious backgrounds of the Australian people' the federal policy shift towards multiculturalism (Matwijiw 2001, p. 782) facilitated the association's renewed attention to cultural activities. Another past president, here called Ming, suggests that this rejuvenation of the association, often lead by new professional migrants from Malaysia, was part of a process of 'coming out' for the Chung Wah and for the Chinese community in Perth. According to Ming, until this period the:

> Chung Wah Association was very much a sleeping sort of organisation... the community was thrive in those days on being inconspicuous, and that came from the necessity to survive in a hostile environment... [but] it came to a stage where they need to 'come out', almost and say, 'yeah, we are here'. (Interview N23)

With a renewed focus on cultural activities, the association began to publish a regular newsletter and established a Chinese class for children on Saturdays.[32] By the 1980s, this had become one of the largest ethnic schools in Western Australia. From the 1970s, the association also began to reach a broader audience by using new media, contributing to a weekly Chinese radio programme. A new fundraising drive raised around $20,000 to renovate of the building's kitchen and construct two new offices in the hall and a new ablution block. From the 1980s, cultural activities were established to 'meet the needs of young families to maintain our language and cultural heritage', including a Chinese orchestra, singing and dancing groups, tai chi classes, a lion dance troupe, a dragon boat group and a literary and arts group (Atkinson and Yee 1986, p. 4).

Many of the Chung Wah's cultural activities were popular among Chinese youth, particularly lion dance, Chinese dance and dragon boat racing. Lion dance was taught at the Chinese Saturday school (Yee 1996, p. 2). In 1990, the Chung Wah's Lion and Dragon Dance Troupe 'performed beyond expectation' in international competition in Malaysia, finishing seventh out of twenty-three teams from eleven countries. The same team made the finals four years later in Hong Kong (Yee 1996, p. 3). The Chung Wah's lion dance troupe is dominated by young people, with the dozen-or-so members in 2007 ranging from ages 13 to 20. While many have Malaysian-Chinese backgrounds, there are a few from other backgrounds such as Hong Kong Chinese or Vietnamese and, according to one member, there is always the 'token Aussie... some Aussie's they just love the Chinese culture' (Interview N17). The troupe, which is financially independent from the CWA and pays for its own expenses from performance fees, performs at a range of events from house-warmings to business openings to festivals and balls. The troupe has also performed for Chinese investors at a mine site outside of Perth. One member of the troupe, Mei Li, in 2007 notes that although the performers are all unpaid volunteers, she enjoys participating because:

> I like to show the community, the public what lion dance is about, it's a really good feeling. So it's like voluntary work, but I don't see it as voluntary work because I like to do it so much... just to show what our culture is about. (Interview N17)

She also enjoys challenging stereotypes by showing that girls can perform in this physically demanding sport and recalls the reaction after her first performance at a large Chinese community event:

> you got out of the lion head and for people to realise that you're a girl—you could see everyone's mouth just drop open. And so just that rewarding feeling of, you know... it's half a feminist thing, but another half to say that you can break the cultural, traditional barriers of just only guys doing these kinds of things. Girls can do it easily as good. (Interview N17)

For one member of the Chinese dancing group Chung Wah Dance, participating in the group has been an important social and cultural activity, allowing her to make new friends as well as providing 'a sense of staying in touch with your culture and from where you came from' (Interview N24). Like the lion dance troupe, Chung Wah Dance is self-supporting financially, providing classes for free or for a minimal charge, and paying its costs through performance fees.[33] The group also pays a Chinese dance teacher and, in 2007, fundraised to pay for a two-week trip to a Chinese school in Shanghai to develop their skills in Chinese dance. With an average of 15 members across a range of ages, the group performs at festivals and balls as well as special events such as the opening of a Chinese garden in Kalgoorlie in 2007 (Interview N24).

In 1990, the formation of a Chung Wah Youth Group brought together all the young members from the various dancing, cultural and sporting groups. Prior to the formation of the youth group, 'any young member [of the Chung Wah] who was not interested in these activities was left out. As a result, the Association suffered a lack of young members' (Yee 1996, p. 3). The youth group organised cultural tours to China in 1990, 1992 and 1994 (Yee 1996, p. 3) and held regular social events such as balls and ballroom dancing classes (Interview N24). By the mid-1990s, the number of young members of the Chung Wah was growing (Yee 1996, p. 4) with increased Chinese immigration. However, while members of the Chung Wah still participated in China tours with groups from the eastern states, the Chung Wah youth group eventually disbanded and groups such as the lion dance troupe began to struggle to attract new members. Mei Li, introduced above, suggests that reasons might include the increased busyness of people's lives (one troupe leader left after he bought a house and got a full-time job) and the tendency of younger children to be more sedentary and choose computer games over more active leisure time (Interview N17). In Mei Li's view, 'everything's happening faster, people are maturing faster', so attracting and keeping members is an increasing challenge. Wang Wei, too, notes that encouraging young people to stay involved in the Chung Wah once they have work and family commitments is 'quite a mammoth task' (Interview N4). However, Mei Li is optimistic that the lion dance troupe can attract new members by targeting teenagers (through 'open days' to introduce them to the sport) and university students, with Chinese international students often finding themselves without 'anything to do' in their leisure time (Interview N17).

As well as developing its cultural activities, in the 1980s the renewed CWA maintained an interest in Chinese politics, passing a motion to support 'public condemnation of the Chinese Government' after the events in Tiananmen Square in 1989 (Yee 1996, p. 3). The association also took on an increasing role in domestic politics in Australia. 1984 had seen growing tensions over Asian immigration, fuelled by comments made by historian Geoffrey Blainey in which he expressed concern about the level of Asian immigration and warned against a 'slow Asian take over of Australia' (Blainey in Foster and Stockley 1988, p. 224). One year later, the anti-Asian Australian National Movement (ANM) was formed in Perth by Jack Van Tongeren. As Graham Chen recalls, during that time:

> people were hostile and increasingly so... there was this undesirable element of Van Tongeren lurking around... where every street you see, you know, posters saying 'Asians out'. (Interview N23)

With the ANM attempting to drum up racism around Perth, the executive committee of the CWA held a special meeting to discuss the appropriate response. They subsequently made a representation to the state minister for multicultural affairs to express their concern about racist posters (Yee 1996, p. 1). With the 1988 suggestion of then Opposition Member of Parliament John Howard that the rate of Asian immigration to Australia was detrimental to social cohesion, and the tragic murder of a Chinese taxi driver in Perth in the same year, 'Anti-Asian feeling was probably at its worst' (Yee 1996, p. 2). While raising money to support the driver's family, the CWA also wrote to the attorney general of Western Australia to raise its concern. It also successfully lobbied Western Australia's parliament to support amendments to the state's legislation that would outlaw the display of material deemed racially inflammatory[34] (Interview N23). In September of 1989 members of the association 'rejoiced' along with the broader Chinese community 'when they received news concerning the arrests of the ANM leaders' (Yee 1996, p. 2), who were later jailed for terms of up to 18 years (Yee 1996, p. 2). As Graham Chen recalls, 'we came out and told people 'hey, we're here', and then we had to tackle [a racist response]... and we survived it all' (Interview N23).

In the 1980s, the CWA developed formal and informal activities to increase 'understanding and awareness of Chinese culture' in the broader community (Yee 1996, p. 1). In 1986, in conjunction with the WA Museum and the WA Multicultural Education Advisory Committee, the CWA held a series of Community Workshops in Northbridge and Fremantle in which Chung Wah members participated in group discussions with private and state school teachers. One former president of the association, Wang Wei, notes that:

> The workshops were particularly important during those days, bearing in mind that there was a frightful and unceasing attack on Asian migration and Multiculturalism. (Yee 1996, p. 1)

Efforts to engage with the non-Chinese community also included participation in the annual Oz Concert series that began in 1990 with the aims of showcasing diverse Australian cultures and generating cross-cultural unity, with the inaugural concert committee chaired by the then president of the CWA (Yee 1996, p. 3). Eric Tan describes that the Oz Concert was part of the 'coming out' of Perth's Chinese community. It was:

> to try and get... all types of people in our community to share their culture, on Australia Day, and it's purpose is to unify all Australians... Oz Concert was in many ways the symbol of when the Chinese 'coming out' they

> want to play a role not just in an exclusive way but in actually helping to reach out and uniting their community... we didn't call it a multicultural concert, we called it the Oz Concert for that purpose. (Interview N23)

In addition, the CWA's cultural activities, such as lion dancing, dragon boat racing and tai chi, were open to both Chinese and the 'wider community' (Atkinson and Yee 1986, p. 4; Yee 1996, p. 2). Non-members were also invited to participate in other cultural events such as painting exhibitions.

The CWA's interest in domestic and Chinese politics was also matched by its interest in the economic opportunities and welfare of its members. One president of the association, Wang Wei, notes that from 1985 the Chung Wah 'recognised its potential economic influence' (Yee 1996, p. 1). Unlike many Chinese associations in the eastern states where early presidents tended to be scholars, presidents of the CWA had tended to be 'professional business people', even in the early days (Interview N25). In the 1980s, the Business Migration Program introduced by the Australian federal government resulted in an 'influx' of Southeast Asian business migrants to Perth as that city became the most popular destination for Malaysians and Singaporeans. Many of these new immigrants joined the CWA and, in response to their needs and interests, the association formed a 'Business and Professional Group' and, in 1987, the autonomous Western Australian Chinese Chamber of Commerce that still functions to this day (Yee 1996, p. 1). Graham Chen notes that the business and professional group, and later the Chinese chamber of commerce, were established to support business and professional migrants:

> partly because a lot of people were... not familiar with the new country, they probably wouldn't understand sometimes what is meant on the contracts, and so some have almost lose their investment before they even start... there are unscrupulous people out there and so these are easy prey, you know, they are not very good at the language, and, particularly legal language. (Interview N23)

Membership of the Western Australian Chinese Chamber of Commerce was open to non-Chinese to create a broad business network and increase opportunities for trade and investment. The chamber hosted trade delegations from China and began a series of 'Coffee Shop Forums' where leading business people and politicians from Asia and Australia spoke to members about topical issues (Interview N23).

While most of the first members of the CWA were from mainland China, as Chinese immigration diversified, so too did the membership of the Chung Wah. From the 1960s, Chinese restaurateurs had moved to Perth from the eastern states to take advantage of Perth's rapid development during the mining boom. The mid-1970s saw the arrival of many ethnic Chinese refugees from Vietnam, many of whom did not speak English (Atkinson and Yee 1986, p. 3). Business migrants in the 1980s further diversified Perth's Chinese population and the balance of membership in the CWA shifted more towards Malaysian Chinese. The first 'Rules and Regulations' of the CWA, as spelled out in the organisation's minute book of April 1909, had stated that 'All persons of Chinese descent are welcome to join' (King 1998, p. 57). This demonstrated a significant difference from cities in the eastern states, where many of the earliest Chinese associations were clan based.

In 1951, the CWA changed the wording in its new constitution to accommodate families of mixed ethnicity, noting that the association aimed to serve 'persons substantially of Chinese descent' (Atkinson and Yee 1986, p. 2). Over the decades, the Chung Wah has continued to 'adapt to the changing ethnic Chinese population' in Western Australia (CWA 1996 in King 1998, p. 94), with membership including people of Chinese descent from Malaysia, mainland China, Taiwan, Hong Kong, Singapore, Indonesia, Burma, Cambodia, Vietnam and Brunei (CWA 2009). While accommodating members from diverse Chinese backgrounds has created new challenges in 'mutual understanding' of cultural differences (Interview N4), the association has adapted its activities to meet the changing needs. For example, when Vietnamese refugees—mainly ethnic Chinese—began arriving in the 1970s and some joined the association, social activities expanded to include music groups to accommodate the 'very talented' musicians among them, while welfare activities were introduced to assist their settlement (Interview N4).

Opening membership of the association to non-Chinese has been more controversial. With the success of the CWA's Dragon Boat Club in the 1980s and 1990s, a motion was put to the association's Executive Committee by a senior member of the Dragon Boat Club to 'accept an amendment to the Association constitution removing the restriction on ordinary membership to persons of non-Chinese descent' (Yee 1996, p. 2). At that time, the motion was rejected by a majority of nine votes to six (Yee 1996, p. 2). However, the constitution was eventually changed and, as of 2009, membership of the Ching Wah Association is open to those with no Chinese ancestry who are 'interested in Chinese culture' (CWA 2009). In addition, the association runs a School Visits Program that 'promotes inter-cultural exchange' and its Saturday classes in Chinese language and cultural activities at the Chung Wah Chinese School are 'open to all Australians' (CWA 2009; Interview N24). As of 2009, the school ran Saturday classes at three campuses and had over 1000 students, having grown from a base of only 12 students in 1974 (CWA 2009; Yee 1996, p. 2).

As well as adapting to a changed ethnic and immigrant mix, the association has also had to adapt to other demographic changes. Since the 1960s, membership and the activities offered have been much more inclusive of families, with the original association geared to the needs and interests of single men (King 1998, p. 94). With many ageing Chinese and recent migrants in Perth—including parents of earlier migrants who have arrived under the family migration scheme—the association has also increased its services in community and aged care. In 1984, the association obtained a Commonwealth government grant to employ a social worker to work with new arrivals, particular those with poor English language skills (Atkinson and Yee 1986, p. 4). Two years later they received another grant to continue the work, with one member of the Chung Wah noting later that 'without the grant it would be difficult for the association to provide its welfare services to the community' (Yee 1996, p. 1). The association had by then a full-time social worker for over twenty years (Interview N25). In 1987, the 'Chung Wah Autumn Centre' was opened to providing 'low cost accommodation and a respite centre for elderly members' (Yee 1996, p. 1). Services for the aged and for non-English speakers also include the Community Visitors Scheme, centre-based day care, Panda Community Aged Care Packages, domestic assistance, social support, transport services, respite care and migrant services. The centre-based day care programme was extended to include Vietnamese, Cambodian and Thai seniors (CWA 2009). English classes are also run for seniors and new migrants (Interview N25). As Kay Phua explains:

> The association has always, and to this day it still does, try to look after the interests of those most vulnerable in the community, and currently now we

> are looking at our seniors and those new migrants that need assistance as well. (Interview N25)

Informal programmes attract elderly Chinese to the Chung Wah hall regularly to eat together, learn conversational English, play mah jong and read Chinese magazines and newspapers (Yee 1996, p. 1; Field notes N08.11.07; Interview N26).

While overall administration of the CWA is still conducted at the James Street hall, formal community and aged care services are run from a separate office in Northbridge's William Street, and many cultural activities take place at a second, larger Chung Wah hall (known as the Chung Wah Cultural Centre) that was built in Balcatta in the mid-1990s. In the 1990s, the association had raised almost $110,000 in three years to contribute to the development, working steadily on fundraising auctions, quiz nights, concerts, dinners and cooking demonstrations as well as collecting donations (Atkinson and Yee 1986, p. 5; Yee 1996, p. 4). Additional funds were raised both to renovate the James Street hall (with significant renovations carried out in 1992) and for construction of the Balcatta cultural centre. The Balcatta centre can hold up to 500 people and is also used for concerts, annual general meetings of the Chung Wah executive committee and a fortnightly 'Canteen Day' during which meals and social services are provided to elderly members (CWA 2009). The original hall (Fig. 4.4) is still in regular use as a meeting space and for fundraising and cultural activities including mah jong, dancing and orchestra practice. Kay Phua notes that:

> there are different activities at our Balcatta site different from what we have at the James Street site. The James Street site tends to be focused more for the seniors because it is so central, it's very easy for them to get transportation in and out of town. (Interview N25)

The Balcatta site also housed a Day Long Respite Centre for seniors that operated six days each week (Kay Phua, pers. comm., 25.05.09). Ideas for the future development of the Balcatta site include developing a museum or repository for archives to properly conserve the association's history, as well as a Chinese garden and a tea house or restaurant. While the James Street hall has remained more popular among many users because of its convenient location and the vibrancy of Northbridge, Kay Phua hopes

Fig. 4.4 The Chung Wah Association, James Street, Northbridge (*Source* Kirrily Jordan)

that such developments might 'encourage people' to utilise the Balcatta site for more events (Interview N25).

With its 100-year history, the association is now the 'longest running ethnic association in Western Australia' (Interview N25) and has emerged as the 'major Chinese-based association' in the state (CWA 1996, in King 1998, p. 94). Kay Phua explains that although Chinese immigration has become much more diverse and new associations have sprung up to represent their different interests, the CWA has remained the peak organisation for Western Australia's Chinese:

> There are a lot more other Chinese associations being formed now… but we [the Chung Wah Association] are considered in the eyes of the government to be the primary group, so whenever anything needs to be done they come through us to try and filter through to the other groups…[we] have the infrastructure to be able cater for a lot of things which the other groups are only just establishing themselves, so they might just be catering for certain needs or interests, but when anything else happens they tend to look to the Chung Wah. (Interview N25)

Hence, the CWA has continued to provide 'collective socio-political representation' for the state's Chinese (CWA 1996, in King 1998, p. 94). According to Wang Wei, it has been 'the strength and soul of the Chinese community in Perth', reflecting:

> the unity of the ordinary people in the Chinese community who share the common desire to protect their interests and well being and to foster and preserve their culture and heritage. (Yee 1996, p. 4)

The objectives of the CWA still focus on the three areas of welfare, education and cultural activities. As of 2009, the broad objectives of the association are to: be an association for persons of Chinese descent living in Australia; look after the welfare and interests of its members and the state's Chinese community; foster the Chinese language, culture, customs, values and way of life; promote cohesion within Australian society; provide its members with accommodation and community centre facilities for leisure activities and education; and provide a home for the aged (CWA 2009). These activities have been carried out by approximately 200 volunteers and a small number of paid administrative and welfare staff (CWA 2009; Interview N4).

The CWA Hall was classified by the National Trust of Australia (WA) in 1998 and adopted in the City of Perth's Municipal Heritage Inventory in 2001. It was listed on the permanent register of the Heritage Council of Western Australia in November 2002 (HCWA 2002). The Heritage Council listing recognises that 'the construction of [the] *Chung Wah Association Hall* demonstrates the development of the Chinese community in Western Australia as a cultural group' (HCWA 2002, p. 1). The CWA has an extensive collection of photographs and historical materials, with additional items—such as a woven banner made in the early 1910s—having been conserved (Yee 1996, p. 2; Field notes N08.11.07). The banner, made of red and blue satin and embroidered with Chinese characters and symbols, is believed to have been made especially for the CWA (HCWA 2002) and to have been used 'during the First World War in parades to support... the Australians and to commemorate the end of the war' (Interview N25). It was restored with over twenty years of work by CWA volunteers (Interview N25) and was classified by the National Trust in 1994 (HCWA 2002). The banner is now in the possession of the Western Australian Museum (Interview N25). Kay Phua reflects on the importance of recognising the heritage embodied in both the Chung Wah hall and the banner. She notes that while the history of the association may be much shorter than the ancient history of China, it is celebrating its 100th anniversary in 2009 and it is important to start somewhere in preserving the association's heritage for the next generations:

> I suppose if we just maintain the building and make sure it doesn't fall down in a heap—which can quite often happen when you have volunteers running things, you are so busy looking after the day to day that you forget about bricks and mortar. And now that it actually has been classified hopefully we might be able to tap into some funding to maintain it... for future generations for the Chinese community for quite a while to come. (Interview N25)

4.1.5.3 Church of Saints Constantine and Helene

The first Greeks in Western Australia are believed to have arrived in 1830, although these early arrivals may have only stayed in the state for a few months and a large Greek population did not settle in the state until the late nineteenth and early twentieth century. The 1881 Census of Western Australia recorded only 14 Greeks. By 1901, the Australian census recorded that the Greek population of Western Australia had reached 148. One early settler of particular importance to Northbridge's Greek history was Athanasios Avgoustis (Arthur Auguste) who arrived in Broome in far north-Western Australia in 1891. Auguste is the first person known to have arrived in Western Australia from Castellorizo, the 'small, remote and parched' Greek island (officially known as Megisti) that lies very close to the southern Turkish coast (Yiannakis 1996, pp. x, 68). Auguste lived and worked in Broome, Perth and Adelaide before settling in Fremantle in 1904 (Yiannakis 1996). His arrival was the beginning a long relationship of chain migration from Castellorizo to the fledgling Western Australian state (HCWA 2005b, p. 5), with estimates suggesting that by 1933 around 89% of the Greek-born population of Perth were Castellorizian (Yiannakis 1996, p. 74). As we shall see in this section, the migration of significant numbers of Castellorizians to Perth and surrounds, particularly in the pre-World War II period, has had important consequences for the built and social environment of Northbridge's Greeks.

Although most early Greek migrants to Western Australia were of the Greek Orthodox faith, the first resident Orthodox priest—Reverend Chysanthos Constantinides—did not arrive until 1911.[35] At that time, there were almost 350 Greek Orthodox men and women in the state, with concentrations in Perth, Fremantle and the Eastern Goldfields (HCWA 2009c, p. 4). Following the arrival of Reverend Constantinides, the Greek Orthodox community in Perth and Fremantle attempted to establish an association to raise funds to build a church. With this initial attempt failing, a temporary arrangement was made to hold Orthodox services in an annex attached to Arthur Auguste's Fremantle home[36] (HCWA 2005b, p. 4). This meant that Fremantle residents could participate in services each Sunday, with Perth's Greek Orthodox residents attending mass 'when they could' (HCWA 2005b, p. 5).

While the earlier attempt at establishing a Hellenic association had failed, by 1912 a local Castellorizian Brotherhood had formed under the presidency of Arthur Auguste (HCWA 2005b, p. 5). It was the first Greek regional association in Australia and the second ethnic organisation established in Western Australia after the CWA (Interview N29). While membership of the brotherhood was open only to Castellorizians, the 'association did strive to handle the affairs of the Greek fraternity of Perth and Fremantle in a pan-hellenic fashion, exhibiting public and private concern for all Greeks' (Yiannakis 1996, p. 83). The primary concern of the brotherhood was the 'linguistic, cultural and religious welfare' of

Greeks (Yiannakis 1996, p. 83) including progressing the idea of building an Orthodox church (HCWA 2005b, p. 5). In this effort, local Castellorizians were able to link their activities to the church which is itself 'a potent symbol of "Greekness"' (Yiannakis 1996, p. 87).

The large proportion of Perth's Greeks who were Castellorizian, and the early formation of the influential brotherhood, contributed to a long-standing dominance of Castellorizians in the 'public affairs' of Greeks in Western Australia that lasted at least until the 1980s (Yiannakis 1996, p. x) and in many respects continues today. However, Yiannakis argues that in understanding the power structures within Perth's Greek population one also needs to acknowledge the influence of certain individuals such as Auguste. These individuals gained special prominence as the 'heads' of migrant chains, with the loyalty of newly arrived family and friends bestowing status and influence. Some 'chains' were stronger than others and marriage into a more influential chain was one 'means of augmenting your socio-economic or political standing' (Yiannakis 1996, p. 75). As Yiannakis explains:

> The large number of Castellorizians in WA does not alone explain how and why they came to be so powerful within the local Greek community. In fact, only a handful of Castellorizians were able to wield considerable influence in the first half of the twentieth century, and they exercised this dominance over Castellorizians and non-Castellorizians alike. Thus it is not just chain migration which is important for Castellorizian control, but the links in the chain that gave some individuals more power than others. (Yiannakis 1996, p. 74)

Throughout the first decades of the twentieth century, the enthusiasm and momentum for building a church grew, particularly as the Greek population and the proportion of women in the Castellorizian community increased (Interview N29). By the early 1920s, the proportion of women in Perth's Castellorizian community had grown significantly—from only 4% in 1911 to around 29% in 1921 (HCWA 2005b; Yiannakis 1996, p. 109). As more families settled and began to raise children in Perth, growing importance was placed on building a church that could offer 'religious and cultural familiarity and... preserve their Greek identity'[37] (Yiannakis 1996, pp. 101–102). Fundraising efforts for the new church (which continued over many years) were often managed by the women, including concerts, dinners, raffles and bazaars.[38] Like the fundraising process for the Katanning Mosque and Griffith's Sikh temple, funds were also raised by direct collections from families, with each Greek family in the community paying a sixpence levy into the building fund 'whenever they could afford to do so' (Yiannakis 1996, p. 106; HCWA 2005b, p. 5).

By 1922, the Castellorizian Brotherhood had raised enough money to buy two lots in Parker Street in what was later to become Northbridge.[39] There is some suggestion that the Northbridge site was chosen over an alternative site in Subiaco due to 'the lobbying of a few influential Castellorizians' who lived closer to Parker Street, including successful entrepreneur Peter Michelides (HCWA 2005b, p. 5). However, as Perth's Greek community diversified, many saw the need for a new, pan-Hellenic association. Father Germanous Illiou (who had replaced Reverend Chysanthos in around 1913) was particularly adamant on this matter. The Castellorizian Brotherhood took the lead in establishing such a group, possibly hoping to have influence over the association's agenda, and elections for the new association—the Hellenic Community of Western Australia (referred to from this point as the Hellenic Community)—were held in 1923[40] (Yiannakis 1996, p. 109). The group's inaugural meeting was held later that same year. Its constitution noted the central importance of building a church, stating that:

> The object of the Association is the erection of a Greek Orthodox church, Greek school and the improvement of the religious, moral, mental and social conditions of its members. (Hellenic Community in HCWA 2005b, p. 6)

The question of ownership of the Parker Street property apparently caused some initial tension, but despite the opposition of some members of the Castellorizian Brotherhood to relinquishing the land title, it seems the brotherhood made a verbal agreement to hand over ownership to the Hellenic Community so the latter organisation could build a church. Title was officially transferred on 2 June 1925. In the intervening period, the Metropolitan of the newly established Orthodox Diocese of Australasia, Archbishop Christophorous Knetes, had arrived in Perth and, seeking to circumvent negotiations about ownership of the site, organised a public ceremony for 27 July 1924 at which the church's foundation stone was laid. The hollow stone had been 'filled with gold coins and various documents' and was laid by two prominent local Greek women—Mrs J Michelides and Mrs T Kalafatas—while the ceremony was officiated by Archbishop Knetes, Reverand Germanos Illiou and the Church of England's Archdeacon Huddleston (HCWA 2005b, p. 6; Yiannakis 1996, p. 110).

Although Reverend Illiou officiated at the ceremony, tensions had been growing between the Castellorizian Brotherhood and Reverend Illiou for some time. While 'personality clashes' and ideological differences appear to have been the main sources of tension, Illiou's independence from the brotherhood also seems to have been a cause of concern. For example, by the early 1920s Illiou had begun holding Greek Orthodox services at Presbyterian and Anglican Church halls in Perth, hence having no need to hold services in Arthur Auguste's Fremantle annexe. In 1917, Illiou had also established a Greek evening school that taught scripture, language, Greek history, geography and literature (HCWA 2005b, p. 6; Yiannakis 1996, pp. 105–106). Since local Greek families at this time were raising Australian-born children, 'parents encouraged, coaxed or forced their children to attend classes' (Yiannakis 1996, pp. 105–106). However, there may have been a perception that Illiou had 'assumed authority of educational matters from the Brotherhood' (HCWA 2005b, p. 6). Illiou had also supported the development of a Pan-Hellenic association and suggested that a regional association like the Castellorizian Brotherhood should not have ultimate responsibility for building a church (Yiannakis 1996, p. 106). In transferring the land title to the Hellenic Community, the Castellorizian Brotherhood included a condition that a request be made to remove Reverend Illiou and replace him with the Castellorizian Archimandrite Nektarios who was then working overseas (HCWA 2005b, p. 7; Yiannakis 1996, p. 111).

By the time Nektarios arrived in 1925, the Hellenic Community had built the Hellenic Hall on the Parker Street site.[41] The hall was designed to be used for religious services on Sundays as a community and cultural centre at other times. Local historian and Castellorizian, John Georgiou, notes that in order to serve its dual function as religious and cultural centre the hall was specially designed to have 'a little altar with the icons and so on' which was 'screened off with a curtain, and then when there was a religious event they pulled the curtain back' (Interview N29). The hall was a single storey, rendered brick building that externally displayed 'little architectural reference to the heritage of its users' (HCWA 2005b, p. 7). However, its cultural, religious and social significance attracted many Greeks to the area, including both new immigrants and those who had earlier settled elsewhere in Western Australia. By the 1930s, the surrounding streets 'had a definite Greek character' (HCWA 2005b, p. 7; see also Interview N29). For example, in 1936 nearby Aberdeen Street housed nine Greek families and Lake Street housed as many as thirty[42] (HCWA 2005b, p. 7).

Through the 1920s and 1930s, the growing Greek population of Perth assisted in the ongoing efforts to raise funds to build an Orthodox church. Fundraising events were often held in the Hellenic Hall, including concerts in which volunteers would perform dances, play music or recite poetry for an admission fee[43] (Yiannakis 1996, p. 113). Funds were also contributed from other Greek associations such as the Hellenic Union[44] (founded in 1918 to provide social and cultural support to young Greek men) and the Hellenic Women's Association (established in 1923). While much of the fundraising involved Castellorizian Greeks, non-Castellorizians also contributed to the cause both as individuals and through the Greek-Macedonian 'Alexander the Great' association (HCWA 2005b, p. 5, 7).

Sufficient funds had been raised by the mid-1930s for the Hellenic Community to seek designs and quotes from local architects. They requested a design based on the Cathedral of Saint Constantine in Castellorizo and settled on a quote from well-known architectural firm Oldham, Boas and Ednie-Brown for £4500.[45] The design was very similar to the Cathedral in Castellorizo, with the main differences being its smaller size and the square (rather than round) columns in the nave (HCWA 2005b, p. 8).

With approval for the building decided at an extraordinary meeting of the Hellenic Community in December 1935, building commenced in January 1936.[46] The new building would be built immediately next to the existing Hellenic Hall. The project was funded by the £1000 already raised through the many years of fundraising, a £2500 bank loan[47] 'secured by mortgaging the Hellenic Hall and surrounding land' and a new fundraising drive that extended to Greek settlements throughout the state (HCWA 2005b, p. 8). This new drive was led by Archbishop Timotheos Evangelinides (who had replaced Knetes in 1928) and Peter Michelides and raised funds from Greek communities in Bunbury, Manjimup, Donnybrook, Pemberton, Bridgetown and Kalgoorlie (HCWA 2005b, p. 8).

The building was completed in 1937 and consecrated by Archbishop Timotheos on 18 April of that year (Yiannakis 1996, p. 116). It was the 'first purpose-built Greek Orthodox Church' in the state (HCWA 2005b,

p. 2) and was a 'pinnacle of Castellorizian achievement' (Yiannakis 1996, p. 116). The ceremony included placing 'relics of saints from Europe, a gold coin and historical documents' under the altar and was attended by the local rector Father Christoforos Manessis as well as other church dignitaries.[48] It was followed by celebrations next door in the Hellenic Hall (HCWA 2005b, pp. 8–9). *The West Australian* reported that on the day:

> The scene was impressive, the priests in their robes of gold, and scarlet, and blue; the acolytes with lighted candles; the interior illuminated by the large, glittering central candelabra; the light of the sun, for a time streaming golden through the windows; the richly-painted altar screen and the music from an invisible choir of men. (HCWA 2005b, pp. 8–9)

The name of the church had special significance. While Peter Michelides wanted to 'continue an accepted Greek practice of church benefactors being entitled to choose an appropriate name for the building' and name the church 'Ayios Spyrithion' (Saint Spiro) after his father, the name decided upon represented the patron saints of Castellorizo, Constantine and Helene (HCWA 2005b, p. 9). This name not only mirrored the name of a significant cathedral in Castellorizo but also signified the influence of Castellorizians among local Greeks and provided 'an identifiable aspect of their heritage and homeland ...re-established in Australia, recognizable not only to Castellorizians but to all Greeks' (Yiannakis 1996, pp. 117–118).

Unlike the Chung Wah Association Hall, the Church of Saints Constantine and Helene adopts a style that demonstrates its specific use—in this case an inter-war Byzantine style with a cruciform plan, a large domed cupola where the nave crosses the transept and two smaller domed cupolas above the entrance (HCWA 2005b). Of course, this deliberate use of symbolic architectural features is very common of religious buildings and in this instance reflects not only the users' cultural and religious heritage but also the traditional design of the 'mother church' in Castellorizo.[49] However, while the design draws on this heritage it also adopts local features, 'translating the requirements of the Latin cross plan and Byzantine stylistic language into local brick and tile' (see Fig. 4.5) (HCWA 2005b, p. 11). John Georgiou notes that this 'red brick makes a difference, you don't get that sort of red brick in Greece' (Interview N29).

Fig. 4.5 Church of Saints Constantine and Helene, view from Francis Street, Northbridge (*Source* Kirrily Jordan)

The richly decorated interior reflects the Orthodox liturgy and includes iconography and a painted altar screen produced by the Castellorizian-born artist Vlase Zanalis. Additional iconography (including the ceiling and wall frescos) was completed by the Greek artist A. Karafilakis in 1952 (HCWA 2005b, pp. 2, 9). Many of the icons inside the church were donated by local Castellorizian families (Yiannakis 1996, p. 119). The major financial contributors to the church are listed on a white marble 'honour board' that was placed on the building's western wall in 1937[50] (HCWA 2005b, p. 9).

In these early years, Greek immigrants and their families from all around Perth would attend Saints Constantine and Helene. As Paul Drakos, the son of Greek immigrants, recalls,

> at the time when it first started, I'm talking '37, you would've had about six hundred Greeks living in this area [Northbridge], predominantly in

> Lake St and all these streets around the area... in this street here there would have been ah, three or four hundred Greeks... if you lived further out, you would have to try and make your transport here. The only way you could get here by trams, [or] if you were lucky enough to have a car. (Interview N27)

The significance of the church was, of course, more than its religious function. It represented many years of hard work and dedication in raising funds as well as a symbol of Greek culture. For Nicholas, the Greek immigrant introduced above, a key aspect of its significance was its role in binding together a Greek community 'because what binds us Greeks is our religion' (Interview N3). John Georgiou also notes that even for those people who are not religious, 'there's elements of the [Greek] culture that are tied to Greek Orthodox' so the church has been a 'a very important means... of maintaining culture' (Interview N29). Similarly, Paul Drakos remembers that going to the church and to Saturday Greek school at the Hellenic Hall were two of the most important parts of the week and were crucial social events:

> We used to go to church... to learn Greek... the most important thing that you did, was you went to school during the week and on... Saturday you would go to Greek school to learn Greek and on the Sunday you went to church... that was a very [important] gathering point for people to mix and congregate... that's how you saw someone you might want to marry, see... the girls would get dolled up like they were a million dollars, and so it was 'Oh, I fancy her', and 'That's my cousin, I'll introduce you' ... the church was a very, very strong thing, it brought people together. (Interview N27)

Paul Drakos also notes that the church was an important place for making business contacts:

> of course a lot of people did business as well, you'd go [to church] and say, 'Well, what are you doing?'... 'Oh, well, I'm selling a fish'n'chip shop.' So lot of business transactions went to church. (Interview N27)

Just like the Hellenic Hall, the new Church of Saints Constantine and Helene reinforced the pattern of Greek settlement in Northbridge. As John Georgiou explains, having:

> a church in this area did reinforce an emerging pattern so that by the '30s, the '40s and the '50s lots of Greeks were congregating in the area. And as you got that critical mass you also started to get Greek run businesses which catered not solely for Greeks... but certainly catering for a southern European element. (Interview N29)

By the 1950s, many of the newly arrived Greek immigrants settling in Northbridge did so because of personal connections to pre-war immigrants in the area. Those without such connections settled further away from the city centre in North Perth or West Perth, and eventually as Greeks in Northbridge became more affluent many also moved further out into the suburbs. The church, though, retained its significance for many of Perth's Greeks who would regularly make the trip into Northbridge to attend mass or meet with friends (Interview N29). On 21 May 1972, the Church of Saints Constantine and Helene was proclaimed a Cathedral[51] by Archbishop Ezekiel Tsoukalas, indicating its significance as the official address of the Bishop for the Archdiocesan District of Western Australia and the 'principal church' of the Bishop's diocese (HCWA 2005b, p. 1).

In 1962, the Hellenic Community of Western Australia purchased an additional property immediately south across Francis Street. This building was used as the rectory and, during the 1970s, for running a Greek School. In 1969, the original Hellenic Hall was replaced with a much larger and more modern building (to a cost of $250,000) that constitutes the Hellenic Community Centre today (HCWA 2005b, pp. 4, 10). The centre is a two-storey concrete and steel building (Fig. 4.6) that included a committee room, kitchen, two classrooms, stage, hall and 'balcony and cocktail area' (HCWA 2005b, p. 15). Since this new venue was built, it has been used for social events, weddings (Interview N29) and as 'a meeting place for Hellenic organisations' and the administrative centre for the Hellenic Community of Western Australia (HCWA 2005b, pp. 10, 11).

A decline in use caused some to suggest the community centre is a 'white elephant'. However, John Georgiou notes that there has been some 'renewal' of usage since around 2007, particularly with bookings for the hall by Vietnamese groups:

> just recently, probably in the last 12 months, starting to get a lot of Vietnamese people booking the hall, 'cause it holds about 400 people, and

Fig. 4.6 The Hellenic Community Centre, Parker Street Northbridge (*Source* Kirrily Jordan)

> they still like those really big old style Greek/Italian type weddings. And there's not many venues, unless you go to a real big fancy hotel, there's not many... venues like that around in Perth anymore. And what they do is they hire the hall and we fixed up the kitchen, so they do their own catering, and it's, I won't say it a rejuvenation but there's a bit of a renewal going on, you know. In the last 6 to 12 months we've probably had a wedding, a Vietnamese wedding there every couple of months. (Interview N29)

In addition, while John Georgiou acknowledges that in 'churches across all denominations... the interest of young people in the church is waning' there is some involvement of young people at the Church of Saints Constantine and Helene as chanters and a young Australian-born man in his late twenties has recently been ordained as a priest. If he eventually takes leadership of the congregation at Saints Constantine and Helene, John Georgiou believes his ability to give sermons in both English and

Greek may encourage more young people to attend, as has been the experience of other Greek Orthodox churches with English-speaking priests (Interview N29).

The original constitution of the Hellenic Community of Western Australia, written in 1924, stated that:

> The object of the Association is the erection of a Greek Orthodox Church, Greek school and the improvement of the religious, moral, mental and social conditions of its members. (Hellenic Community of Western Australia 2007)

Having built the Church of Saints Constantine and Helene relatively early in its now almost 85 year history, the voluntary association has continued to work towards the original broad aims, including ongoing fundraising to restore and conserve the church building. The current constitution lists the association's objectives as including not only maintaining and preserving the church but also ensuring 'the promotion of the religious, moral and intellectual education and learning' of members and of all persons of Greek Orthodox faith and/or Greek origin; promoting 'the teaching of the Greek language and the catechism and dogma of the Greek Orthodox Faith'; and promoting the welfare of people of Greek origin or the Greek Orthodox faith (whether necessitated by 'social or psychological problems, old age, poverty, illness, disease or otherwise'). The association's objectives also include assisting the 'integration' of migrants and preserving and maintaining 'the Greek culture and community spirit' while promoting 'a closer friendship between the members of the Community and other Australians generally' (Hellenic Community of Western Australia 2007).

In order to achieve its aims, the Hellenic Community of Western Australia has established several subcommittees and external bodies. One subcommittee of the association, the Hellenic Community Media Board, manages broadcasts of Hellenic Community Greek language programmes on Perth community radio. The youth subcommittee is 'charged with the responsibility of creating youth orientated events and learning activities, in accordance with Hellenic ideals' and two youth representatives sit on the Hellenic Community Management Board (Hellenic Community of Western Australia 2007). In 1992, the Hellenic Community of Western Australia built the 40 bed Villa Hellas Aged Care Hostel (now called Hellenic Community Aged Care) in the northern Perth suburb of Dianella. The facility caters to Greeks as well as people from a 'mixture of cultural and religious backgrounds' and is owned and managed by the Hellenic Community Benevolent Association (Hellenic Community of Western Australia 2007).

The Hellenic Community Aged Care facility is co-located with St Andrew's Grammar school which is owned by the Hellenic Community of Western Australia. The school is governed by a board that includes representatives from the Hellenic Community of Western Australia, the Greek Orthodox Archdiocese, the Greek government (through the Consul of Greece) and the school's parents' association, and was formed to be 'a multi-cultural school… providing affordable educational opportunities for families seeking a Christian ethic for their children' (Hellenic Community of Western Australia 2007). St Andrew's offers classes from Kindergarten to Year 12 and was opened in 1991 with seven students who were taught at a temporary site made available to the school by the State government until permanent facilities were built at Dianella. With the 27-acre Dianella site acquired from the State government, the school grew quickly and had soon expanded into pre-primary and high school education. Along the way, substantial new developments on the site proceeded with significant financial contributions from the community[52] (St Andrew's Grammar 2007). Each year the Greek government sponsors and fully funds a group of St Andrews students to visit Greece for their cultural education (Interview N2). The school's first group of year 12 students began their studies in 2005 and by the end of 2007 the total number of students at the school had reached 480 (St Andrew's Grammar 2007). The school also offers Saturday Greek language classes that are open to all children, including those who do not attend St Andrews during the week (Interview N29).

Since the Church of Saints Constantine and Helene was built there have been several more Greek Orthodox churches established in Perth and elsewhere in the state. The second of Perth's Greek Orthodox Churches, the Annunciation of Our Lady (Evangelismos), was opened in 1959 in a former Anglican Church in West Perth. This building was replaced in 1970 by a new church that incorporated the distinctive features of an Orthodox church (Fig. 4.7). The church was founded by the newly formed Greek Orthodox Community of WA (Evangelismos) which had been formed by a number of post-war immigrants who felt that the existing church was too small for the local Greek population. Although many among this group were Castellorizian, they also resented

Fig. 4.7 Greek Orthodox Church of the Annunciation of Our Lady (Evangelismos), Corner Charles and Carr Streets, West Perth (*Source* Kirrily Jordan)

what they saw as the arrogance of the pre-war Castellorizians who dominated the existing church (Yiannakis 1996, p. 122). While they had initially proposed that the new church come under the jurisdiction of the Hellenic Community, that association rejected the proposal outright and the new group not only formed their own association but took some parishioners (and a former priest) of Saints Constantine and Helene with them. They were later joined by many more non-Castellorizians (Yiannakis 1996, pp. 122–125) such that the congregation became mostly non-Castellorizian and mostly post-war immigrants (Interview N29). Both the Greek Orthodox Community of WA (Evangelismos) and the Hellenic Community claim to represent the Greek population of Perth (Yiannakis 1996, p. x).

In the founding of this second church, John Yiannakis's (1996) concern to highlight the regional loyalties and cultural differences among Greeks—their super-diversity as Vertovec would call it—from particular regions, islands or towns is significant. The patronage of the Church of Saints Constantine and Helene had been heavily dominated by Castellorizians from the church's inception and Yiannakis notes that 'as recently as 1979 non-Castellorizian Greeks, not necessarily newcomers to the community, were referred to by the Castellorizian establishment as *xenoi* or foreigners', demonstrating the existence of 'animosities' even within an ethnic group (Yiannakis 1996, p. 117). Within the Church of Saints Constantine and Helene, hostility towards *xenoi* was sometimes shown through seating arrangements. When not in use by those involved in special ceremonies (such as christenings, weddings or funerals) the two rows of high-backed chairs close to the altar were reserved for 'those upon whom church honours [had] been bestowed' (Yiannakis 1996, p. 120). In an 'unwritten law' held by many in the laity the *xenoi* were not welcome in these seats and 'a non-Castellorizian who unknowingly sat in the first few pews was made to feel uncomfortable'[53] (Yiannakis 1996, p. 121). While such behaviour was not the main reason for establishing the new church, many local Greeks had certainly 'found the Castellorizian domination of the Cathedral of Saints Constantine and Helene quite intimidating' (HCWA 2005b, p. 9) and some non-Castellorizians saw its establishment as a chance to 'break away from and even challenge Castellorizian hegemony' (Yiannakis 1996, p. 125). For Paul Drakos, differences that arose within the Church of Saints Constantine and Helene mean that it was not only a place that brought people together but also a place that 'split a lot of people', 'cause then a lot of people did have their beliefs in how to run these things' (Interview N27).

The third of the Greek Orthodox churches to be established in Perth was Saint Nektarios in the northern suburb of Dianella. Consecrated on 14 January 1990, St Nektarios differs from the earlier two churches in that it was initiated by and is still controlled by the Archdiocese. This highlights another source of enmity among some Greek immigrants, with tensions between community-controlled churches and the Archdiocese having long been a feature of Greek Orthodox communities in Australia's eastern states. The establishment of Saint Nektarios was seen by 'large numbers' of Orthodox Greeks in Perth (especially Castellorizians) as 'a possible erosion of the freedom of the local community and its church' (Yiannakis 1996, p. 119). Greek Orthodox parishes in Western Australia now also include the Church of Archangels Michael & Gabriel in Geraldton, the Parish of St Nicholas in East Bunbury and the Parish of Pantocrator in the southern Perth suburb of Bibra Lake (Greek Orthodox Archdiocese of Australia 2007; Greek Orthodox Archdiocese of Australia [WA], n.d.).

The Greek Orthodox Archdiocese in Australia has also auspiced aged care services in Perth since 1997 through the not-for-profit organisation St Basil's Aged Care Services[54] and has a Central Youth Committee that is open to all young people and young adults in the Greek Orthodox community in the state. Western Australia has had a Greek Orthodox Monastery, the Holy Monastery of St John of the Mountain, since approximately 2004. Built in the eastern Perth suburb of Forrestfield, the monastery has a small monastic community of three monks including the Abbot Heiromonk Evagrios Koutouzis (Greek Orthodox Archdiocese of Australia 2007; Greek Orthodox Archdiocese of Australia [WA], n.d.). Saints Constantine and Helene retain significance as the 'first purpose built church constructed by and for the Western Australian Greek community' (HCWA 2005b, p. 16).

According to the Heritage Council of Western Australia, while additional Greek Orthodox churches have been built in the state since the completion of the Church of Saints Constantine and Helene, and 'notwithstanding… the drift of Greek people away from the area north of the city' (HCWA 2005b, p. 11), the latter church 'remains the spiritual focus of the Greek community' in that state (HCWA 2005a, p. 2). Indeed, for some local Greeks, even though they have moved away from Northbridge they still return to the Church of Saints Constantine and Helene.[55] Nicholas, for example, notes that:

> a lot of people too they are traditionalists, like myself, I don't go to the other churches, I go here… because it was the first one and, ah, it's the one I know, it's where I grew up. (Interview N3)

The Church of Saints Constantine and Helene was identified as 'a highly significant example of architecture from the Inter-War period' by the Art Deco Society of Western Australia (HCWA 2005b, p. 11). It was classified by the National Trust of Australia (WA) in 1996 and adopted into the Municipal Heritage Inventory of the City of Perth in 2001 with a recommendation it be considered for inclusion in the City's Register of Heritage Places. The church was listed on the permanent register of the Heritage Council of Western Australia in 2005 (HCWA 2005b, p. 11, 2009c). Ongoing fundraising by volunteers and through donations (ranging from spare change to very significant donations in the tens of thousands of dollars) have allowed restorations of the building in recent years (Fig. 4.8). With the church now heritage listed, restorations are done carefully to maintain the building's heritage value (Interview N27).

Fig. 4.8 Extensive restorations at the Church of Saints Constantine and Helene, view from Parker Street (*Source* Kirrily Jordan)

4.1.5.4 St Brigid's Catholic Church

St Brigid's Catholic Church (Fig. 4.9) reflects the heritage of several immigrant groups in Northbridge: first the Irish, then Italians and later other groups including Polish, Spanish and Chinese. It is part of a larger complex that includes St Brigid's Convent (built in 1896/1897), St Brigid's Parish Hall (1899), presbytery (c. 1902), St Brigid's Church (1904) and St Brigid's Convent School (1921). The group of buildings sits on a number of separate allotments bounded by Aberdeen, Fitzgerald and John Streets. While it is formally in North Perth, the church is immediately to the west of Northbridge, with the suburb boundary at Fitzgerald Street. It is an example of the transformation of the built environment by successive immigrant minorities over time.

The St Brigid's Convent site was first occupied by the Sisters of Mercy in 1888. An Irish Catholic religious order established in Dublin in 1831 to educate poor women, the Sisters of Mercy quickly spread through Ireland and into England, North America, New Zealand and Australia. They were soon the second largest female order in the world, smaller only than the French Daughters of Charity. In 1846, a small group of 'pioneers' from the order travelled to Western Australia's young Swan River Colony[56] on the invitation of the Catholic Bishop John Brady (HCWA 2004). Upon arriving in Fremantle, the Sisters sailed up the Swan River to Perth and within a month they had established their first school and convent at Victoria Square (Commonwealth of Australia 2008a).

With the arrival of more Sisters from overseas and interstate, the Sisters of Mercy continued to establish schools[57] in regional Western Australia (York, Toodyay, Bunbury, Coolgardie), nearby Fremantle and several Perth suburbs (Guildford, Subiaco, North Perth, Victoria Park, West Perth). The Sisters opened their West Perth convent and school in 1888. Named St Brigid's after the Irish saint of the same name, the convent and school were first housed in a small cottage on John Street[58] (Commonwealth of Australia 2008a; HCWA 2004; Hickey 2007). With Irish immigrants having been settling in Western Australia since at least the 1840s (see Fitzpatrick 2001; Reece 2001), by 1888 the area surrounding the new school had a significant Irish Catholic population[59] (Hickey 2007). The mixed school opened with 58 students, both boys and girls[60] (HCWA 2004). Enrolments grew rapidly and over the next decades the Catholic Church acquired the adjoining lots and progressively had new buildings constructed to meet their growing needs.[61] Within six months

Fig. 4.9 St Brigid's Catholic Church, front view from Fitzgerald Street (*Source* Kirrily Jordan)

of the school opening the foundation stone for a new larger school had been laid on the lot at the corner of John and Fitzgerald Streets. Tenders were called in early 1889 and by mid-year the new primary school, consisting of a hall and two classrooms, had been completed (HCWA 2004, p. 6). Between 1889 and 1894, a chapel, new rooms and a laundry and drill shed were also added to the convent site to keep pace with the growing number of students and staff (Commonwealth of Australia 2008b; HCWA 2004, p. 6).

By 1896, the convent was again too small and plans were made for a new building. Seven living rooms were built by mid-year, as well as a significant expansion of the chapel. In 1897, a building fund was launched to raise money to build a 'new' convent, although the 'new' building would also incorporate the work undertaken the previous year. By the end of 1897, the new convent had been completed,[62] with the iron and stone fence added in around 1900 (HCWA 2004, p. 7). By 1905, St Brigid's school had 413 students and had become the largest Catholic school in Perth[63] (Hickey 2007, p. 2). With the new school building and convent completed, the convent and adjacent cottages (the latter since demolished) could be used as a high school for young ladies. The high school also functioned as a boarding school until 1929. In 1913, the high school expanded into another cottage on one of the existing lots,[64] and in around 1920 one cottage was demolished to make room for new tennis courts. At around the same time, it was deemed that the existing primary school no longer meet the requirements of the state department of education. Drawing on funds raised by the St Brigid's building committee, the new two-storey St Brigid's Convent School (Fig. 4.10), designed to accommodate 450 students, was opened in 1921. The primary school building was converted into parish hall, complete with new kitchenette, and at its opening in 1921 was lauded as 'one of the best equipped in the city' (*The WA Record* in HCWA 2004, pp. 9–10).

The Sisters of Mercy group at St Brigid's had originally been established as a branch order of the first Sisters of Mercy convent in Western Australia that had opened in Victoria Square in 1846. In 1896, the St Brigid's Sisters of Mercy assumed a separate identity from the Sisters of Mercy at Victoria Square, becoming the Sisters of Mercy West Perth[65] (Commonwealth of Australia 2008a). That allowed the group to appoint their own mother superior and establish their own novitiate (Commonwealth of Australia 2008b), and from 1901 the parish was administered separately from the St Mary's Cathedral that had been opened in Victoria

Fig. 4.10 St Brigid's Convent School, Fitzgerald Street, North Perth (*Source* Kirrily Jordan)

Square in 1865. Anselm Bourke, an Irish immigrant who had arrived in Australia in 1855, was appointed the first priest of the West Perth (now Northbridge) parish (HCWA 2004).

In around 1902, a two-storey brick presbytery was built to house the new priest. By early 1904, 'the children of the Parish were busily raising funds for the church building appeal' (HCWA 2004, p. 8). The foundation stone was laid in May 1904 and a grand church was envisioned. Finished in 1904 and opened in 1905, the new church could accommodate 758 people. It was designed traditionally in the form of a Latin cross—with an entry lobby, nave, aisles, transepts, sanctuary, sacristy and belltower—and was built in the Federation Gothic style in brick and stucco with a tiled roof. A new alter and sacristy were added in 1957 (HCWA 2004).

While the convent and school were run by Irish Catholic nuns and the church overseen by Irish Catholic priests, by the 1920s the local area had become popular among new Italian immigrants. As described above, the influx of Italians from around the 1920s (and particularly after World War II) and the growing Greek population gave Northbridge and surrounds a strong Mediterranean feel. In addition to establishing their own institutions such as the Casa d'Italia, Italians quickly adopted the local Catholic Church and school. Martino, the son of Italian immigrants who grew up in Northbridge and attended St Brigid's primary school, notes that since most of the Italians in the neighbourhood were of the Catholic faith St Brigid's church was 'a good and proper place to go' (Interview N21). Moreover, most of the priests could speak some Italian, having studied at the Vatican for part of their training. This was a great advantage for newly arrived immigrants and helped to establish strong bonds with St Brigid's church. As Martino explains:

> it was good for people who had just arrived in Australia who had no English language skills whatsoever, and had to work so hard, and who didn't even have time to go and take up courses because they were all working… so to actually have someone who spoke a little bit of Italian was good. And also the Italian families… were very very generous in opening up and allowing… the priest and others to come and have meals in their houses and so on. (Interview N21)

Of course, St Brigid's Church served an important religious function for these new Italian immigrants. Another son of Italian immigrants who grew up going to St Brigid's primary school and church is Robert Conti (introduced above). Torre was born in Northbridge and retains a strong association to the area. He suggests that access to the church and the ability to practice their Catholic faith was very important for many of the early Italian immigrants because it was a common link between Italy and Australia and was 'something to cling to' (Interview N15). In that sense, the church was 'fundamental' for Italian immigrants in trying to find their 'niche' when they arrived (Interview N15). Religious events were also important social occasions. Torre explains that equally important to the first two parts of the Catholic mass, which include the religious teaching, is the third part, or community, when parishioners can sit down and 'actually talk to one another':

> there's supposed to be three parts to the mass, the liturgy of the word, the communion and community… the last part of the mass is community.

> It doesn't stop when the mass stops, it is your interaction between one another in your day-to-day life. (Interview N15)

Meanwhile, many Italian children in the area, and those born to Italian parents, attended St Brigid's primary school. And since Italian men were not allowed to bring out a partner unless they were married, many arranged proxy marriages through St Brigid's in order to bring their new wives to Australia (Hickey 2007).

From the late 1940s or early 1950s, St Brigid's church began to offer an Italian mass on Sundays (Interview N21). Later, following a string of Australian-born priests Italian priests were sent to oversee the congregation. By the late 1950s, the majority of parishioners were immigrants from Italy and other European countries including then Yugoslavia, Poland and the Ukraine.[66] The assistant priest at St Brigid's from 1959 to around 1965, the Australian-born Most Reverend Barry Hickey, suggests that as immigration from these countries increased, Irish parishioners moved away:

> I had a sense, confirmed by others around at the time, that many Irish parishioners drifted to the Redemptorist Monastery in Vincent Street because St Brigid's had taken on a distinctly Italian flavour... The very large post-war immigration wave could have been too overwhelming for some whose own traditions were being threatened. (Hickey 2007, p. 2)

The first Italian priest to arrive at St Brigid's, Father Gaetano Nanni, was parish priest between 1977 and 1988. While he now resides in Fremantle, Father Nanni was recognised for his importance to the Northbridge community with the naming of Piazza Nanni that was built next to St Brigid's Church in 1999 (Fig. 4.11). Commissioned by the East Perth Redevelopment Authority, Piazza Nanni was designed to be 'reminiscent of a mediterranean courtyard' and reflect 'the European character of the community' (Ellul 1999). According to Torre, Father Nanni became the piazza's namesake for his vision and tireless work for the church, particularly when adjoining land was reclaimed for the Northbridge freeway project in the 1970s and 1980s and many Italians moved away. At that time, the Italian mass went from 'only standing room outside' to starting to go 'into decay', but 'it was Father Nanni who was persistent and kept

Fig. 4.11 Piazza Nanni and St Brigid's Catholic Church, view from Aberdeen Street, North Perth (*Source* Kirrily Jordan)

going' (Interview N15). He also worked hard, along with church parishioners, to save the church buildings themselves from demolition (Ellul 1999).

Father Nanni's presence as parish priest in the 1970s and 1980s reflects the ongoing importance of the church to the local Italian community during that period. With the growing Italian influence in the church through the mid-twentieth century, Torre laughs that it took on the new name of 'Santa Brigita' (Interview N15). As noted above, many Italians and their families have since moved further out into the Perth suburbs. However, elderly Italians who remain in Northbridge as well as some of those who have moved away still attend the church's Italian mass on Sundays[67] (Interview N15; Interview N21; Interview N22). Martino notes that he still sees a lot of these people at St Brigid's:

> because some of them have maintained that link and still go to the Italian mass every Sunday morning… some have felt, I think, that they had this home that was away from home, and it's still important for them and they just don't want to leave it…. (Interview N21)

Similarly, Robert Conti notes that St Brigid's remains important for people because it is 'where they were baptised, where they were married or where they [are] going to be buried. That will always hold an important part in their life because that was their roots' (Interview N15). He sees this process as ongoing 'cause the kids will be baptised there because their parents will take them there. Kids will remember that' (Interview N15). For Torre, the connection to the past through the church is particularly important in the face of such rapid change in Northbridge as the area is progressively redeveloped. He suggests that many of the original buildings, and the Italian feel of the area, are being lost:

> with the sinking of the railway line coming, you'll find that the CBD… can only go North… the whole place you can see by the new developments all coming, you know, all those houses being knocked down, all those multi-storey buildings are coming… the feel the Italians had for it before will be forgotten with that generation who live here. (Interview N15)

However, since St Brigid's is heritage listed, Torre is confident that it will be preserved and remain significant for Italian immigrants in retaining their early Australian heritage:

> It won't be the [other] buildings because the buildings will move with the times, they will be knocked down… [but] for the Italians it will be Santa Brigita. (Interview N15)

While St Brigid's Italian heritage remains important, Torre notes that it has also become much more multinational, with mass now said in four languages: Italian (twice a week on Sunday mornings and Sunday afternoons), English, Spanish and Polish.[68] According to Torre the Spanish, Italian and Polish mass are all well attended, with the English mass growing in recent years as more English-speakers have moved to the area[69] (Interview N15).

While St Brigid's school had been booming in the early and mid-twentieth century, by the 1970s enrolments had dwindled and the residential population of the areas was in decline. The high school was closed in 1972 and in 1976 the Sisters of Mercy West Perth moved out of the area and relocated the primary school to Craigie, some 20 kilometres to the north. While St Brigid's church continued operating, the Sisters sold the convent to the State Government and it was used by the Western Australian Department of Corrections as a work release hostel for working prisoners (Commonwealth of Australia 2008b; HCWA 2004). In 1978, the St Brigid's primary school building and parish hall were converted into a studio and teaching space for Perth Technical College's Department of Art and Design[70] (HCWA 2004). During this period, the rear wing and first floor of the convent were not used and 'fell into disrepair' (John Taylor Architect 2000). In the early 1980s, the state government proposed demolishing the convent to replace it with a 'purposes built hostel' for working prisoners (HCWA 2004), and with the plans to develop the freeway through Northbridge the future of the church building also looked uncertain. However, in the face of community protests against demolishing the convent, in 1988 the government sold the convent back to the Catholic Church (Commonwealth of Australia 2008b; HCWA 2004). Italian and other parishioners on the parish council joined with Father Nanni and the Sisters of Mercy to preserve and restore the church buildings, including the convent, the cottage and the church. Torre suggests that without this effort:

> the convent wouldn't be there, the old cottage where the nun's wouldn't be there, the hall of the primary school wouldn't be there, restoration of the church wouldn't be there, the church would've been gone, land behind would've been sold off. (Interview N15)

With a community grant, the Sisters contracted an architectural firm to restore the convent to its original condition in consultation with both the City of Perth and the Heritage Council of Western Australia[71] (John Taylor Architect 2000; Commonwealth of Australia 2008b), with the restorations uncovering an original 1986 mural on the maim wall of the chapel (HCWA 2004). The Sisters moved back into the convent in 1998 (Commonwealth of Australia 2008b) and the chapel was reopened to the public in 2000 (HCWA 2004). The convent now functions as the Sisters of Mercy's administration offices. The original cottage occupied by the Sisters in 1888 houses their historical collections (Commonwealth of Australia 2008b).

The St Brigid's school, church and presbytery were classified by the National Trust of Australia (WA) in 1991 and the entire St Brigid's group of buildings were included in the City of Perth's Municipal Inventory in 2001 (HCWA 2009d). The Municipal Inventory recommended that the group be considered for listing in the State Register of Heritage Places, and they were listed by the HCWA in 2004. The Heritage Council of Western Australia notes that although many of the buildings were completed in different styles (including Federation Gothic, Federation Arts and Crafts, Federation Free Style and Federation Queen Anne) (HCWA 2009d), they are visually harmonious, contribute to a sense of place and have significant social and historic value (HCWA 2004).

4.2 Minority Immigrants and the Built Environment in Fremantle

Fremantle is a port city at the mouth of the Swan River, only 20 kilometres east of Perth. Long a meeting place for Aboriginal people, its role as a working harbour has attracted several waves of immigrants who have often found work in the fishing industry. Fremantle has also been the first port of call for many immigrants arriving on passenger ships from abroad. The city's multicultural heritage is evident today in its Italian and Greek cafés and restaurants (especially in its famous 'cappuccino strip') and is celebrated in public monuments and the annual Fremantle Festival (Fig. 4.12). The city and surrounds also house several ethnic clubs and welfare associations.

4.2.1 Fremantle's Immigration History

Fremantle has always been an important site for its traditional Nyoongar[72] owners. It sits alongside the mouth of the Swan River, the huge riverbed created by the Rainbow Serpent, or Wagyl, during the Dreaming as it slithered across the land. As in most parts of southern Australia, the local Nyoongars were dispossessed of their land when Europeans arrived. European occupation began with the arrival of eighteen British ships in 1829, with Captain Charles Fremantle of the HMS Challenger, the first ship to arrive, declaring the land south of the river as the Swan River Colony[73] Fremantle became the colony's first major settlement, with Perth settled later that same year Unlike the eastern states that were populated with convicts, the early British arrivals in the Swan River Colony were free

Fig. 4.12 Fremantle Festival parade (*Source* Kirrily Jordan)

settlers who were 'granted' land by the British Crown. The land around Fremantle was quickly divvied up by the colonists, with the Aboriginal population dispersed by the land acquisitions as well as decimated by violence and disease (Morgan 2000, p. 3). Before long, Aboriginal men would return to Fremantle, this time under duress as they were rounded up in other parts of the state and sent to Fremantle prison. Many of them were then transferred to the notorious Aboriginal prison on nearby Rottnest Island where hundreds lost their lives (see Morgan 2000, p. 2).

With the settlements in Fremantle and Perth struggling to survive, convict ships were sent to boost Western Australia's labour supply from 1850 until 1868. The population of the townships during that time remained largely Anglo-Celtic, although there were other immigrant minorities even in the settlement's early days. For example, there is evidence that a Greek family settled in the Swan River Colony as early as 1830. Early Italian immigrants included a missionary who arrived in 1836 and a small number of tradespeople who arrived in the following decades (Stransky 2001, pp. 492–493). At least one Italian arrived as a convict deported from England, landing in Fremantle in 1866 (Cresciani 2003, p. 39). By 1880, enough Italians had arrived that Fremantle hosted a consular agent for Italy (Stransky 2001, p. 493). While the number of non-Anglo-Celtic immigrants in Fremantle remained low, the settlement boasted one of the fledgling state's major ports, and its pivotal role in shipping meant that it soon became Australia's 'western gateway' and the first port of call for many new immigrants (see Ewers 1971). In 1897, the mouth of the Swan River was dredged and re-engineered to allow the entry of large vessels, including passenger ships. By 1906, a new immigration building had been established on the waterfront (Dowson 2001, p. 1).

The first major wave of voluntary immigrants arrived in Fremantle in the 1890s with the onset of the Western Australian gold rush. These included many British, Dutch and German immigrants as well as those from southern Europe including Italians, Slavs and Greeks. Most new arrivals saw Fremantle as only their first port of call, soon heading out to the goldfields or elsewhere, including the eastern states. However, many chose to remain in Fremantle. In 1885 an Italian fisherman, Cono Glorioso, from Capo d'Orlando in Sicily arrived in Fremantle on a passenger ship. He decided to stay and establish a fishing business and was soon followed by more fishermen from Capo d'Orlando and the adjacent Lipari Islands who made Fremantle 'an alternative locus for their fishing activities' (Pascoe 1987, p. 69). According to historian Robert Pascoe (1987, p. 69) this was 'the beginnings of a colony of Capo d'Orlandesi... in the Western Australian seaport'. They were soon joined by more Italians, this time Apulians from Molfetta on the Adriatic Coast (Pascoe 1987, p. 69). By the first decade of the twentieth century, Fremantle had become home to a sizeable population of Italian fishermen.[74] The group of around 150 men were 'unusually homogenous', with roughly half from Capo d'Orlando and the other half from Molfetta (Stransky 2001, p. 493). Based around the Fitzgerald Terrace area in South Fremantle, they sold their catch of fish and rock lobster through the Rockingham Fishing Company, a fishing co-operative established by Cono Glorioso that survived until after World War II (Stransky 2001, p. 493). Throughout the early 1900s, these Italian fishermen dominated the local industry (see Pascoe 1987, p. 53). By the turn of the twenty-first century, descendants of those early fishermen were still key players in the

Fremantle Fishermen's Co-operative and the state's lucrative rock lobster industry (Stransky 2001, p. 493).

Through the early 1900s, Fremantle's Italian population grew in a process of chain migration. The peak period of immigration from Molfetta was the 1920s, when 229 Molfettesi arrived. These were mostly wives, children or other relatives of the fishermen who had arrived earlier. Immigration from Molfetta then slowed: there were only 26 new arrivals from that city over the next decade. Prior to their families arriving, many of the fishermen slept on their boats (Pascoe 1987, p. 54). The Capo d'Orlandesi and Molfettesi often worked separately but began working together in earnest in the late 1940s, bonded together by 'their occupational linkage as much as anything else' (Pascoe 1987, p. 53).

With the Sicilian and Apulian populations of Fremantle came Italian cultural institutions. An Italian welfare association was established in Fremantle in 1902. In 1908 the *signori*, or educated middle-class Italians such as consular representatives, attempted to start an Italian school for the fishermen in Fremantle, most of whom were illiterate. However, hostile to the *signori*, the fishermen 'wanted nothing to do with it' and the school failed (Cresciani 2003, p. 60). In the 1930s, the international political climate had changed substantially. Fascist consuls, veterans' associations and newspaper editors established fascist associations in many Australian cities and towns, including Fremantle (Pascoe 1987, p. 89). During World War II, the authorities 'relentlessly shut down any Italian institution', fascist or not (Pascoe 1987, p. 90). Fremantle became home to a new group of Italians: officers from the captured Italian ship *Remo* were interned at Fremantle Prison from 1940. The crew were interned on nearby Rottnest Island (Rottnest Island Authority 2005).

In 1947, following the suspicions and trauma of the war, the Italians who still dominated Fremantle's fishing industry established the Fremantle Fishermen's Co-operative (Western Australian Museum, n.d.; Pascoe 1987, p. 133). This signalled a shift in attitude among the fishermen, 'throwing off the poor years and becoming more political, more united' (Pascoe 1987, p. 148). It allowed the men to fight the 'unfairness and inequities within the fishing industry', organising for better conditions such as freedom to choose how their catch was sold and distributed (Western Australian Museum, n.d.). The fishing industry at this time also branched out into crayfishing, a lucrative business begun in the 1930s that took off following the war (Pascoe 1987, p. 149). The post-war period also heralded the arrival of Italian shops in downtown

Fremantle. Benny Roncio's coffee bar, opened on South Terrace in 1960, led to the establishment of the major Western Australian firm Benny's Gelati (Pascoe 1987, p. 152). The Italian cafés along South Terrace were the origins of Fremantle's contemporary 'Cappucino Strip', its al fresco dining contributing to the city's tourist appeal.

Italian cultural institutions in Fremantle in the post-war period also included a Miss Italy Quest, established in 1956. The funds raised through the pageant helped to found the Italo-Australian Welfare Centre. The centre was opened in 1965 and included child-minding facilities and a 'villa' for ageing Italians, as well as facilitating the activities of a welfare worker. It was funded by the 'tireless work' of voluntary committees (Pascoe 1987, p. 69). One committee, including Rita Scolaro who had been born in Capo d'Orlando, coordinated the development of an Italian Club in Fremantle. The club was 'housed in a handsome building on the waterfront' and was opened in 1974 (Pascoe 1987, p. 70). In an interview with a local newspaper Rita explained the purpose of the club: 'It is important for Italians to have somewhere to go, somewhere to take their friends, and somewhere to meet new friends' (Pascoe 1987, p. 70). She particularly encouraged women to attend, with the club including a separate women's room designed to appeal to women who had become housebound. These women 'must realise that things are changing in Italy, and they have to change here as well' (Scolaro in Pascoe 1987, p. 70).

In the early 1900s, the Italian fishermen in Fremantle were also joined by other European immigrants including Slavs and Greeks. Like the early Italians, some came during the gold rush but decided to stay in the port town. By 1904, an inspector of the Fremantle fisheries stated that:

> The number of licenses issued has been 354 men and 124 boats, about 10 boats being engaged chiefly in the cray fishing. I regret to say that the industry is chiefly in the hands of the Greeks and Italians, both afloat and ashore. These prefer the small class of boats and work together in batches and send their fish to market by the same boat. (Western Australian Museum, n.d.)

The records of fishermen in Fremantle prior to 1947 include the names of 373 men who worked regularly in the local industry. Most were Italian but there were also Greeks and Slavs[75] (see DPI 2005). Many of the early Greek immigrants in Fremantle were Ithacans but by the first decade of the twentieth century their numbers had dwindled, with many moving east or back to Greece. At the same time, however, the number of Castellorizian immigrants was increasing, often via chain migration (Yiannakis 1996, p. 137). Like the Italians in Fremantle, many of these Greeks were familiar with fishing and were attracted to the port city because 'its working force looked to the sea rather than the land for employment, to ships, cargoes, imports and travellers... [and] had its own discrete community' (*A City on Its Own*, in Yiannakis 1996, p. 137). However, finding employment in the fishing industry was apparently difficult, with some reports suggesting that discrimination against non-British immigrants in working-class Fremantle was worse than anywhere else in Western Australia (see Yiannakis 1996, p. 137). Some Greeks established themselves in fish dealing rather than fishing itself. Others did find work as fishermen, although they remained outnumbered by Italians in the industry[76] (Yiannakis 1996, p. 135).

Today, Fremantle's Greek heritage is still evident in its fishing and seafood industries. Kailis restaurant in Fishing Boat Harbour is one of the contemporary enterprises in the business empire established by Castellorizian immigrant George P. Kailis, who arrived on the west coast of Western Australia aged fourteen in 1914. He established the fish trading business G.P. Kailis and sons in 1928, opening a fish shop in Perth that survived from 1936 until 1990. During the 1960s, George's sons expanded the business into fish wholesaling, retailing and exporting, as well as other industries such as farming and fast food franchises, and created 'the largest privately owned fishing company in Australia' (Yiannakis 1996, p. 136). Also in the 1960s, Michael Kailis, born in Australia to Castellorizian immigrants of a different Kailis family, established the highly successful MG Kailis Group that is based in Fremantle and runs prawn, lobster and pearling operations along the Western Australian coast.

Greeks in Fremantle also established other local businesses. Many had found work as employees in catering companies as 'shop assistants, waiters, cooks or kitchenhands', but often worked long hours or for little financial return (Yiannakis 1996, pp. 137–138). As a result, a number stepped out into self-employment, establishing their own cafes, shops or restaurants. These included several 'eating houses' near the centre of town along South Terrace, High Street and Market Street (Yiannakis 1996, p. 138). One of these was the Greek coffee house or *kafenion* on High Street, opened by another Castellorizian Greek immigrant, Bartholemew Kakulas, in the early twentieth century. Next to the *kafenion* was the now-iconic Kakulas Brothers grocery store. In 1929, the Kakulas family moved to Perth and established a new grocery store, of the same name, on William Street in Northbridge (Yiannakis 1996, p. 138). This store still operates today and has more recently been joined by an additional store, Kakulas Sister, opened in Fremantle in 2004. Many of the Greek-owned business in Fremantle were sold after World War II or during the Great Depression (Yiannakis 1996, p. 138).

While Italians, Greeks and Croatians had established themselves in Fremantle in earlier decades, the first Portuguese did not arrive until after World War II. The first two of these men, Francisco Correia and José da Silva, both arrived from the Madeira archipelago in 1951. Having previously left Madeira for work as crayfishermen in South Africa, they had learned of the export potential of the crayfishing industry and the opportunities for crayfishing in Western Australia. After making their way to the Australian coast (presumably Fremantle), they were able to secure a contract with the Australian government for themselves and 16 of their countrymen to establish a crayfishing business. While da Silva stayed in Fremantle to buy the necessary boats, Correia returned to Madeira to gather the workers. These 16 men (and one five-year-old boy) arrived as a group aboard the small ship the North Cape in 1952.[77] Just under half of the men were single, the others had left wives at home. The married men brought their wives and families to Australia some years later while, in time, some of the single men married women from Madeira by proxy and also brought them to Australia once they had established homes. Of the first 16 arrivals, some had experience as fishermen but others had been farmers, soldiers or small-scale entrepreneurs. Within a few years of their arrival, several of the men had left the crayfishing industry and found work as far afield as the banana plantations of Carnarvon and the coal mines of Collie[78] (Dias 2002). The men who remained in crayfishing eventually became as central to Fremantle's fishing industry as the Italians, and over the next decades chain migration saw the numbers of Portuguese in Fremantle rise rapidly. By 1980, there were around 6000 Portuguese immigrants and their descendants living in and around Fremantle (York 2001, p. 632) and many of the more recent immigrants were from the Portuguese mainland (Interview F2). Significant numbers of Portuguese have also settled in the neighbouring suburbs of Beaconsfield, Spearwood and Hamilton Hill (York 2001, p. 632).

While they usually worked separately, some of the early southern European immigrants found comfort in each other's presence. For example, while most of the first Portuguese men to arrive in Fremantle could not speak English, one of the men, Manuel Pereira, recounted his greater ability to communicate with Italians:

> When I came to this land, there was nothing, except a few bushes here and there. There were some Italians already working here. We could nearly talk to each other. The Latin helped, I guess, as our conversations went a bit further than they did with the English. (Dias 2002)

There was a 'traditional emphasis on sharing and reciprocity' among the Italian fishermen, whose willingness to share boats, equipment and information was one factor in their success and dominance in the industry[79] (Pascoe 1987, p. 133). However, the Sicilian and Apulian fishermen worked separately. Following World War II, key individuals such as Molfettese Frank Del Rosso worked to 'reconcile any difference' between the Apulians and Sicilians and the two groups became more unified, symbolised by their joint participation in the new Blessing of the Fleet ceremony which occurred annually from 1948 (Pascoe 1987, pp. 148, 214). Following their arrival in the 1950s the Portuguese fishermen also joined in this celebration. Pascoe (1987, pp. 50–54) notes that Fremantle's Blessing of the Fleet incorporates the traditional Molfettese religious festival of *Madonna dei Martiri*. In Molfetta, this would involve the statue of the fishermen's patron, the *Madonna dei Martiri* being brought out from the church. Fishermen, even those at sea, would celebrate the Madonna's day as a:

> form of invocation, calling upon the Virgin in this aspect of her many-sided powers to help the fishermen to haul in bountiful catches and to protect their lives at sea. The Madonna's day was second in importance only to Christmas. (Pascoe 1987, p. 50)

During the Blessing of the Fleet in Fremantle fishermen carry a replica of the original statue of the Madonna in Molfetta from Fremantle's St Patrick's Basilica to the harbour. The procession also includes marching bands and key community figures. As Pascoe (1987, p. 214) describes, the statue of the Madonna is adorned with a 'crown of gold, a flowing cape, diamond earings, and a blue sash upon which is pinned gold ornaments and votive offerings', and the procession:

> snakes around Fremantle's streets, as it makes its way from church to pier. All the fishing boats are at the moorings, decked in flowers and adorned with fluttering pennants of all nations. The statue is taken aboard the pilot ship and the flotilla of craft circle around the harbour, their crews singing Marian hymns. Then the procession rewinds its way back, taking the statue in the reverse direction back to the church, after which the participants party the rest of the afternoon in a fair set up on the Esplanade.

While participants in the first Blessing of the Fleet in Fremantle were ridiculed by the local Anglican priest and other onlookers (Pascoe 1987, p. 214), it has become an important cultural institution in Fremantle that is now promoted by the City Council as a 'quintessential part of our cultural melting pot' and 'an integral part of our identity' (Tagliaferri in *Fremantle Focus* 2007).

The last dedicated migrant ship to arrive in Fremantle Port was the Australis in December 1977 (Welcome Walls 2004). As in other parts of the country, the arrival of southern European immigrants in Fremantle has slowed significantly. Since the 1990s, the large majority of immigrants have come from the UK (ABS 2016). However, in the 2016 Census Italians still made up the largest immigrant group in Fremantle from outside the main English-speaking countries. On this measure, Italians were followed by New Zealanders and South Africans (Table 4.3). The longstanding nature of Italian settlement in Fremantle is evidenced by ancestry data (Table 4.4): in the 2016 Census there were nearly 1142 resi-

Table 4.3 Country of birth of Fremantle residents, top ten countries, 2016

Country of birth	*Persons*
Australia	4439
England	663
Italy	235
New Zealand	167
South Africa	81
Scotland	73
United States of America	72
Ireland	70
Canada	53
France	51
Total residents	14,846

Source Author's calculation based on ABS (2019a)

Table 4.4 Ancestry of Fremantle residents, selected groups, 2016

Ancestry	*Responses*
English	5969
Australian	3890
Irish	2025
Scottish	1667
Italian	1142
German	549
Dutch	296
Chinese	221
French	213
Croatian	193
Welsh	191
Australian Aboriginal	25
Total responses	14,846

Source Author's calculation based on ABS (2019a)

dents in Fremantle who claimed Italian ancestry, many times the number of Italian immigrants.

It should also be noted that a significant number of southern European immigrants live in nearby suburbs such as Spearwood and Hamilton Hill. In 2016, in these two suburbs alone there were over 706 immigrants from Italy and Croatia. While the largest immigrant group across the two suburbs was those from England (577 people), Italians numbered only slightly fewer at 468. Croatians were the next largest immigrant group with 238 people (ABS 2019a).

Fremantle's Italian and Greek heritage remains prominent in the local built and social environments. Fremantle and Funchal, the latter a city on the island of Madeira, became sister cities in 1996 (Dias 2002). Streets and landmarks such as Fremantle Fishing Boat Harbour's Capo d'Orlando Drive and Molfetta Quays and the monument to Portuguese navigator and explorer Vasco da Gama in The Esplanade park are public symbols of the city's immigrant heritage (see Fig. 4.13). The businesses lining the Fishing Boat Harbour demonstrate the dominance of southern Europeans in Fremantle's fishing history, from Cicerello's restaurant[80] to Kailis Café. The Fishermen's Monument, erected in 2004 to recognise the contribution of Fremantle's pioneer fishermen also takes pride of place in the harbour.

Fig. 4.13 Monument to Vasco da Gama, The Esplanade, Fremantle, 2008. The inscription reads: 'The Portuguese navigator, Vasco da Gama, whose voyages linked Europe with the Indian Ocean' (*Source* Kirrily Jordan)

4.2.2 Cosmopolitan Monuments in Fremantle

4.2.2.1 WA Portuguese Club

In his research on Portuguese immigrants in Australia, Barry York (2001, p. 632) suggests that since the number of Portuguese immigrants is not large 'it is currently very easy for Portuguese children to lose their cultural heritage and be rapidly assimilated into Anglo-Australian culture'. In addition, he argues that 'the Portuguese are a sociable people who in their homeland enjoy meeting in cafes and squares to play cards or simply to talk' (York 2001, p. 632). It is not surprising then, that in seeking to maintain their cultural heritage Portuguese immigrants in Australia have sometimes established Portuguese clubs. These include clubs in south-west Sydney, Wollongong and Melbourne (York 2001, p. 633). Portuguese immigrants in Fremantle and surrounds have also established a club, the WA Portuguese Club in Hamilton Hill (Fig. 4.14).

The club premises were opened in 1969 as a place for Portuguese immigrants and their families to meet and socialise. It grew out of a tradition of regular monthly dances that had been held in local halls since the late 1960s. A young mother whose family are now heavily involved in the club, here called Cristina, remembers these dances from when she was a child:

> before this club was established, the Portuguese community used to congregate once a month. They used to have a dance at St Pat's church in Fremantle. They had a parish hall, so once a month they used to have a dance there. Then after St Pat's all got a bit too small for them they moved to Pageant Street [community hall], so once a month again they'd have dances there and get everyone together, and you'd get up to five, six hundred people in there, you know, once a month, and everybody would go right through from babies, you know *everybody*. (Interview F2)

Meanwhile, funds were being raised within the community to establish their own clubhouse, with land and a building eventually purchased in Hamilton Hill. Adjacent land was also leased from the state department Main Roads Western Australia (via the local council) to provide room for a soccer oval. As Cristina explains, fundraising included a number of activities, such as dinner dances and a 'buy a brick' scheme:

> They did dances and dinner dances and all that sort of stuff. And then a few of the more affluent members of the community put in extra. We had

Fig. 4.14 Entry to the W.A. Portuguese Club, Hamilton Hill (*Source* Kirrily Jordan)

stuff like buy a brick, so for a hundred dollars your family could buy a brick. So yeah, that sort of stuff. That's how we did it. (Interview F2)

The purchase of the property was a substantial investment, and while the cost was minimal compared to the value of the land today, at the time there was some concern that the community had over-committed:

> I know at the time they all said it was expensive and we shouldn't have done it, but yeah, they did it. And [now] we're sitting on a fair bit of land. (Cristina, interview F2)

While a small building already existed on the site, it was substantially renovated. The existing building was fitted out as a bar, pool room and offices and a large hall was added on one side (see Fig. 4.15). There have been several more renovations over the years, including the more recent addition of an outdoor barbeque area. As Cristina recounts:

Fig. 4.15 The large dance hall that was added to the original building on the site, W.A. Portuguese Club (*Source* Kirrily Jordan)

> We keep renovating as [we] need. The barbecue area also got added on and built on, so that's where we have our barbecues and small functions. The bar's been renovated at least four times. This original section has stayed the way it was because it's pretty solid, so we haven't had to do, you know, the roof and that sort of thing. So yeah, just mainly the wet areas, bar, hall and that we've had to do. (Interview F2)

The renovations were done in the common style of the day and did not include any identifiably 'Portuguese' features. Cristina explains that this was a deliberate decision to prevent the risk of friction among club members about what constituted a Portuguese style:

> *Interviewer*: Are there any aspects of the design or the fit out that are particularly 'Portuguese'?
>
> *Cristina*: No, not at all. It's hard because Portugal has such a vast... because there's different villages and different villages have different things that are meaningful to them and because we've got such a diverse community, you know, there's people from the north, people from the south, people from the mainland, people from the island, so it's hard to say 'OK this is what we're having that's Portuguese,' because they'll say 'well this is what we think's Portuguese and we're not from your area,' you know, so it was just easier not to do it, to save complications.

However, a small wooden boat just outside the club, the *Grupo Alegre*, does bear witness to the fishing heritage of Fremantle's early Portuguese pioneers (Fig. 4.16).

Despite the regional differences between members of the club, it has never been split into regional factions and there have never been plans to build separate Portuguese clubs. The one exception is the recent creation of a second Portuguese club,[81] with around 20 or 30 members, which Cristina suggests stemmed from the personal preference of one woman who 'splintered off to do her own thing' (Interview F2). This second club provides some services to the aged.

In the early years of the WA Portuguese club's operation, it was extremely popular among the local Portuguese immigrants and their families. It was open most nights, with bingo and cards nights held late in the week. The club established soccer teams and Sunday soccer tournaments became a huge family event, with the teams competing on the club's own soccer oval and the trophies and photos from each year's teams being displayed on the walls of the club's pool room and bar (Fig. 4.17).

Fig. 4.16 The *Grupo Alegre* outside the entrance of the W.A. Portuguese Club (*Source* Kirrily Jordan)

Cristina describes the atmosphere of the Sunday soccer tournaments:

> Everybody used to come. If you were Portuguese this is where you came. We used to have Sunday soccer, we got some soccer teams together. We had an oval down there. We used to start probably nine o'clock on a Sunday morning and finish at about five in the afternoon. And

Fig. 4.17 Pool room and bar, W.A. Portuguese Club. The walls are adorned with trophies and photographs of the club's many soccer teams over the years (*Source* Kirrily Jordan)

> again, everyone who played soccer, their families, the grandmas, the kids, everyone came along. We'd open the kitchen and make hotdogs and hamburgers. It was just where you went. You didn't have to think about what you were going to do on the weekend, it was just 'we're goin' to the club'. (Interview F2)

The early members of the club were mainly Portuguese immigrants and their spouses and children. Other non-Anglo-Celtic families used to come to the club's events from time to time, particularly the Sunday soccer tournaments, where 'you'd get your occasional Spanish family... or you know an Italian family that knew a Portuguese family, they'd sort of come along and see what it was all about' (Interview F2). For Cristina, the importance of the Portuguese club for members in those early years was clear. It was about:

> staying connected to your own people. It was the base of the Portuguese community—it didn't matter where you lived or where you wandered off to, this was the centre, and you knew that you'd always find someone that you knew here. You could always talk your own language and you knew that someone was going to understand you. You could find your own food. Yeah, it was grounding for them. (Interview F2)

Like many ethno-specific clubs established in earlier decades when immigrants had recently arrived, the membership of the WA Portuguese club has declined in recent years. There are still a number of young people involved in the club, particularly since participation in the club committees tends to be family based, with several generations of the same family taking an active role in the club together and responsibility passing from family to family. So, young people who are involved in the club tend to come in through a longstanding family connection to it (Interview F2). Since early 2007 younger people have also begun to get more involved in the club through the regular Friday night barbeques that give young men somewhere to go out that is not too expensive. The barbeques have also begun to bring in non-Portuguese patrons. As Cristina explains:

> We do Friday night barbecues, every Friday night, cheap as chips, you can come in and get a really decent feed for sixteen dollars. Lots of the younger guys are now starting to do that 'cos it's, you know, by the time you actually go out into town and have a few drinks it costs you a fortune. So they come here have a big feed, few drinks and then they're done [laughs]. But then they're actually bringing their friends in, so it's not just Portuguese anymore, there's Italians, there's Slavs, you know, they're starting to bring in the outside community as well now, so it's quite good. (Interview F2)

A lot of these new, young patrons have also become members of the club, which entitles them to free or discounted meals on special occasions throughout the year. For these young members, the annual cost of membership is $40.00. However, the majority of members are now pensioners, who pay a discounted membership fee of $27.50 per year. Hence, while as of late 2008 there are still in excess of 600 members, the ageing profile of the members has significantly reduced the club's annual income. This has created some financial stress. As Cristina explains, while most members now pay a reduced membership fee, 'they expect you to still run the club the way you did 15, 20 years ago… So yeah it's just really hard' (Interview F2). While membership has tipped towards the elderly, there is a fairly even spread of male and female members, with the women probably slightly outnumbered by the men (Interview F2).

The ageing membership of the club has also shifted the emphasis of the services provided in the premises. The club is still open most days for members to come and socialise at the bar. The club still sponsors a soccer team, but as the team has improved and moved into the A grade competition it has outgrown the club's basic oval and now plays at a better-quality oval in Cockburn. One of the main uses of the club premises is now a support service for the elderly through the Portuguese Community Care Association. This service is used by most elderly Portuguese (whether members of the club or not) who live in the area. While the community care association is a separate entity from the club, some of the organisers also serve on the club committee. Every Monday, elderly Portuguese can come to the club for a full day of activities. They are served morning tea and can then knit, crochet or play cards and Portuguese games until lunch. After being served the free lunch, they play bingo and then stay on for afternoon tea. Many of the members also use the time to get support with practicalities such as making doctor's appointments. Cristina helps to provide the service each Monday, and as she explains, people appreciate this service because while many of them don't speak fluent English it means they don't have to keep asking their busy families for help:

> Quite often they'll bring me a list of, you know, 'I need to go and see the doctor for this on that day so can you ring and make my appointment, or can you check when this is on.' So to them it's not relying solely on their family for doing stuff, 'cos a lot of them are at the stage when their family have moved on and don't have the time to spend with them and do the things for them, so that's when they think that we've covered that for them—they can come in and if they need to go and see a doctor or if they need someone to ring social security or they need someone to ring council to come and cut the tree at the front of their house they can ask us to do it and we're quite happy to do it for them. And they don't feel like they're burdening their family. (Interview F2)

On some days, other service providers are invited to the club to explain to the elderly Portuguese what services are available to them, while Cristina and others translate as best they can:

> We actually get people from like Fremantle Migrant Resource Centre[82] come out and talk to them about where they can look at going for aged care… as they're getting on they're going to have to start thinking about that sort of thing, [so they can be told] 'there's your avenues, this is who you can call, these are the places that have Portuguese-speaking people, these are the ones that cater for Portuguese.' So we encourage that, so they're actually told by government agencies what's available to them, how to do it.

Until recently, around once a month the elderly members were also taken on day trips to the casino. As Cristina laughs, 'half of them can't read or write but they can gamble! Seriously they are illiterate but put them in front of a machine and they know exactly what to do' (Interview F2). The transportation was via a community bus, purchased by the aged care association with $10,000 of donations from local businesses. The bus was also used to transport the elderly to the club for special events, such as Saturday night dances when singers came out from Portugal. However, the bus has recently 'fallen apart' and, according to Cristina, 'we need a new bus desperately but no one's got any funding to give us a bus' (Interview F2). Significantly, the second, small Portuguese association mentioned earlier has recently received grant funding from the state government agency Lotterywest to buy a bus and Cristina believes that has influenced Lotterywest's decision not to fund the aged care association's similar request for grant funding. She is reluctant about asking the same businesses who have previously donated to provide more funding, asking 'how many times can you bleed a stone?' (Interview F2).

Other than the regular Monday events with the aged care association, the busiest times at the WA Portuguese club are the special feast days. These include religious festivals such as for Our Lady of the Mount, celebrated in August, and other significant feasts such as the remembrance of famous Portuguese poet Luís de Camões on 10 June. Cristina explains that since 'religion's a big part of Portuguese culture', club members appreciate the opportunity to celebrate them in Australia:

> Religion is huge in the Portuguese community, they have a very strong faith…to them their religious feasts are huge. So to be able to celebrate them, in our own club, know that the food's going to be like back home, and the dances are going to be the same as home, and the music's gonna be the same as home, just gives them that extra connection to what they believe in. (Interview F2)

The celebrations are extravagant. For example, for Our Lady of the Mount in August 2008, the club brought out a priest from Portugal to oversee the celebrations. Along with the feast of Saint Amaro in January, this is the biggest celebration of the year, when the morning mass at a local church (where there is a Portuguese priest) is followed by a procession and then lunch at the Portuguese club. The afternoon is filled with music, dancing and eating Portuguese food at the club, and in the evening fireworks are let off on the club's old soccer field. The entire event is run by volunteers, including the preparation of all the food and the decoration of the club. While the club lays out the funds for the fireworks and preparations, the costs are recouped by people paying for the lunch. Cristina notes that voluntary labour is the ethos of the club:

> It's never been a profit, make money sort of thing, it's just getting by day by day. So, you know, the guys that work the bar are all volunteer... they all take a turn and work the bars. (Interview F2)

Although membership has declined since the early days of the club, day-to-day running costs are covered and the club now has a significant asset in the land and premises. However, the club committee considered selling the property and moving to a newer facility. There are concerns that the club building is ageing and that it doesn't have appropriate facilities for a younger generation. In addition, while there is plenty of room with the soccer field, since that piece of the land is rented from Main Roads Western Australia it could be resumed at any time. Cristina describes some of the existing concerns, and hopes for the club's future:

> It looked pretty daunting there for a while, whereas you couldn't get any young people in here at all. But we've actually got a bit of hope now that the younger people are starting to come in ... if we moved away from here and did something different we could get playing fields for netball and basketball and stuff that younger kids again could actually get interested in... give the kids something to [say] 'oh well we'll go to the club with mum and dad 'cos we can go and play basketball, we can go and do this,' or, you know, instead of 'oh I don't want to go to the club there's nothing to do'. (Interview F2)

In order to move ahead with this option, Cristina notes that the committee will need the approval of the club members at an extraordinary annual general meeting, as well as support from the local council in the form of an affordable lease on new land.

4.2.2.2 Fishermen's Monument

The Fishermen's Monument is set on a purpose-built jetty in Fremantle's Fishing Boat Harbour. Finished in late 2004, the monument was the original idea of three men of Italian ancestry whose fathers had been pioneers in Fremantle's fishing industry. Claude Basile, Ross Merlino and Guido Micalizzi, who had all continued in their fathers' line of work, decided that since many of the early fishermen were ageing or had already passed on, their feats on the early fishing boats should be recognised. As one of these men recalls, he was having coffee with the others, both of whose fathers had recently passed away:

> and they said it's pretty sad, very soon we won't have any old people left. And they said let's do something… So I said let me think about it. And I thought if we can build a monument to honour these forefathers that put a lot of work into the fishing industry it would be great. (Interview F3)

The three men consulted with other local fishermen to gauge the level of support and, finding enthusiasm for the idea, established an organisation—the Fremantle Fishermen's Memorial Trust (FFMT)—to try to turn it into a reality. The first task of the FFMT was to get a commitment of funds for the project. Basile explains that they first approached the then premier of Western Australia, Dr Geoff Gallop:

> So I went to the government, premier at the time, and I said 'I need you to help me out'… and he said 'OK', he says 'go away, see what you can raise, and when you [reach the limit of] your fundraising, come and see me and… we'll give you the rest.' Which he did, he give me $80,000… from the West Australian Government. (Interview F3)

The primary approach to FFMT took in raising funds was requesting sponsorship from local and state businesses and business associations. Business sponsorship could be at a range of levels and the names of sponsors would be visible on the monument. The group also approached other governments and government agencies and secured funding from the City of Fremantle, the state Department of Fisheries and Department for Planning and Infrastructure, and the Government of Portugal. The local Fremantle papers, the *Fremantle Gazette* and *Fremantle Herald*, also supported the project and did a series of articles on the proposed monument. Basile particularly remembers the enthusiasm from the Portuguese community:

> The Portuguese community was very, very good. Even the Portuguese government turned around and give us ten grand... Yeah, the Portuguese supported us a hell of a lot. They even had people from America come over, you know, relations of the fishermen who were already here, for the opening. It was great. (Interview F3)

Despite the generally positive response, Basile recalls that raising the funds was a long and difficult job: 'it was hard work, it took a long time, took a lot of meetings and a lot of knocking on a lot of doors' (Interview F3). He estimates that it cost him and another member of the trust around $25,000 each from their own funds 'taking... people to lunch and trying to get money out of them. And without doing that it would never have happened' (Interview F3).

To develop the design of the monument the FFMT asked for expressions of interest from artists and worked with arts consultants and a project manager from art source, the artists foundation of Western Australia. Being unable to decide between two of the submissions—one from local artist Greg James who would create two life-size bronze figures of fishermen with their catch, and another from Jon Tarry who had proposed building a jetty in Fishing Boat Harbour—the FFMT asked the two artists to collaborate to produce one monument. In Basile's words, 'we said if you can work together you've got the job' (Interview F3). As a result, the final design incorporated both the bronze statues and the jetty.

From the original idea to the date of completion the project took around three years and cost around $1.4 million, including the cost of donated and materials and labour. The FFMT raised around $800,000 in cash donations and the sale of name plaques to be included on the monument. The concrete (worth around $100,000) and jarrah timber (worth around $300,000) were donated, with the timber having to be specially cut and prepared because beams in the required size were no longer made. The engineering work for the jetty was also donated, with the supplier charging only for the paperwork. That represented a further saving of over $100,000. The money left at the end of the project was donated to the Western Australian Department for Planning and Infrastructure for ongoing maintenance costs (Interview F3).

Each feature of the monument plays an important part in telling the story of the roots of Fremantle's fishing industry. The jetty itself creates a timeline from the heritage of the pioneer fishermen before they migrated to Australia to the modern fishing industry of Fremantle today. The stone steps are the first stage, reflecting the early fishing villages such as those in Molfetta and Sicily where there were stone fishing walls. The next stage is the timber, representing the early construction of jetties in Australia. And, finally, the concrete along the side and at the far end of the jetty represents modern Australian jetty construction (Field notes F12.08.08). The colours on the jetty are also designed to represent the main ethnic groups who were involved in Fremantle's early fishing industry—the Italians, Croatians, Portuguese and Greeks—with blue, red, white and green representing colours of those four national flags (Interview F3).

The 'timeline' along the jetty also corresponds to the bronze figures, with the figure on the stone steps representing one of the pioneer fishermen and the farther figure depicting a modern crayfisherman. The two fishermen are looking directly at each other, illustrating the connection between the two. According to artist Greg James, it is very common for today's crayfishermen in Western Australia to have a grandfather or father among the region's fishing pioneers (Field notes F12.08.08). The detail on the bronze figures is also representative of Fremantle's fishing history. Each figure was based on months of research with local fishermen in order to get the style of clothing, the fishing equipment and the type of fish in the catch accurate for the era being represented. So, for example, the older fisherman is dressed in the style of early Italians in the industry while the younger fisherman is dressed like a modern worker in the crayfishing business. The fish in the first man's basket are local species that would have been caught in the early days of Fremantle's fishing industry.[83] Each element was painstakingly produced using lost wax casting (Field notes F12.08.08).

Greg James describes the significance of the two figures:

> We looked at where [the fishing industry] started and where it is now... It started with line fishing: the fishermen would go out in small boats, catch what they could in local waters, bring it back, have a basket of fish and take it to the local market. Now we have a multi-million dollar crayfishing

> or lobster fishing industry. So, we wanted to look at both of those. So, the older fisherman represents the pioneers and he's wearing the gear they would have been wearing at that time, he has a basket of fish and the fish represent the types of fish that were caught in this area... the other fisherman... represents lobster fishing... So, more of a today kind of character. (Perkins 2008)

Perhaps the key element in the monument that brings the viewer's attention to its significance is the row of 12 poles along the jetty that are inscribed with the names of the pioneer fishermen. These 12 poles represent the 12 months of the year. There is a total of 608 names listed on individual plaques on the poles, including the 373 fishermen whose names could be gathered from Department of Fisheries records up to 1947.[84] These latter names were included free of charge. Additional names of more recent fishermen were added where fishermen, their families or friends purchased a name plaque for $600.00 (Interview F3). The first pole along the jetty tells the history of the Fremantle's fishing industry and pioneer fishermen and shows a map of the early fishing grounds along the Western Australian coast.

The monument was unveiled on 29 October 2004, with the ceremony attended by the then Premier of Western Australia, Dr Geoff Gallop, the local member for Fremantle and other dignitaries. The jetty was blessed by a visiting Italian archbishop.[85] The local Italian women's choir sang and the eight surviving pioneers of Fremantle's fishing industry were honoured and introduced to the premier. Hundreds of people attended the event, including many local fishermen and their families, many of whom had Italian, Croatian, Portuguese and Greek heritage. As Basile recalls:

> we had a great opening where we spend a fair bit of money, we had the premier, we had the archbishop from the town where I was born to open it, bless it... the premier opened it, and it was great. We had... a helium balloon for each person, and it was all covered over, and there was two cray boats tied up over there, which when the premier cut the ribbon, they pulled it and all these balloons floated away... they made a really big thing. (Interview F3)

Today, the monument is a key feature of Fishing Boat Harbour. It is very interactive, drawing passing pedestrians out on to the jetty, with many of them stopping to read the plaques, inspect the sculptures or pose for photographs (Fig. 4.18). In the year it was officially unveiled, it won the award for best monument in Western Australia. It was also a factor in Claude Basile being awarded the Order of Australia for his services to the fishing industry. It is briefly mentioned in three of the City of Fremantle's heritage walk guides: the Art and Culture Trail; the Waterfront Trail; and the Discovery Trail. For one of the founders, the monument brings him both joy and sadness, reflecting on the 'oldies' who have passed away. While there were eight of the pioneer fishermen at the monument's unveiling, by late 2008 there were only two surviving men:

> I think the best thing is when I come down here [to the monument] that I can see so many people photographing, you know, apparently it's the most photographed monument in Australia... to me, it just feels good to come down here. And my sort of wish was that I was going to put

Fig. 4.18 Visitors reading inscriptions at the Fishermen's Monument (*Source* Kirrily Jordan)

> a chair down there, you know, a nice chair... that every fisherman that come here, old fisherman want to sit and... talk about the past, they'd go there and they'd get a free coffee [from nearby Cicerello's café]... but unfortunately there's no oldies left, they all passed away, they all gone. So that wish or that dream, it will never come true... To me [the opening was] very moving and very emotional... but if it would have happened five years before it would have been great, there would have been a lot more of the oldies around that could have appreciated it... and said 'there's some young people that appreciated what we done for them.' And maybe they're up there now looking down and saying 'this is great, we got acknowledged for all the hard work that we did'. (Interview F3)

While the monument garnered widespread community support and has become a popular feature of the local environment, there was some community politics involved in the early stages including tensions over who was asked to be involved (Field notes F12.08.08). Cristina, from the WA Portuguese Club discussed above, thinks the monument is great but suggests that, although there were many Portuguese in the fishing industry, the monument has 'very much taken on an Italian feel' (Interview F2). While the commissioned sculptor went through a detailed process of research in designing the clothing of the early fisherman, Cristina points out that:

> our fishermen didn't dress like that... Ours always wore shorts, short sleeved tops, hardly *ever* wore caps. Never wore a cap. To them it was distraction—having a cap on their head was distraction. They couldn't feel the air. And if they can't feel the salt air, they're not working. (Interview F2)

The Italian style of the older fisherman's clothing probably reflects the earlier entry of Italians into Fremantle's fishing industry, with the Portuguese not arriving until after World War II. Nevertheless, it does indicate the difficulties of representing ethnicity and ethnic history in the landscape in a complex and multi-ethnic cosmopolitan or super-diverse environment.

The founding fisherman interviewed also hints at some people being disappointed that they missed out on including their own of their forebears' names on the poles (Interview F3). He suggests that while the amount of media coverage for the project meant that everyone knew about it and had the chance to get involved at the time, he might consider a 'second stage' of the project in the future. He has been given an old 1950s fish processing boat that belonged to 'one of the best fishermen that was in those days', and while he is currently busy with other commitments he suggests that:

> maybe when I get rid of that [commitment] I might do something else, and all these people who want to put their name on, you know, maybe I'll do it, [and] put the boat there in the side, or somewhere else further down. (Interview F3)

He stops short though, of supporting recent artists' proposals to add a statue of a woman and child waiting for the return of the fishermen. Reflecting on these proposals he asks 'hang on, where do you stop?' (Interview F3). And while not everyone has had their wishes met, Basile feels the project has been worth the three years of work:

> the amount of people on weekends, you see the amount that go there and get their photo taken... I'm pretty proud of it anyway. All the hard work, when you see something like that you think 'hey, it wasn't that bad, it was worth it at the end of the day'. (Interview F3)

4.3 Minority Immigrants and the Built Environment in Kalgoorlie

Kalgoorlie (Fig. 4.19) is a remote regional mining town in Western Australia's Eastern Goldfields, about 600 kilometres from the State's capital city of Perth. Kalgoorlie forms part of the city of Kalgoorlie-Boulder which, with a population of just under 30,000 people (ABS 2019a), is the largest inland city in Western Australia and the biggest urban centre in the massive Goldfields-Esperance region that runs from the Nullarbor Plain in the east into central Western Australia. It is 'a pivotal service centre' catering to this vast area of close to 800,000 square kilometres (Laurie 1995, p. 5).

4.3.1 Kalgoorlie's Immigration History

Unlike the inland centre of Katanning that developed around agricultural industries, Kalgoorlie's primary industry has been mining. It was

Fig. 4.19 Kalgoorlie skyline (*Source* Kirrily Jordan)

first settled by Europeans in 1893 when an Irish gold prospector, Paddy Hannan, discovered gold in the area, prompting the flood of thousands of men to the region—up to 2000 within a week of the reward claim being lodged (Blainey 2003, p. 179). The township of Kalgoorlie was declared in 1894. In that same year, its population reached as high as 15,000 on some estimates, and by 1901 it had settled at 30,000 (Laurie 1995, pp. 3–4). At its highest, in 1896, the population of the Western Australian goldfields was reported to be over 65,000 (Blainey 2003, p. 195). Conditions in the early years were poor: there was no running water until 1903 when a 560 kilometre pipeline was built to pump water from Mundaring Weir (near Perth) and, until the arrival of the railway in 1896, the supply of goods depended on camel trains. In these first years of the settlement:

> Fresh food was almost non-existent, even onions were tinned, and the camel-loads of basic foodstuffs such as oatmeal and sugar were enormously expensive. Water cost about 2 shillings and 6 pence a gallon, and there was never enough of it. (Laurie 1995, p. 2)

What water there was—often sourced from small depressions in rocks or mines or condensed from salty lakes—seemed barely fit for consumption: it 'teemed with insects, it turned white damper to yellow, and diggers vowed a bucket of water wanted an ounce of Epsom salts to make it drinkable' (Blainey 2003, p. 179).

Illnesses and accidents were common and the hard work and tough conditions broke many men: a large proportion of the early graves in Kalgoorlie tell of deaths by dysentery, typhoid, mine accidents or suicide (Argus 2005; see also Casey and Mayman 1964; Laurie 1995, p. 2; Thomson 2004; Whittington 1988). However, the extent of the gold deposits in and around Kalgoorlie—sometimes referred to as the richest goldfields on earth—meant that many men found enormous wealth. Kalgoorlie became a prosperous 'frontier town', its main streets dominated by large and elaborate buildings including dozens of pubs and ornate administration buildings (see Laurie 1995). It also became the engine of economic growth for the whole of Western Australia, with individual prospecting making way for a large-scale, capital-intensive industry based around underground mines run by large mining firms.

The rapid growth of the mining industry brought many immigrants from the eastern states as well as overseas. Indeed, through the 1890s most residents in the Eastern Goldfields were 'T' Othersiders' from Australia's eastern colonies (Strickland 2003, p. 123; Casey and Mayman 1964, p. 105). When Western Australia tossed up the possibility of remaining separate from a united Australian federation, a strong movement formed in the Eastern Goldfields to cede from Western Australia as the colony of 'Auralia' in order to join the proposed Australian nation (Strickland 2003, p. 123; Casey and Mayman 1964, p. 105).

Most of those who arrived from the east had their origins in Britain and Ireland, but some were Italians who had gained experience in gold digging in the goldfields of Victoria or New South Wales. Italians also arrived direct from overseas, hoping to make a quick fortune and return to Italy with their newfound wealth. Almost all were from the southern regions including Campania, Calabria and Sicily and many found work either in the gold mines or in the surrounding regions cutting wood for mine construction (Stransky 2001, p. 493; see also Bunbury 1997). Other immigrant groups included Slavic peoples from the Austro-Hungarian Empire, including Dalmatians, Croatians and Serbians.[86] Together these Slavic immigrants were often referred to as 'Austrians' (Bunbury 1997, pp. 31–32). Most of the Italians and Slavs lived just outside Kalgoorlie in an area known as 'Dingbat Flat',[87] or in a small area around Kalgoorlie's main street (Strickland 2003, p. 139). A small number of Greek immigrants had also settled in Kalgoorlie, some of them travelling from the eastern colonies where they had also worked in the goldfields and others coming directly from Greece (see Gilchrist 2001; Yiannakis 2001). Early Greek arrivals in Western Australia were mostly from the island of Ithaca, with others from Crete, Samos and Santorini (Yiannakis 2001, p. 406). By the early 1900s, most Greeks in Australia had turned to wholesale or retail businesses (Gilchrist 2001, p. 391). Those in Kalgoorlie and Boulder were no exception, establishing delicatessens and cafés along the main streets. While the goldfields in the eastern colonies, particularly Victoria, had had a sizeable Chinese population, fierce opposition to Asian immigration in the Western Australian goldfields kept the number of Asian immigrants in Kalgoorlie relatively low.

The restriction of immigration in Australia is generally linked to the *Immigration Restriction Act 1901*—known as the White Australia policy—which was passed by the fledgling nation soon after federation. However, the Western Australian parliament had passed their own restrictive laws several years earlier, including the *Goldfields Act 1886* (Atkinson 2001, p. 214) and the *Immigration Restriction Act 1897* (Stransky 2001, p. 493). The latter Act could be used to prevent the entry of prospective immigrants who could not 'write out a passage... of 50 words, selected from an English author' and also excluded 'paupers, criminals and lunatics' (Hansard of the House of Commons 1898). In 1901, the goldfields branch of the Trades and Labour Council of Western Australia complained to the State's premier about the increasingly 'large influx of Italians and Austrians' and requested that the government apply the 'education test' under the 1897 Act (Stransky 2001, p. 493). The goldfields were strongly unionised (see Blainey 2003) and, being unskilled and speaking little English, Italian labourers were often prepared to accept lower wages than the unionised Anglo-Celtic workers. Concerns that Italians were undercutting wages were inflamed by suggestions that agents or mine bosses had contracted them in (Stransky 2001, p. 493; see also *The Sun* 1901, in Milentis and Bridge 2004, pp. 73–75; Pascoe 1987, p. 110), presumably to reduce operating costs. Resentments were also raised by accusations that Italians were bribing shift bosses to ensure they got regular shift work or reducing safety standards in the mines because of their limited English (Bunbury 1993, p. 107; Strickland 2003, p. 139). While there was some recognition that a minority of Italian immigrants might be 'decent law-abiding citizens', it was believed that their arrival was bound 'sooner or later, to bring down white men's wages' (*The Sun* 1901, in Milentis and Bridge 2004, p. 74). Moreover, the majority could not be regarded as 'desirable citizens' and would, according to a local newspaper of the time:

> bring with them the turbulence and lawlessness that they drunk in with their mother's milk. Unlike the emigrants from the northern parts of Europe, they do not assimilate with the Saxon stock. Like the Chinamen, they are among us but not of us. (*The Sun* 1901, in Milentis and Bridge 2004, p. 74)

The Sun newspaper further warned that:

> If Australia is to be flooded with Italians, we may one of these days witness a repetition of the New Orleans riots of 1891... If the Italian is getting himself disliked, he has himself to blame for it. (*The Sun* 1901, in Milentis and Bridge 2004, p. 75)

Many of the goldfield's 'Austrian' immigrants were seen as enemy aliens and interned on Rottnest Island and later in Holdsworthy, New South Wales, during World War I. A similar fate awaited many of the goldfield's Italian immigrants in the next great war when, in 1940, they were also interned (Bunbury 1997, pp. 32–33).

While Anglo-Celtic workers petitioned governments to limit the arrival of Italians from the first days of the Western Australian gold rush, they were often more vitriolic in their opposition to Asian immigrants. The *Goldfields Act 1886* specifically prohibited Asians from entering the gold mining industry in Western Australia. Many of the miners in Kalgoorlie had heard of, or even worked alongside, Chinese immigrants in the goldfields of the eastern colonies, and there was a widespread perception that, if left unchecked, the Chinese would 'take over' the goldfields of Western Australia (Atkinson 2001, p. 214). Anti-Asian sentiment was also targeted at the 'Afghan' cameleers,[88] with an Anti-Afghan League (sometimes referred to as the Anti-Asiatic League) established in 1894.[89] Like resentment towards the Chinese, resentment towards the cameleers was increased by their industrial success: the horses and bullocks used by Anglo-Celtic operators were no competition for camel trains in the desert regions.[90] Stevens (1989, pp. 139–141) reports that raids on camel camps, verbal attacks on Afghans and even fist fights were common as horse teamsters tried to protect their former monopoly on bulk transport from the threat of competition from the 'Afghan camel invasion'.[91]

The Anti-Afghan League, with the support of 2000 miners across nine branches, aimed to have Afghans and other Asians removed from the goldfields (Stevens 1989, pp. 144–145). Residents of Kalgoorlie also petitioned the government to prevent further Asian immigration, citing 'the serious danger to the health, morality and general wellbeing of the white population, through the presence and continuous influx of Asiatics into this colony' (King 1998, p. 43). A small number of Asian (mostly Japanese) men did settle in Kalgoorlie but found work in niche areas outside the mining industry, including operating laundries or working as cooks (see *The Sun* 1902, in Milentis and Bridge 2004, p. 82; Field notes Kal17.11.05). Japanese women (referred to in one local newspaper as 'Asiatic humpies of pleasure') also worked in Kalgoorlie's many brothels[92] (Milentis and Bridge 2004, p. 175). These Japanese prostitutes worked alongside French and Anglo-Celtic women, with the French and Japanese women often the victims of organised international syndicates that brought them to work in Kalgoorlie's sex trade against their will (McKewon 2005, pp. 17–18). While the 'Afghan' cameleers who serviced Kalgoorlie established a settlement and a mosque in the neighbouring town of Coolgardie in the 1890s (see Cigler 1986, p. 65), when the rail line came to Kalgoorlie their services were no longer needed and many disappeared from the region.[93]

Although Asian immigration was severely curtailed by local resistance and state regulations, resistance to Italian immigration did not prevent the arrival of more Italians in the Eastern Goldfields. When the United States imposed restrictions on Italian immigration in the early 1920s, many thousands of Italians who would otherwise have settled in the Americas came to Australia. By 1933, there were over 4500 Italians in Western Australia (Stransky 2001, p. 494), many of them in the goldfields. As more Italians settled in Kalgoorlie many of them joined the miners and woodcutters unions. Others bought up local businesses, including a number of hotels. One such hotel was the All Nations Hotel in Kalgoorlie's main street, infamous now for its role in two pivotal events: the race riots of 1919 and 1934.[94] The All Nations Hotel had long been seen as a 'dago drinking den', "tabooed' by respectable people' but frequented by:

> a beery, jabbering crowd of ruffians, whose appearance suggest the lowest scum of Mediterranean or Levantine seaports. Whether they be Austrians, Italians or Greeks, they reflect little credit on any nationality… Several notorious bludgers are valued patrons of the All Nations Hotel. (*The Sun* 1901, in Milentis and Bridge 2004, p. 74)

In 1919, a strike had been organised to demand better pay and working conditions for the woodcutters, most of whom were Italian (Strickland 2003, p. 141). This Italian dominance of the woodlines had become a sore point in Kalgoorlie: when Anglo-Celtic soldiers returned to the town after World War I they found that Italians 'had taken many of their places down the mines and on the woodline' (Bunbury 1997, p. 33). During, or perhaps before, the strike (see Strickland 2003, p. 141 and Bunbury 1997, p. 35), a 'melee' broke out between Italians and a group of Anglo-Celtic men in Kalgoorlie in which a returned soldier was stabbed and killed by an Italian. At a large meeting of returned soldiers the following day, the soldiers demanded that:

> all Italians on the Goldfields be deported, all Italian hotels and businesses be closed and that all Italians leave the Goldfields by Saturday night… Unless the authorities met these conditions, [the returned soldiers] declared they would not hold themselves responsible for the consequences. (Bunbury 1997, p. 38)

After the meeting 'a couple of hundred' Anglo-Celtic men (*The West Australian* 1919, in Bunbury 1997, p. 38) decided they could not wait until Saturday night. They made their way to the All Nations Hotel, smashing the windows (Bunbury 1997, p. 38) then setting it alight (Strickland 2003, p. 141). Several other Italian-owned businesses in Kalgoorlie and Boulder were vandalised or burned (Strickland 2003, p. 141). *The Sun* newspaper reported that 'the activities of the disturbing element among the foreigners had reached a level that created a breaking point, with the inevitable results' (Milentis and Bridge 2004, p. 76). Apparently, the Police advised Italians in Kalgoorlie to leave town, and many went to the wood lines, to Perth or even back to Italy (see Bunbury 1997, pp. 39–42).

The events of 1919 were played out again, on a larger scale, in one of Australia's 'worst ever displays of xenophobia' in 1934 (Bunbury 1993, p. 102). Not all Italians had left the goldfields, and in a remarkably similar demonstration of the earlier unrest, violent anti-Italian sentiment was stirred up when the Italian manager of the Home from Home hotel ejected a young Anglo-Celtic man from the establishment. In the scuffle outside the hotel the young man had fallen backwards, fracturing his skull on the kerb. He died a few hours later, creating 'the catalyst needed for years of simmering ill-feeling towards "foreigners" to reach boiling point' (Strickland 2003, p. 139). This time, the years of simmering ill-feeling had included escalating resentments as the Great Depression took hold and jobs had become scarce (Bunbury 1997, p. 103), with Italians again blamed for taking jobs that were not rightfully theirs. When the young man from the Home from Home died from his injuries, rumours spread that the hotel manager had killed him 'in cold blood' (Strickland 2003, p. 139).

By the following evening—which happened to be Australia Day (Bunbury 1997, p. 102)—an angry mob of hundreds of people had gathered outside the Home from Home. A young boy threw a stone through a window of the hotel, the trigger that started a 'frenzied mob attack' (Strickland 2003, p. 139). The Home from Home was set on fire and when fire fighters arrived the angry mob cut the fire hoses with axes to prevent them putting out the blaze. The rioters quickly spread throughout Kalgoorlie, looting and then setting alight businesses owned by Italians, Greeks and other 'foreign nationals', ignorant of the fact that most of these immigrants had become naturalised Australians years before (Strickland 2003, pp. 139, 141). The properties targeted included the All Nations, now a boarding house following its resurrection after the riots of 1919. As the crowds looted hotels, they got increasingly drunk on the stolen liquor, and with the fire fighters disabled and the police vastly outnumbered there was little the authorities could do to stop the chaos. Having ransacked the southern European shops and businesses in Kalgoorlie, hundreds of rioters moved on to Boulder, commandeering trams or following on bikes and in cars. There they set alight more Italian-owned businesses including the Main Reef and Cornwall hotels.

The following day the rioters temporarily dissipated. Many southern-European families took refuge out in the bush and the manager of the Home from Home hotel found a safe-house in Coolgardie (Strickland 2003). Journalists from *The West Australian* newspaper surveyed the damage:

> From the twisted iron-work, galvanised iron, and charred timbers and brickwork, smoke still issued. Bedding, mattresses, iron bedsteads, broken

> bottles, empty wine and beer casks, covered the roadway, and several foreigners could be detected surreptitiously salvaging what remained of their belongings. Battered cash registers taken from the hotels and the shops were also in evidence, and the marks of violence revealed that the looters had endeavoured to purloin any money that they might have contained... In the Rex Café and the premises owned by G. Kalafatas two new refrigerators had been wrecked and the electric motors wrenched out of them. In all the shops attacked in Kalgoorlie the interiors were wrecked beyond repair, and the furniture smashed to splinters... At 1 o'clock this morning hordes of men and women streamed through Kalgoorlie. Several were laden with goods that they had taken from the destroyed buildings. (Strickland 2003, p. 140)

But the riots were not over. In the afternoon, mine workers gathered at a mass meeting in Boulder, addressed by government ministers appealing for calm. However, a small party headed to Dingbat Flat to raze the Italian camps and homes and fighting broke out with the Italians who had dug into protect their property. Hearing the fighting, the crowds ran to Dingbat Flat, some armed with rifles they had stolen from a Kalgoorlie sports store. The Italians had armed themselves with home-made bombs. The ensuing violence saw two men killed—a young Anglo-Celtic man and a Slav—and many others were injured. Parts of Dingbat Flat was ransacked and set alight. As the riots continued senior police and volunteer civilian 'special constables' were sent by train from Perth (Strickland 2003, pp. 140–141). When things finally quietened down, the damage was added up:

> three men had been killed, many shops, cafes and hotels had been vandalised, looted and burnt. An entire district, home to many Yugoslav and Italian families, had been raked with gunfire, homes destroyed and their inhabitants forced to flee, either into the bush, or as far from Kalgoorlie as their feet could carry them. (Bunbury 1993, pp. 105–106)

In total the mayhem had lasted four days, but the racial tensions lingered on. Relief for the victims was sent from Mussolini in Rome and the state government provided some compensation (Strickland 2003, pp. 140–141). However, many southern European families took whatever belongings they had left and moved off the goldfields for good (see, e.g., Stransky 2001, p. 494).

While Italian immigration to Western Australia increased after World War II, the tendency of new immigrants to head to the goldfields declined. Until 1921, the greatest concentration of Italians in Western Australia was in the eastern goldfields. By 1930, Italians were equally split between the goldfields, the agricultural districts south of Perth and the Perth metropolitan area. By the 1960s, most Italians lived in the coastal cities, particularly Perth and Fremantle, and by the late 1970s they were 'far more urbanised than the total population' (Stransky 2001, p. 494).

Today, the Italian-born population of Kalgoorlie-Boulder is very small. The 2016 Census recorded that of Kalgoorlie's 29,873 residents only 29 were Italian immigrants (ABS 2019a). The vast majority were Australian-born and most immigrants were from England and India (Table 4.5). However, close to 1033 Kalgoorlie or Boulder residents identified that they had Italian ancestry (Table 4.6), making Italians one of the larger ancestry groups in the city (after Australian, English, Irish, Scottish, German and Maori).

Kalgoorlie's Aboriginal population is probably underestimated in the census as many people are very transient. Kalgoorlie is the traditional land of the Wongai people who had 'hunted amongst the region's gimlet gums and sandalwood, conserved its sparse waterholes, and known its searing summer heat and intense night cold for tens of thousands of years' (Bunbury 1993, p. 24). With the onset of the Western Australian gold rush in the early 1890s, they were rapidly excluded from large tracts of their land as thousands of European men flocked to the region and hastily

Table 4.5 Country of birth of Kalgoorlie/Boulder residents, top ten countries, 2016

Country of birth	*Persons*
Australia	10,203
England	367
India	189
China	117
Ireland	73
Fiji	55
Germany	34
Italy	29
Croatia	24
Indonesia	24
Total residents	29,873

Source Author's calculation based on ABS (2019a)

Table 4.6 Ancestry of Kalgoorlie/Boulder residents, selected groups, 2016

Ancestry	*Responses*
Australian	10,987
English	10,393
Irish	2820
Scottish	2615
German	1148
Maori	1091
Italian	1033
Filipino	714
New Zealander	645
Australian Aboriginal	513
Indian	478
Dutch	396
Total responses	32,833

Source Author's calculation based on ABS (2019a)

registered claims for land title. The new arrivals carried guns and knives and were willing to use them on 'blacks' they encountered in prospecting expeditions (*The West Australian* 1894, in Argus 2000, p. 26). In time, the Aboriginal peoples of the Eastern Goldfields became subject to the same 'protectionist' laws that saw them confined to missions and government settlements in most parts of the country.

In 1981, following the shift in policy towards Aboriginal self-determination and the beginnings of land rights legislation, a permanent Aboriginal settlement called Ninga Mia was established on crown land on the outskirts of Kalgoorlie. Ninga Mia was named in honour of Mr Jim Brennan, whose Wongatha name is Ninga, who was largely responsible for securing the land and funding necessary to establish the settlement (Western Australian Planning Commission [WAPC] 2006, p. 1). The land is close to Nanny Goat Hill which has special significance for local Aboriginal people. The Ninga Mia Village Aboriginal Corporation was set up in 1983 and today the settlement houses at least 85—and probably more like 100—people (Indigenous Studies Program 2007; WAPC 2006). Surrounded by industrial land use and mine sites, including the huge, open cut Kalgoorlie Consolidated Gold Mines Super Pit gold mine, the settlement consists of several homes and limited facilities including a playground and cricket pitch, though some of the facilities are in need of repair or renovation (WAPC 2006). There have been serious health concerns at Ninga Mia relating to pollution from the nearby mines and industries, although improvements have been made over the last few years and pollution levels are now well-monitored. Most residents are from the Wongatha language group and have kinship ties with people from several goldfields towns including Coolgardie, Leonora and Laverton, as well as the Aboriginal community of Warburton. Ninga Mia's population can swell substantially as Indigenous people from these towns or the desert regions come to the settlement, often camping on adjacent vacant crown land known as 'Silver City' (WAPC 2006). Others who come to town temporarily—often referred to as 'fringe dwellers' (Weber 2001)—sleep out in Kalgoorlie's parks or roadsides.

4.3.2 Cosmopolitan Monuments in Kalgoorlie

4.3.2.1 The Eastern Goldfields Italian Club

In the early days of Italian settlement in the Eastern Goldfields, Italians tended to congregate at the Italian-owned hotels such as the All Nations and the Home from Home. Several of the Italian-owned hotels were clustered at the lower end of Hannan Street, the main street running through Kalgoorlie's town centre. In the early twentieth century, the concentration of Italian businesses and Italian and Slav homes in this area was about three blocks long up Hannan Street and one-and-a-half blocks deep, leading some historians now to refer to this area as Kalgoorlie's early 'Little Italy' (Field notes Kal24.11.05).

Throughout the early 1900s Italian and Anglo-Celtic mine workers usually kept their distance socially, even if they formed closer bonds through their work. According to historian Bill Bunbury (1993, p. 107):

> Despite individual tolerance and even friendship underground, at street level the Italian preference for games such as bocce over cricket, and their other, unfamiliar, customs came in for criticism by the Australian majority.

The tradition of Italians congregating at hotels owned by their countrymen continued through the mid-twentieth century, with Italian immigration to Kalgoorlie continuing in the post-war period. At this time, Kalgoorlie was a 'party town', with most men working regular eight-hour shifts and having the weeknights and weekends to meet at their preferred hotel (Field notes Kal23.03.07).

In 1978, a group of Italian immigrants who had arrived in the preceding decades decided that a new venue was needed to match their changing circumstances. Now with young children, they wanted a place where they could meet together while still spending time with their families. As one of these men, here called Alessandro, describes, 'we were all young, with young kids and we couldn't go nowhere' (Interview Kal1). Their solution was to form the Eastern Goldfields Italian Club. Perhaps surprisingly, this was the first formally constituted Italian club on the goldfields.

The club first met in a rented room at the Palace Hotel in Hannan Street and began a fundraising drive in order to purchase their own premises. The fundraising effort, led by the women, included organising special events such as a 'walk-a-thon' and a 'dance-a-thon', the latter continuing over a whole weekend. Individuals also contributed large sums, and as one of the early club members, here called Helen, explains, some contributions were donations and others were loans:

> When the club was financial they would get the money back that they put in, they really only leant it. But there were others that left money there, that, you know, said, 'no, I don't want it back'. (Interview Kal1)

When they had decided on a premises—an old night club on Lane Street—volunteers got to work to on its transformation. The building had been bought outright for $10,500, paid in cash with the proceeds of the fundraising effort. Now the walls—which had been painted black—had to be repainted, damp spots had to be repaired, and a new bar had to be built. Two volunteers spent 'every spare minute' for thirteen months on the renovations, assisted by others who came to help as they could (Interview Kal1). When the club was opened in July 1979, the total estimated cost had been $50,000 (*Kalgoorlie Miner* 1979a). The fit out included a bar, kitchen, outdoor barbecue area and multi-purpose hall with a dance floor, and the stage from the original building was retained for performances. While the architecture of the building does not include any specifically Italian features, the large green, white and red sign above the door identifies it clearly as the Eastern Goldfields Italian Club (see Fig. 4.20).

The official opening of the club was on 28 July 1979. The club was full beyond capacity, being able to comfortably seat 180 people. As Helen

Fig. 4.20 Eastern Goldfields Italian Club, Lane Street, Kalgoorlie (*Source* Kirrily Jordan)

and Alessandro recall they had to seat people wherever they could, even in the corridor:

> *Helen*: The opening night we had 350.
> *Alessandro*: Stand up, was it?
> *Helen*: (while laughing) No, we had them sitting down, but we had them across the dance floor and we had to clear the tables off the dance floor so people could dance, 'cause everybody wanted to dance. We had them in the passage ... I don't think they realised how many tickets we'd sold, until they got there.
> *Alessandro*: And people wanted to come, and this town they get upset if 'oh yeah, why not me there?' and this and that, they say, and you try, you don't want to offend anybody so what do you do? (Interview Kal1)

The opening night was also attended by several dignitaries and guests of honour, including the Italian Consul in Western Australia Mr Stefano Stefanini and his wife, the Speaker of the Western Australian Legislative Assembly, the Catholic parish priest Father Bianchini, Mr Nunzio Castiglione from the Perth Italian Club, the Mayor of Kalgoorlie and the

Shire President of Boulder (*Kalgoorlie Miner* 1979b). Speaking at the opening, Mr Stefanini expressed both surprise and delight at how quickly the club members had transformed the old building into its new guise, noting that 'this is not a particularly big or wealthy Italian community' and 'the members and committee are to be congratulated' (*Kalgoorlie Miner* 1979b).

Following its opening, the club was used as a meeting place after work and on weekends, with dances or 'cabarets' held every six weeks. It was a vibrant place for drinking, dancing and socialising. For Alessandro, it was a key part of his social life:

> I really I tell you, since day one I really enjoyed to be there... we used to have a beautiful time... we spend some wonderful times there. When you got the good crowd and the good friends, and that's what it's all about you know. (Interview Kal1)

At the cabarets the committee members would prepare the food and the club would be full, with around 100 people attending. While the original membership was around 75% Italian, the club was open to everyone of good character:

> *Alessandro*: It used to be full, full, I mean four or five deep [at the bar], you know. As I say, you know, Italians and Australians used to come there. The beauty of this club here is it's not like many other clubs, this club has been open to anybody if you know what I mean, any nationality you know. It's a, you want to come, as long as you, if they become a member they get scrutinised—if you a crook or.... (Interview Kal1)

The access to membership for people of all national backgrounds was important. As described above, Kalgoorlie had a history of racial tensions that had occasionally bubbled over into physical violence. While the events of 1919 and 1934 were never repeated on anything like the same scale, some of the early members of the Eastern Goldfields Italian Club remember that ethnic tensions still existed in the 1970s. Most Italians, Yugoslavs and other immigrants drank at certain hotels, but Alessandro recalls that if 'even one Aussie' turned up there was often a problem, since Anglo-Celtic Australians were 'still carrying the burden of the war' (Field notes Kal23.03.07).

While non-Italians could join the Eastern Goldfields Italian Club, the atmosphere was usually convivial. The cabarets and dances were restricted to adults, but on Sundays the members could bring their children for a barbecue. Following a Saturday night function at the club, the adults would spend the Sunday cleaning up the premises, finishing off the left overs, and letting their kids play:

> *Alessandro*: We got a family club here, it is not a gamble club, it's a family club, that's what we want... most of the time you can bring your kids down there and do whatever you want to do, you know, play... You know, kids are kids, kids are priority and that's it. So like for Sundays you'd want to go down to the club and maybe have a couple of drinks or could have a barbecue or whatever, you'd take your kids, you keep an eye on the kids and... used to be a little bit different those days you know we had a big lawn and other things... that's how we done, to get together, there was quite a few Australians with us too. (Interview Kal1)

Helen also remembers the Sunday barbecues fondly:

> Well, the cabarets on the Saturday night was only for the adults and the Sunday we'd go back and clean it up, take the family, and the kids would all play and, you know have a great time while we were cleaning up... and we'd stay for lunch, there would used to be a lot left over, we'd eat that for lunch, but it served the purpose of mixing and it served the purpose of cleaning and everything else that went with it, no it was a great time. We would put music on and have a bit of a dance and the kids would dance all together. (Interview Kal1)

During the early 1980s, the club also had a pool team and darts team that participated in local tournaments, as well as a soccer team for teenagers. The club also organised fundraising events, such as for the relief effort following the 1976 earthquake in Italy's north.

Unlike Griffith (Sect. 2.3), Kalgoorlie has never had separate Italian clubs for those from different regions: as well as being open to non-Italians, the Eastern Goldfields Italian club was open to all Italians. Most of the early Italian immigrants to Kalgoorlie were from the southern regions, but in later years there were also immigrants from the north (see Bunbury 1993). The Italian club's current committee members include those from northern and southern Italy and while jokes are occasionally made about each other's regional backgrounds it is usually in good humour (Field notes Kal23.03.07). The Italian club has also been used by Kalgoorlie's Slavic immigrants. For example, when the Socialist Federal Republic of Yugoslavia broke up in the 1990s, a Croatian dignitary came to visit Croatians in Kalgoorlie and, since there was no Croatian or Slavic club, Kalgoorlie's Croatian residents held the official function at the Italian club (Field notes Kal23.03.07). For Alessandro and Helen, the Italian club was a place to meet new people and make good friends:

> *Helen*: The difference it made [to have the Italian club was that] we met lots of people... Lot of those people we really didn't know before we got involved in the club. We became friends with them, very good friends. (Interview Kal1)

Alessandro also values the friendships made through the club, even though there were sometimes disagreements, too:

> We meet a lot of people, the company was beautiful and we all got on together well... We, we had arguments, we had arguments like anybody else, we used to have one on the committee we use to call him peg leg—he lost a leg underground. One day there was a big argument and he pulled his leg out and bashed it on the table, and everybody shut up (laughing). No really, that's what he done!... You know, we build [the club] for us actually, to pass a bit of time and in company... we become all good friends. (Interview Kal1)

As Italian immigration to Australia has slowed over the last few decades, and as Italian immigrants in Kalgoorlie have aged and either moved to Perth or passed on, the membership of the Eastern Goldfields Italian Club has declined. From a peak of several hundred members, there are now only around 50. The committee has dwindled to only around six, including a president, a secretary and a treasurer. In earlier years there had to be 12 people on the committee and there were more positions, including vice president. In Alessandro's words, the committee is 'just barely there' now (Interview Kal1).

The biggest night of the year for the club is the annual ball, held in June or July. At this event, residents of Kalgoorlie and Boulder who have Italian heritage but do not attend the club on a regular basis 'come out of the woodwork' (Field notes Kal23.03.07). There are also several other big events each year, when the club hires a band and puts on a meal. For example, in March 2007 the club hosted 100 visitors including several dozen from a Perth Italian club and a bus load who had come from Italy to join a commemorative service for Modesto Varischetti, an Italian miner who became famous in 1907 after being rescued from a Coolgardie mine collapse (see below). The Eastern Goldfields Italian Club held a welcome reception on the Friday night for both groups of visitors, as well as a dinner dance on the Saturday night for the visitors from Perth.

The small club committee organised everything from setting up the tables and chairs to decorating the hall, preparing the food, and hiring music, waitresses and bar staff. They also returned to clean up on Sunday. The time invested by the committee is all voluntary. As Helen notes, 'it's always been voluntary, every person works... every, the kitchen, nobody gets paid you know, we do it all for nothing' (Interview Kal1). While the club's treasurer—who fondly remembers playing at the club as a child—is in his twenties, there are very few young members to fill committee positions (Field notes Kal24.03.07). So, Alessandro laments, it is always the same handful of (ageing) people doing the work to host functions and keep the club going:

> Things always the same two or three people doing the job you know... we all work, where now I mean there is two or three, you can work as much as you like, after certain times you get sick and tired. (Interview Kal1)

Large functions, though, are crucial to the club's survival, with local people renting the hall for birthdays and weddings:

> *Alessandro*: We have a few weddings, quite a few weddings.
> *Helen*: And 21sts, and 50th and 60th's you know, people hire the hall.
> *Alessandro*: I think that's what keep the club alive, because is many people go there... It's the functions at the moment are a saving the Italian club at the moment, but otherwise it would have been shut a long time ago. (Interview Kal1)

According to both Helen and Alessandro, the difficulty in attracting new members stems not only from the declining number of locals with Italian heritage. It is also the result of changing patterns of work, with the eight-hour day replaced by shift work so that working people have less opportunity to participate in a club. As Helen explains:

> Twelve hour shifts we have here, we work twelve hour shifts… you know, before at least you worked five days a week and you had Saturdays and Sundays off. Now you don't, you know… so I mean, yeah, it's made it very hard. (Interview Kal1)

Alessandro notes the added difficulty this represents for work-life balance, reflecting on one young past president of the club who tried to engage more young people but struggled with his own commitments to work, a young family and the club:

> He is still a member, he is a past president too, but you know commitments, now he's a got a young family, and job wise he's always busy… plus he used to go down there [to the club]. It's too much for him you know, you know when you got a young family and you gotta try to do the best you can… alright club is beautiful but the family's first you know, so, you know, so that's the way we go. (Interview Kal1)

With club members ageing, the membership is also increasingly non-Italian. While the ratio of Italian-born to non-Italians used to be about 3 to 1, non-Italians now outnumber those with Italian heritage. According to Alessandro, the club is now really Italian largely by name:

> Now the majority they all, say, for argument sake it's Aussie. We only got the name left, that's all—Italian Club, but in a way it's not Italian Club. Well, as long as the name stays there maybe mean something, you know. (Interview Kal1)

The Italian flavour is also very clear among the members who regularly attend the club, with most having Italian heritage or being married to an Italian. Two exceptions are the Scottish-born barman, a life member of the club, and his wife. In Alessandro's words:

> We got a few good Aussie, or non-Aussie, like the barman, he been with us for 20 or more years… he's a Scotsman, you know, he's a life member, so, he work hard for the club, he's always there when behind the bar, he stocked the bar, or when there is a function or something. (Interview Kal1)

An Italian flag still adorns the bar and at functions Italian food and music accompany more 'Australian' dishes and popular songs. And despite the largely non-Italian membership, the name of the club is cherished by the original members: when some of the non-Italians on the committee a few years ago were talking about changing the name of the club Alessandro 'got very upset', recalling 'all our sweat and tears that went into there' (Interview Kal1).

However, Alessandro does predict that the club will soon fold and, aside from hoping that the proceeds from the eventual sale of the club go to a Kalgoorlie charity, he is accepting of, though sad about, this possible fate:

> *Alessandro*: I'm a life member, I don't like to see the club shut… [but] I think eventually will close down, I thought it was maybe this year, but still going…anyway, we just hoping you know, it's a, it's a pity to go, if the club shut, but I think eventually maybe, if it's not this year, next year maybe,…
> *Interviewer*: How would you feel if it did close?
> *Helen*: Pretty upset I'm sure.
> *Alessandro*: I would be very sorry really, but, life will go on. I mean, if there is a nobody there what can we do? (Interview Kal1)

4.3.2.2 Tribute to the Rescue of Modesto Varischetti

As well as the Eastern Goldfields Italian Club another location that strongly identifies the region's Italian heritage is the site of the rescue of Modesto Varischetti (Fig. 4.21). Varischetti was an Italian immigrant from Gorno, in the province of Bergamo in Italy's north. Along with his two brothers he had moved to Western Australia's eastern goldfields and, in the early 1900s was working in the underground mines. On 19 March 1907, Varischetti was working deep underground on the Westralian and East Extension mine at Bonnievale, 12 kilometres north of Coolgardie. At level 10, he was over 200 metres below the surface. A thunderstorm caused a sudden deluge of 100 millimetres of rain, causing the local creek to overflow with 54 million litres of water flooding three working mines in the area (Porter 2008), including the Bonnievale mine.

The floodwater poured into the mine and flooded it to level nine—above where Varischetti, a widower with five children (*Bacchus Marsh Express* [BME] 1907), had been working. By the evening, the other 40 or so workers in the mine had managed to make their way to the surface, but Varischetti remained missing. A team of men, including Varischetti's

Fig. 4.21 Site of the Westralian and East Extension mine and Varischetti's rescue, Bonnievale (*Source* Kirrily Jordan)

brothers, worked through the night bailing water out of the mine, fearing the worst.

However at mid-morning the next day the group of men heard knocking coming from deep in the mine. The Italian miners had developed a system of morse code to tap out messages to each other underground, and one descended to level nine to send a signal. Varischetti replied. Knowing they had to move fast if they were to reach him alive, the rescuers called for a team of deep-sea divers to travel from Perth. While a pump that could clear out 20,000 litres of water a day had been sent from Coolgardie, they knew this would not be enough: even the best pump would take 10 days to empty the flooded mine shafts. On 21 March, four divers and their equipment reached Coolgardie. They had travelled by train from Perth in the record time of 11 hours and 44 minutes, the train driver doing his best to get them there in time. A fifth man, Frank Hughes, an experienced miner and diver who worked in Kalgoorlie, joined the team.

Early the next day the divers were lowered to a rescue base at level nine. From there, they were able to dive down to level 10 and on the first dive established that Varischetti was alive. On the second dive, they made contact and delivered supplies of food and candles, finding Varischetti huddled in an air pocket on a small rise. Over the next five days, the divers continued to deliver fresh food and provisions to Varischetti, unable to get him out of the mine because the water level was still too high. A letter sent up with the divers from Varischetti expressed his fears:

> There is no man that can form an idea what speed the water was rising from the time I first noticed it, and I made up my mind absolutely that God wanted me in the other world. I was prepared to accept death. Between all of you, help me. (BME 1907)

Above ground the crowds were anxiously anticipating Varischetti's rescue, 'all the inhabitants of Bonnievale ... clustered round the mine, and they were supplemented by a large contingent from Coolgardie ... and it was only with the greatest difficulty that the large staff of officials could keep the eager crowd back' (BME 1907). But more water had to be pumped out of the mine to make the rescue possible. The crowd included representatives of Italian residents on the fields who 'left Kalgoorlie for Bonnievale ... in order to be present when the rescue of their countryman was effected. Some came from Kalgoorlie and Boulder, others from Kanowna wood line, while others again flocked in from Bulong, Broad Arrow, and adjacent centres' (ibid.).

On 28 March, nine days after the mine was flooded, Hughes was able to lead Varischetti through the still partly-flooded level 10 and out to safety. When he emerged from the mine just after 6.00 p.m. 'the crowd could not contain themselves and, after the skip was fairly on top, cheer after cheer was given for Varischetti and for Hughes' (ibid.). Varischetti 'did not speak. He was lifted from the skip, wrapped in a blanket, ... put to bed, and carefully attended to' (ibid.).

The news of the rescue made headlines around the world. Varischetti, and his rescuers, became legendary both in Australia's goldfields and in Varischetti's home town of Gorno. While a makeshift sign has long marked the site of the mine (Fig. 4.22), on 25 March 2007, Gorno Mayor Gianpiero Calegari officially dedicated a new commemorative plaque marking the 100th anniversary of the rescue. The new plaque recognises:

> the heroism and bravery of all the men who played their respective parts in this rescue. A special mention is made of the innovative and forward thinking of Inspector Crabb to bring a team of divers into the arid environment of Coolgardie to dive into a tangle of fallen timbers and rock, mixed with turbid waters of a recently flooded mine. We also pay tribute to those divers Hughes and Hearn that went fearlessly into the unknown, with only their skill and bravery to support them.

4.4 Minority Immigrants and the Built Environment in Katanning

Katanning is a small regional centre in a rural area dominated by farming industries. With a population of just over 4000 people, it has a degree of cultural diversity usually associated with Australia's major cities. Although Katanning is home to immigrants from almost 70 countries, its largest non-Anglo-Celtic group are those who migrated from Christmas Island and the Cocos Islands (both Australian territories) who have Malay ancestry. As in the previous case studies, this section begins with a brief introduction to Katanning's history of Indigenous peoples, immigration and ethnic diversity. It then turns to a discussion of multicultural place-making, focusing in particular on the Katanning Mosque that was built by Malay residents in the late 1970s.

Fig. 4.22 Makeshift sign at the rescue site, Bonnievale (*Source* Kirrily Jordan)

4.4.1 Katanning's Immigration History

Katanning is a small rural town—about 280 kilometres south-east of Perth—in Western Australia's Central Great Southern sheep and wheat belt. While Griffith sits in the traditional lands of the Wiradjuri, Katanning is in Nyoongar country. The Katanning district is the traditional land of the Kurin Bibbulmun, or the east Bibbulmun people, but prior to European arrival was the meeting ground for two dialect groups and three distinct 'tribes' (Bignell 1981, p. 2).

The British colonisation of Katanning occurred in much the same way as it did in Griffith, with the arrival of pastoralists in the mid-nineteenth century meaning the land was increasingly alienated from the Kurin Bibbulmun. British and Irish immigrants and their descendants, along with itinerant Chinese market gardeners, took over the land for agricultural production and were soon joined by a number of German settlers[95] (Field notes Kat21.11.06). By the early 1900s, the district had become an important agricultural region with Katanning its major centre (Bignell 1981, p. 235). The town also remained highly significant for the Aboriginal people of Western Australia's south west, with an Aboriginal camping ground and school established in around 1905.[96]

From the late 1940s, Katanning's population was boosted with both soldier-settlers and new immigrants, the latter predominantly from Italy. Italian immigrants came as part of Australia's post-war immigration programme that eased restrictions for Italians wishing to enter the country and encouraged their arrival through recruitment schemes and assisted passages (Stransky 2001; ABS 2005). Like in Griffith, early Italians who arrived in Katanning are regarded as 'pioneers' who helped to build services in the town (Ayers in Turiyo 2005). In Katanning, however, many of the early Italian immigrants have since moved away and evidence of Italian settlement in the built environment is much less apparent than it is in Griffith.

Just as Katanning's Italian population was beginning to decline in the mid-1970s, the town's first Malay residents arrived from the Cocos and Christmas Islands. Katanning has since become home to a large number of Malays from these islands, with estimates putting the number at around 300 families (Ayers in Turiyo 2005). Malays have a long history in Western Australia[97] and in the Cocos and Christmas Islands.

The Cocos (Keeling) Islands, around half-way between Australia and Sri Lanka, have been Australian territories since 1955. They have been home to Malays since the early nineteenth century when European traders brought Malay workers to the islands to farm coconut and harvest copra. The islands were annexed to the British Empire in 1857 and control was vested to Australia in the 1950s[98] (Cocos Solutions 2008; National Archives of Australia 2007). Christmas Island, which lies around 1000 kilometres north-east of the Cocos (Keeling) Islands and is closer to

Indonesia than mainland Australia, has a very similar history. Annexed to the British Crown in the 1890s, Christmas Island became home to many Chinese and Malay indentured labourers recruited to mine phosphate (National Archives of Australia 2007). It became a territory of Australia in 1958.

According to the 2016 Census, the Cocos (Keeling) Islands are home to around 544 residents. Over 84% of Cocos Islanders were born in Australia and only around 4% were born in Malaysia[99] (ABS 2019a). Malays are now into their eighth generation on the islands and have maintained strong religious and cultural traditions and speak a distinct dialect of Malay[100] (Cocos Solutions 2008).

Christmas Island has a larger population than the Cocos, with around 1843 residents. Just over half of the population was born in Australia and almost a third born in Malaysia. Christmas Island is officially multilingual, with the principal languages being Mandarin, Bahasa Malay and English (Shire of Christmas Island 2008). There is significant migration between the Cocos and Christmas Islands, with many Malays from the Cocos having moved to Christmas Island to find work (Murphy 1978).

Malays from the Cocos and Christmas Islands first arrived in Katanning in 1973 when a Christmas Islander was employed to drive earth-moving equipment on a nearby dam construction site. Returning to Christmas Island, he resigned from his job and moved his family to Katanning (Murphy 1978). In the following year, several more Malay families moved from the islands to mainland Australia and made their way to the town, attracted by news of employment opportunities at the halal export abattoir, then called Southern Meat Packers (SMP).[101] A number of these early Malay families shared a house while they established themselves in Katanning, and many got jobs at SMP (Mydie in Turiyo 2005).

Emigration from the Christmas and Cocos Islands continued through a process of chain migration: by 1981 there were more Christmas and Cocos Islander Malays living in mainland Australia than on the islands themselves (National Archives of Australia 2007, see also Ayris 1981). On the mainland, they established communities in Port Hedland, Katanning, Geraldton and Bunbury. Over the last thirty years Malays in Katanning have become firmly established, building their own mosque and madrasa which provide a focal point for the community and, combined with employment prospects at the abattoir (now called WAMMCO), have attracted more recent immigrants from countries such as Malaysia and Indonesia. Dominic Pontillo, an Italian immigrant who arrived in

Katanning after World War II, suggests that with their strong community orientation and regular community activities the Malays have developed a similar presence in the town as the Italians had at their peak in the early 1970s (Pontillo in Turiyo 2005).

Over recent decades, Katanning's non-Anglo-Celtic immigrants have grown to include new settlers from Myanmar, Thailand, Afghanistan, China and India (ABS 2019a). Many, such as those from Afghanistan, are refugees. Others have come as skilled migrants. Still others have come to Australia on temporary work visas known as 457s. For example, many of Katanning's Chinese immigrants were granted 457 visas with sponsorship from WAMMCO to work at the abattoir (Field notes Kat17.03.07).

Like the Aboriginal population in and around Griffith, Nyoongars in Western Australia's south west were moved around between a number of reserves and missions until only a few decades ago, with those remaining at the nearby Marribank Family Centre moved to 'scatter homes' in Katanning in the late 1980s (Flowers in Turiyo 2005).

Table 4.7 illustrates that of the approximately 4560 Katanning residents counted in the 2016 Census, almost 67% were born in Australia. Among those born elsewhere, the largest group are those born in the Myanmar, followed by New Zealand. There are significant immigrant populations from Thailand and Afghanistan, with smaller numbers from India, Malaysia, Italy and several other countries. Bruce Gilbert, formerly

Table 4.7 Country of birth of Katanning residents, top ten countries, 2016

Country of birth	*Persons*
Country of birth	Persons
Australia	3043
Myanmar	154
New Zealand	144
England	134
Thailand	72
Afghanistan	66
South Africa	42
China	29
Philippines	26
India	24
Total residents	4559

Note Excludes Hong Kong, Macau and Taiwan
Source Author's calculation based on ABS (2019a)

the Community Development Officer with Katanning Shire Council, has estimated that Katanning is one of the most culturally diverse rural towns in Western Australia (Turiyo 2005).

However, census information on country of birth tells us little about the cultural diversity of Katanning. Katanning is unique in the sites studied in this section as its largest cultural minority—Christmas and Cocos Island Malays—have come from Australia's external territories. So, while they have retained a strong and distinct culture and religious practices and many have learnt English as a second language and speak Malay at home, a large proportion of the community are not immigrants. Those who were born in the Christmas Islands after it became an Australian territory in 1958 are Australian citizens by birth and are included in the Australian-born census count (Pereira 2008). The same is true of Cocos Islanders who came to Australia after 1978, when almost all residents of the Cocos Islands opted to take Australian citizenship.[102]

As we have seen, the census also provides information on ancestry. Respondents can list up to two ancestries, both of which are treated with equal weight. In Katanning, self-reported ancestry information gives a slightly better picture of the town's ethnic and cultural makeup. The majority (64%) of residents claim Australian, English, Scottish or Irish ancestry (ABS 2019a). However, here we see more people identifying Italian and Aboriginal ancestry than is apparent from the country of birth data alone (Table 4.8).

While ancestry information begins to provide a clearer picture of Katanning's ethnic makeup, the figures for residents with Aboriginal ancestry still seem quite low. Some of the disparity between these estimates and the census ancestry data may be due to a high rate of non-responses among Nyoongar residents in answering this question: there were 587 non-responses for the census' ancestry question in Katanning in 2016. The census also indicated that 24 Katanning residents were Muslim (ABS 2019a). Most, but not all, of Katanning's Islamic community are Malay (Field notes Kat21.11.06).

Multiculturalism in Katanning is touted by many as very successful. In a film produced by local residents about Katanning's cultural diversity, town residents from Malay, Nyoongar, Italian and western European backgrounds express their desire to learn from each other and to understand and appreciate each other's cultures (Turiyo 2005). The cultural diversity of Katanning is celebrated every year with the Katanning Multicultural Festival, and some believe cultural diversity has become a 'selling

Table 4.8 Ancestry of Katanning residents, selected groups, 2016

Ancestry	*Responses*
Australian	1768
English	1410
Scottish	285
Irish	229
German	178
Italian	118
Maori	83
Chinese	57
Dutch	52
New Zealander	52
Australian Aboriginal	49
Total responses	4559

Note This question in the Census is multi-response—total responses may not equal total number of persons
Source Author's calculation based on ABS (2019a)

point' in attracting new residents to the town (Gilbert in Turiyo 2005). Proponents of Katanning as a multicultural success story often make reference to the original meaning of 'Katanning' as being 'meeting place', and suggest that while it was once a place where neighbouring Aboriginal groups would congregate, that tradition has been continued through the peaceful meeting of new immigrant groups.

However, the reality is somewhat more complex. Just as the original meaning of the word 'Katanning' is actually far from clear (Bignell 1981), multiculturalism in Katanning cannot be simply understood as a story of 'smooth sailing' and acceptance. Of course, as elsewhere in Australia, the history of Indigenous and non-Indigenous contact in Katanning is one of significant tension and flagrant racism, with a continued legacy in socio-economic disparities. In addition, while in past decades Katanning has been relatively free from sustained and overt racism towards cultural minorities, racist attitudes have not been eliminated. For example, Alep Mydie, a Malay from Christmas Island who arrived in Katanning in the early 1970s, remembers that at that time 'some people like us here and there were people who didn't. But… I guess that's their choice' (Turiyo 2005).

While there have been occasional expressions of resentment or hostility towards some of Katanning's non-Anglo-Celtic groups, locals report that when such situations have arisen, tensions have quickly subsided. For example, despite the initial resistance from some of the town's residents to the arrival of Malays, most people soon accepted their presence, particularly because Katanning residents realised that Malay labour ensured the survival of the local meatworks by allowing export of meat to Asia and the Middle East. As Mydie recalls, 'Katanning people soon understood and respect our culture and why are we here to cut halal meat' (Turiyo 2005).

The events of September 11 and the rise of anti-Islamic sentiment had some impact in Katanning. One who holds a senior position in the Katanning Mosque, explains that post-September 11 some local people expressed negative attitudes towards their Malay neighbours. Again, though, such tensions seem to have subsided without much lasting effect:

> When September 11 occurred, a lot of resentment, not directly but indirectly about our faith...Osama Bin Laden came along, they call me terrorist, they call me, um, 'where's you bomb?'... Sometime you gotta swallow it, yeah, especially if it's said in front of other people and then you gotta have a thick skin ... it's hard... people call me Bin Laden in the supermarket in front of other people. (Interview Kat1)

The mosque leader responded by politely confronting them:

> I say 'you're mean saying that', 'you're mean to me.' I said 'you know you shouldn't say that', and, you know, I think they felt it. You know, I wasn't saying anything bad to them, like I just said 'you shouldn't say that, you are mean to me'... I stood up and give them indirect criticism. (Interview Kat1)

In an effort to defuse tensions the leader also raised with others at the mosque the possibility that they may be insulted. The local Catholic priest also encouraged acceptance among his parishioners. As the mosque leader explains, the priest:

> stood up and tell [his congregation], he told them 'there's good and bad of anything, you know... if you point the finger at other Muslims are we better than them?'... So yeah, he stood up and explained to them how he felt, as a person, as a priest, as a person who has been involved with Muslims... I thank him very much for that. (Interview Kat1)

The mosque leader believes these efforts were successful: 'sooner or later the... sentences they stop ... Yeah, and you know, we become friends' (Interview Kat1).

Tensions have also existed in Katanning over staffing practices at the meatworks, with some local men feeling that the employment of Chinese workers on 457 visas has reduced the job opportunities for young people in the town (Field notes Kat17.03.07). Others suggest that these recent immigrants lack enough social support (Phillips 2007) or are being exploited, losing too much of their income on company-provided transport and accommodation (Field notes Kat17.03.07).

4.4.2 Cosmopolitan Monuments in Katanning

The impact of non-Anglo-Celtic residents on Katanning's built environment is less immediately apparent than in some other locations like Northbridge. This is probably explained by Katanning's relatively small size and, concurrently, the smaller size of many of its non-Anglo-Celtic groups. However, a number of sites do stand out as places of multicultural heritage. These include the Nyoongar Mungart Budja Art Gallery and a number of sites linked to Christmas and Cocos Malays, most notably the Katanning Mosque and madrasa but also two commercial sites—a small Malay deli in the town centre called Norni Trading and a Malay and Indonesian take away food store. Chinese immigrants have a presence in the built environment too, with Hun Wing's Chinese restaurant opening in what was once a Baptist church. The Katanning Mosque and madrasa are explored in this section.

4.4.2.1 Katanning Mosque

Katanning's Malay residents are Sunni Muslims. They maintained strong religious traditions on the Cocos and Christmas Islands that have been carried over to the mainland. With several families arriving in Katanning at once, there was immediately a need for a place for prayer. They first gathered in old vacant buildings and then rented halls while raising funds to build their own mosque. Alep Mydie was among the first Malays to arrive in Katanning and recalls the many movements of the Malay community before they established their own premises:

> the first time we had a [prayer] session with the Katanning people... we all gathered at this place called the 'winery'—it's opposite the BP [British

> Petroleum] service station now. The winery had lots of pigeons and it was very cold. That's where we would pray. We were there for about twelve months, then we [went to] the RSL [Returned and Services League] hall, in town. After the RSL hall we went to the Katanning showgrounds hall… Every year it would rotate, we were finding a place that we can pray to worship, and still no one helped us to get the land for the mosque. (Mydie in Turiyo 2005)

The growing Malay community sought support from government agencies as well as implementing a formal fundraising strategy among their own members. As Mydie describes:

> We met the Minister of Agriculture at Perth. We asked to help us to get a land… [And] we decided that the people that work on the [mosque] committee should pay five dollars per week, and still we do now. After a while we had enough money to buy the land and then we built the mosque and started praying there. (Mydie in Turiyo 2005)

In the end, most Malay families have contributed five dollars each week for the land purchase and mosque construction (Field notes Kat21.11.06), with the initial construction costing just under $60,000 (Murphy 1978). Additional funds were raised through the sale of food prepared by local women at food stalls (Interview Kat1), while a significant proportion of the original capital ($30,000) was provided by a loan from Saudi Arabia through the Australian Federation of Islamic Councils[103] (Murphy 1978). Donations were also made by Islamic groups both in Australia and overseas (*Indonesian Observer* 1981).

The land where the mosque has been built was very cheap because it had become highly salinated and was interrupted by a creek (the land was levelled with the assistance of the shire council prior to building). While the poor quality of the site helped to reduce initial costs, it has meant that the mosque needs regular repairs from salt damage. As the mosque leader elaborates:

> We bought it off the government, it was crown land… it cost us about fifteen-hundred dollars, I mean, no one want it, like it was… full of salt… we bought it [for] nothing… handed to us I suppose… And you know we fill up all the creeks with rocks and soil and level it, and the Shire… Council, they helped us to level the land. What we see now… before it was a creek so deep and so high you know, full of water, and the water

just flow from the field down through the Mosque... about four years or six years ago we have to change... the foundations of the facial bricks of the Mosque, underneath it we have to change it because it had been eaten because of corrosion from the salt. (Interview Kat1)

In his research on minority places of worship in urban Australia, David Beynon (2007, p. 5) has argued that the siting of these places on marginal land (in his case studies including sites adjacent to major freeways and council rubbish tips) is evidence of the resistance of established residents to multicultural or cosmopolitan place making and their belief that such buildings 'belong elsewhere'. This may well be so, but in Katanning it appears the decision was primarily based on the limited financial resources of residents who had arrived relatively recently and had little access to capital. In addition, according to the mosque leader, the site had special meaning and, despite its problems, had always been intended as a place for the mosque. To him, the pre-existing presence of the surrounding palm trees—an iconic image of the Cocos and Christmas Islands—indicates that the plans for a mosque there had already been laid out even before Malays arrived in the town:

Mosque Leader: In Australia if you see a palm tree... it's something unique. It's like there's this God, or Creator, that knew someone's coming here [laughs].

Interviewer: So, the palm trees were already there?

Mosque Leader: Yeah, I think they're about ninety years old that palm tree. You know, people will say, who planted that? It's been there 90 years, and then we, it's like someone knew, you know, someone's coming to Katanning (Interview Kat1).

The construction of the building relied heavily on volunteer labour. As the mosque leader recalls:

The only labourers that we hired was the... brick layers and the plumber—a registered plumber—and the electrician and that's about it, the rest was done by the community... it's a big job. (Interview Kat1)

The Katanning Mosque was officially opened in 1981 by the then president of the Regional Islamic Council for South-East Asia and the Pacific and former Prime Minister of Malaysia, Tunku Abdul Rahman. The opening ceremony was also attended by Federal and State parliamentarians, local shire councillors and representatives from state and national

Islamic associations. When it was opened, the Katanning Mosque was the only mosque in Western Australia outside of the State's capital city (*Indonesian Observer* 1981). According to the mosque leader, the Katanning Mosque has become central to the town's Islamic community not only as a place where 'people can gather together', but was also 'a landmark for us' and a 'contribution to the community now' (Interview Kat1).

Since the original mosque was built the ongoing fundraising has been bolstered by a business deal with WA Meat Marketing Co-operative Limited (WAMMCO) under which the Katanning Islamic Society is paid for conducting halal certifications that allow WAMMCO to export meat to Asia and the Middle East. The Katanning Islamic Society also provides halal certifications to a number of other abattoirs (Interview Kat4). As the mosque leader explains, this income from halal certifications is returned to the mosque and is 'the reason why we continue to survive... otherwise it's going to be very hard' (Interview Kat1). In addition, he notes the broader benefits to the town since without the mosque 'there'd be no halal food... there would be no meat exported to the Middle East' (Interview Kat1). As well as providing income to the mosque through halal certifications, WAMMCO has donated money to the mosque, including \$20,000 to build a car park.[104]

The ongoing income from halal certifications and community fundraising has also allowed the purchase of purpose-built domes and minarets from Indonesia and the construction of a madrasa, or Islamic school, and children's playground behind the mosque. It also supports a funeral fund that covers the funeral costs whenever one of the mosque's congregation passes away (Interview Kat1) and assists Malays both from Katanning and the Cocos Islands to make their pilgrimage to Mecca (*Great Southern Herald* 2003, p. 3). The mosque, with its silver domes and palm trees, is shown in Fig. 4.23.

The Katanning Islamic Society have further plans to build basketball courts and a cricket pitch at the side of the mosque. They also have council approval to build a covered area between the mosque and the madrasa that will be used to hold functions like the celebrations for Hari Raya[105] and graduations from the madrasa, both of which are currently held in the Katanning town hall (Interview Kat4).

Young people are heavily involved in the Katanning Mosque and the Islamic culture of the town's Malay community has remained strong. The madrasa (Fig. 4.24), operating since the early 1990s, is used for weekend

Fig. 4.23 Katanning Mosque (*Source* Kirrily Jordan)

Fig. 4.24 Katanning Madrasa (*Source* Kirrily Jordan)

school where children learn the basic precepts of Islam. Classes run for two hours every Saturday and Sunday and are taught by three volunteer teachers, all in their late twenties or early thirties, who have trained overseas. One member of the Katanning Islamic Society and teacher at the madrasa is Mohammad A. Born in Australia of Malay heritage in the 1970s, Mohammad A explains the role of the madrasa:

> We used to have like the Sunday and Saturday school in the mosque, so we started at a very young age, like 5 years old, we start going to the Malay School... we'd learn about religion and stuff... also we'd learn the Koran every night... every weekdays at the mosque... But now we study [the Koran] at the teacher's house... [and] weekend classes we have here [at the madrasa]...[where children learn] the basic fundamentals of our religion, Islam. (Interview Kat4)

Most of the Malay children in Katanning attend the weekend school, until 'after year twelve when they start working—they all stop coming then because they have jobs to go to' (Interview Kat4). That means that the classes also have a social aspect:

> The kids they get to see their friends, because we have three schools in Katanning and they don't go to the same schools, so when they come here everybody meets here and... they catch up. (Interview Kat4)

Mohammad A suggests that not only do most of the younger generations attend the madrasa but they also remain actively involved in the mosque, as do all age groups right up to the elderly. One young mosque user, here called Abidin, thinks the Katanning mosque remains the 'heart' of the town (Interview Kat2). Mohammad A hopes that this attachment to the mosque continues:

> I hope [the mosque continues] to be just the way it is, a place for our community to get together. I hope like our kids and grandkids would do the same as we did—a place where we all share to pray and we all get together [for] our celebrations. (Interview Kat4)

The regular celebrations at the mosque include prayer during Hari Raya and at the end of an annual march through Katanning to commemorate the Prophet Mohammad's birthday. At these times, the whole Malay community—young and old—get involved. The mosque leader describes the scene at the end of Ramadan:

> The end of Ramadan for example... it's just like Christmas. Everybody comes. And that mosque fills... maybe from say four hundred to six hundred people like for one Ramadan... it's just full, everything, little spaces that we can... get into ... It's so amazing that... the Mosque can fill up that much with that many people. (Interview Kat1)

The march that celebrates Prophet Mohammad's birthday proceeds through the town to the mosque and occurs annually on the 31st of March. As the mosque leader explains:

> We be marching the Prophet Mohammad's birthday. It's not compulsory but we do it the last 30 years, and it's about unity, getting together, that's what it's all about... family, people... it's what we do, it's part of our community... part that [brings] people together. (Interview Kat1)

On a more regular basis, the mosque is open every day for prayer, and people can also come for social support—to ask for help with politics, business, or just 'to be together so we can talk, we can share a problem, you can talk fishing together, this or that you know?' (Interview Kat1). On Fridays there is a lecture at the mosque, where people take it in turns to give the sermon. For the leader, an important message that the mosque conveys is about education—it can play a role in emphasising not only values such as 'honesty, sincerity and trust' but also the importance of applying oneself to education and work:

> Religion is not just based upon what we believe in hereafter... what about the life that we're in now? So we have to associate with others as well... we need to work together, we need to achieve, achieve education which is important in life... money doesn't come from trees... you've gotta work for it ... Education is very important... in Islam. (Interview Kat1)

The mosque leader accepts that this may mean young people leaving Katanning to further their education and careers, but believes they will succeed if they take with them a strong grounding in Islam—since a strong faith helps people to withstand the 'pressures of life'—as well as the best of both Malay and western cultures and values (Interview Kat1). That way, one can:

> preserve our beliefs... [and] at the same time... adapt other values into our values... If there is a better values within western values that would benefit my values... I take it... It's not wrong. (Interview Kat1)

This is particularly important since, according to the leader, one needs 'a white mentality to study, not an Islander mentality':

> So that's where your education comes in—[if] you translate from your mother tongue to English, you can't get anywhere. You have to... be able to think like a white man think, then you can achieve what the white man achieve... That's why some of the Islanders are a bit backwards, because they still translate it from the Malay or Chinese to English, you can't do that. (Interview Kat1)

While the Katanning Mosque has remained important for the younger generations of Malays, it has not been adopted by all of the town's Islamic groups. In particular, the Afghan population have chosen not to use the mosque on a regular basis (Field notes 21.11.06). This reflects the differences between Sunni and Shia Islam. Mohammad A notes that while 'we welcome all the Muslims if they want to come', the Afghans 'haven't come yet'. However, the Afghans in Katanning 'do come to some of our special occasions, like we had Hari Raya—like our Christmas—and they came and celebrated it with us' (Interview Kat4).

The mosque is used more regularly by others outside the Malay community, predominantly Indonesian and Malaysian immigrants but also a number of Nyoongars and others who have married into Malay families and adopted Islam (Field notes 21.11.06; Interview Kat4; Murphy 1978). A small number of Pakistanis also use the mosque, including one visitor from a neighbouring town and a local teacher (Interview Kat4). The mosque is occasionally used by non-Muslims when they are invited for special events like Hari Raya. School groups and senior citizens groups are also shown through the mosque on appointment, with the mosque leader or a member of the Katanning Islamic Society giving a talk and answering questions about the mosque and Islam. As Mohammad A describes, the mosque is:

> well known in Katanning, we have open days for the schools, like recently, last Thursday, we had the Bayside Primary School, having a day trip, and they came here to see the mosque and... [to get] more of an understanding of our culture and our religion. So that's why in Katanning we're

> very comfortable here, because the whole community they understand our culture and our religion so it's not like an alien thing to them. Yeah, so it has a very big effect, having the mosque here, and we open it to other people and schools, and we have some seniors from Wagin and Narrogin come a few months ago, come to Katanning to have a look at the mosque. (Interview Kat4)

Tourism in Katanning is less well developed than in Griffith, reflecting both Katanning's smaller size and Griffith's increasing promotion of cellar door sales at local wineries. However, a number of tourist brochures and websites list Katanning Mosque as a tourist attraction, including state-sponsored guides such as *Hidden Treasures of the Great Southern.*[106] The *Hidden Treasures* guide lists Katanning Mosque as one of fifteen 'sight-seeing' stops in the town, along with heritage sites, galleries and the Katanning sale yards. The Katanning Tourist Association has produced postcards of images of the mosque and the annual march for Prophet Mohammad's birthday, advertising them both as unique images of their town.

Notes

1. The name 'Northbridge' was not given to this area until 1981. However, it is used throughout this section for convenience.
2. While some initial contact between Perth's Nyoongars and European settlers was friendly, competition over land soon saw relations become more hostile. The Europeans devised and enforced policies that prevented Nyoongars from entering the city and forced them to the outskirts of the settlement (Town of Vincent 2004, pp. 2–3).
3. Nyoongar was the word used by Aborigines in this area to refer to themselves. At the time of European settlement of the Western Australian (Swan River) colony, there were an estimated 3000 Aboriginal people living in the areas alongside the Swan and Canning Rivers, and groups camped regularly at the lakes to the north of the Swan. One campsite beside the upper Swan River has been dated at over 38,000 years old (Town of Vincent 2004, p. 1).
4. Chinese indentured labourers, or 'coolies', were employed 'in the pearling industry, and as domestic servants, farm labourers, carpenters, gardeners, shepherds, station hands and cooks' (HCWA 2002, p. 3, see also Atkinson 2001, p. 214).

5. By 1901, there were 1521 Chinese in Western Australia (only 18 of them women), with just under half living in the Perth metropolitan area (Atkinson 2001, p. 215).
6. Like in Sydney, trade unions in Perth lobbied hard to restrict Chinese enterprise. The Western Australian *Factories Act 1904* and subsequent acts of state parliament legislated for such restrictions (Atkinson 2001, p. 215; King 1998).
7. The Chung Wah Association was the first ethnic association formed in Western Australia and is still active, and based in James Street Northbridge, today.
8. Following the introduction of the White Australia Policy the country's Chinese population fell considerably in Australia from just under 30,000 in 1901 to 9000 in 1947 (Choi 1975, p. 27). Numbers also fell in Western Australia, from over 1500 in 1901 to only 152 in 1954 (King 1998, p. 47).
9. Many Chinese market gardens in the area were purchased by the city authorities and, by the late 1920s, where converted into public parks (Town of Vincent 2004, p. 20).
10. While the club building was opened in 1937, the club had actually been established in 1934 (WA Italian Club 2009).
11. The name 'Little Italy' was not commonly used among Italians (Interview N21).
12. One local entrepreneur suggests that backpacker accommodation has become 'one of the largest industries in Northbridge' (Interview N13).
13. Working in conjunction with the local TAFE (Technical and Further Education College) members of the local business and residents' association the BigN (Business Improvement Group of Northbridge) provide 'liquor and hospitality' training to many of these tourists to encourage their employment locally (Interview N13).
14. As will be seen shortly the *paifang* on Roe Street has gained limited attention.
15. While the use here is not clear 'half caste' was a term used to refer to Indigenous Australians until recent decades and is now considered by many people to be offensive.
16. EPRA has significant powers under the East Perth Redevelopment Act including the power to acquire, redevelop, subdivide or sell land, develop a master plan for an area, retain assets for particular purposes and issue planning approvals. The boundaries covered by EPRA can be extended as long as the new area is joined to an existing EPRA area, with the local town planning scheme in the new area repealed to allow EPRA's entry. When EPRA projects are completed control is returned to the local planning authority (Interview N19).

17. Officially, Northbridge ends at Newcastle Street. However, the concentration of Vietnamese, Chinese and South Asian shops extends as far north as Brisbane Street, and many people see that as the 'real' boundary.
18. The Town of Vincent was created only in the 1990s, with the areas within its boundaries having formerly been part of the City of Perth (Town of Vincent 2004, p. 31).
19. In other parts of Northbridge EPRA has bought back some retail floor space once developments have been completed in order to have control over the type and quality of businesses that operate there (Interview N19).
20. EPRA consulted with representatives from the Hellenic Association of WA, Italian Chamber of Commerce, Chung Wah Association and Aboriginal Advancement Council.
21. There is some suggestion that a Greek square was developed because Greek houses were demolished in the freeway development (see Interview N29).
22. Via Torre commemorates a well-known Italian family and their renowned butchery 'Carl Torre & Sons', while Kakulas Crescent recognises the prominent Greek family and their iconic 'Kakulas Brothers' grocery store. Hoy Poy Street honours the Chinese Hoy Poy family, with Mrs Edie Hoy Poy having been named a member of the Order of Australia in 1988 for her services to the Chinese community (Yee 1996, p. 2).
23. The Plateia originally included a number of large painted panels depicting Greek scenes from Northbridge, but they were always intended to be temporary and have since been removed.
24. As noted earlier, the boundaries of Northbridge are interpreted differently by different people, and while the Perth Mosque is officially within North Perth, many people see this area as the northern outskirts of Northbridge.
25. Adelaide Mosque was not used as a place of worship for a period until the 1950s, when it was reopened as a mosque with the support of Bosnian immigrants (Dunn 1999, p. 239).
26. Stevens (1989, p. 144) uses 'Anti-Afghan League' while Cigler (1986, p. 81) uses 'Anti-Asiatic League'.
27. Cigler (1986, p. 86) also notes that the hostility towards the cameleers was fueled by the incompatibility of camels and horses, with horsemen being thrown off horses and horse-teams bolting at the sight or smell of camels.
28. Some estimates put the number of 'Afghans' on the Western Australian goldfields at up to 2000, although the number was more likely in the high hundreds (Stevens 1989, p. 24). By 1896, there were 4000 camels servicing Western Australia's eastern goldfields (Stevens 1989,

p. 147). As well as hostilities directed at the cameleers from Anglo-Celtic Australians, there were also tribal conflicts among the cameleers themselves (Stevens 1989, pp. 157–158).

29. The practice of donating (in cash or in kind) that is a fundamental pillar of Islam.
30. The Perth Mosque was included in the Assessment Program of the Heritage Council of Western Australia in 2003 (HCWA 2009a).
31. The mortgage of £1300 was raised with the Diocesan Trustees of the Church of England and total cost of construction reached over £2000 (HCWA 2002, p. 5).
32. The Chung Wah Association received some financial support from the state to establish the Chinese school and a local school lent the association the use of school classrooms (Interview N23).
33. Classes are free for members who participate in paid performances (Interview N24).
34. These changes to the *Criminal Code Act Compilation Act 1913* were sought in response to the widespread racist graffiti and poster campaigns in Perth and some rural areas of Western Australia. They were enacted into legislation with the passage of the *Criminal Code Amendment (Racist Harassment and Incitement to Racial Hatred) Act 1990*.
35. Prior to 1911 Orthodox priests visited Perth from the eastern states, performing Christenings and marriages in people's homes. It is believed that the first Greek Orthodox marriage in Western Australia occurred in 1906, with the Greek Orthodox section at Karrakatta Cemetery consecrated in the same year (HCWA 2005b, p. 4). Reverend Constantinides moved to Darwin in 1913 and was replaced by Germanos Illiou (HCWA 2005b, p. 5).
36. Yiannakis (1996, p. 104) notes that with this arrangement Auguste was not only making his home available to Reverend Crysanthos and the Orthodox community, but also raising his own standing and reputation among local Greeks and 'laying the foundations of the powerful, even hegemonic, role that Castellorizians in W.A. would have with the formal practice and operation of the Greek Orthodoxy in this state'.
37. Yiannakis (1996, p. 102) highlights the cultural importance placed on building a church by early Greek immigrants, noting that 'for nearly 400 years while under Turkish domination, the Orthodox Church openly and clandestinely had worked to maintain Greek language, culture and religion'. Now, in a host society that was 'frequently hostile' they believed the church could again play this role.
38. Since these early days of fundraising to build a church local Greek women have played a key part in the church's development and operation. Excluded from the power structures of the church many have

nonetheless worked tirelessly in fundraising, cleaning, baking ceremonial bread, teaching Sunday school and other functions. Although some women have recently expressed discontent at this obvious inequality in gender roles, many local Greeks have remained very traditional and in some ways 'more Greek than the Greeks of Greece' (Yiannakis 1996, p. 126).

39. Northbridge at this time was 'still largely undeveloped' (HCWA 2005b, p. 6).
40. The Hellenic Community of Western Australia displaced the Castellorizian Brotherhood as the 'key Greek organization' in Perth. However, the association was dominated by Castellorizians for several decades and the fact that it was officially a Pan-Hellenic organisation simply enhanced the legitimacy of Castellorizian control of local Greek affairs (Yiannakis 1996, p. 113).
41. There had been some tension within the Hellenic Community about whether to proceed with earlier plans to immediately build a church or to begin by building a hall that could also be used for church services. The association's president, Peter Michelides, had threatened to resign his position if his preference for the hall was not adopted (Yiannakis 1996, p. 111).
42. The Mediterranean character of the area continued to develop through the inter-war period as Greeks were also joined by Italians and other immigrants (HCWA 2005b, p. 7).
43. Andrew notes that a lot of people were unhappy with the hall's dual function and 'the idea that the place where you were having concerts and wedding receptions served as a venue for a church'. The benefit of such an arrangement was that it was 'manageable' and gave the community time to raise more funds to build a church (Interview N29).
44. The Hellenic Association (Union) first met above the Greek-owned oyster saloon at 507 Wellington Street, Perth, with the saloon having become an important site in the local Greek social scene. They later transferred to the new hall in Parker Street when it was built in 1925 (HCWA 2005b, p. 5).
45. The plans were based on the Hellenic Community's request but designed by architect Harold Boas (HCWA 2005b, p. 8).
46. The builders were F.J. Deacon & Co (HCWA 2005b, p. 8).
47. The mortgage was cleared by 1942 (Yiannakis 1996, p. 113).
48. Dignatories included Illiou who had been preaching in Adelaide after leaving Perth (HCWA 2005b, p. 8).
49. Yiannakis suggests that while people have often suggested this link to the Saint Constantine Church in Castellorizo, the designs are similar largely because both are in a byzantine style and the Northbridge church

also has features similar to the Church of Saint George on Castellorizo (Interview N29).

50. Depending on the amount donated to establishing the church donors listed on the honour board were given the status of 'donors, great donors, benefactors and great benefactors' (HCWA 2005b, p. 9).
51. According to the Heritage Council of Western Australia, the Greek Orthodox Archdiocese of Australia is 'endeavouring to cease the use of this term and wishes the place simply to be known as a church' (HCWA 2005b, p. 10).
52. For example, the first stage of the 'middle school' development was built with over $800,000 raised through pledges (St Andrew's Grammar 2007).
53. While such unwritten laws have since broken down, Yiannakis (1996, p. 120) notes that close association with the church can still be a source of power and prestige. The origins of such animosity towards non-Castellizians may be linked to a Castellorizian parochialism that was exaggerated by the distance of Megisti from other parts of Greece and the presumed superiority of Castellorizian identity and customs over those of other Greeks (see Yiannakis 1996, p. xi). However, it is important to acknowledge that that this behaviour was not universal among Perth's Castellorizian population and that while Castellorizians admit that 'some of their kind were unnecessarily aloof towards other Greeks' they argue there was 'no real malice intended' (Yiannakis 1996, p. 122).
54. St. Basil's Aged Care Services provide in-home help to the aged and can offer Greek-speaking carers. The organisation is subsidised by the Commonwealth Department of Health and Ageing.
55. Peter Kalaf, on the other hand, suggests that many Greeks who have moved away from Northbridge now attend the other churches because of ease of access and parking. He also notes that some people attend both the Church of Saints Constantine and Helene and the nearby Church of the Annunciation of Our Lady (Evangelismos) (Interview N27).
56. The seven Sisters of Mercy women on this voyage were joined on the boat by 21 other missionaries including an Irish Catholic bishop and Spanish Benedictine priests, brothers and lay catechists (Commonwealth of Australia 2008a).
57. In this period, state-sponsored primary school education was not yet widely accessible in Western Australia (HCWA 2004).
58. It is reputed that the original cottage was given to the Sisters of Mercy by an inmate they had visited in Fremantle Prison. On the inmate's death, the title was passed to Bishop Gibney who was himself an Irish immigrant and the Catholic Bishop of Perth from 1887 to 1910 (HCWA 2004).

59. While the Irish population of Northbridge was significant, most Irish settled in the nearby suburbs of Highgate, Subiaco, Leederville or Wembley (Hickey 2007).
60. Girls could continue at St Brigid's all the way through their education, while boys had to leave for another school after year four (Interview N21).
61. The new buildings were designed by prominent architects in Western Australia, including Cavanagh and Cavanagh (who designed the convent and church), J. J. Talbot Hobbs (parish hall) and R. Dennehy (convent school).
62. Further substantial additions to the convent were made in around 1925. At some time prior to 1950, the brick façade was rendered (HCWA 2004).
63. It is interesting to note that in 1902 the majority of students to the high school were Protestant (HCWA 2004, p. 7).
64. In 1902, the high school had 26 day students and 10 boarders. By 1928, there were more than 600 students attending the high school, with around 150 of them boarders. In 1929, the boarders were transferred to a newly purchased property in Lesmurdie, around 25 kilometres to the east (HCWA 2004).
65. Later the Sisters of Mercy Northbridge.
66. There were also a number of Nyoongar parishioners at St Brigid's in the late 1950s and early 60s, many of whom had connections to the Benedictine mission at New Norcia (Hickey 2007).
67. Nonetheless, the former assistant priest at St Brigid's church (and now Catholic Archbishop of Perth) the Most Reverend Barry Hickey suggests that with the residential decline and commercialisation of Northbridge over the last few decades St Brigid's has become 'less of a Parish Church' and is increasingly 'a Chapel for the cosmopolitan… inner-city restaurant and metro-social hub' of Northbridge (Hickey 2007, p. 2).
68. Until recently the church also held mass in Chinese (Hickey 2007). Like the Italians, most of the Polish immigrants in Perth were Roman Catholic and local Poles negotiated to have mass said in Polish as early as the 1950s. Halina Szunejko (2007, p. 5) notes that 'it was very important for the new arrivals to start their family life by having Polish priests officiate at their weddings and baptisms of their children… Later on funeral services were held there'. Between 1952 and 1953, St Brigid's housed a Polish school in the parish hall.
69. Some parishioners from British backgrounds also have a long family history with the church. English mass continued throughout the twentieth century and many Anglo-Celtic parishioners remained heavily involved in the church and school through religious services, social events, tennis and church-based clubs (see, e.g., Slyth 2006).

70. Perth Technical College left the site in 1998 (HCWA 2004).
71. Funding for the restorations included a $20,000 grant from the state government's Heritage Grants Program (HCWA 2004, p. 12).
72. Also Noongar, Nyungar.
73. The Swan River Colony was officially referred to as Western Australia from 1832.
74. Robert Pascoe (1987, p. 53) dates the pioneers of this fishing community as arriving in 1885 but suggests that a 'permanent community' of Italians was not established in Fremantle until the early 1920s. Stransky (2001, p. 494) notes that some early Italian immigrants also established market gardens in Spearwood, about 7 kilometres south of Fremantle.
75. They were also joined by a smaller number of fishermen from Scandinavia, Spain, Estonia, Germany, Austria, Japan, Britain and Australia (see DPI 2005; Tagliaferri in *Fremantle Focus* 2007). The founding fisherman interviewed, who followed his father into Fremantle's fishing industry, argues that while there were a few Norwegians and English who worked in the local industry for many years, it was usually the Italians, Croatians and Greeks who stayed on. Most of the others may have held licenses for a year or so but were really just passing through (Interview F3).
76. The numbers of Greeks who settled in Fremantle were also fewer than the Italians: until World War I the biggest concentration of Greeks was in Fremantle but Perth soon became the biggest Greek centre. For most of the late 1920s there were around 70 Greeks living in Fremantle (Yiannakis 1996, p. 138).
77. These men first traveled on a passenger ship to Cape Town, then transferred to a 77 foot sardine boat for the 73 day journey to Fremantle. The boat and its passengers nearly did not survive the journey as rough seas damaged the engine and blew the boat 300 miles off course (Dias 2002).
78. These men left the fishing industry after their boat caught fire and sank off Cervantes. It was 'a tragedy, but an excuse [to leave the industry] if you had never been a fisherman' (Pereira in Dias 2002).
79. One example of such collectivity in the early years was Cono Glorioso's Rockingham Fishing Company which collectively owned boats and fishing equipment (Pascoe 1987, p. 137).
80. The Cicerello fish markets became an institution in Fremantle in the mid-twentieth century (see Pascoe 1987, p. 148).
81. The WA Portuguese Community Council for Justice (Peace and Social Welfare) (Interview F2).
82. Now the Fremantle Multicultural Centre Inc. The centre offers these services under the Community Partners Program in its Aged Care Project.

83. There are two exceptions: one fish is a mangrove jack from much further north on the Western Australian coast that a fisherman mistakenly brought into the sculpture studio; the other is the addition of two prawns to the bronze basket. While the prawns are not an accurate reflection of the species caught, they were a special request from a donor (Field notes F12.08.08).
84. The founding fisherman interviewed noted that while there were around 2000 names listed up to 1947, the FFMT decided to include only those names the 'looked like they were genuine' workers in the local industry. That is, where men held licenses only for a year or so their names were not included in the list. With each individual name plaque costing around $300, including more names would have significantly increased the cost of the project (Interview F3).
85. The archbishop was visiting Fremantle for the annual Blessing of the Fleet which was to occur the following day (Interview F3).
86. Researcher in Slavonic studies, Peter Hill, also notes that by the 1960s Kalgoorlie had become a centre for Macedonian settlement, although it is not clear when the first Macedonians arrived in the region (Hill 1989, p. 57).
87. This reflected the derogatory term 'ding' that, along with 'dago', was often used by Anglo-Celtic Australians at that time to refer to immigrants from Southern Europe. While 'dago' was used across the continent, the use of the word 'ding' was limited to Western Australia (Baldassar 2001, p. 850).
88. While many of the early 'Afghan' immigrants were indeed from Afghanistan (Stevens 1989, p. viii), others were from areas now known as Pakistan (Interview N1; Dunn 1999, p. 227). Still others were from Iran, Egypt and Turkey. The term 'Afghan' was 'used principally to differentiate between camel-handlers and the other migrants from the Indian subcontinent who were employed as agricultural labourers principally on the east coast of Australia' (Dunn 1999, p. 227).
89. Stevens (1989, p. 144) uses 'Anti-Afghan League' while Cigler (1986, p. 81) uses 'Anti-Asiatic League'.
90. Cigler (1986, p. 86) also notes that the hostility towards the cameleers was fueled by the incompatibility of camels and horses, with horsemen being thrown off horses and horse-teams bolting at the sight or smell of camels.
91. Some estimates put the number of 'Afghans' on the Western Australian goldfields at up to 2000, although the number was more likely in the high hundreds (Stevens 1989, p. 24). By 1896, there were 4000 camels servicing Western Australia's eastern goldfields (Stevens 1989,

p. 147). As well as hostilities directed at the cameleers from Anglo-Celtic Australians, there were also tribal conflicts among the cameleers themselves (Stevens 1989, pp. 157–158).

92. While the Kalgoorlie newspaper *The Sun* campaigned against prostitution in Kalgoorlie, it regarded the presence of 'the unspeakable Asiatic' as a greater problem. In 1908, an article titled 'Amongst the Afghans' asked 'why, in combating the lesser and necessary evil of prostitution, should we shut our eyes to the deeper degradation that is caused by the existence in our midst of a race of people with the salacious and disgusting instincts of the east, and the freedom, unchecked by law, to carry their revolting customs into practice?' (Milentis and Bridge 2004, pp. 169–170).
93. As the demand for camel transport declined, many of the cameleers returned to their homelands. Others found alternate sources of work. The transport of goods by camel was almost completely superseded by 1925 (Stevens 1989, p. 26). It is clear from local newspaper reports that some 'Afghans' remained in Kalgoorlie until at least 1908 (see Milentis and Bridge 2004, pp. 169–170).
94. There were several other instances of race-related attacks in Kalgoorlie in the early 1900s. For example, 1916 saw anti-Greek rioting in Kalgoorlie and Boulder in response to the battle between Greek troops and English and French soldiers at Piraeus during World War I. Resentment towards Greeks at that time, fanned by the press, had its worst expression in Kalgoorlie and Boulder where 'a mob led by soldiers from a nearby camp wrecked a dozen Greek shops, leaving their owners destitute' (Gilchrist 2001, p. 391). Following these riots, many of the Greeks in the Eastern Goldfields, particularly those from Ithaca, moved to the eastern states or back to Greece (Yiannakis 2001, p. 406).
95. German settlers arrived around the turn of the century (Field notes Kat21.11.06) and by the early 1900s Chinese immigrants had established several market gardens in the area (Atkinson 2001, p. 215).
96. Katanning also became the site of early Aboriginal political organisation. The Australian Aborigines Mission were actively encouraging Aboriginal people to move to the town to attend their Katanning Aboriginal School (Department of Indigenous Affairs WA [DIA] 2004, p. 35). With the reserve's population growing rapidly, Katanning's Anglo-Celtic residents became increasingly disturbed by the presence of Aboriginal people in the town and what they saw as their 'uncivilised' behaviour (Chandler and Layman 1998, p. 57). In response to these concerns, some local Aborigines called a large public meeting that drew attendance from all over southern Western Australia. They agreed to establish their own police force and magistrates and develop new laws for Aboriginal people to abide by that would help them cohabit more successfully

with Europeans (Chandler and Layman 1998, p. 57). These regulations included limitations on gambling, drinking and fighting and obligations to earn their keep and assist the elderly. However, the plans failed, largely because of an inability to enforce the laws (DIA 2004, p. 37).

97. As early as the 1870s Malays had become an important source of labour in Australia's pearling industry, particularly on vessels operating out of the Western Australian towns of Broome and Port Hedland. By the 1960s, most of the Malays living in Australia were still employed in the pearling industry, although others had found work in mining, agriculture and the Queensland sugar cane fields (Manderson 2001, p. 579).
98. While annexed by the British government the islands were, for the most part, administered by the Scottish trader John Clunies Ross and his family until control was given to Australia.
99. Percentages are calculated after non-responses are excluded.
100. The two inhabited islands of the Cocos are West Island and Home Island. The latter is known as the Malay village or *kampong* and most *kampong* residents are Cocos Malays.
101. Since the Cocos Islands currency was plastic money that could not be tendered off the islands, some of the migrants had their airfares paid by John Clunies-Ross (see Mahmood in Turiyo 2005). Some of those who came from Christmas Island were aided financially under the British Phosphate Commission's resettlement scheme (Murphy 1978).
102. In 1978, the Cocos Islands were sold to the Australian government by the Clunies-Ross family. At that time, residents of the Islands could voluntarily take up Australian citizenship and all but one did (Bell 1981, p. 13).
103. The General Secretary of the World Islamic League, Saudi Arabian Dr Ali Ketani, had previously visited Katanning and assured the Malay community that he would help secure the funds (Murphy 1978).
104. Metro Meat, as it was then known, also donated $5000 to the original construction of the mosque in the late 1970s (Murphy 1978).
105. Hari Raya literally means 'day of celebration' and is the Malay term for the celebrations at the end of Ramadan, in the form Hari Raya Aidilfitri. It can also refer to the commemorations at the end of Hajj in the form of Hari Raya Aidiladha.
106. The *Hidden Treasures of the Great Southern* is produced with the support of the Great Southern shire councils, the federal Department of Transport and Regional Services and a number of Western Australian state government agencies.

References

Anderson, K. (1990, October). 'Chinatown Re-oriented': A Critical Analysis of Recent Redevelopment Schemes in a Melbourne and Sydney Enclave. *Australian Geographical Studies, 28*(2), 137–154.

Argus, H. J. (2000). *The Long Road to Siberia*. Kalgoorlie, WA: H. Argus.

Argus, H. J. (2005). *The Forgotten Pioneers of the Eastern Goldfields: Information on the Historic Cemeteries of the Eastern Goldfields of Western Australia*. Kalgoorlie, WA: H. Argus.

Atkinson, A. (2001). Chinese in Western Australia. In J. Jupp (Ed.), *The Australian People: Encyclopedia of the Nation, Its People and Their Origins* (pp. 213–215). Cambridge: Cambridge University Press.

Atkinson, A., & Yee, K. Y. (1986). History of Chung Wah Association Part One: 1909–1985. *Chung Wah 75th Anniversary Magazine 1910–1985*. http://www.chungwah.org.au/history.html. Accessed 20 February 2009.

Australian Bureau of Statistics (ABS). (2005). Australia's Top Four Overseas Birthplace Group. *Year Book Australia, 2005*, cat. no. 1301.0. http://www.abs.gov.au/AUSSTATS/abs@.nsf/allprimarymainfeatures/8382A5CD718AA7B0CA2570FC00118529?opendocument. Accessed 1 October 2008.

Australian Bureau of Statistics (ABS). (2019a). *Community Profiles*. https://www.abs.gov.au/websitedbs/D3310114.nsf/Home/2016%20Census%20Community%20Profiles. Accessed 10 March 2020.

Australian Bureau of Statistics (ABS). (2019b). *QuickStats*. https://www.abs.gov.au/websitedbs/D3310114.nsf/home/2016%20QuickStats. Accessed 9 April 2020.

Australian Bureau of Statistics (ABS). (2019c). *Australia's Population by Country of Birth: Key Statistics*. https://www.abs.gov.au/ausstats/abs@.nsf/Latestproducts/3412.0Main%20Features22017-18?opendocument&tabname=Summary&prodno=3412.0&issue=2017-18&num=&view. Accessed 9 April 2020.

Ayris, C. (1981, June 22). Will WA Malays Decide Destiny of the Cocos? *The West Australian*.

The Bacchus Marsh Express (BME). (1907, April 6). The Rescued Miner. *The Bacchus Marsh Express*.

Baldassar, L. (2001). *Visits Home: Migration Experiences Between Italy and Australia*. Carlton South: Melbourne University Press.

Bell, J. (1981, April 17). Islanders Now Control Their Own Destiny. *Western Mail*, p. 13.

Beynon, D. (2007). Centres on the Edge: Multicultural Built Environments in Melbourne. In S. Velayutham & A. Wise (Eds.), *Everyday Multiculturalism Conference Proceedings, Macquarie University 28–29 September 2006*. Sydney: Centre for Research on Social Inclusion, Macquarie University.

Bignell, M. (1981). *A Place to Meet: A History of the Shire of Katanning Western Australia*. Nedlands: University of Western Australia Press.

Blainey, G. (2003). *The Rush That Never Ended: A History of Australian Mining* (5th ed.). Carlton: Melbourne University Press.

Blagg, H., & Valuri, G. (2004, December). Aboriginal Community Patrols in Australia: Self-Policing, Self-Determination and Security. *Policing & Society, 14*(4), 313–328.

Body-Gendrot, S. (2003). Cities, Security, and Visitors: Managing Mega-Events in France. In L. Hoffman, S. Fainstein, & D. Judd (Eds.), *Cities and Visitors: Regulating People, Markets, and City Space* (pp. 39–52). Oxford: Blackwell.

Bunbury, B. (1993). *Reading Labels on Jam Tins: Living Through Difficult Times*. South Fremantle, WA: Fremantle Arts Centre Press.

Bunbury, B. (1997). *Timber for Gold: Life on the Goldfields Woodlines*. Fremantle: Fremantle Arts Centre Press.

Burayidi, M. (2003). The Multicultural City as Planners' Enigma. *Planning Theory & Practice, 4*(3), 259–273.

Burnley, I. H. (2001). *The Impact of Immigration on Australia: A Demographic Approach*. South Melbourne and Oxford: Oxford University Press.

Casey, G., & Mayman, T. (1964). *The Mile That Midas Touched*. Adelaide: Rigby Limited.

Chandler, L., & Layman, L. (1998). *Report on historical background for 'A Heritage of Endeavour—Central Great Southern Heritage Trail'*. Great Southern Development Commission.

Chinatown. (1982). *Chinatown: A Submission to the Federal Minister for Immigration and Ethnic Affairs* (Unpublished).

Choi, C. Y. (1975). *Chinese Migration and Settlement in Australia*. Sydney: University of Sydney Press.

Chung Wah Association. (2009). Chung Wah Association. http://www.chungwah.org.au/home.html. Accessed 19 February 2009.

Church, J. (2005). *Per L'Australia: The Story of Italian Migration*. Carlton, VIC: The Miegunyah Press.

Cigler, M. (1986). *The Afghans in Australia*. Melbourne: AE Press.

City of Perth. (1989). *Northbridge Study: Discussion Paper Number One, Issues*. Perth, WA.

City of Perth. (2007). *Northbridge Piazza*. http://www.perth.wa.gov.au/web/Council/Plans-and-Projects/Current-Projects/Northbridge-Piazza/. Accessed 9 January 2008.

Cleland, B. (n.d.). *A History of Islam in Australia*. http://islam.iinet.net.au/channel/islam_australia.html. Accessed 1 January 2009.

Cocos Solutions. (2008). *Cocos (Keeling) Islands*. Cocos (Keeling) Islands Tourism Association Inc. http://www.cocos-tourism.cc/. Accessed 6 October 2008.

Collins, J. (2013). Rethinking Australian Immigration and Immigrant Settlement Policy. *Journal of Intercultural Studies, 34*(2), 160–177.

Collins, J., & Castillo, A. (1998). *Cosmopolitan Sydney: Explore the World in One City*. Sydney: Pluto Press.

Collins, J., Gibson, K., Alcorso, C., Castles, S., & Tait, D. (1995). *A Shop Full of Dreams: Ethnic Small Business in Australia*. Leichhardt: Pluto Press.

Collins, J., Noble, G., Poynting, S., & Tabar, P. (2000). *Kebabs, Kids, Cops and Crime: Youth, Ethnicity and Crime*. Sydney: Pluto Press.

Commonwealth of Australia. (2008a). *Sisters of Mercy Perth*. Collections Australia Network, Australian Cultural Heritage Collections Online. http://www.collectionsaustralia.net/org/1513/about/. Accessed 10 April 2009.

Commonwealth of Australia. (2008b). *Sisters of Mercy West Perth*. Collections Australia Network, Australian Cultural Heritage Collections Online. http://www.collectionsaustralia.net/org/1518/about/. Accessed 10 April 2009.

Cox, S. (2003). *North of the Line: The 'Demonisation' of Northbridge Youth and the 'Exclusion' of Aboriginal and 'Asian' Youth* (Unpublished thesis). Curtin University of Technology, Perth.

Cresciani, G. (2003). *The Italians in Australia*. Cambridge: Cambridge University Press.

de Lepervanche, M. (1975). Australian Immigrants 1788 to 1940: Desired and Unwanted. In E. L. Wheelwright & K. Buckley (Eds.), *Essays in the Political Economy of Australian Capitalism* (Vol. 1). Sydney: Australia and New Zealand Book Company.

Department for Planning and Infrastructure (DPI) Western Australia. (2005). *The Jetty: The Fishermen's Monument*. Fishing Boat Harbour, Fremantle. www.dpi.wa.gov.au/imarine/gfx/challenger/monument/the%20jetty.doc. Accessed 15 November 2008.

Department of Indigenous Affairs (DIA) Western Australia. (2004). *Lost Lands Report*. Perth, WA: Department of Indigenous Affairs.

Dias, E. (2002). *A Chegada Do Português*. Fremantle, WA: E. Dias.

Dowson, J. (2001). *Fremantle: The Immigration Story*. Fremantle, WA: The Fremantle Society.

Dunn, K. M. (1999). Mosques and Islamic Centres in Sydney, Representations of Islam and Multiculturalism (Unpublished PhD thesis). The University of Newcastle.

Dunn, K. M. (2003). Using Cultural Geography to Engage Contested Constructions of Ethnicity and Citizenship in Sydney. *Social and Cultural Geography, 4*(2), 153–165.

East Perth Redevelopment Authority (EPRA). (2000a). *The History of Northbridge*. East Perth: East Perth Redevelopment Authority.

East Perth Redevelopment Authority (EPRA). (2000b). *The Master Plan—October 2000 Fact Sheet*. East Perth: East Perth Redevelopment Authority.

Edensor, T. (1998). *Tourists at the Taj; Performance and Meaning at a Symbolic Site*. London: Routledge.

Ellul, M. (1999, July 24). Priest Leaves Mark on Piazza. *The West Australian*.

Ewers, J. K. (1971). *The Western Gateway—A History of Fremantle*. Perth: UWA Press.

Fazal, A. K. (2001). Afghans. In J. Jupp (Ed.), *The Australian People: Encyclopedia of the Nation, Its People and Their Origins* (pp. 164–165). Cambridge: Cambridge University Press.

Fitzpatrick, D. (2001). Irish Immigration 1840–1914. In J. Jupp (Ed.), *The Australian People: Encyclopedia of the Nation, Its People and Their Origins* (pp. 451–456). Cambridge: Cambridge University Press.

Fremantle Focus. (2007, October 8). Blessing of the Fleet: A Wish for Fish on Freo's Streets. *Fremantle Focus*. http://www.fremantle.wa.gov.au/news/html/blessing2007.cfm. Accessed 15 November 2008.

Foster, L., & Stockley, D. (1988). *Australian Multiculturalism: A Documentary History and Critique*. Clevedon, UK and Philadelphia: Multilingual Matters Ltd.

Gabaccia, D. (1998). *We Are What We Eat: Ethnic Food and the Making of Americans*. Cambridge, MA: Harvard University Press.

Gilchrist, H. (2001). Greek Settlement Until 1940. In J. Jupp (Ed.), *The Australian People: Encyclopedia of the Nation, Its People and Their Origins* (pp. 387–392). Cambridge: Cambridge University Press.

Government of Western Australia. (2008). Taking People Out of Harms Way. *InterSector*. http://intersector.wa.gov.au/article_view.php?article_id=80&article_main=33. Accessed 21 April 2008.

Great Southern Herald. (2003, February 20). Spirit of Mecca at mosque. *Great Southern Herald*, p. 3.

Greek Orthodox Archdiocese of Australia. (2007). Greek Orthodox Archdiocese of Australia. http://www.greekorthodox.org.au/general/. Accessed 15 March 2009.

Greek Orthodox Archdiocese of Australia (WA). (n.d.). Greek Orthodox Archdiocese of Australia, Fifth Archdiocesan District of Western Australia. http://members.optusnet.com.au/~goawa/index.html. Accessed 15 March 2009.

Gregory, J. (2007, May 12). *Northbridge and Carlton: A Tale of Two Inner City Suburbs*. Paper to the Northbridge History Studies Day, Perth.

Hansard of the House of Commons. (1898). *British Indians in Western Australia*. HC Deb 14 March 1898 vol 54 cc1521-2. http://hansard.millbanksystems.com/commons/1898/mar/14/british-indians-in-western-australia#S4V0054P0-02719. Accessed 6 November 2008.

Hellenic Community of Western Australia. (2007). Hellenic Community of Western Australia. http://helleniccommunity.net/index.php. Accessed 15 March 2009.

Heritage Council of Western Australia (HCWA). (2002). *Register of Heritage Places, Permanent Entry, Chung Wah Association Hall* (Assessment documentation). http://inherit.stateheritage.wa.gov.au/Admin/api/file/61684ebd-82e6-fef8-6725-16d6cf86694f Accessed 23 March 2020.

Heritage Council of Western Australia (HCWA). (2004). *Register of Heritage Places, Permanent Entry, St Brigid's Group, Perth* (Assessment documentation). http://register.heritage.wa.gov.au/viewplace.html?place_seq=23605&offset=4&view=regentries. Accessed 10 April 2009.

Heritage Council of Western Australia (HCWA). (2005a). *Register of Heritage Places, Permanent Entry, Cathedral of St. Constantine and St. Helene (1935–37, 1969)* (Register document). http://register.heritage.wa.gov.au/viewplace.html?place_seq=25660&offset=0&view=regentries. Accessed 9 March 2009.

Heritage Council of Western Australia (HCWA). (2005b). *Register of Heritage Places, Permanent Entry, Cathedral of St. Constantine and St. Helene (1935–37, 1969)* (Assessment documentation). http://inherit.stateheritage.wa.gov.au/Admin/api/file/206e88a4-aca4-31d9-8c34-952aea494408. Accessed 23 March 2020.

Heritage Council of Western Australia (HCWA). (2009a). *Register of Heritage Places, Perth Mosque, Place No. 02156* (Data base entry). http://register.heritage.wa.gov.au/viewplace.html?place_seq=2156&offset=0&view=location. Accessed 18 February 2009.

Heritage Council of Western Australia (HCWA). (2009b). *Register of Heritage Places, Chung Wah Association Hall, Place No. 02027* (Data base entry). http://register.heritage.wa.gov.au/viewplace.html?place_seq=2027&offset=0&view=location. Accessed 19 February 2009.

Heritage Council of Western Australia (HCWA). (2009c). *Register of Heritage Places, Cathedral of St Constantine & St Helene, Place No. 04641* (Data base entry). http://register.heritage.wa.gov.au/viewplace.html?place_seq=25660&offset=0&view=location. Accessed 19 February 2009.

Heritage Council of Western Australia (HCWA). (2009d). *Register of Heritage Places, St Brigid's Group, Place No. 02030* (Data base entry). http://register.heritage.wa.gov.au/viewplace.html?place_seq=23605&offset=4&view=location. Accessed 19 February 2009.

Hickey, B. (2007, May 12). *Irish to Italian: The Changing Northbridge—A Personal Perspective*. Unpublished memoir presented to the Northbridge History Studies Day, Perth.

Hill, P. (1989). *The Macedonians in Australia*. Carlisle, WA: Hesperian Press.

Hoffman, L., Fainstein, S., & Judd, D. (Eds.). (2003). *Cities and Visitors: Regulating People, Markets, and City Space*. Oxford: Blackwell.

Indigenous Studies Program. (2007). *Ninga Mia Indigenous Community*. Agreements, Treaties and Negotiated Settlements Project, Indigenous Studies

Program, The University of Melbourne. http://www.atns.net.au/agreement.asp?EntityID=3049. Accessed 2 November 2008.

Indonesian Observer. (1981, July 1). Islamic Religion Grows Rapidly in Australia. *Indonesian Observer*.

Ip, D. (2005). Contesting Chinatown: Place-Making and the Emergence of 'Ethnoburbia' in Brisbane, Australia. *GeoJournal, 64*, 63–74.

Iveson, K. (2000). Beyond Designer Diversity: Planners, Public Space and a Critical Politics of Difference. *Urban Policy and Research, 18*(2), 219–238.

John Taylor Architect. (2000). *St Brigid's Convent Northbridge*. http://www.architecture.com.au/awards_search?option=showaward&entryno=20006033. Accessed 12 April 2009.

Kalgoorlie Miner. (1979a, July 28). Italian Club, Country Club, Open Tonight. *The Kalgoorlie Miner*.

Kalgoorlie Miner. (1979b, July 31). Consul Opens Club. *The Kalgoorlie Miner*.

Keith, M. (1995). Shouts of the Street: Identity and the Spaces of Authenticity. *Social Identities, 1*(2), 297–315.

King, S. (1998). *Restricted Entry: Investigating Chinese Immigration to Western Australia*. Perth, WA: National Trust of Australia.

Kinkead, G. (1993). *Chinatown: A Portrait of a Closed Society*. New York: Harper Perennial.

Kringas, P. (2001). Post-war Greek Immigration. In J. Jupp (Ed.), *The Australian People: Encyclopedia of the Nation, Its People and Their Origins* (pp. 392–395). Cambridge: Cambridge University Press.

Laurie, K. (1995). *Hannan Street, Kalgoorlie "Our Golden Heritage"*. Kalgoorlie: Kalgoorlie-Boulder Tourist Centre.

Mac Arthur, C. (2007). *'The Emperor's New Clothes': The Role of the Western Australian Press and State Government in Selling the Story of the Northbridge Curfew* (Unpublished thesis). Murdoch University.

Maiorana, G. (1997, April 24–25). Reflections on the Italian Influence in Northbridge. *The Western Review*.

Manderson, L. (2001). Malays. In J. Jupp (Ed.), *The Australian People: Encyclopedia of the Nation, Its People and Their Origins* (pp. 579–580). Cambridge: Cambridge University Press.

Matwijiw, P. (2001). Public Policy Towards Immigrants. In J. Jupp (Ed.), *The Australian People: Encyclopedia of the Nation, Its People and Their Origins* (pp. 782–785). Cambridge: Cambridge University Press.

McKewon, E. (2005). *The Scarlet Mile: A Social History of Prostitution in Kalgoorlie, 1894–2004*. Crawley, WA: University of Western Australia Press.

Milentis, S., & Bridge, P. J. (Eds.). (2004). *The Scarlet Stain: Harlots, Harridans and Hellholes of Old Kalgoorlie*. Carslisle, WA: Hesperian Press.

Morgan, S. (2000, September 18–20). *Ngulak Ngarnk Nidja Boodja—Our Mother, This Land*. Paper to the AIATSIS Conference, AIATSIS, Canberra.

Multicultural and Ethnic Affairs Commission of WA (MEAC) and Commonwealth Office of Multicultural Affairs (OMA). (1989). *Diversity Is Great, Mate! A Study of Community Relations in an Inner-City Area of Perth, Western Australia*. Perth: MEAC.

Murphy, T. (1978). Islanders Build a New Life and Money Is No Object: Katanning Gets a Mosque. *Great Southern Herald*.

National Archives of Australia. (2007). Muslim Journeys, Arrivals, Malays. *Uncommon Lives*. http://uncommonlives.naa.gov.au/contents.asp?cID=89. Accessed 2 October 2008.

Northbridge History Project (NBHP). (2005). *Northbridge History Project Community Consultation Plan June 2005*. Perth, WA: Department of Premier and Cabinet.

Northbridge History Project (NBHP). (2007). Northbridge History Project. http://www.northbridgehistory.wa.gov.au/. Accessed 9 January 2008.

Northbridge History Project (NBHP). (2008). Northbridge History Project Reference Panel. http://www.northbridgehistory.wa.gov.au/index.cfm?event=whoReferencePanel. Accessed 7 March 2009.

Organisation for Economic Co-operation and Development (OECD). (2019). *International Migration Outlook 2019*. https://www.oecd.org/migration/international-migration-outlook-1999124x.htm. Accessed 9 April 2020.

Paddenburg, T. (2017, July 16). Migrants Make Up 60 Per Cent of Residents in Some Perth Suburbs. *Perth Now*. https://www.perthnow.com.au/news/wa/migrants-make-up-60-per-cent-of-residents-in-some-perth-suburbs-ng-cfb9f2f5305b156a4e3b375a3beb46d3. Accessed 9 April 2020.

Pascoe, R. (1987). *Buongiorno Australia: Our Italian Heritage*. Richmond, VIC: Greenhouse Publications.

Pereira, L. (2008, October7). *Citizenship Inquiry*. Shire of Christmas Island (email), personal communication.

Perkins, M. (2008, April 23). *Fremantle's Fishermen's Memorial*. ABC Perth local radio (transcription). http://www.abc.net.au/local/stories/2008/04/23/2199906.htm. Accessed 4 December 2008.

Peters, N. (2007, May 12). *On the Street Where You Live: Inner City Immigrant Enterprise*. Paper to the Northbridge History Studies Day, Perth.

Phillips, J. (2007, January 11). *Moving On*. Department of Community Development Katanning (email), personal communication.

Porter, L. (2008). *No Modest Rescue*. http://www.abc.net.au/local/stories/2007/02/09/1843472.htm. Accessed 23 March 2020.

Poynting, S., Noble, G., Tabar, P., & Collins, J. (2004). *Bin Laden in the Suburbs: Criminalising the Arab Other*. Sydney: Sydney Institute of Criminology.

Price, C. (1963). *Southern Europeans in Australia*. Canberra: Australian National University Press.

Productivity Commission. (2016). *Migrant Intake into Australia*. https://www.pc.gov.au/inquiries/completed/migrant-intake/report. Accessed 9 April 2020.

Rayner, M. (2003). Northbridge Curfew. *Indigenous Law Bulletin, 5*(27), 9–13.

Reece, B. (2001). Irish Convicts. In J. Jupp (Ed.), *The Australian People: Encyclopedia of the Nation, Its People and Their Origins* (pp. 447–451). Cambridge: Cambridge University Press.

Rottnest Island Authority. (2005). *Rottnest Island a 'Little Italy' During WWII*. http://www.rottnestisland.com/en/About+Rottnest+Island+Authority/Rottnest+Island+a+little+Italy+during+WWII.htm. Accessed 15 November 2008.

Sandercock, L., & Kliger, B. (1998a). Multiculturalism and the Planning System, Part 1. *Australian Planner, 35*(3), 127–132.

Sandercock, L., & Kliger, B. (1998b). Multiculturalism and the Planning System, Part 2. *Australian Planner, 35*(4), 223–227.

Shire of Christmas Island. (2008). *Welcome to the Shire of Christmas Island*. http://www.christmas.shire.gov.cx/ Accessed 2 October 2008.

Slyth, M. (2006). *Early Slyth History in Northbridge*. Unpublished memoir, Perth.

St Andrew's Grammar. (2007). St Andrew's Grammar. http://www.sag.wa.edu.au/. Accessed 15 March 2009.

Stannage, C. T. (1979). *The People of Perth: A Social History of Western Australia's Capital City*. Perth: Carroll's for Perth City Council.

Stevens, C. (1989). *Tin Mosques and Ghantowns: A History of Afghan Cameldrivers in Australia*. Melbourne: Oxford University Press.

Stewart, S., Hanna, B., Thompson, S., Gusheh, M., Armstrong, H., & van der Plaat, D. (2003). Navigating the Sea of Diversity: Multicultural Place-Making in Sydney. *International Journal of Diversity in Organisations, Communities and Nations, 3*, 239–252.

Stransky, C. (2001). Italians in Western Australia. In J. Jupp (Ed.), *The Australian People: Encyclopedia of the Nation, Its People and Their Origins* (pp. 492–495). Cambridge: Cambridge University Press.

Strickland, B. (2003). *Golden Quest Discovery Trail Guide Book*. Kalgoorlie, WA: Golden Quest Discovery Trails Association Inc.

Szunejko, H. T. (2007, May 1). *Polish Connection to Northbridgue*. Paper to the Northbridge History Studies Day, Perth.

Thompson, S. (2003). Planning and Multiculturalism: A Reflection on Australian Local Practice. *Planning Theory & Practice, 4*(3), 275–293.

Thomson, T. (2004). *Kalgoorlie Cemetery Heritage Walk Trail 2004*. Kalgoorlie: Kalgoorlie-Boulder Cemetery Board.

Town of Vincent. (2004). *Town of Vincent Heritage Inventory—Thematic History*. Report prepared by Hocking Planning and Architecture, Town of Vincent, Perth.

Town of Vincent. (2006, August 29). *New-Look William Street*. Media Release. http://www.vincent.wa.gov.au/cproot/1247/11207/Williampercent20Streetpercent20Upgrade.pdf. Accessed 9 January 2008.

Turiyo, S. (2005). *Our Stories: A Tribute to Multicultural Harmony, Katanning, Western Australia*. Supported by the Living in Harmony Initiative, Department of Immigration and Multicultural and Indigenous Affairs.

Vertovec, S. (2007). Super-Diversity and Its Implications. *Ethnic and Racial Studies, 30*(6), 1024–1054.

WA Italian Club. (2009). *The History of the WA Italian Club Perth*. http://www.waitalianclub.com/content/history-wa-italian-club-perth.php. Accessed 10 April 2009.

Warde, A., & Martens, L. (2000). *Eating Out: Social Differentiation, Consumption and Pleasure*. Cambridge: Cambridge University Press.

Weber, D. (2001, April 10). Town Drunkenness Upsets Kalgoorlie Locals. *The World Today*, ABC radio, reporter David Weber (transcription). http://www.abc.net.au/worldtoday/stories/s275376.htm. Accessed 7 November 2008.

Welcome Walls. (2004). *Inscription, Welcome Walls*. WA Museum, Fremantle.

The West Australian. (2005, June 25). $122,000 Funding Cut to Nyoongar Patrol. *The West Australian*.

The West Australian. (2009, June 2). Northbridge Businesses Want Police Focus Shifted. *The West Australian*. http://www.thewest.com.au/default.aspx?MenuID=77&ContentID=145395. Accessed 12 June 2009.

Western Australian Museum. (n.d.). *Fremantle's Italian Fishing Fleets*. http://www.museum.wa.gov.au/collections/maritime/mhist/italianfish.asp. Accessed 15 November 2008.

Western Australian Planning Commission (WAPC). (2006). *Ninga Mia Community Layout Plan No. 2*. Prepared by the Department of Planning and Infrastructure in partnership with Ninga Mia Village Aboriginal Corporation, Western Australian Planning Commission Planning for Aboriginal Communities Project. http://www.wapc.wa.gov.au/Initiatives/Planning+for+Aboriginal+communities/CLP+maps/1244.aspx. Accessed 2 November 2008.

Whittington, V. (1988). *Gold and Typhoid, Two Fevers: A Social History of Western Australia 1891–1990*. Nedlands, WA.: University of Western Australia Press.

Wise, A. (2005, February–May). Hope and Belonging in a Multicultural Suburb. *Journal of Intercultural Studies, 26*(1–2), 171–186.

Yee, K. Y. (1996). History of Chung Wah Association Part Two: 1985–1995. *Chung Wah 85th Anniversary Magazine 1910–1995*. http://www.chungwah.org.au/history.html. Accessed 20 February 2009.

Yiannakis, J. (1996). *Megisti in the Antipodes*. Carlisle, WA: Hesperian Press.

York, B. (2001). Portuguese. In J. Jupp (Ed.), *The Australian People: Encyclopedia of the Nation, Its People and Their Origins* (pp. 632–633). Cambridge: Cambridge University Press.

Zukin, S. (1995). *The Cultures of Cities*. Cambridge, MA: Blackwell.

CHAPTER 5

Minority Immigrants and the Australian Built Environment

Global mobility of people is one of the characteristics of the current (pre COVID-19) age. People move from their country as permanent, temporary or undocumented immigrants, refugees or asylum seekers. They also move as tourists, and to visit family and friends. All countries experience population inflow, but few have a history of sustained large-scale immigration to match the Australian experience. Since white settlement/invasion in 1788, immigration has been central to nation building in Australia. This is particularly the case since World War II when Australia joined the United States of America, Canada and New Zealand to become settler immigration nations: immigrants and their families were actively sought to increase population growth and to settle over many generations as members and citizens of their new host nation. These new immigrants settled into new urban, regional and rural neighbourhoods that became their home. Consequently, new immigrants literally changed the face of Australia. This is particularly the case given that the immigration net was cast increasingly widely. Initially most immigrants came from England, Scotland, Ireland and Wales, given Australia's Colonial history, though even those arrivals on the First Fleet included many from a non-British background. The Gold Rushes on the East Coast of Australia from the 1850s changed this: many Chinese male sojourners arrived seeking fame and fortune on the New Gold Mountain (Gao 2017). At one stage one adult male in four in Victoria was Chinese. Here the very racism and prejudice that led to the pronouncement of Australia as *terra nullius* (no

J. Collins et al., *Cosmopolitan Place Making in Australia*,
https://doi.org/10.1007/978-981-15-8041-3_5

one's land) and led to the marginalisation and dispossession of the Indigenous peoples (who had inhabited the land for some 40,000–60,000 years) led to strong and explicitly racist responses to the Chinese. The very first immigration policy was that of Chinese exclusion in New South Wales (NSW), Victoria and Queensland. When the new Australian nation was born at Federation in 1901, the common denominator—the policy that saw most agreement among the former colonies—was the White Australia policy, a policy designed—effectively, as it turned out—to restrict entry of Chinese and other 'coloured' immigrants (Price 1974). Hence the White Australia policy restricted the diversity of the Australian population by restricting the diversity (national, religious, linguistic, cultural) of immigrant arrivals. But it also constructed, by default, the notion of immigrant minorities in Australia: all immigrants of non-British/Irish background.

After World War II, the first Minister for Immigration, A. A. Calwell, announced a large-scale immigration programme that was to attract enough new immigrant settlers to add a further 1% to population growth per year. 'Populate or perish' was the slogan adopted to win support for this programme, with Calwell promising that nine out of every ten post-war immigrants would come from Britain. In other words, the explicitly racist White Australia policy would be the cornerstone of the post-war immigration programme, designed to assuage racist opposition to the arrival of large numbers of new immigrants. But British immigrant arrivals could only fill just over half of the planned intake, so that Australia's post-war immigration policy was facing a crisis just as it was beginning. The Australian government was faced with a stark choice: either cut the immigrant intake in half or permit non-British immigrants to arrive. The weight of numbers won over racial purity concerns. Many refugees—Displaced Peoples—from Eastern Europe entered in this period. The government then sought the most 'white' and 'civilised' non-Brits to come to Australia. In the 1950s and 1960s, this meant that Australia tried to attract first northern (German, Dutch) and then southern Europeans (Greeks, Italians, those from the former Yugoslavia) to its immigration net. It was not until the 1970s that the White Australia policy was formally and finally abandoned. The 'boat people' fleeing Vietnam after the fall of Saigon in 1975 were the first 'Asian' immigrants to arrive in Australia in large numbers since Federation.

In the decades since the introduction of non-discriminatory immigration policy, Australia has been able to cast its net to immigrants from all corners of the globe. Today immigrants from China and India outnumber British and New Zealand immigrants in annual intakes. Most immigrants who arrive under the permanent programme—that is those who arrive with permanent residency rights and (after four years) citizenship rights—are highly-educated young migrants, recruited under the skilled component of the programme, as Australian immigration policy has been continuously fine-tuned to meet the needs of the increasingly globalised economy. At the same time, increasing numbers of immigrants have arrived on temporary immigration visas as temporary skilled workers, international students or working holiday makers. Today the number of temporary migrants who arrive annually outnumber those who arrive under the permanent programme by a factor of three to one. The big change in Australia in the past two decades has been this apparent shift from a settler migration policy to a guest-worker migration policy. But the big change over the past seven post-war decades has been the increasing diversity of the immigration intake: immigrant minorities arrive in increasing numbers from increasingly diverse backgrounds. In this way, immigration has been the key driver of the increasing super-diversity of Australia and of the neighbourhoods into which new immigrants settle.

In order to appreciate the nature of this super-diversity, we need to adopt the lens of cosmopolitanism. When Australia abandoned assimilation policy and introduced multiculturalism—after a brief inter-regnum of integration policy—in the 1970s the key focus was to respect and recognise cultural diversity. A whole series of policies and programmes were introduced under the new multiculturalism framework to reduce the socio-economic disadvantage of minority immigrant groups and their children in the spheres of education, the labour market, health, the law and other aspects of Australian life. Multicultural broadcasting and media were established and promoted. Religious, linguistic and cultural diversity—multiculturalism's five Ds of dance, diet, dress, devotion and dialect—were no longer something for migrants to be ashamed of but something to be encouraged, celebrated and supported.

At the centre of multiculturalism was ethnicity: ethnic community associations were the organisational base of the new multiculturalism (Castles 2000). Multicultural programmes were designed in consultation with ethnic communities who were in turn recruited to participate in the delivery of these programmes and services. The Federation of Ethnic Community Councils (FECCA) became a powerful voice inside the Hawke/Keating Labor Government (1982–1996). This was a great advancement for minority immigrant communities in Australia: they had agency, they had voice, they had (some) power, they had rights, they had access to programmes and services. However, at the same time as ethnicity became a vehicle for the rights and outcomes for minority immigrant communities it also became a constraint. Ethnic identity was but one aspect of an immigrant's super-diversity but it became the defining one. Ethnicity was constructed as mono-dimensional: all Greeks did this; all Italians ... The very freedom that government recognition of ethnicity under multiculturalism granted minority immigrants also became a trap that denied other aspects of diversity *within* ethnic groups. An essentialist approach both recognised and valued ethnicity at the same time as it reduced individuals of minority immigrant background to cultural stereotypes that limited the individual and community (Castles 2000).

It is here that *cosmopolitanism* provides insights to the multivocal dimensions of super-diversity. Just as majority immigrants of British origin were comprised of great difference and diversity so to were minority immigrants of non-British origin. A cosmopolitan approach compels us to investigate and value this super-diversity. It demands a more nuanced, complex and contradictory analysis of the impact of immigrants on Australia society, including their impact on the built environment. The other important advantage of cosmopolitanism for this book is that it necessitates an acknowledgement of the Indigenous history and presence in Australia. Australia was not an empty land but had a long and rich cultural history of Indigenous settlement and development. Importantly, Indigenous Australians were themselves very diverse: 250 Indigenous Australian languages including 800 dialectal varieties were spoken on the continent at the time of European settlement in 1788 (AIATSIS 2019).

Another important point of departure for this book is the *agency* of new immigrant settlers. New immigrants not only settle in new urban, regional or rural neighbourhoods of Australian society, they also *transform* these neighbourhoods (Castles et al. 2015). Minority immigrants have often faced many formal and informal barriers that constrain their settlement opportunities and outcomes. But despite these constraints, immigrants make their own history in Australia. The central concern of this book has been to document and understand the ways that minority immigrants transform the built environment of suburbs, regional cities or rural towns. The important point here is that these transformations take time and can only be appreciated through the lens of history, a history that always has an Indigenous past and present and has a changing British and minority immigrant aspect.

There are two key drivers of the transformation of the built environment by minority immigrants. The first is by way of the immigrant or ethnic community associations and organisations that immigrants form in the countries where they settle. This is a form of ***ethnic community capital*** (Lalich 2003) and is perhaps most visible in terms of the building or repurposing of places of worship to respond to the religious diversity that accompanies immigrant settlement. It is also evident in the transformation of buildings to act as the places where members of that minority community can safely gather for community meetings and gathering of a cultural, recreational, leisure, educational or sporting nature. Here social capital is mobilised by minority immigrant communities—local and diasporic—to raise capital to purchase, build or renovate a building for their purposes.

The other key driver is that of minority immigrant entrepreneurship—or what Dana (2007) and his colleagues call 'ethnic minority entrepreneurship'. Wherever immigrants have settled they have established restaurants, shops and other businesses providing goods and services, initially to their co-ethnic community—the ethnic market niche—and, in most cases, later to the mainstream community of their neighbourhood. Immigrant entrepreneurs have been the most visible agents of change in the built environment of main streets of suburbs, cities and towns across Australia.

The final key point of departure is that the diverse history of large-scale Australian immigration has transformed Australia to an increasingly cosmopolitan country. Even in the areas of greatest immigrant density no one immigrant or non-immigrant community dominates the neighbourhood. In one of the most concentrated local government areas of immigrant concentration, Hurstville in Sydney, Chinese-born represent 56% of the total population. But the other 44% come from all corners of the globe and include Indigenous peoples. There are no ethnic ghettoes in Australian cities or towns (Jupp et al. 1991; Johnston et al. 2007). Rather, the suburbs of Australian metropolitan areas are very cosmopolitan in terms of the cultural diversity. This cosmopolitan character is also evident in regional cities and rural towns, though generally to a less extent in terms of minority immigrant population and to a variable extent in terms of the Indigenous population. A cosmopolitan focus also highlights the great diversity within different immigrant communities: diversity in terms of the region/town/island from whence community members came, their ethnic backgrounds, their age, their language and dialect, their religion, their class background and the class resources that they can mobilise, their length of stay in Australia and the human and social capital that they possess.

5.1 Cosmopolitan Heritage

The research for this book was funded by the Australian Research Council and Industry Partners that were part of the National Trust organisations in NSW and Western Australia (WA) and Multicultural policymakers in Queensland. National Trusts have a key concern for the heritage of significant buildings and sites. Most of these heritage sites are those of British immigrants and their ancestors, since buildings constructed in the early periods of white settlement have the weight of history on their side, not to mention architectural distinction. An unkind view of heritage organisations is that they are overly concerned about architecture and architectural value from the past to be preserved for the future. The number of buildings or sites from Indigenous or minority immigrant history in heritage lists is very small indeed. In part this is because the contribution of minority immigrants to the built environment is often more recent and the buildings themselves perhaps more significant in social rather than architectural terms. This book has attempted to redress this gap with its focus on minority immigrants and the Australian built environment. But we hope that our contribution *does more* than fill a gap. Rather our approach situates the study of the built environment of suburbs, cities and towns in the changing social processes that underlay the transformation of Australian neighbourhoods over time. A key theme has been that the history of white settlement is a history of the increasing super-diversity of Australian society in general and of Australian neighbourhoods in urban, regional and rural areas in particular. Super-diversity existed prior to white settlement—as seen in the great diversity within Australia's First Peoples—but increased over time as the size and diversity of the immigration net continued to transform the cultural, linguistic, religious and ethnic characteristics of the Australian people. While most immigrant settlement has been in Australia's metropolitan areas—its capital cities—reinforcing the urban concentration of the Australian population, regional and rural Australia also has an immigrant and cosmopolitan past, present and future. Indeed, one of the big recent changes in Australian immigration policy has been to encourage an increasing number of new immigrant arrivals to settle in regional and rural Australia.

The methodology adopted in this book is that of urban, regional and rural case studies in three states—NSW, Queensland and WA—as a way of understanding the larger issues and processes at the national level. This is not to say that the sites chosen are in any way representative of all other areas, but rather that the ways of seeing the changing impact of minority immigrants and the Australian built environment in these sites presents a lens through which the broader Australian experience can be researched and studied. In each site, we looked at the (changing) Indigenous history, an ever-present though often ignored aspect of heritage and the built environment. We then looked at changing patterns of immigrant settlement in each site. Key informants from different minority immigrant communities narrate their history in each case study. The focus then shifted to different aspects of the built environment of each site: those built or transformed by private enterprise in the form of immigrant entrepreneurs (often shops and restaurants); those built or transformed by ethnic or immigrant community groups, or what we would now call social enterprise or not-for-profit organisations (often places of worship, ethnic or migrant community clubs or centres for community meetings and educational, sport and recreational purposes); and those monuments and other landmarks erected to symbolically honour minority immigrant heritage.

We were interested to identify how minority immigrants transformed the Australian built environment. A key player in this has been local government—the regulators—whose permission is required for development of the establishment of new community services and community spaces. In all instances, we drew on key stakeholders as key informants to narrate the social processes that underlay the dynamics that led, eventually, to new or transformed places or spaces that reflected the iconography of new minority immigrant communities.

We were also conscious that there are strong cultural stereotypes about minority immigrant groups in Australia. These are in part a product of the historical and contemporary racialisation of immigrant minorities in a country that was not ashamed to proudly enact explicitly racist immigration policies nor ashamed about its racist responses to the First Peoples of the land. For these reasons, in some sites we interviewed people selected from the passing parade of consumers/visitors to get their take on the *authenticity* of the minority immigrant shops, restaurants, places of worship and ethnic precincts.

5.2 Theoretical and Conceptual Implications

Our intention in conducting the fieldwork for this book was to broaden the theoretical and conceptual framework of our understandings of the built environment. Because the research questions related to the impact of minority immigrants on the built environment of urban, regional and rural Australia, we draw on several literatures. Firstly, there is the literature related to *immigration* per se, and to *minority immigration*. The changing political economy of immigration (Goldin et al. 2011; De Hass et al. 2019) has led to dramatic changes in the size, character, composition and settlement patterns of Australian immigrant intakes over time. These changes are then reflected in the changing population of urban, regional and rural Australia (Productivity Commission 2016) and, in turn, their impact on the built environments of the neighbourhoods into which they settle. This requires the historical lens of the *racialisation* of immigration policy and formal and informal responses to minority—that is, non-British—immigration by governments, institutions and individuals. It also requires an elevation of the concept of migrant *agency*, that is, the capacity of migrants to make their own decisions within constrained economic, political and social environments. Central to this is the way that migrants are both transformed by the migration experience and, in turn, transform the society into which they settle. This transformation is a two-way process and lays at the heart of understanding the contemporary migrant experience (Castles et al. 2015).

Secondly, the *cosmopolitan* framework compels us to consider Indigenous histories of the places that are our case studies as well as keeping an alert eye to the super-diversity within different ethnic or immigrant communities as well as between minority and British immigrants. This approach rejects the essentialist, homogenous conceptualisation of ethnic groups that lays at the heart of the multiculturalism literature.

Thirdly, since the greatest agents of change in the built environment of urban, regional and rural Australia are immigrant entrepreneurs, the literature on *immigrant entrepreneurship* is an important conceptual framework for this book. Not all immigrants move into entrepreneurship: some immigrant groups (Koreans, Lebanese, Greek, Italians) have relatively high rates of entrepreneurship while others (Indian, Chinese, British) relatively low rates of entrepreneurship. Uneven rates of immigrant entrepreneurship in Australia are shaped by differences in the group characteristics of immigrants and the employment and other opportunity structures that they face when they arrive in Australia (Waldinger et al. 1990) as well as by the different ethnic and class resources (Light and Gold 2000; Light and Rosenstein 1995) that immigrants can accumulate and mobilise once settled in Australia. The research presented in this book suggests that the theory of immigrant entrepreneurship needs to place greater emphasis on the changing and uneven processes of the racialisation of immigrant minorities than it currently does. Many immigrant entrepreneurs have an individual and/or family experience of entrepreneurship prior to emigration to Australia. In addition, different immigrant groups at different times in different countries face different regimes of regulation and different experiences of immigrant settlement—what Kloosterman and Rath (2001) refer to as mixed embeddedness—that impact on their immigrant entrepreneurial experiences. In our story, the national government shapes the opportunities for immigration—how many come and from where—while the state (provincial) and local governments determine rules and regulations that shape access to business opportunities by new immigrants and regulate changes to the built environment.

One subset of the immigrant entrepreneurship literature relates to *ethnic precincts*, that is, geographic clusters of immigrant entrepreneurs from the same ethnic group, such as Chinatown, Little Italy, Asiatown, Koreatown and the like (Collins 2007; Collins and Kunz 2007; Collins and Shin 2014). It reflects on notions of the cultural and symbolic economies (Zukin 1995; Urry 2002). The streetscape of ethnic precincts and other clusters of immigrant entrepreneurs is often dominated by associated visual signs and symbols of the area's ethnic character, including foreign language signs (see, for example, Lou 2007; Wise and Velayutham 2009; Wise 2011, 2010) and ethnically themed public art, shopfronts and street furniture (Kunz 2005). As Dunn (1999, p. 16) describes, these areas 'may develop a feel, a reputation or an identity linked to a non-hegemonic culture'. Ethnic precincts are key sites of the commodification and marketing of ethnic diversity in cities of significant immigration. They are a prime focus for the production and consumption of the ethnic economy, a commodification of place and space where the symbolic economy of space (Zukin 1995) is constructed on representations of ethnicity and 'immigrantness'.

The built form of ethnic precincts is often quite different from the surrounding neighbourhood, being characterised by clusters of small businesses associated with an ethnic group. In NSW, Queensland and WA, the urban case study chosen related to Chinatowns in Sydney, Brisbane and Perth, respectively. The prominence of Chinatowns in most cities of Chinese immigrant settlement reflects the long history of Chinese settlement in Australia from the gold rushes beginning in the 1850s in eastern Australia. Despite—or perhaps because of—the changing nature of Chinese immigration to Australia (Wang et al. 2018), Australia's Chinatowns have changed over time. But they retain traditional forms of Chinese iconography: the dragons, the Chinese lanterns, the Chinese language signage. Here is a contradiction identified thirty years ago by Anderson (1990) between the stereotypical notion of 'Chineseness' and the dynamic super-diversity of ethnic Chinese peoples around the globe.

The other leading forces at the forefront of the change minority immigrants make to the built environment are ethnic and migrant community organisations. They established ethnic clubs and ethnic associations for political, educational, cultural, recreational and sporting activities, and helped build places of worship for their newly-arrived immigrant communities (Lalich 2003). In many instances, these immigrant community organisations receive assistance from Diasporic networks and governments. While immigrant entrepreneurs represent the transformation of local built environments by private enterprise, ethnic clubs and ethnic associations are a form of transformation by social enterprise or ethnic community capital.

Another literature that intersects with our study of the impact of immigrant minorities on the built environment of Australia's metropolitan and regional cities and rural towns is that of governance and regulation: local area plans and planning processes. Regulation theory (Fainstein et al. 2003, p. 240) explores the way that different regulatory frameworks and institutions shape the development of the built environment within a 'complex matrix of economic, political, cultural and spatial interactions and illustrates the interplay of sectors and scales—local, regional, national and international…without sacrificing the possibility of agency or overlooking the complex role of culture'. The Federal Australian government shapes the overall contours of immigration policy, including the numbers, ethnic composition and other characteristics of immigrant arrivals. State governments enact all sorts of policies that regulate private businesses and community sector organisations. It wasn't until the 1980s that cafés and restaurants were able to have street tables, for example, changing dramatically the built environment of downtown and suburban areas. Local government oversees the makeover of public spaces and places of the city, the holding of festivals, the erection of monuments and so on. The city councils of Sydney, Brisbane and Perth regularly review the Chinatown developments in each city, consulting widely and producing new local area plans that include the incorporation of new public iconography, furniture, signage and display. The key problem here is that each minority immigrant or ethnic group is in fact quite diverse, so that the challenge becomes one of identifying which part of the immigrant community to consult and who to ignore.

5.3 Chinatowns

In our chapters, we have traced the transformation of Chinatowns in Sydney, Brisbane and Perth by presenting their history, narrated by key informants in the Chinatown communities. In all cases, the history is one of (changing) Chinese immigrant settlement with the private and social Chinese immigrant entrepreneurs the key agents of the changing face of Chinatown over time. Chinatown is an ethnic precinct that has been found in many cities of immigrant settlement around the globe (Anderson 1990, 1991; Lin 1998; Wong et al. 2016; Rath et al. 2018). Other ethnic precincts such as 'Little Italy' (Collins 1992; Conforti 1996; Collins and Castillo 1998), 'Little Korea' (Min 1996, 2008; Park 1997; Collins and Shin 2014), 'Little India' (McEvoy 2003; Chang 2000), 'Little Bavaria' (Frenkel and Walton 2000), 'Little Sweden' (Schnell 2003) and 'Finntowns' (Timothy (2002) have emerged across many continents. A key feature of ethnic precincts is the provision of ethnic food and ethnic restaurants (Gabaccia 1998; Warde and Martens 2000).

Recent research on Sydney's Chinatown (Wong et al. 2016, p. 8) emphasises its rapid change and transformation, a cause and effect of the increase in Chinatown's super-diversity, and makes the case for a reconceptualisation of Sydney's Chinatown. The area has transformed greatly in the past two decades because of strong permanent and temporary migration intakes leading to a population growth of 800%, accompanied by strong development of high-rise apartment buildings in the area. Many Asian international students and working holiday makers live in Haymarket. Asian migrant settlement in Haymarket—where Chinatown is located—increased to 64%, the highest ethnic concentration density of all suburbs in greater Sydney. Wong et al. (2016, p. 8) argues that

'[C]hinatown is no longer a self-contained ethnic enclave, but a "nodal meeting place" for different kinds of transnational human, economic and cultural flows between Australia and Asia'. Chinatown is no longer an exclusively Chinese area, they argue, though it could be argued that Chinatowns—their population, their business owners and community leaders—are rarely exclusively Chinese. Our other case studies of Chinatowns in Brisbane and Perth also demonstrate an increasing diversity of people and businesses. In Fortitude Valley, there is a culturally diverse population with many European and Asian immigrants running small businesses including Korean supermarkets, Indonesian and Thai grocery stores, Asian/Chinese supermarkets and Thai, Korean, Japanese, Vietnamese, Chinese and Italian restaurants as well as Chinese herbal medicine practitioners and other services. In this sense, there are at least two layers of businesses in ethnic precincts. One is the street level, the most visible part of the built environment. Here restaurants and retail shops predominate. Ethnic iconography, non-English language scripts and other markers of cultural difference predominate as visual cues—dragons, lanterns, gates—to go with the sounds and smells of the ethnic precinct that accompany them. But go upstairs and you will find many Chinese and other Asian immigrant professionals: doctors, lawyers, accountants, dentists. Here the cultural markers of the professionals' ethnic background may be more subtle. This level is less for the tourists and lunch-time customers and more for the co-ethnic Chinese/other Asian resident population.

Northbridge is an interesting example of a 'failed' Chinatown. In Chapter 4, we outlined in some detail the historical change of Northbridge as an ethnic precinct and ethnic cosmopolitan neighbourhood over more than a hundred years of (changing) immigrant settlement. By the early 1980s, with the influx of Asian immigrants in the area, a small group of Malaysian Chinese businesspeople began to plan a Chinatown for Northbridge. Local Government has elaborate planning processes and procedures that govern such a proposed development. A Northbridge Board of Management was established but the original plan—to purchase surrounding properties to include over 30 specialist Asian food stalls, a Chinese theatre, a 49-bed hotel, entertainment facilities and professional offices—was never fully implemented because of three key factors: poor positioning, the reluctance of property owners to sell to the developers and the blow-out in interest rates in the late 1980s. Twenty years later a second attempt to create a formal 'China Town' in Northbridge was spearheaded by Town of Vincent Mayor, Nick Catania, who wanted to

develop a 'readily identifiable and popular precinct' that 'for want of a more appropriate name might be called "China Town"' (Town of Vincent 2006, p. 1). However, the proposal had limited support from business owners and residents. Many of the businesses in Northbridge were owned by non-Chinese entrepreneurs, including Vietnamese, Thai, Greek, Italian and Japanese, while some ethnic Chinese entrepreneurs felt little connection with China, having been born in South-East Asia. The proposal was also opposed by some members of Perth's peak Chinese organisation, the Chung Wah Association, who felt that establishing a formal Chinatown did not accurately reflect the area's history and ran the risk of both alienating members of the non-Chinese community and stereotyping Chinese.

Put crudely, it was the historical and increasing contemporary cosmopolitan diversity of Northbridge that was the Achilles heel in the Chinatown proposal: how can you identify an area with one ethnic community when many others live and have businesses there. Similarly, the very diversity within Northbridge's ethnic Chinese community meant that while some promoted Chinatown others opposed it. In the historical development of Sydney's and Brisbane's Chinatowns local government—the city councils—consulted with the local Chinese community as part of their local area development planning process. This was to make sure that the proposal had community support and thus legitimacy. But the key problem then becomes who are the legitimate representatives of the local ethnic Chinese community? Wong et al. (2016, p. 47) cites an informant who estimated that there are over 300 Chinese community organisations in Sydney's Chinatown. Who is to be consulted, and who is to be ignored? What is evident in this contradiction about legitimacy in the impact of minority immigrants on the built environment is the tension between differentiation and homogeneity, as Fainstein et al. (2003, p. 246) put it, from the perspective of cultural tourism research. The cosmopolitanism framework is more alert to these underlying complexities and contradictions than the stereotyped construction of ethnicity under Australian multiculturalism theory and policy.

5.4 Cosmopolitan Place Making

There is another contradiction that is inherent in appraising the impact on the built environment of minority immigrants in Australia. This relates to the problem of credibility and authenticity of an ethnic precinct or individual building's claim to reflect/represent some cultural diversity. There is a large body of cultural tourism research concerned about this from the tourist's perspective. International and domestic tourists visit the Chinatowns of Sydney and Brisbane and Northbridge in Perth. What do they expect to see in a Chinatown? Is their experience the authentic ethnic Chinese experience?

In order to investigate this further, we conducted fieldwork with tourists in Sydney's Chinatown and in Northbridge. There are very different responses to Chinatown's marketing and ethnic iconography and symbolism. We found that for many survey respondents 'boundaries' of ethnicity, ancestry and identity can be blurred. Kunz (2005) found that Chinese and Asian consumers were more likely to experience Chinatown's built environment as 'fake' and 'kitschy', while other consumers were more likely to experience it as 'authentically Chinese'. The survey of 100 passers-by in Dixon Street conducted as part of the research for this book also revealed a range of responses to Chinatown's built environment, from those who felt it was 'very authentic' to those who felt it was 'a bit kitsch'. However, contrary to the findings of Kunz (2005), there was no clear pattern between people's response to the built environment and their ethnicity. A survey of Sydney's Chinatown consumers conducted in 2015 found that while there is a popular belief that people go to Chinatown mainly for Chinese cuisine due to its 'authenticity' in taste, Chinatown's most popular ethnic cuisine among 43% of student respondents to the survey was actually Japanese. Overall, 90% of the survey respondents answered that they enjoyed going to Chinatown with 'Asian food'—not Chinese food—the key reason for students going to Chinatown (Wong et al. 2016, pp. 42–43). This is a key reason why Wong et al. (2016) argues that Chinatown has been transformed into an Asiatown.

As we argued in Chapter 1, heritage assessments of the built environment have tended to emphasise historic, scientific and archaeological value rather than social value, with the concept of social heritage significance inadequately understood (Armstrong 1994, p. 480; see also Sandercock and Kliger 1998). The argument is that official definitions of heritage have prioritised 'elite' or 'western' heritage at the expense of the heritage places of socially marginalised groups.

In this book, we have adopted an approach that recognises that what constitutes 'heritage' is socially constructed and should give equal value both to places deemed significant by heritage 'experts' and those felt to be heritage by local communities. The impact of minority immigrants on the built environment cannot be fully appreciated if the focus is solely on building development that is grand and distinctive in architectural or heritage terms. Often the everyday plain building is purchased for minority community purposes to play a central role in the life of that immigrant community as well as other communities in the neighbourhood. For example, in Cairns a modest house was purchased in 2000 as the site of the new Islamic Mosque. Donations from the Islamic community in Cairns and Islamic Associations from all over Australia helped pay for this transformation from house to mosque. Similarly, in Griffith a very modest house was brought to become the new Mosque, the Riaz Mosque, very near the centre of Griffith but quite inconspicuous. Located in a largely commercial area, the mosque is architecturally unremarkable and set some way back from the street with only the sign above the door giving its presence away. Both modest buildings play a vital role in the social life of the immigrant communities of Cairns and Griffith.

Often the super-diversity within minority immigrant communities imposes constraints on the appearance of a building because different regional groupings of migrants have a different take on what constitutes ethnic authenticity. For example, when renovations were done to transform an existing building into the Portuguese Club in Freemantle they were done in the common style of the day and did not include any identifiably 'Portuguese' features. As one Portuguese community informant put it, 'this was a deliberate decision to prevent the risk of friction among club members about what constituted a Portuguese style…because we've got such a diverse community, you know, there's people from the north, people from the south, people from the mainland, people from the island… they'll say "well this is what we think's Portuguese and we're not from your area", you know, so it was just easier not to do it, to save complications' (Interview F2).

This is an important point because when immigrant communities construct a place of worship, an ethnic club or community hall, or a monument to the immigrant history of the area, the underlying politics is often that of competing regional immigrant groups. For example, in the Greek Orthodox Church of Saints Constantine and Helene in Northbridge, Castellorizian Greeks have played the leading role in its development to the relative exclusion of non-Castellorizians. In Griffith, both the Italian community and the Sikh community are rife with complex internal politics. At the Italian Museum some informant members of the museum committee criticised the dominance of northern Venti Italian immigrants, evident they say in the Museum contents' northern Italian bias. In the Sikh community, intra-group rivalries are played out within the management committee of the Gurdwara Singh Saba (itself comprised only of men), with two groups of roughly equal numbers jostling for power at the committee's elections for officeholders.

When what is being built is a monument to a broader immigrant heritage the contestation over authenticity is even sharper. In WA, the Freemantle Fishermen's Monument was constructed in 2004 to celebrate the pioneering role of southern European immigrant groups (Greeks, Italian, Portuguese) in establishing the fishing industry out of Freemantle. While consultation with all communities preceded the design and construction of this monument, the Portuguese community were less than enthusiastic about the outcome. Some Portuguese informants felt that the monument has 'very much taken on an Italian feel' while another informant points out that 'our fishermen didn't dress like that'.

Similarly, the Gold Water Mouth Fountain was constructed in Sydney's Chinatown in 2000 as a gift from Sydney to the Chinese community to celebrate the 2000 Sydney Olympic Games. Designed by Chinese artist Lin Li, who won the public design competition held by the City of Sydney, Gold Water Mouth Fountain consists of a 200-year-old dead gum tree reinforced with steel on the inside and lined externally in gold in its top half, with recycled water flowing out of the one remaining branch at the top and trickling down the tree. However, some Chinese entrepreneurs in Chinatown argued that a dead tree with water flowing out is bad *feng shui*, particularly for a commercial precinct, because it symbolises the loss of money. The controversy over the Golden Water Mouth Fountain not only confirms Meethan's (2001, p. 27) argument about the multivocal, ambiguous and contradictory meanings that symbols of ethnicity can carry, but also highlights the significant influence of those that have input into the council decisions of the day. With the complexity and diversity within Chinatown's business community, let alone its other stakeholders, these decisions can rarely claim to represent most constituents' views.

Other buildings are transformed many times. For example, the first Chinese Temple built in Innisfail in 1886 was damaged by a cyclone in 1918, repaired, and remained standing for another twenty years. In 1940, the original temple was demolished, land was purchased with the money and a new temple was built. St Brigid's Catholic Church was initially a development of the Irish catholic community and later the Italian immigrant community, as changing migration settlement patterns transformed the parishioners.

Social usage and significance are the strong suites of many of the buildings constructed or renovated by minority immigrant communities. Many ethnic community groups collectively raise capital—ethnic community capital—for the purpose of financing a new building or transforming an existing one for different purposes. For example, the Sikh temple, Gurdwara Singh Saba, which opened in Yoogali just outside Griffith, NSW, in 1993, at the old Coronation Hall site. After around six months of fundraising from Sikh families in Griffith, Melbourne and Brisbane it was purchased outright with cash. To build the Katanning Mosque, most Malay families in Katanning contributed five dollars each week for the land purchase and mosque construction.

Often the façade of a building is transformed, but always the social interaction within the building changes. The buildings that these institutions are housed in make a significant though often undervalued contribution to the built heritage. Many buildings built by immigrant communities often serve the broader cosmopolitan community in the neighbourhoods. In Cairns, for example, Polish, Italian, Russian, Romanian, Bulgarian, Serbian as well as Indigenous communities meet at St John's Community Care.

The impact of minority immigrants on the built environment of Australian suburbs, cities and towns is profound. This is what we mean when we talk about cosmopolitan placemaking. While many changes to the built environment by immigrant entrepreneurs and minority immigrant community groups might not be of striking architectural significance, their social significance is unarguable. The social processes that underlie this changing built environment are complex, often contradictory and represent as much conflict within minority immigrant communities as co-operation within and between them. This is but one dimension of the super-diversity of contemporary Australian cosmopolitan society. This book has presented the historical and contemporary story of the way that immigrant communities have transformed Chinatowns in Sydney and Brisbane and failed to establish a Chinatown in Perth's Northbridge. We have looked at similar stories in the regional centres of Cairns, Freemantle, Port Kembla and Kalgoorlie and the rural towns of Griffith, Katanning and Caboolture. As Australia's history of migration continues to change the face of Australian society, it also transforms the built environment of

Australian suburbs, cities and towns, perhaps the most visible affirmation of Australia's (changing) cosmopolitan society. In each urban, regional and rural case study addressed in this book we have seen the way that not only have the lives of immigrant minorities been transformed by immigration to Australia but in turn these immigrants have transformed the Australian neighbourhoods into which they settle. This is but one expression of the agency of immigrants. While we have selected a few places and a few key minority immigrant groups for our fieldwork, the demographic and social fact is that Australian neighbourhoods are super-diverse and increasingly cosmopolitan. In each place new immigrant minorities arrive to change the face of what is already a cosmopolitan suburb, city or town. Private and social enterprises are the key agents of this changing physical and social landscape as immigrant entrepreneurs and immigrant community groups add their touch to the changing built and social environment of the places where they settle. This is at the same time a process mediated by politics and an expression of the politics of everyday multiculturalism. Federal governments shape the contours—the numbers and the class, religious and ethnic characteristics—of new immigrant arrivals. Local and state government authorities impose and change planning rules and regulations that shape what changes to the built environment of these new immigrant communities is and is not possible. Community groups organise to raise funds for a new place of worship, a new social or sporting club or agitate and mobilise for a new monument, place or space to represent the past, present or future needs of their community. A key argument of this book is that it is the changing, complex and often contradictory social relations that occur within the facades of buildings in suburbs, cities and towns that is the most important legacy of cosmopolitan place making in Australia today.

References

Anderson, K. (1990, October). 'Chinatown Re-oriented': A Critical Analysis of Recent Redevelopment Schemes in a Melbourne and Sydney Enclave. *Australian Geographical Studies*, 28(2), 137–154.

Anderson, K. (1991). *Vancouver's Chinatown: Racial Discourse in Canada, 1875–1980*. Montreal: McGill–Queens University Press.

Armstrong, H. B. (1994, July 13–15). Sustaining Urban Heritage in Multicultural Cities. In S. Neary, M. Symes, & F. Brown,*The Urban Experience: A People-Environment Perspective* (pp. 479–485). Proceedings of the 13th

Conference of the International Association for People-Environment Studies, University of Manchester. London: E & FN Spon.
Australian Institute of Aboriginal and Torres Strait Islander Studies (AIATSIS). (2019). *Indigenous Australian Languages: Celebrating 2019 International Year of Indigenous Languages*. https://aiatsis.gov.au/explore/articles/indigenous-australian-languages. Accessed 14 April 2020.
Castles, S. (2000). *Ethnicity and Globalisation*. London: Sage.
Castles, S., Ozkul, D., & Arias Cubas, M. (Eds.). (2015). *Social Transformation and Migration: National and Local Experiences in South Korea, Turkey, Mexico and Australia*. London: Palgrave Macmillan.
Chang, T. C. (2000). Singapore's Little India: A Tourist Attraction as a Contested Landscape. *Urban Studies, 37*(2), 343–368.
Collins, J. (1992). Cappuccino Capitalism: Italian Immigrants and Australian Business. In S. Castles, C. Alcorso, G. Rando, & E. Vasta (Eds.), *Australia's Italians: Culture and Community in a Changing Society* (pp. 73–84). Sydney: Allen and Unwin.
Collins, J. (2007). Ethnic Precincts as Contradictory Tourist Spaces. In J. Rath (Ed.), *Tourism, Ethnic Diversity and the City* (pp. 67–86). New York: Routledge.
Collins, J., & Castillo, A. (1998). *Cosmopolitan Sydney: Explore the World in One City*. Sydney: Pluto Press.
Collins, J., & Kunz, P. (2007). Ethnic Entrepreneurs, Ethnic Precincts and Tourism: The Case of Sydney, Australia. In G. Richards & J. Wilson (Eds.), *Tourism, Creativity and Development* (pp. 201–214). New York and London: Routledge.
Collins, J., & Shin, J. (2014). *Korean Immigrant Entrepreneurs in the Sydney Restaurant Industry*. A final report to Sushi Bay Pty Ltd. Sydney: UTS Business School.
Conforti, J. M. (1996). Ghettos as Tourism Attractions. *Annals of Tourism Research, 3*(4), 830–842.
Dana, L. (Ed.). (2007). *Handbook of Research on Ethnic Minority Entrepreneurship: A Co-evolutionary View on Resource Management*. Cheltenham, UK: Edward Elgar Publishing.
De Hass, H., Castles, S., & Miller, M. (2019). *The Age of Migration*. London: Macmillan Education.
Dunn, K. M. (1999). *Mosques and Islamic Centres in Sydney, Representations of Islam and Multiculturalism* (Unpublished PhD thesis). The University of Newcastle.
Fainstein, S. S., Hoffman, L. M., & Judd, D. R. (2003). Making Theoretical Sense of Tourism. In L. M. Hoffman, S. S. Fainstein, & D. R. Judd (Eds.), *Cities and Visitors: Regulating People, Markets, and City Space*. Oxford: Blackwell.

Frenkel, S., & Walton, J. (2000). Bavarian Leavenworth and the Symbolic Economy of a Theme Town. *The Geographical Review, 90*(4), 559–581.

Gabaccia, D. (1998). *We Are What We Eat: Ethnic food and the Making of Americans*. Cambridge, MA: Harvard University Press.

Gao J. (2017). Rediscovering the New Gold Mountain: Chinese Immigration to Australia Since the Mid-1980s. In M. Zhou (Ed.), *Contemporary Chinese Diasporas*. Singapore: Palgrave.

Goldin, I., Cameron, G., & Balarajan, M. (2011). *Exceptional People: How Migration Shaped Our World and Will Define Our Future*. Princeton: Princeton University Press.

Johnston, R., Poulsen, M., & Forrest, J. (2007). The Geography of Ethnic Residential Segregation: A Comparative Study of Five Countries. *Annals of the Association of American Geographers, 97*(4), 713–738.

Jupp, J., McRobbie, A., & York, B. (1991). *Metropolitan Ghettoes and Ethnic Concentration*. Working Papers on Multiculturalism no. 1 (2 vols.). Wollongong: Office of Multicultural Affairs and the University of Wollongong.

Kunz, P. (2005). *Ethnic Entrepreneurs, Ethnic Precincts and Tourism: Missed Opportunities from Sydney* (Unpublished PhD thesis). University of Technology, Sydney.

Lalich, W. F. (2003). *Ethnic Community Capital* (Unpublished thesis). University of Technology, Sydney.

Light, I. H., & Gold, S. J. (2000). *Ethnic Economies*. San Diego: Academic Press.

Light, I. H., & Rosenstein, C. (1995). *Race, Ethnicity, and Entrepreneurship in Urban America*. New York: Aldine de Gruyter.

Lin, J. (1998). *Reconstructing Chinatown: Ethnic Enclave, Global Change*. Minneapolis: University of Minnesota Press.

Lou, J. (2007). Revitalizing Chinatown into a Heterotopia: A Geosemiotic Analysis of Shop Signs in Washington, D.C.'s Chinatown. *Space and Culture, 10*(2), 170–194.

McEvoy, D. (2003, September 15–19). *The Evolution of Manchester's 'Curry Mile': From Suburban Shopping Street to Ethnic Destination*. Paper presented to Eighth International Metropolis Conference, Vienna.

Meethan, K. (2001). *Tourism in Global Society: Place, Culture, Consumption*. New York: Palgrave.

Min, P. G. (1996). *Caught in the Middle: Korean Merchants in America's Multiethnic Cities*. Berkeley: University of California Press.

Min, P. G. (2008). *Solidarity for Economic Survival: Korean Greengrocers in New York City*. New York: Russell Sage Foundation.

Kloosterman, R., & Rath, J. (2001). Immigrant Entrepreneurs in Advanced Economies: Mixed Embededdness Further Explored. *Journal of Ethnic and Migration Studies, 27*(2), 189–201.

Park, K. (1997). *The Korean American Dream: Immigrants and Small Business in New York City*. Ithaca and London: Cornell University Press.

Price, C. (1974). *The Great White Walls Are Built: Restrictive Immigration to North America and Australasia 1836–1888*. Canberra: Australian National University Press.

Productivity Commission. (2016). *Migrant Intake into Australia*. https://www.pc.gov.au/inquiries/completed/migrant-intake/report. Accessed 9 April 2020.

Rath, J., Bodaar, A., Waagemakers, T., & Yan Wu, P. (2018). Chinatown 2.0: The Difficult Flowering of an Ethnically Themed Shopping Area. *Journal of Ethnic and Migration Studies, 44*(1), 81–98.

Sandercock, L., & Kliger, B. (1998). Multiculturalism and the Planning System, Part 2. *Australian Planner, 35*(4), 223–227.

Schnell, S. M. (2003). The Ambiguities of Authenticity in Little Sweden, USA. *Journal of Cultural Geography, 20*(2), 43–68.

Timothy, D. (2002). Tourism and the Growth of Ethnic Islands. In C. M. Hall & A. M. Williams (Eds.), *Tourism and Migration: New Relationships Between Production And Consumption* (pp. 135–151). Dordrecht: Kluwer Academic.

Town of Vincent. (2006, August 29). *New-Look William Street*. Media Release. https://www.vincent.wa.gov.au/cproot/1247/11207/Williampercent20Streetpercent20Upgrade.pdf. Accessed 9 January 2008.

Urry, J. (2002). *The Tourist Gaze*. London: Sage.

Waldinger, R., Aldrich, H., & Ward, R. and Associates (Eds.). (1990). *Ethnic Entrepreneurs: Immigrant Business in Industrial Societies*. Newbury Park, CA: Sage

Wang, S., Sigler, T., Liu, Y., & Corcoran, J. (2018, November). Shifting Dynamics of Chinese Settlement in Australia: An Urban Geographic Perspective. *Geographical Research, 56*(4), 447–464.

Warde, A., & Martens, L. (2000). *Eating Out: Social Differentiation, Consumption and Pleasure*. Cambridge: Cambridge University Press.

Wise, A. (2010). Sensuous Multiculturalism: Emotional Landscapes of Inter-Ethnic Living in Australian Suburbia. *Journal of Ethnic and Migration Studies, 36*(6), 917–937.

Wise, A. (2011). 'You Wouldn't Know What's in There Would You?' Homeliness and 'Foreign' Signs in Ashfield, Sydney. In K. Brickell & A. Datta (Eds.), *Translocal Geographies: Spaces, Places, Connections*. Farnham: Ashgate.

Wise, A., & Velayutham, S. (Eds.). (2009). *Everyday Multiculturalism*. Houndmills, Basingstoke, Hampshire and New York: Palgrave Macmillan.

Wong, A., Anderson, K., Ang, I., & McNeill, D. (2016). *Sydney's Chinatown in the Asian Century: From Ethnic Enclave to Global Hub: A Research Report*. https://www.westernsydney.edu.au/__data/assets/pdf_file/0009/1086885/sydneys_chinatown_in_the_asian_century_research_report.pdf. Accessed 15 April 2020.

Zukin, S. (1995). *The Cultures of Cities*. Cambridge, MA and Oxford: Blackwell.

Index

J. Collins et al., *Cosmopolitan Place Making in Australia*,
https://doi.org/10.1007/978-981-15-8041-3

R

S

T

U

The manufacturer's authorised representative in the EU is Springer Nature Customer Service Centre GmbH, Europaplatz 3, 69115 Heidelberg, Germany. If you have any concerns regarding our products, please contact ProductSafety@springernature.com

Printed and bound by CPI Group (UK) Ltd, Croydon, CR0 4YY

30/09/2026

02225286-0015